PUBLIC VALUES & PRIVATE POWER IN

AMERICAN POLITICS

PUBLIC VALUES & PRIVATE POWER IN

AMERICAN POLITICS

EDITED BY J. DAVID GREENSTONE

The University of Chicago Press ★ Chicago and London

The University of Chicago Press, Chicago 60637
The University of Chicago Press, Ltd., London

Library of Congress Cataloging in Publication Data
Main entry under title:

Public values and private power in American
    politics.

    Includes index.
    1. Pressure groups—United States—Addresses,
essays, lectures.   2. Public interest—United
States—Addresses, essays, lectures.   3. United
States—Politics and government—Addresses,
essays, lectures.   I. Greenstone, J. David.
JK1118.P82   322.4'3'0973   81-16416
ISBN 0–226–30716–6   AACR2

Contributors ★

Peri E. Arnold, associate professor in the Department of Government and International Studies, University of Notre Dame, is a specialist on the American presidency and national bureaucracy, and has written several papers on Herbert Hoover's contribution to the development of American politics.

Matthew A. Crenson, professor in the Department of Political Science, Johns Hopkins University, is the author of *The Un-Politics of Air Pollution* and *The Federal Machine*.

J. David Greenstone, professor in the Department of Political Science and the College, and member of the Committee on Public Policy Studies, University of Chicago, is the author of *Labor in American Politics*, and coauthor of *Race and Authority in Urban Politics* (with Paul E. Peterson), both published by the University of Chicago Press.

Ronald C. Kahn, associate professor in the Department of Government, Oberlin College, specializes in urban politics and constitutional law, and has published papers on the politics of police accountability in Chicago, New York, and Philadelphia.

Mark Kesselman, professor in the Department of Political Science, Columbia University, is the author of *The Ambiguous Consensus: A Study of Local Government in France*, and coauthor of *The Left Academy: Marxist Scholarship on American Campuses*.

Karen Orren, associate professor in the Department of Political Science, University of California, Los Angeles, is the author of *Corporate Power and Social Change: The Politics of the Life Insurance Industry*, and a number of articles on interest groups and the American economy.

Paul E. Peterson, chair of the Committee on Public Policy Studies and professor in the Departments of Political Science and Education, University of Chicago, is the author of *School Politics Chicago Style* and *City Limits,* both published by the University of Chicago Press.

Michael Paul Rogin, professor in the Department of Political Science, University of California, Berkeley, is the author of *Fathers and Children: Andrew Jackson and the Subjugation of the American Indian,* and *Subversive Genealogy: Politics, Family, and Fiction in Herman Melville* (Knopf, forthcoming).

Contents ★

Introduction   ix   The Public, the Private,
and American Democracy:
Reflections on Grant McConnell's
Political Science

J. David Greenstone

Part I   **Perspectives on the Study of
American Politics**

One   3   The Transient and the Permanent
in American Politics:
Standards, Interests, and the
Concept of "Public"

J. David Greenstone

Two   34   The Conflictual Evolution of
American Political Science:
From Apologetic Pluralism
to Trilateralism and Marxism

Mark Kesselman

Part II   **The American Executive**

Three   71   The King's Two Bodies:
Lincoln, Wilson, Nixon, and
Presidential Self-Sacrifice

Michael Paul Rogin

Four   109   Ambivalent Leviathan:
                               Herbert Hoover and
                               the Positive State

                               Peri E. Arnold

Part III   **Interest Groups**

Five   139   Political Change in America:
                               Highway Politics and Reactive
                               Policymaking

                               Ronald C. Kahn

Six   173   Liberalism, Money, and the
                               Situation of Organized Labor

                               Karen Orren

Part IV   **Cities in a Federal System**

Seven   209   Urban Bureaucracy in
                               Urban Politics:
                               Notes Toward a
                               Developmental Theory

                               Matthew A. Crenson

Eight   246   Federalism, Economic
                               Development,
                               and Redistribution

                               Paul E. Peterson

Index   277

Introduction ★

The Public, the Private, and American Democracy: Reflections on Grant McConnell's Political Science

J. David Greenstone

Perhaps the most enduring feature of American domestic politics during recent decades has been the continuing ideological struggle over the passage and implementation of redistributive, egalitarian welfare-state policies. Yet this broad programmatic cleavage does not represent a truly permanent feature of American politics. At least until the Civil War, it was the egalitarian left that raised laissez faire objections to state intervention in the economy. And in our day, the many welfare-state goals that have been met are no longer salient issues, while other goals now appear to raise new and more complicated questions.

A chief merit of Grant McConnell's political science, one more fully explicated in the Greenstone, Kesselman, and Kahn papers, is his emphasis on a more permanent political cleavage that pits the welfare of the public or community against the interests of private individuals or groups. In its specific form, of course, this conflict has changed over time. In the first New England colonies, the tension was between individual saint and invisible church; a century later it was a matter of individual rights in a republican regime; in our time it is the problem of private versus public interests on which McConnell himself has focused. Yet important continuities link these different conceptions. Negatively, each version, including McConnell's, contrasts the individual or narrowly defined group with the whole polity, so that there is little room for larger collectivities, such as social classes or oligarchies, that seek to rule their social inferiors. Positively, collective action is limited to group politics in which the key actors reject comprehensive social goals in favor of narrower objectives that cannot be readily described in terms of either class conflict or elite theory.

These remarks suggest the essential tension that has made McConnell's position so intriguing to his many students. For if his vision of American politics can be traced back to the Progressives' belief that political activity is motivated by the narrow private regarding pursuit of group interests, McConnell's moral stance is rooted in a still older—indeed Puritan—conception of the community, the common good, and what is now called the public interest. From this tension follow the series of dualisms that characterize McConnell's work. Although his empirical analysis emphasizes a pluralist account of interest-group activity, his normative position views that pluralism as fatally private regarding. Consequently, he typically combines a microlevel emphasis on individual and group behavior with a macrolevel concern for that behavior's impact on the regime and political institutions. And though he expects almost all groups to be private regarding, he insists on the existence and importance of public values in the political process and argues that these values will fare best at the hands of large diverse constituencies—the presidency (and perhaps the Senate) rather than the House; the national government rather than the states and the local governments.

In this volume, eight of McConnell's students explore, develop, and critique this political perspective in the course of elaborating on several of his most important analytic themes: the private regarding character of group politics, the institutional and structural constraints on policymaking, and, finally, the basic tension between public and private values.

In developing the first theme, Ronald Kahn and Karen Orren bring new data and perspectives to the study of group interests. As Kahn recognizes, one might well assume, for example, that federal highway policy issues since the mid-1950s have been fought ideologically, with the crucial decisions primarily reflecting the shifting balance of congressional power between liberals and conservatives. In fact, however, Kahn shows that, as McConnell might expect, most though not all of the real battles were between the House of Representatives, with its small homogeneous constituencies, and the Senate and president, whose constituencies are more diverse. Regardless of their many ideological and personal differences, each presidential administration typically supported public regarding (e.g., pro-mass transit) policies against the narrower (pro-trucker and anti-mass transit) orientation of the House.

However narrow the objectives of groups active in highway politics, McConnell's analysis of interest groups might seem inapplicable to organized labor given the unions' vigorous support since the 1930s for broadly based egalitarian welfare policies. Although Orren recognizes labor's position on these issues and its alliance with the Democratic party, she uses a very different set of data to give an account of union political behavior, both before and after the New Deal, that confirms McConnell's own view of labor politics. At each economic turning point, she suggests, unions have adjusted their goals and actions to changes in the business cycle and, most important, the American and international monetary systems. And these adjustments have been designed to protect their own organizational security and their members' income. Just as broad-gauged party-related ideologies played a very limited role in highway politics, so too the intensity of labor's commitment to social welfare policies reflects narrower, more self-regarding objectives. And just as McConnell maintains, these narrow concrete material objectives have, in fact, proved extreme rather than moderate, for they have seriously distorted fiscal and especially monetary policymaking, thus undermining the nation's economic well-being.

As Kahn points out, McConnell believes that the influence of private regarding interest groups varies with the institutional context. And as Peri Arnold and Matthew Crenson argue in their papers on Herbert Hoover's view of the presidency and urban bureaucracy, this context itself varies over time. Although McConnell stresses his contribution to an orthodoxy that legitimates business influence on the government's attempts at economic regulation, Hoover's political thought is primarily remembered as a laissez faire critique of welfare-state policies. While Arnold accepts McConnell's qualifications, he believes that neither of these interpretations fully captures the complexity of Hoover's political thought and practice. Confronted with pervasive administrative problems in an increasingly complicated society, Hoover forcefully (if not always consistently) favored the development of a strong, rationalized administration. Perhaps unintentionally, he thus accepted the logic of a broad constituency public regarding politics (to use McConnell's terms) at considerable variance with his other political and ideological values.

Issue-oriented conflicts in urban politics have typically turned less on welfare-state policies than on the competing goals of machine and reform politicians. But as Crenson shows, the importance of even this urban ideological cleavage can also be overemphasized. In fact, machine and reform politicians sought to centralize urban bureaucracies and discourage the capture of particular agencies by organized interests. In this way, Crenson draws heavily on McConnell's public/private distinction, but from McConnell's own perspective the results are paradoxical. First, even if local interest groups are more homogeneous and thus more private regarding than national organizations, Crenson maintains that they have had less power to capture government agencies. Not only are local groups poorly organized, but, at least until recent years, the relatively centralized bureaucracies of local government have been better able to resist group pressures. Second, this distinctively urban character of city government began to give way to the national pattern of effective interest group pressure only when local politics itself began to be "nationalized"—that is, when the new federal welfare programs of the 1960s sought to create powerful organized clientele groups in local politics.

Although he believes that public regarding values are better served in some institutional contexts rather than others, McConnell also focuses on structural features of the American regime—especially its deep-seated hostility toward the exercise of public power that helps privileged private groups seize power at the expense of the politically unorganized and socially disadvantaged. In their papers, both Paul Peterson and Mark Kesselman develop this emphasis on structural limits. Peterson, for example, provides his own explanation for the generalization that federal policies are typically more egalitarian and redistributive than those of local governments, since in his view, the American federal system forces most local governments to compete with each other for economic resources. In this respect, localities have distinctively homogeneous interests, since, in the long run, all residents of a locality are better off if their government attracts prosperous, taxpaying individuals and businesses while discouraging low-income consumers of public services. By contrast, federal policies are not subject to the same constraints, and the government consequently has more freedom to pursue redistribution. Regardless of their ideological commitments, then, local officials will try to undercut the egalitarian effects of redistributive federal welfare programs, even when they are not locally funded. In McConnell's terms, these officials will act on narrow private regarding values in ways that discourage the economically disadvantaged from moving into their communities.

As Kesselman sees it, radical egalitarian change is unlikely, not because of American federalism or the fact that conservatives typically triumph in explicitly ideological, class-oriented political struggle but rather because of the imperatives of a capitalist economy based on production for private profit. Like McConnell, Kesselman insists that the American state is not simply the creature of a cohesive capitalist class. A need for legitimation and worker acquiescence, and a need to limit divisions among capitalists and counteract their sometimes self-defeating impulses, can produce public policies that many in the business community oppose. Nevertheless, just as local governments benefit by attracting prosperous residents and businesses, so too a successful national government depends on a prosperous, capitalist economy. The important point, therefore, is not who wins overt class conflicts, or the fate of particular welfare-state policies. Rather, given the specially privileged position of those pursuing private profit, the polity and economy are partially insulated from each other, so that the most fundamental questions of political economy are not considered.

For all their differences, I believe that, taken together, these six papers strongly support McConnell's basic perspective on American politics. Despite the obvious importance of contemporary ideological and partisan debates, other crucial features are better understood in terms of an enduring tension between public values and narrow private regarding interests.

This tension is itself a central theme in Michael Rogin's paper on Lincoln, Wilson, and Nixon. Where McConnell sees the presidency as the public's bulwark against private regarding politics, Rogin sees each of these presidencies as problematic just to the extent that the presidents' self-regarding ambitions were not informed by a legitimate public purpose. Moreover, each of these presidents ended his public life in failure or tragedy after having acted in time of war to expand his powers at the expense of constitutional rights. Nevertheless, unlike Wilson and Nixon, Lincoln did successfully share and speak for his community's moral values. This success in turn depended on an authentic public rhetoric, a concretely meaningful language, with which Lincoln articulated both his own political objectives and the moral significance of his nation's trials. Wilson's rhetoric, to be sure, also invoked morality and self-sacrifice, but partly because he indulged his personal racial and ethnic animosities, and partly because his vision was abstracted from the moral experience of his community, he communicated, but—as he discovered in 1919—he could not persuade. Nixon's failure, of course, was still more complete. Confronted with the Vietnam crisis, his behavior was so entirely self-serving, so preoccupied with his own private inner secrets, that he found no effective rhetoric at all. Both his private and public speech displayed an unalloyed ambition that led to crime and disgrace.

Although Rogin's paper is less concerned with social and economic policies than the other papers I discussed, I argue in my paper that this ethical and cultural concern with self and community reflects a major theme in McConnell's own work. To be sure, McConnell's crucial concept of "public" does embody basically consequentialist or utilitarian criteria for the equitable satisfaction of individual needs and preferences (of concern in the other six papers), but as I try to show, the concept has a cultural and ethical dimension. From this perspective, the individual's responsibility is not just to treat others fairly, or even generously, but to contribute to a common life in ways that maximize each person's opportunity to develop cultural, intellectual, and moral faculties according to substantive standards of excellence and competence.

Thus the interest of the community (or public) must be to encourage this self-development, which indeed is only made possible by establishing and upholding appropriate standards. For only if these norms of competence or excellence are determined intersubjectively, rather than individually, can one distinguish between meeting a standard and simply following a personal, perhaps whimsical, inclination. Since these two orientations frequently recur in American political history—for example, before the Civil War, during the Progressive era, and during the 1960s and early 1970s—McConnell's concept of "public" thus parallels a fundamental bipolar feature of American politics.

As the reader will quickly perceive, these eight papers differ in rhetoric, political commitments, and fundamental assumptions; nor does any one of us simply reproduce Grant McConnell's own methods and conclusions. Our very differences, however, testify both to the richness of his scholarly vision and intellectual interests and to his remarkable openness as a teacher and mentor. Thus we honor him in this volume not just for contributing so signally to our political understanding but also for teaching each of us, by precept and example, to chart an independent course in exploring the complex character of American democracy.

Part I

★

Perspectives on the Study of American Politics

One

The Transient and the Permanent in American Politics: Standards, Interests, and the Concept of "Public"

J. David Greenstone

Heaven and earth shall pass away; but my words shall not pass away." With this sentence from Luke 21, Theodore Parker began perhaps the most controversial theological manifesto of New England Transcendentalism, his 1841 "Discourse of the Transient and Permanent in Christianity." For Parker, the permanent elements of Christianity are ethical and religious truths, which for him can produce important social and political implications: "the divine life of the soul, love to God, and love to man." Contrary to orthodox Unitarian and Calvinist creeds, only these truths —and not historically transient "forms and doctrines"—can show a religion's validity.[1] For these transient elements, even the incidents in Christ's life, cannot justify belief if the fundamental ethical and religious teachings are false.

Transience and Permanence in Political Analysis

Despite his nineteenth-century religious idiom, Parker's contrast can be taken over into political analysis. In politics, the transient includes the flow of events, actors, and preferences as well as the actions, decisions, and, in particular, the crucial causal relationships that differentiate one

A number of friends and colleagues have provided encouragement and helpful criticisms and suggestions for improving this paper. I should like to thank in particular John Brigham, Peter Frett, Russell Hardin, Robert Hawkinson, Ira Katznelson, Mark Kesselman, Robert Meister, Karen Orren, Benjamin Page, Paul Peterson, Michael Rogin, and Bart Schultz.

political era from another. The politically permanent, by contrast, cannot designate causal (e.g., economic) factors that produce specific political outcomes. Strictly speaking, no unchanging feature of a social situation can cause a change in some feature as long as a "cause" is understood to mean a change in one element that produces a subsequent (or possibly coincident) change in another. Instead, a concern with the permanent emphasizes those enduring features of a political system that exclude some outcomes as impossible or infeasible by limiting the practical and conceptual tools with which individuals and groups interpret and act on their experience.

Parker's theological epistemology suggests one way in which this limitation might occur. In considering the New Testament, Parker by no means rejects its account of the transient events of Christ's life. What he denies, however, is that this account—specifically, the reports of Christ's miracles—provides definitive evidence for the Gospel's general validity. For what, in turn, makes these reports believable? Accordingly, Parker insists that we must first have some method with which to evaluate this empirical account itself. Thus Parker reverses the orthodox position that the miracles prove the Gospel's validity. For him, the decisive point is the Gospel's teaching about the excellence of the human soul and the ethical duties that follow. It is because these standards of human conduct are so permanent and undeniable that Parker accepts the Gospel as (permanently) truthful and, in turn, accepts the reports of the (transient) miracles. In sum, the permanent truths of the Gospel's ethical teachings justify our believing its reports about the miracles rather than the other way around.

But why does Parker take Christ's religious and ethical teachings about the human soul to be permanently true? Although his sermon does not explicitly address this question, it can be answered by rendering his argument in a more contemporary philosophical idiom, in which he is understood to be making claims *both* about human souls as entities or objects (as they exist in the world) *and* about the meaning of the concept "soul," that is, its central place in our language.[2] For Parker would not call an object a soul (not *see* that it was a soul) unless—consistent with our use of the word "soul"—that object exhibited the distinctive rational and moral features of the human personality. Moreover, such complexes of fundamental beliefs, ethical commitments, and conceptual meanings are enduringly valid. To abandon these beliefs and meanings would mean changing our basic world view and thus our language.[3] But these basic assumptions and meanings necessarily change much less frequently than our specific empirical beliefs. For instance, it is only because the *word* "constitution" has a relatively stable meaning that we can make specific empirical statements about how and why the American Constitution has changed.[4] For without stable meanings there would be no way to make such before and after comparisons.

There is, in sum, a crucial sense in which the most permanent features of our language and thought embody our most unshakable beliefs about the world. Thus Parker's language commits him to the belief that there are souls, just as a physicist's language commits him to the belief that there are atoms and nuclei. And given these beliefs, we can observe what happens to particular souls, atoms, or nuclei. Just as the quotation from Luke suggests, it is indeed Parker's "words," and standards, that signify the relatively permanent, as will be shown presently with reference to our concept of "public."

This type of permanence, in turn, implies limitation. Because they help classify our flow of transitory sense impressions, these relatively stable concepts and standards—and their associated practices—limit the kinds of experiences a group, individual, or political community can have. For example, certain actions are not possible, cannot have real significance for us, as long as our language and practices cannot classify them meaningfully. Given our concepts of "chess" and "presidential election," throwing a piece of wood in the air cannot be counted as a move in chess, and shooting a bullet at a voting machine cannot be counted as a vote.[5] And, as Parker himself shows, members of a political culture cannot understand even the most rapacious capitalist economic practices in class terms—as one class collectively exploiting another—if their language lacks such concepts as "class conflict."

Permanence and Bipolarity in American Liberalism

In political analysis, accounts of just such permanent limits differ from one perspective to another. In the American case, for example, a neo-Marxist view of American politics might stress the permanence of a capitalist political economy that limits working-class power and influence. An institutional analysis might focus on the limits that a presidential—as compared to a cabinet—system imposes on party unity. And as we shall see, a consensus approach might emphasize the extent to which the liberal American tradition limits the emergence of social class conflict.

In these particular examples, and unlike the orthodox Marxist stress on continuing bourgeois-proletarian struggle, limits are thought to be imposed by a basically monolithic set of permanent attitudes and behaviors. Here, however, I wish to assert a different view of the permanent features of American politics—a recurring, and philosophically based, bipolar opposition that nevertheless occurs within a common liberal commitment to freedom, individualism, and pluralism. What has been (relatively) permanent about American political life and conflict, from at least Parker's Jacksonian era to the present, is not a single set of limiting concepts and practices but two opposed—although equally liberal—traditions. One side of this opposition involves a broadly *empiricist* or utilitarian politics that seeks to maximize rights, interests, and preferences. The other side involves a politics of humanitarian reform that emphasize individual self development, that is, the capacity to master certain *substantive standards* of excellence or competence essential for a shared moral, social, and cultural life. My claim here, it must be emphasized, is that this bipolarity has limited American politics as a whole—not that every individual is a liberal, nor that every liberal permanently adheres to one side of this bipolarity or the other, nor that the beliefs of the two sides have remained fixed over the years. What is permanent, instead, is an opposition of the most basic philosophic values that operates within, as well as among, individuals. This opposition in turn helps us to understand, for example, the shift from a primary concern with humanitarian reform and substantive standards in the 1960s to the more privatistic, materialistic politics of the 1970s. There have been, of course, other recurrent oppositions in American politics, such as the struggles over equality and the economic role of the state. But unlike the liberal bipolarity considered here, these tensions do not reflect any fundamental philosophic disagreement over the character of social community, individual personality, and human knowledge. And it is for this reason, I contend, that the bipolarity continues to pose the major political alternatives.

Since no one paper can fully establish this thesis, my goal here is simply to show the permanence of this bipolarity by establishing its relevance for both Parker's pre–Civil War intellectual and political career and Grant McConnell's theoretical and empirical perspectives on contemporary American group politics.[6] But the bipolarity assumes different forms in these two periods. Because Parker's concerns were fundamentally theological, at the theoretical and conceptual level his position was unipolar, and he held that only a liberalism of substantive standards had a permanent place in American culture. But at the level of political practice, Parker saw and denounced the empirical, acquisitive liberalism of his time. Thus he recognized the importance of both liberal perspectives.

By contrast, McConnell's concerns are scholarly and analytical, and, unlike Parker's unipolar position, his crucial concept of "public," which he takes over from contemporary political discourse, embraces both sides of American liberalism. On the other hand, McConnell's empirical account emphasizes the dominance of empiricist or utilitarian values in contemporary American political practice. Consequently, his empirical view of American politics, unlike Parker's is unipolar.

By failing to be consistently bipolar, each of these positions partially distorts our understanding of American politics. This paper, therefore, makes two closely related and consistently bipolar claims. First, the concept of "public" in American political discourse and analysis has *two* sets of criteria: an empiricist set concerned with inclusiveness and equity, and a set of substantive standards which has animated humanitarian reform. Second, American politics itself, at least in the case of Parker's Jacksonian era, reveals a fundamental, philosophically grounded division within the American liberal tradition.

Parker's Transcendentalism: Conceptual Permanence and Ethical Commitment

The core ideas of humanitarian substantive standards liberalism include the ethical truths that Parker himself took to be permanently valid, for example, the potential dignity, morality and rationality of every human soul, and certain consequent standards of human conduct, such as duties toward others that follow from these truths. Parker's own ethical position then is broadly idealist, if not Kantian. For insofar as human beings rationally use these permanent concepts and standards to make their experience intelligible, they demonstrate their moral and intellectual worth. And it is this "excellence" of man's "nature," in Parker's words, that creates the obligation to treat others with "humility, reverence . . . charity . . . and active love."[7] This position in turn suggests Parker's Transcendentalist view of human community. Not only do these norms make it a duty to treat others as objects of ethical concern (rather than as means to obtaining one's own goals), but adherence to these norms is in itself a sign of membership in a genuinely moral community.

The permanent validity of these standards, however, by no means implies their general acceptance. Parker himself attacked many dominant features of his own society and participated in "every possible reform movement, the Sabbath, capital punishment, crime, prostitution, temperance, jails, women's rights, marriage," and finally in the all-consuming "slavery controversy."[8] Although some Transcendentalists shunned political activism, Parker's insistence that all men and women have—and must be treated as having—the capacity for human excellence led him to challenge politically the acquisitiveness and materialism, that is, the predominant empiricist liberalism, of Jacksonian politics. Indeed, he persuasively articulated a liberal politics of moral reform that powerfully appealed not only to many younger Transcendentalists but to (generally antislavery) reformers with New England Calvinist backgrounds.[9] The reformers' own struggles, then, illustrate the permanently dual character of American political ideas. For described in less ethically pejorative terms than Parker's, Jacksonian electoral politics was centrally concerned with how best, and most equitably, to organize the pursuit of each individual's often material interests and preferences. This equally permanent but empiricist feature of American politics is illustrated by one side of Grant McConnell's bipolar concept of the "public."[10]

Empirical and Conceptual Elements in McConnell's Analysis

McConnell's conceptual distinction between public and private, and his implicitly bipolar criteria for "public," are essential for both his explanatory generalization that specifies the conditions determining whether private or public regarding outcomes occur, and his empirical observation that private regarding outcomes typically predominate. Like other "critical pluralists" (such as Lowi and Schattschneider), McConnell observes empirically that particular pieces of public power have been captured by many smaller, narrow, self-interested groups, each dominated by a relatively homogeneous geographical- or functional-based elite, such as the rich farmers in a rural area or the largest companies in an industry. By controlling the appointment or behavior of the relevant public officials, these elites maximize their benefits from government programs at the expense of the less-advantaged (e.g., poor farmers, sharecroppers, or workers) and protect certain practices (e.g., collusion on prices, poor product quality, or industrial pollution) which hurt the less-involved general public. American politics, then, is usually private regarding, where "private" ordinarily refers to the preferences of particular individuals or groups at the expense of those excluded from the benefits of, or influence on, some particular policy. The opposite concept of "public," thus, seems plainly connected to an idea of generality that extends to many, if not all, of the members of the political community.

In explaining the character of American public policies, McConnell then argues that powerful private interests will be opposed only by constituencies, such as the president's, so large and internally diverse that they will seek such common values as product safety and environmental protection.[11] Since these large national constituencies usually fail to exert much influence, public policy typically remains in the hands of powerful, acquisitive, and materialistic private interests—and thus exhibits a privatistic version of empiricist liberal values.[12]

It is, then, McConnell's use of such concepts as "public" and "private" (his words) and not his observations or generalizations that apparently form the permanent aspect of his argument. Certainly it is hard to see how McConnell's analysis could illuminate the bipolar character of American politics, as I believe it does, unless there is some substantial connection between the way he uses these concepts and the framework with which political participants assess and act on vital political issues. Since we have seen that McConnell's concept of "private" typically designates only empiricist liberal values while his concept of "public" can be shown to be genuinely bipolar, our discussion will focus on this latter concept.

It may be objected, however, that this claim—that McConnell's permanent concept of "public" refers to, reflects, and thus helps illuminate important features of American political practice—cannot be sustained. If the concept of "public" has an important, meaningful place in the American political process, it must be intelligible to those who participate; it must be both rather widely accepted and have at least a tolerably clear and settled meaning. Yet this condition, the objection runs, does not seem to be satisfied. Establishing a satisfactory definition of "public" has proved notoriously difficult, and, as McConnell himself admits, his own use of "the public interest" is obscured by "large uncertainties of meaning."[13] How then can McConnell's key concept reliably indicate any salient feature of American politics, bipolar or otherwise? My goal here, consequently, is to show that McConnell's bipolar concept of "public," when properly elaborated, is meaningful and indeed is determined by sufficiently clear criteria to have a central place in American political practice. But because McConnell's criteria unfortunately remain indirect and implicit, I can make this argument only by elaborating his concept in a way that brings these criteria to the surface.

Standards and the Social or Philosophical Sense of "Public"

"Public" can function as an adequate linguistic tool only if we have appropriate criteria with which to apply it. McConnell himself makes just this point when he criticizes the Progressives for failing to achieve their explicitly public regarding goals because they either entirely destroyed relevant standards (i.e., criteria with which to assess policies), or adopted ones too vague to prevent the triumph of private interests.[14]

Unfortunately, however, McConnell does not explicitly indicate what those standards or criteria are. To identify such criteria, we must first establish a general social and philosophical meaning of "public" and then distinguish it from the more specifically political, and bipolar, usage in McConnell's analysis of American politics.

Now, in establishing this first meaning, an important point is that effective standards are necessarily social because they are both indispensable for and dependent on social practices—those patterned economic, religious, social, institutional, and intellectual activities that make up public life. One side of this relationship may be rather evident. Social practices require stable expectations about individual behavior that are based in turn on mutually accepted standards. To participate in a particular practice, in other words, we must have constituent rules that define the appropriate activities—for example, casting a valid vote or making an acceptable move in chess—and also indicate what behaviors are not valid or acceptable. These standards are also relevant for the sometimes larger public of nonparticipants who witness the practice. For if someone violated these standards, for example, by trying to move the queen in chess as if it were a knight or trying to vote after the polls had closed, we could not use our concepts of "playing chess" or "voting" to describe their activities.[15] These standards, in other words, make it possible to criticize each participant's behavior and goals as acceptable, illicit, or irrelevant.

Although effective standards are thus necessary for social practices essential to a public life, the opposite relation also holds; such practices are equally, if perhaps less obviously, necessary for the development of effective meaningful standards. Consider the attempt of any single person to develop a genuinely effective standard, but one that is only for his or her individual use—for instance, when to obey a particular rule of behavior. The problem here is that no verbally stated norm or standard can anticipate every exceptional or troublesome case to which it might apply. For example, it would not ordinarily be appropriate to follow the rule "faithfully open the door when a superior so orders" if opening the door meant spreading a raging fire. This case, however, is but one of an unlimited number of such possibly unanticipated circumstances that can conceivably be thought of as extenuating. Consequently, in every case where someone appears to violate a norm or standard, that person can always try to show that an exceptional circumstance, for example, a raging fire, made the apparent violation appropriate. Now, if the standard is socially shared, others can decide if the excuse is valid. But if the standard is for a single person, then the individual in question is both the author of the standard and the sole authority on its interpretation. There is, therefore, no choice but to defer to his or her claim that there were extenuating circumstances, even if this seems implausible. For the only interpretation that counts is that of the person whose action is being questioned, and there is no reliable way to distinguish between a person always conforming to an individually developed standard and one merely acting out a series of discrete private preferences.[16]

For standards or rules to be useful, then, we must be able to interpret them *independently* of the single actor's own (sometimes conveniently rationalized) justifications. We require *socially* effective interpretations based on the reaction of many actors who participate in the relevant social practices—that is, *a public of significant others*. For it is the judgments on which this public acts that show whether and when an apparent deviation really violates a standard (or alternatively preserves or improves the social practice that standard regulates).[17]

In sum, one condition for our calling some policy or decision public regarding is that it can be located in a social practice, or (to make the same point) can be appraised in terms of shared standards by the actors in question and a public of significant others. And it is this social or philosophical meaning of "public," this need for widely shared standards of conduct, that I believe McConnell evokes when he argues that the absence of standards effectively undermined the Progressives' pursuit of the public interest.

By itself, however, this broadly social or philosophical perspective on the content of "public" is insufficient for political discourse, because it fails to exclude some standards which are *socially* or intersubjectively shared but are politically privatistic. Some practices, for instance, may be flagrantly private regarding in their concern for the "few"—either in terms of who can participate or in their specific content. Polo, for instance, has shared standards of conduct but is restricted to a privileged minority. Other practices like embezzlement and murder for hire are simply antisocial. Even if we somehow specify that the chosen practices (and their associated goals) must be altruistic, they may still be much too abstract and formalistic to be genuinely public regarding.[18] (Parker himself, e.g., criticized the capitalism of his time and urged merchants to be less selfish,[19] but his positive prescriptions were quite unspecific, and after the Civil War a similar abstractness left most of his fellow abolitionists unable to help the poor and politically defenseless exslaves.)[20]

To be public regarding in a politically meaningful way, then, a practice must apply to all members of the political community, or at least to as many as feasible. In other words, the political sense of "public" must first be concerned with *socially shared standards and practices*, and then concerned with *generality*, with the "many" as opposed to the few. Indeed, I shall argue that McConnell's use of "public" has just this feature but that his idea of generality is bipolar in that it points in two different directions. If one begins *procedurally*, generality applies to persons, and the essential distinctions among practices turns on the degree to which their relevant rules apply to all those who do (or might) participate in them. The question is how equitably all the participants are treated. If one begins *substantively*, generality applies to the activities and skills that one must master in order to participate in a social practice. Thus the decisive question about any such practice is not one of equity. Rather, it is how generally important is the mastery of that practice's skills and activities both for those who directly participate in it and other members of society? It is this difference between these procedural and substantive concerns in McConnell's concept of "public," as I shall try to show, that is closely connected to the opposition in American liberalism.

The Political Sense of "Public": Procedural or Empiricist Criteria

The first, procedural, set of standards, as McConnell himself notes in discussing the American commitment to liberty,[21] concerns the impact a person's or group's pursuit of privately determined goals has on the efforts of others to achieve their objectives. On this view, the ends themselves cannot be validly criticized; in this crucial sense each actor is sovereign. Epistemologically, this position seems to be rooted in the empiricist belief that human beings are decisively shaped by individually (i.e., privately) experienced sensations. Since a desirable or pleasurable experience for one person may not be so for another, social activity must be organized to promote the individually defined desires or pleasures of as many people as possible. Insofar as individuals do determine their own goals, socially shared norms are therefore restricted to questions of means, that is, insuring that the methods each person uses must not unduly interfere with others pursuing their preferences.

In this procedural sense, a practice is minimally public regarding if its basic rules and norms are generally binding on all, so that each person pursues his own goals but no on is free to change or invent rules to suit their immediate convenience or personal advantage. But even if rules do bind everyone, they may still treat some persons much more favorably than others, for example, by providing special privileges which unequally aid some individuals at the expense of others. Consequently, some practices will be somewhat more public regarding than others to the extent that the procedures are universalistic. But these more impartial standards remain procedural in that the individuals within this framework are free to pick their own goals.

Even the most genuinely universalistic procedural standards, however, may still allow or even contribute to social and economic inequality in a competitive, acquisitive society. Accordingly, the most public regarding procedural standards call for policies and political arrangements that have explicitly egalitarian distributive objectives. McConnell suggests three such distributive or "inclusiveness" criteria when he examines the consequences ordinarily, but not invariably, associated with large constituency politics.[22]

1. Egalitarian policies that help weaker groups (minorities or the poor, or workers subjected to powerful local elites) by imposing general, impartial, or universalistic standards, for example, in the administration of justice or economic benefits.[23]

2. Policies that provide such relatively public goods as clean air or lower prices that, if supplied to anyone, will typically be available to all (or many).[24]

3. Policies that generally promote freedom, for example, genuine opportunity to pursue different social, political, or economic preferences, by reducing or eliminating the control powerful actors (in, say, a geographic area or industry) exercise over less-powerful ones.[25]

Partly because it may not even be possible to define absolute equality or freedom, and partly because few goods may be perfectly public (i.e., equally accessible to all), these criteria clearly cannot be used as labels that designate permanently public regarding policies. Instead, they function as normative tools with which we can compare policies and political arrangements, although we shall see that the electoral politics of Parker's own time make clear that these norms may not always agree. To be sure, these inclusiveness criteria do specify goals for the government (such as reducing inequality). But from the standpoint of the individual they remain procedural; they restrict the means individuals may use in pursuing goals, but leave the goals themselves to be individually determined.

McConnell's Substantive Reservations about the Inclusiveness Criteria

The most interesting point about McConnell's usage of "public" is that it is not exhausted by these inclusiveness criteria. In each case, the fundamental problem is that the particular criterion specifies how persons and groups are to treated distributively, how particular goods or benefits are to be allocated, but ignores the more substantive question of what those goods or benefits ought to be—and therefore what activities, that is, what substantive ends or goals, a politically public regarding practice ought to pursue. Once again McConnell most explicitly raises this problem in his discussion of the Progressives. Although their conservationist policies were devoted to protecting the natural environment, they relied on the distributive Benthamite goal of "the greatest good of the greatest number in the long run." But because "good" had no substantive definition, each private interest was free to interpret the concept for itself, and government officials, left to their own discretion, typically listened to the most powerful economic interests. This same problem applies to the inclusiveness criteria themselves. For example, because the equality criterion says nothing about the particular goals a group pursues, a group that secures more equal treatment may then use its new position to pursue its own self-regarding interests. This problem underlies the skeptical attitude of McConnell and other critical pluralists toward trade unions. Even though McConnell recognizes that some unions serve egalitarian values by protecting individual workers against powerful employers, he argues that the union organizations have used their power to defend their own private interests, often at the expense of both those still unorganized and the broader public.[26]

Similarly, the freedom criterion, insofar as it encourages individuals to pursue whatever preferences they happen to have without arbitrary restraint, may in fact encourage private regarding, even selfish, behavior, for these preferences may simply reflect an individual's or group's privately determined values. Indeed, an appeal to autonomy and private choice is a central tenet of the self-regarding pluralist orthodoxy McConnell attacks.[27]

The public goods criterion suffers from a comparably serious though quite different problem. Both general economic prosperity and clean air, for example, can be considered public or near public goods, at least in the sense that if these benefits are supplied to anyone they are supplied to many others. Yet in many cases additional increments of either can be secured only at the cost of the other. Of course, one may try to sacrifice only small amounts of environmental protection for substantial economic gains, and vice versa. But when we ask if a given economic gain is "large" compared to a given environmental loss, we are driven back to the relevant preferences, to the private views of the partisans on each side. Yet McConnell typically favors environmental values, in part because increased prosperity primarily increases the material resources with which individuals and groups can in turn pursue goals that in themselves remain private.[28] For McConnell, in other words, it is not simply the public goods feature—the general availability—of, say, clean air or parks but some other attribute that makes environmental policies so eminently public regarding. (Indeed, in some cases, such as the protection of wilderness areas against commercial development, the effect may actually be to exclude most of the public.)

McConnell's unease with the inclusiveness criteria suggests the limitations of an empiricist liberalism that focuses on formal or procedural criteria for equitable treatment and considers the question of substantive ends as a matter of private judgment. Thus his concept of "public" is indeed bipolar. As some black and feminist activists warned in the 1960s, their protests might only succeed in gaining entry to a society that would remain as substantively privatistic as ever. (The political goals of Parker and his fellow humanitarian reformers exhibits a parallel problem. To insist on including the less-advantaged in Jacksonian economic competition was all very well, but this norm only specified who would participate, not what goals they should seek—what they should do with their material wealth—once they were included.)[29]

Self-Development and Substantively
Public Regarding Social Practices

McConnell does not explicitly consider the substantive criteria for the concept of public in American political discourse. But we shall see that the essential step is to link the concern with generality important for procedural criteria to the philosophic or social sense of the concept that emphasizes the shared standards of a social practice. For the decisive point, which procedural standards and empiricist liberalism ignore, is that almost any important and complex social practice, be it gardening, playing chess, or speaking English, requires the mastery of certain essential rules, precepts, and skills. The issue here is fundamental; for on the substantive standards view the human personality is not most importantly characterized, as in empiricist liberalism, by a set of primitive wants or preferences (and perhaps rights) that should be maximized. What is important instead is the capacity to develop one's faculties—in Parker's terms, to cultivate one's soul—according to culturally specified standards that make experiences more intelligible and intentional actions more coherent.[30] Precisely because this capacity is common to all members of a polity, social practices are substantively public regarding just to the extent that they generally contribute to this self-development.

In the American case, this concern with fundamental self-development has characterized the substantive standards approach to both political and social reform. For some groups, the central issue has been to make education not just a matter of vocational training but an attempt to develop the child's moral, intellectual, and esthetic capacities.[31] For other groups, the central objective has been to make American democracy participatory, not just as a means for securing one's preferences but also as an area in which to develop the individual's ability to deliberate collectively about common issues. (It was just this concern with the integrity of democratic principles that animated much of the civil rights movement during the 1960s).[32] For still others, notably McConnell himself, the goal has been to preserve the integrity of the natural environment, not just as an economic resource but out of an almost religious belief that communion with nature is the source of true self-understanding and regeneration.[33]

Indeed, if one takes as a guide those political objectives McConnell associates with large constituency or public regarding politics, it seems that this contribution to self-development can occur at two levels. First, because the mastery of all complex social practices depends upon a basic cultural competence, some social practices are especially public regarding to the extent that their skills are fundamental for meaningful participation in the relevant culture. Although the character of these practices may vary across societies, they will everywhere include the use of language, the education of the young, and other specific skills necessary to act effectively and intelligently in a particular natural and cultural environment. McConnell's discussion indicates that such practices are substantively public regarding, however, only to the extent that they are universalistic or available to all citizens. One may stipulate that "education" refers to merely custodial child care, yet even if run efficiently this activity is not public regarding from the substantive standards perspective. It does not transmit and enrich the practices that make common life possible. As another example, a large majority may favor, and indeed be benefited by, lowering the quality of care for the insane in order to reduce taxes. Yet this policy is not substantively public regarding if it violates the society's observable norms of humane treatment.[34]

At least in American society, McConnell's work suggests, a second set of practices are especially public regarding in substantive terms because they require a mastery that involves more than just performing competently. Although one can learn English just well enough to speak with ordinary facility, and learn chess just well enough to play adequately, the norms that control these activities also provide standards of excellence. The concept of "mastery," in other words, rightly includes grand masters in chess and literary masters of the English language—and thus an ideal of "excellence" in terms of which these social practices may themselves be extended and transformed. But these substantive standards of excellence can be considered public regarding only if they are sufficiently general to be both exemplary and engaging. To be *exemplary*, the practice must be sufficiently difficult, as in the case of chess and English literature, so that true mastery clearly exhibits craftsmanship, creativity, and development that go beyond mere proficiency. For a practice to be *engaging*, all of those members of society who do not participate directly (or creatively) must be able to appreciate its achievements, not just passively or even contemplatively but by empathetically taking the role of those who excel.[35] English literature or chess satisfies this second condition, but antisocial activities do not; engaging practices do not have victims.

At least in the American case, substantive standards liberalism, from Parker's Transcendentalism through Dewey's pragmatism to the reform politics of our own time, has been concerned (to give an illustrative list) with such cultural institutions as schools, museums, orchestras, and more recently the architectural achievements of the American past. Once again these practices are substantively public regarding only insofar as they are either genuinely fundamental or both exemplary and engaging. For example, some phase of a culturally valuable activity may be monopolized by a privileged few or even commercialized in the pursuit of private profit. But in terms of substantive standards, the issue is not quantitative inclusiveness, that is, how many or how few can presently enjoy (or profit from) a building, painting, or even a scenic area. Instead the question is whether the practice preserves an opportunity for self-development and self-understanding—that is, its general significance for both present and future generations.

Here, I believe, we reach a decisive difference between the two sets of conceptual criteria for the concept of "public," and thus between the two poles of American liberalism.[36] As it identifies more public regarding activities, the substantive standards perspective becomes more specific and restrictive about goals or ends, insisting that the activities be (1) fundamental or (2) both exemplary and engaging. By contrast, the question of means, how one is to achieve success, continues to be treated as a matter of private creativity and initiative. Precisely because questions of ends are fixed by the relevant social practice, the substantive standards perspective has been much more open than the interest tradition to experimentation about means.[37] Indeed, this openness with respect to means may well be more obvious the more one is committed to excellence rather than merely competence. Although there are esthetic criteria for evaluating good and bad art and for protecting and displaying it effectively, the methods for achieving creativity vary widely, and imaginativeness and originality are highly valued.

For empiricist liberalism the situation is very different. As they assert more explicitly public values, the relevant procedural criteria for the concept of "public" become more specific and restrictive in the choice of permissible means, ultimately rejecting any policy that fails to meet McConnell's inclusiveness criteria. But as McConnell's uneasiness about these criteria suggests, this perspective leaves the substantive question of ends to individual or group choice.

Substantive Standards, Inclusiveness, and the Concept of "Public"

In many cases, procedural and substantive criteria either coincide or supplement each other. Both sets, of course, reject as private regarding such practices as murder by hire, or policies that cater to a small group's material interests through, say, special tax and tariff preferences. There are also cases where one set of criteria supplements the other. Given two competing but comparably inclusive policies, for example, economic development and the protection of a widely used cultural institution such as a museum, one can consistently invoke the substantive standards criterion to favor the latter. Again, where the substantive standards criteria do not indicate a clear choice, say between policies favoring art museums and private art collectors (assuming each would take excellent care of their works of art), the inclusiveness criteria would clearly favor the museums.

Nevertheless, the two sets of criteria sometimes directly conflict. Meaningful opportunities to participate in democratic assemblies decrease as the number of participants grows, since each individual has less time to speak and profit from the reactions of others. Similarly, the quality of a musical performance may decline as the audience grows too large for an acoustically suitable auditorium, just as the ecological character of a public park may be damaged by large numbers of visitors. Nor are such conflicts limited to these questions of "jointness of supply."[38] Contemporary politics, for example, is marked by a direct clash between consumer demands for energy and the environmentalist opposition to strip mining in scenic rural areas that only a small fraction of the population is ever likely to visit. Given these conflicts, it seems plain that these two uses of "public" cannot be entirely reconciled. Rather than settling such issues, McConnell's complex usage reemphasizes the basic bipolarity that has characterized American liberalism since Parker's time.

The Permanent Features of
American Liberalism:
Consensus or Bipolarity?

I believe this emphasis on substantive criteria is consistent with
McConnell's own use of "public" and his understanding of how that
concept sometimes functions in American politics. Consider especially
his clear support for the ecology movement and his distaste, shared with
Parker, for group goals that are "narrow and concrete" and "usually
economic and material in character."[39]

As we have seen, however, in McConnell's empirical analysis, private interests are so powerful that little room is left for public regarding,
standards-oriented groups such as environmentalists. In accounting for
this monolithically privatistic pattern, McConnell emphasizes a pervasive American fear of governmental or public power, and explicitly in-
vokes Louis Hartz's Lockean interpretation of American liberalism.[40]
But Hartz's interpretation is consensual rather than bipolar, exhibiting
only an empiricist concern for interests, rights and preferences.[41] Just
as Parker's bipolar view of political practice seems more satisfactory
than his insistence that only the Transcendentalists' substantive standards are permanent, so too McConnell's implicitly bipolar use of the
concept of "public" must be vindicated against his more monolithic
Hartzian, or broadly empiricist, interpretation of American political
practice. Accordingly, I shall now briefly assess Hartz's thesis which
argues both that the American liberal tradition is consensual and that
this consensus is empiricist in character.

Hartz's Consensual Interpretation
of American Liberalism

Although Hartz's thesis is much too rich and complex to be fully sum-
marized here, it is feasible to outline his argument, defend some of his
claims about the pervasiveness of American liberalism, (and its non-
feudal origins) and, finally, criticize his position from a bipolar perspective. Following one of Tocqueville's basic insights, Hartz observes that
the British American settlers represented only a liberal middle-class
fragment of European society.[42] Given their liberal values and their
effective freedom from the constraints of the English crown, English
aristocratic society, and England's feudal past, these settlers formed a
consensually liberal community. All white immigrants were free to pursue individual goals—to practice a politics of "atomistic social
freedom"—save only where they interfered with the similar rights of

others. Indeed, the weakness of their feudal institutions meant that American Lockeans were even more opposed to a powerful state than Locke himself (who valued it as a weapon with which to smash feudal social arrangements),[43] thus creating the very fear of state power McConnell finds so important. Applied to the late eighteenth century, this argument rejects any interpretation of the rebellion of 1776 as a genuinely bourgeois social revolution. Applied to Parker's Jacksonian era, that is, to the individualist society that Tocqueville visited, this analysis views the conflict over suffrage extension as a narrowly political matter in which all parties were committed to basically liberal values. As an analysis of later American politics, Hartz's thesis seems most persuasive in identifying a permanently limiting language and practice that excludes from American politics any nonliberal (i.e., socialist or hierarchical conservative) mass movements. On one side, Americans lack the categories with which to recognize basic social divisions and the political example of a revolutionary bourgeois class, both of which are necessary to sustain a militant working-class politics. As a result, where a socialist might see class confrontation, most Americans see only pluralist, empiricist liberal conflict among narrow, typically economic, interests. For all the workers' suffering and exploitation, American socialists have evoked only a limited, sporadic response.[44] On the other side, this same inability to think systematically about class differences, and thus to defer to those with inherited social status, has left many Americans uninterested in the traditionalist use of state power to limit individual freedom. Strongly attached to laissez faire economics, American conservatism has remained deeply suspicious of the powerful, permanent state apparatus so attractive to the European right.[45]

If this brief and selective survey suggests the persuasiveness of Hartz's argument, it also indicates three general lines of criticism which themselves differ in their validity. First, American liberalism has not been as pervasive as Hartz claims. Second, he overemphasizes the importance of America's nonfeudal past. Third, his consensus thesis misdescribes the character of American liberalism. Although the concern about pervasiveness is warranted, I believe it typically qualifies rather than rebuts Hartz's thesis. Hartz's stress on the liberal norm of atomistic social freedom, for example, does obscure the collectivist impact of industrialization and corporate growth on both political activity and public policy. Some socialist presidential campaigns have been relatively successful (e.g., 1912 and 1932); as McConnell notes, there have been some notable local victories. Within the two-party system itself, an influential prowelfare state alliance between most of organized labor and the national Democratic party has supported collectivist welfare-state programs since the New Deal.[46] Socialist successes, nevertheless, have been transient at best, and electoral politics has never been organized around the class-based cleavages that are so common in Western Europe. Similarly, both the union-Democratic party alliance and the welfare state it supports are weaker and less collectivist than their Western European counterparts. And this difference is clearly consistent with Hartz's thesis.

Again, as Hartz himself recognizes, American political leaders—from Hamilton, Clay, and Webster through the New Deal to our own time— have endorsed a policy of state intervention in the economy inconsistent with the norms of atomistic social freedom.[47] Yet this point is not fatal to Hartz's argument. Both Clay and Webster (and indeed Roosevelt's New Deal) shared with their laissez faire opponents a Lockean commitment to liberal democracy and private enterprise. For the Jacksonians, the real political issue (as framed in terms of McConnell's inclusiveness criteria) was a choice among liberal means: whether the Democrats' stress on economic freedom and equal opportunity, or the Whig's stress on public goods such as roads, canals, and a national bank, would best achieve the shared goal of capitalist economic development.

The second line of criticism emphasizes other sources than a non-feudal tradition for the strength of American liberalism. Socialist weakness, for example, may perhaps be attributed to the early onset of white male suffrage (which limited the workers' strictly political grievances); or to the basic pluralism of the American colonial experience, compounded by later, ethnically diverse immigration (which divided the working class); or to the country's unparalleled natural riches (which limited the workers' economic grievances); or, finally, to the often violent repression of workers' movements.[48] But these factors cannot be fully distinguished from those Hartz emphasizes. For example, colonial pluralism, diverse ethnic migration, and the early spread of suffrage may simply show the importance of both nonfeudal liberal values and a liberal theory of citizenship. Again, the repression of worker protest may indicate the unquestioning self-confidence of the industrial bourgeoisie in a thoroughly liberal culture. Hartz himself points out that, while American economic wealth by itself could hardly be a sufficient condition for a liberal consensus, it did provide the necessary material basis.[49] From a bipolar perspective, then, the real problem with Hartz's thesis is less its assertions about the pervasiveness of American liberalism than its insistence on consensus—which itself ignores the distinction within empiricist liberalism between interests and rights. Consider again Hartz's account of socialist weakness. Even if America did not inherit categories congenial to class-based politics, why weren't these categories invented, particularly after the plight of industrial workers became obvious?

One possible answer is that Parker's substantive standards provided enduring and thoroughly liberal categories with which the American capitalist economy could subsequently be criticized. On one side, this tradition remained pluralist and individualist, and thus nonsocialist, in orientation. Indeed, because its fundamental concern was cultural and social, it remained open to any economic system, capitalist or otherwise, that could be made more genuinely humane. Nevertheless, given its concern with the moral, intellectual, and social development of every individual, this perspective would find many of the self-regarding, privatistic features of American capitalism simply unacceptable. As a result, Parker's substantive standards tradition—as articulated, for example, by the Knights of Labor or left-wing Progressives—could absorb and channel much of the anticapitalist energy and outrage that socialist movements effectively mobilized elsewhere.

Jacksonian Politics: Liberal Consensus or Liberal Bipolarity?

This criticism of Hartz holds only if American political practice can be validly described in bipolar terms. Now the bipolarity seems to describe the contrast between the rather privatistic politics of the 1970s, and the civil rights, feminist, public interest, and environmental protest politics of the 1960s. But Hartz developed his consensual thesis before the 1960s, and he devotes four of his eleven chapters to Parker's own Jacksonian era—the period which saw Tocqueville's visit, the first mass-based parties and workingmen's political organizations, an explosion of acquisitive capitalism, and conflict over the state's economic role. It is in terms of this period, therefore, that I shall argue for the relative advantages of a bipolar view of American liberalism.[50]

The most obvious problem for a liberal consensus interpretation of the Jacksonian era is the bitter sectional conflict that destroyed the Whig party, ended the Democrat's electoral dominance, and finally produced civil war. On first impression the problem seems especially serious, since contrary to a consensus thesis much of the conflict appears to have taken place within the American liberal community. Indeed, Hartz himself seems to admit that the conflict actually divided American liberals, since he identifies many bourgeois features of Southern society and liberal features of Southern thought.[51] Not only did Southerners, including their leading politician John C. Calhoun, hold major positions in national politics and government, but they used liberal arguments to defend their regional position.[52] And as Hartz recognizes, Calhoun's

Lockean assertion of minority rights has been widely considered a major statement of American liberal and especially pluralist theory.

Faced with this apparent difficulty, Hartz tries to interpret the sectional conflict as a struggle between the liberal consensus which remained intact in the North and the South's aberrant "feudal," therefore nonliberal, "dream." Properly spelled out, this argument depends on at least four subsidiary claims of which Hartz explicitly makes only the first and third:

1. That the South's major coherent defense of slavery was cast in nonliberal terms.

2. That one could consistently attack slavery with Lockean (or more generally empiricist liberal) arguments.

3. That as a matter of theory, liberal attempts, by Calhoun and others, to defend slavery can be ignored because they are intellectually incoherent.

4. That as a matter of practice, empiricist liberals—and not those adhering to substantive standards—dominated the antislavery movement.

As I shall try to show, however, Hartz's argument fails because claims 3 and 4, on which it depends, cannot be sustained.

With respect to the first claim, as Hartz rightly maintains, some Southern intellectuals did oppose Yankee materialism and liberalism with their own romantic vision of tradition, hierarchy, family, and order (themes that can be traced back at least to John Randolph of Roanoke).[53] And it is also true that others, primarily in the South, defended slavery or tolerated its persistence on the racist ground of black inferiority and made nonliberal, even protosocialist attacks on the economic oppression of Northern workers. Thus Hartz plausibly observes that some Southerners did abandon liberal premises in order to defend their "peculiar institution." And it is equally true, as Hartz implicitly holds, that one could consistently use empiricist liberal (and specifically Lockean) appeals to human experience in order to condemn slavery. Thus, one might follow Richard Hildreth in weighting the slaves' pain so heavily that a utilitarian calculation of total human happiness might justify outright opposition. Or one could join Hinton Helper, Webster in his famous reply to Hayne,[54] and some abolitionists in empirically comparing the economic and social development of free societies and slave societies in order to criticize slavery. Finally, one could argue that, precisely because blacks were culturally disadvantaged by their experience as slaves, their emancipation could be expected to promoted their educational and economic progress.

Hartz is quite mistaken, however, when he moves from these considerations to the much stronger claim that empiricist liberalism is inconsistent with a proslavery position. In his view, Calhoun's reconciliation of liberal freedom with slavery (his distinction between governmental coercion and constitutional liberty) produced a contradictory, even "disintegrated," theory. Even with respect to Calhoun himself, this judgment may have been made too quickly, since empiricist liberal principles can nonarbitrarily exclude the slaves from citizenship and thus, from the protection of membership in a liberal community.[55] Specifically, such an exclusion seems consistent with an empiricist epistemology which holds that each individual's personality and future behavior are fundamentally shaped and limited by the content of their sense experience. Provided one believed that the specific experience of slavery (together perhaps with that of African tribal culture) left the blacks unable to participate responsibly or effectively in a free society, continued coercion could have consistently been seen as legitimate and necessary.

Whatever the coherence of Calhoun's position in particular, a generally consistent empiricist case was made for a defensive, or at least tolerant, attitude toward Southern interests. Although all the major variations cannot be stated here, this argument took roughly the same form whether it primarily emphasized rights (as with Thomas Jefferson), or interests and utility (as with John Taylor of Caroline and Daniel Webster),[56] or both (as with Henry Clay). In each instance the argument includes: first, empirical observations about the Africans' experiences as slaves; second, an empirical prediction about their behavior if emancipated; third, empirical observations supporting the prediction; and, finally, an ethical evaluation of that predicted behavior from either a rights or utilitarian perspective.

From a natural or individual rights perspective, the decisive observation was the slaves' experience of outrage at the denial of their liberty and property. Given their feelings, one could predict that emancipation would produce an orgy of vengeance followed by white retaliation and racial conflict, and could support the prediction by citing several celebrated slave rebellions. This prediction in turn justified opposition to abolition. As Jefferson wrote in his famous letter to John Holmes of Massachusetts, the South had "the wolf by the ears" and had to balance the liberty of the black race against the life and safety of the white. Or as Clay said a generation later, while he was "no friend of slavery," nevertheless, "I prefer ... the liberty of my own race to that of any other race. The liberty of descendents of Africa in the United States is incompatible with the safety and liberty of the European descendents."[57] Substantial emancipation, then was precluded (1) because the right to life was more fundamental than the right to liberty, and (2) because the whites' right to life implied the duty of securing their own self-preservation, even if it meant keeping blacks enslaved.

From the standpoint of utility or interest, the crucial observation was that the slaves' experiences on the plantation had left them uneducated and ignorant. Accordingly, one could empirically predict that freed blacks would contribute little to economy and be unable to provide for their own needs. To support this prediction, Southern apologists such as Taylor and moderates such as Clay made the claim that freed blacks typically lived immoral, idle lives. Ethically, emancipation could be rejected on utilitarian grounds as economically inefficient, costly to the slave owners, and cruel to the free but impoverished ex-slaves, especially those too old or sick to fend for themselves. Indeed, this suffering could be depicted as all the more unnecessary, since on a utilitarian account rational slave owners had every incentive to treat cooperative slaves well and would do so more regularly if only abolitionist agitation could be stopped. To sum up with respect to the third claim on which Hartz's position depends: although liberal empiricist premises neither compelled nor entailed tolerant or defensive attitudes toward slavery, these premises clearly permitted and may well have encouraged just such a pro-Southern position.

As for the fourth subsidiary claim, contrary to Hartz's implicit position, the slavery issue did *not* first develop as a struggle between slavery's defenders and its empiricist (Lockean) liberal opponents. On the contrary, the early formative conflict over slavery actually took place *between* the two poles of American liberalism, with substantive standards liberals insisting on emancipation. In fact, Hartz's own persuasive claims about the consensual character of Jacksonian electoral politics actually undercut his treatment of slavery and sectionalism. To be sure, as Hartz's broader thesis maintains, the second (Jacksonian) party system was dominated by Democrats and Whigs whose egalitarian laissez faire versus state-interventionist debate over economic policies rested on empiricist, if not specifically Lockean, assumptions. But the most important of these party leaders in both regions tried to block any serious challenge to slavery through compromises designed to keep it off the national issue agenda while allowing it to expand into some federal territories.[58] Although many of them personally abhorred slavery, these empiricist liberal leaders rightly saw the issue as a threat, not just to national unity but to the familiar set of largely economic issues on which Jacksonian party conflict politics was based.

Not surprisingly, then, demands for emancipation in this period primarily developed within the broader humanitarian reform movement that mainly developed outside the two-party system. And whatever their personal religious beliefs, the antislavery activists (including Parker) almost all came from a generally Calvinist background and espoused a humanitarian liberalism of substantive standards.[59] Indeed, save only perhaps for the notable exception of Richard Hildreth, no leading utilitarian or natural rights–oriented writer saw slavery as sufficiently intolerable to take a leading role in the antislavery movement's formative period through the mid-1840s. Hartz, to be sure, somewhat offhandedly recognizes just this point when he characterizes the leading opponents of slavery, such as Garrison, Channing, and Parker, as "romantics."[60] But he fails to note that, contrary to his general argument, Parker and other antislavery Transcendentalists explicitly rejected Locke's empiricist epistemology and, at least implicitly, any contractarian or utilitarian political thought.

The contrast here between empiricist and substantive standards liberalism is clear. At least in the egalitarian form espoused by Parker and his humanitarian reformer contemporaries, the basic premises came very close to entailing an antislavery position, since personal slavery denied the African the opportunity to achieve self-development, to exercise choice in the crucial area of moral conduct.[61] And for the morally conscientious white, this denial created a duty to work for emancipation, to put an end to national sin. At least on the question of slavery, American liberalism exhibited a philosophically rooted polarization rather than consensus.

Conclusion: Conflict, Change and Political Permanence

But in what way can a permanent bipolarity help explain a transient event such as the coming of the Civil War or, in the next century, the emergence of McConnell's militant environmentalist movement? In the case of the antislavery movement, Parker and many other activists outside electoral politics at first worked for other humanitarian reforms, including temperance, education, and the prisons. Yet, as they came to concentrate on slavery, they retained the same ethical commitments. Again, many antislavery electoral politicians first participated in Antimasonry, a movement that shared with antislavery a Protestant evangelical style, a universalistic insistence on moral equality, and a constituency geographically concentrated in rural New England, Western New York, and areas of the Midwest where New Englanders settled.[62] In both instances the focus on slavery represented a shift within a general and continuing substantive standards tradition. Since the tradition persisted it cannot be the cause of this shift in focus, at least if "cause" means the change in one factor that produces a change in another. The causes must be other, more transient factors—including, perhaps, changes in plantation agriculture that made slavery's future

seem more secure, capitalist growth that linked the Eastern and Western free states and threatened the South's relative economic and demo-
graphic importance, territorial expansion that repeatedly raised the
issue of slavery's extension, and finally, the spread of democratic, universalistic values that made it harder to rationalize slavery.

On this issue, the link between the permanent features of a political
culture and its more transient causal patterns, Hartz's discussion may
be revealing. In his view, the Lockean consensus effectively prevented
the emergence of a socialist or collectivist working-class movement,
even when the American capitalist economy became heavily industrialized. Thus in terms of causal theory the consensus was a culturally
constituted boundary condition that both precludes certain outcomes
and affects those causal relationships that do occur. Industrialization,
for instance, did help produce working-class political protest, but it was
relatively moderate (witness the CIO unions during the 1930s and
1940s). Thus the consensus weakened the causal link between economic
change and political behavior.

Although Hartz is less explicit on how this cultural boundary condition operates, his emphasis on political values suggests the importance
of the political actors' intentional behavior, including their perceptions,
beliefs, and purposes. For if fundamental political and ethical values
have been consensually fixed, actors in American politics would find
their range of intentional choice sharply restricted. As a result, any
economic or social change would tend to be seen in terms of its immediate impact; each issue would be reduced to a clash of specific
interests,[63] rather than part of a broader class-based struggle over the
character of the regime. As Hartz himself suggests, this pattern may
help account for the dearth of American political theory.[64]

The situation changes, however, when we assume a permanent but
bipolar, rather than consensual, liberal culture. In the case of slavery,
for instance, important social and economic changes were interpreted
very differently by adherents of the two liberal traditions. On one side,
both Northern capitalists and empiricist liberal politicians were able to
interpret the major economic developments of the time as warrants for
sectional harmony. Consider both the westward spread of cotton plan-
tations and the North's greater economic growth.[65] Insofar as the
Southern slave economy continued to grow in absolute terms, it
qualified for protection as an established substantial interest. Yet insofar as the institution was threatened by the North's more rapid economic growth, there was ample precedent for treating this important
interest with special consideration. Empiricist, interest-oriented liberalism thus encouraged the compromises of 1850 and 1854 that
sought to still the sectional quarrel while preserving slavery's access

to some Western territories. Just as the consensus thesis argues, empiricist liberals understood the potentially divisive consequences of social-economic change as limited, negotiable issues that provided them the option of compromise and conciliation.

On the other side, humanitarian, substantive standards liberals like Parker interpreted these same economic changes very differently. First, the North's economic superiority could be seen almost providentially as a sign of the virtues of a free society. Second, the very strength of the plantation system made slavery's persistence so probable that a crusade for emancipation became ethically mandatory. From this perception came the conflicts within the North and between the sections over such issues as the Wilmot proviso, "Bleeding Kansas," and the fate of fugitive slaves—issues which eventually divided the churches, the parties, and the union itself.

The bipolar approach, then, also specifies a cultural boundary condition that shaped the impact of social and economic change by encouraging radically opposed descriptions of social and economic changes, that is, as a threat to an established and valued interest, *or* as further entrenching slavery. In Charles Taylor's phrase, these two descriptions "secreted" the evaluations that led to political conflict.[66] Consequently, American politics faced not just a clash of discrete and limited interests but a fundamental choice that called for purposive, self-reflective political action.

This discussion suggests that the consensual and bipolar accounts may fundamentally differ on the place of social and economic interests in determining American political life. For the consensus thesis, the settled character of fundamental political issues means that interests typically have a stable and dominant role in influencing political behavior. For the bipolar approach, the political importance of these interests varies from case to case, and, as the slavery issue shows, they lose some of that importance when humanitarian substantive standards liberals persuasively articulate alternative descriptions of American political life.

Even on this bipolar account, however, the range of such intentional descriptions is clearly limited. In particular, neither liberal pole is well equipped to describe social-economic conflicts as fundamental oppositions. Just as few Northern whites after reconstruction recognized and acted on the desperate plight of the ex-slaves, so too the fate of the nineteenth-century proletariat was not seen in class terms. Many empiricist liberals, to be sure, saw these workers as an important interest group, and some substantive standards liberals believed the treatment of the working class violated their ethical and cultural values. But neither group could accept a nonliberal description of the working class as the radical side of a social conflict that would doom or transform capitalism. Neither the liberal tradition that followed Parker nor that which followed his empiricist opponents offered the sustenance vital for a successful American socialist movement.

It is within just these limits, imposed by a bipolar liberal tradition, that Grant McConnell has analyzed American politics. Despite his sensitivity to the political consequences of social-economic change, for example, his discussion of American agriculture, McConnell has insisted on the permanent importance of an acquisitive private regarding group politics—while his conceptual framework suggests the possibility of a substantive standards politics concerned with the quality of American public life.

This parallel between McConnell's perspective and Theodore Parker's, I have maintained, suggests the enduring importance of a liberal bipolarity that constrains the development of more transient issues, parties, and ideologies. Yet permanence in McConnell's work is both more complex and more relative than it was for Parker. Although the first sources of the liberal bipolarity can be traced back beyond colonial America to the beginning of modern Western culture,[67] this split itself appears to have taken clear shape only in Parker's time (after the Second Great Awakening).[68] Equally important, as I have suggested elsewhere, the content of each pole has changed since then.[69] Among substantive standards liberals, for instance, Parker's Transcendentalism gave way to a more secular and sophisticated pragmatist philosophy and a Progressive politics that McConnell in his turn perceived as simplistic. Seen more generally, the transition from Parker's perspective to McConnell's exhibits a move from theology to a concern with the meanings of concepts such as "public," from religious belief to those presuppositions of speech and practice with which Americans continue to make their political experience and action intelligible. As a result, the American liberal bipolarity exhibits not a strict continuity of particular beliefs but the persistence of a more fundamental, philosophical opposition between two contrasting views of human nature and cognition.

The question for the 1980s, of course, is whether this liberal division has now finally ended; whether substantive standards liberalism can continue to play the creative critical role with respect to American capitalism that it has played for Parker and McConnell. But as the career of each man suggests, there is no easy answer. We must respond to this question, as they have done, in our political practice as well as our political theory.

Notes

1. Theodore Parker, "Discourse of the Transient and Permanent in Christianity," in *The Transcendentalists,* ed. Perry Miller (Cambridge, Mass.: Harvard University Press, 1971), p. 263.

2. Stanley Cavell, *Must We Mean What We Say?* (New York: Charles Scribner's Sons, 1969), pp. 19–21.

3. Parker, "Discourse," pp. 273, 277–78. This point is made more explicitly in Theodore Parker, "The Previous Question between Mr. Andrews Norton and His Alumni," in Miller, ed. (n. 1 above), pp. 226–31.

4. On this point, see Hanna F. Pitkin, *Wittgenstein and Justice* (Berkeley: University of California Press, 1972), pp. 106 ff.; Cavell, *Must We Mean What We Say?* p. 19, and "The Claim to Rationality" (Ph.D. diss., Harvard University, 1961–62), p. 214. In the main, their position is derived from Ludwig Wittgenstein, *Philosophical Investigations,* 3d ed., trans. G. E. M. Anscombe (New York: Macmillian Publishing Co., 1968), pt. I, pars. 20, 28–32.

5. Cavell, *Must We Mean What We Say?* p. 25.

6. Grant McConnell, *Private Power and American Democracy* (New York: Alfred A. Knopf, Inc., 1966). This work will serve as the primary focus of this analysis, but see also Grant McConnell, *The Decline of Agrarian Democracy* (Berkeley: University of California Press, 1953), and his *Steel and the Presidency* (New York: W. W. Norton & Co., 1953). For works with a similar perspective, see E. E. Schattschneider, *The Semisovereign People* (New York: Holt, Rinehart & Winston, 1960); Theodore Lowi, *The End of Liberalism: Ideology, Policy and Crisis of Public Authority* (New York: W. W. Norton & Co., 1969); and Robert Engler, *The Politics of Oil* (Chicago: University of Chicago Press, 1961).

7. Parker, "Discourse," pp. 273, 277–78.

8. Miller (n. 1 above), p. 449.

9. George M. Frederickson, *The Inner Civil War* (New York: Harper & Row, 1968), pp. 12–14.

10. There is, of course, an extensive literature on the concepts of the "public" and the "public interest." To cite just a few examples: Brian Barry, *Political Argument* (New York: Humanities Press, 1965); Richard Flatham, *The Public Interest* (New York: John Wiley & Sons, 1966); Carl J. Friedrich, ed., *The Public Interest,* Nomos ser., vol. 5 (New York: Atherton Press, 1962); John Dewey, *The Public and Its Problems* (New York: Henry Holt & Co., 1927).

11. McConnell develops his argument throughout *Private Power.* For general summaries, see pp. 4–8, 157–65, 344. For his negative appraisal of claims about a monolithic power elite, see pp. 336 ff.

12. Ibid., pp. 235–36, 351. Compare this view with the argument developed by Ronald Kahn in his contribution to this volume.

13. McConnell, *Private Power,* p. 368.

14. Ibid., pp. 46–50.

15. Cavell, *Must We Mean What We Say?* pp. 25, 16. Nor could we go on to say "Tom is playing chess fairly well" or "Joan is voting responsibly" without involving additional, more complicated norms or precepts, such as "Protect your king early" or "Vote for a candidate with congenial policy views."

16. "Private persuasion (or personal appeal) is not the paradigm of ethical utterance" (Cavell, *Must We Mean What We Say?* p. 23). This general perspective follows the basic thrust (although by no means the precise arguments) of Wittgenstein's critique of an entirely private language. See Wittgenstein, pt. I, pars. 243 ff.

17. See Wittgenstein, "... every course of action can be made out to accord with [a] rule.... [Therefore] there is a way of grasping a rule which is *not* an *interpretation*, but which is exhibited in what we call 'obeying the rule' in actual cases ... [and] it is not possible to obey a rule 'privately'" (pt. I, pars. 201–2; his emphases).

18. I am indebted to Michael Rogin for making this point to me.

19. Theodore Parker, "Sermon of Merchants," in Miller, ed. (n. 1 above), pp. 449–57.

20. Frederickson, *The Inner Civil War*, pp. 190 ff.

21. McConnell, *Private Power*, pp. 52–53, 89.

22. For a balanced discussion of Jacksonian politics, see Glyndon G. Van Deusen, *The Jacksonian Era: 1828–48* (New York: Harper & Bros., 1959). Cf. Rush Welter, *The Mind of America 1820–1860* (New York: Columbia University Press, 1975). For McConnell's use of the term "inclusiveness," see *Private Power*, p. 365.

23. McConnell, *Private Power*, pp. 356, 365.

24. Ibid., pp. 366; cf. pp. 227–28.

25. Ibid., pp. 356, 365.

26. Ibid., pp. 301 ff., 332–33.

27. Ibid., chap. 3, esp. pp. 89–90, and chap. 9.

28. Ibid., pp. 227–30.

29. See Ralph Waldo Emerson, "Politics," in *Ralph Waldo Emerson: Selected Prose and Poetry*, ed. Reginald L. Cook (New York: Rinehart & Co., 1955), pp. 193–207.

30. The most forceful and celebrated statement of this position in Parker's time may well be found in the work of Ralph Waldo Emerson. See esp. his "Self-Reliance," Cook, ed., pp. 165–92.

31. Jane Addams, *Twenty Years at Hull-House* (New York: New American Library, 1961), chap. 18; John Dewey, *Democracy and Education* (New York: Macmillan Publishing Co., 1916).

32. J. David Greenstone and Paul Peterson, *Race and Authority in Urban Politics* (New York: Russell Sage Foundation, 1973), chap. 4. Although much of what I have to say in this essay is consistent with this earlier argument, I now believe that that discussion must be somewhat revised, since it was cast in terms of regime interests.

33. McConnell, *Private Power*, p. 228.

34. See my discussion of the treatment of the indigent insane in Parker's time, in "Dorothea Dix and Jane Addams: From Transcendentalism to Pragmatism in American Social Reform," *Social Service Review* 53 (1979): 527–59. In the limiting case, even a change that every member of society preferred, e.g., simplifying some game such as chess or reducing the obligations of democratic citizenship, would not be public regarding insofar as it damaged the quality of public life. This point, I believe, parallels Rousseau's distinction between the General Will and the will of all.

35. This point is taken directly from Dewey's argument that esthetic sensibility involves the active appreciation of the process by which it was produced. See John Dewey, "Art and Esthetic Experience," in *Pragmatic Philosophy*, ed. Amelie Rorty (New York: Doubleday & Co., Anchor Books, 1966), pp. 297–304.

36. This difference, of course, may still be denied if one insists on treating any course of intentional conduct as the expression of some utility or preference, for in that case all human action can be interpreted in interest terms. Our discussion, however, has suggested three problems with this move. First, while utilities and preferences can be determined by individuals, standards are necessarily public in origin. Second, if one defines utility so broadly, as a necessary feature of all intentional human action, it is no longer possible to distinguish between utilitarian and nonutilitarian sources of behavior. In other words, the concept of utility does not enable us to distinguish one type of behavior from another. Finally, if we abandon this distinction between interests and standards, we

must devise some other description that accounts for both McConnell's different conceptions of "public regarding" and the political conflicts between the standards and interests traditions (e.g., over slavery) so important since Parker's time.

37. The standards tradition has been marked by a propensity to experiment since at least the 1830s; in Parker's time, such experimentation took the form of utopian communities, many of which were bastions of antislavery sentiment. See, in particular, Lewis Perry, *Radical Abolitionism* (Ithaca, N.Y.: Cornell University Press, 1973), pp. 139–42. A concern for experimentation was also characteristic of Emerson's individualist and self-reliant Transcendentalism (see his "Self-Reliance"). A similar spirit pervaded pragmatism. Indeed, as Louis Hartz has rightly remarked, both pragmatism (as exemplified at least by John Dewey) and important components of the New Deal reflected a more persuasive moral consensus which led, in Roosevelt's words, to "bold persistent experimentation" (Louis Hartz, *The Liberal Tradition in America* [New York: Harcourt, Brace & Co., 1955], pp. 271, 263). This same experimental attitude and style characterized the behavior of Jane Addams, perhaps the most important turn-of-the-century Pragmatist reformer, who stressed the importance of the settlement houses "as a method" (Addams, p. 115).

38. Jointness of supply is discussed in Mancur Olson's classic study, *The Logic of Collective Action* (Cambridge, Mass.: Harvard University Press, 1971), p. 14 n. 21, p. 38 n. 58, p. 40 n. 61 See also John Head, "Public Goods and Public Policy," *Public Finance* 17 (1961): 197–219.

39. McConnell, *Private Power*, p. 6.

40. Ibid., pp. 33 and 38; for McConnell's reference to Hartz, see p. 25.

41. Hartz, *The Liberal Tradition*, passim.

42. Ibid. See also Louis Hartz, *The Founding of New Societies* (New York: Harcourt, Brace & World, 1964), chaps. 1–4.

43. Hartz, *The Liberal Tradition*, passim.

44. Ibid. McConnell explicitly agrees (see his *Private Power*).

45. Hartz discusses the American revolution in pt. II of *The Liberal Tradition*, Jacksonian politics in pt. III, and socialist weaknesses in chap. 9. On the importance of group politics, see pp. 30 and 250; on the liberal, often laissez faire and antiauthoritarian character of American conservatism, see pp. 7 ff. and chap. 8, esp. pp. 211 ff.

46. McConnell, *Private Power*, p. 25. And J. David Greenstone, *Labor in American Politics* (New York: Alfred A. Knopf, Inc., 1969), passim.

47. Hartz, *The Liberal Tradition*, p. 100.

48. On the impact of white male suffrage, see Ira Katznelson, *City Trenches* (New York: Pantheon Books, 1980), esp. chap. 3. On colonial pluralism, see Michael Kammen, *People of Paradox* (New York: Random House, 1972). On American wealth, see David Potter, *People of Plenty* (Chicago: University of Chicago Press, 1954). And on the repression of union activity, see Robert Goldstein, *Political Repression in Modern America* (Boston: G. K. Hall & Co., 1978), passim.; and Lewis Lorwin, *The American Federation of Labor* (Washington, D.C.: Brookings Institute, 1933), p. 355; and Greenstone, *Labor in American Politics*, p. 19. See also Mark E. Kann, "Challenging Lockean Liberalism in America: The Case of Debs and Hillquist," *Political Theory*, (1980): 103–222.

49. Hartz, *The Liberal Tradition*, pp. 17–18.

50. For a balanced discussion of Jacksonian politics, see Glyndon G. Van Deusen (n. 29 above). Cf. Rush Welter (n. 29 above).

51. Hartz, *The Liberal Tradition*, pp. 154–55. see also *The Founding of New Societies*, p. 102.

52. Hartz recognizes this point quite explicitly in *The Foundation of New Societies*, (p. 60), where he remarks that "Locke is turned upside down, and he is a defender of the chattelized Negro rather than the Negro person."

53. See Russell Kirk, *John Randolph Roanoke: A Study in American Politics: With Selected Speeches and Letters* (Indianapolis: Liberty Press, 1951); William Taylor, *Cavalier and Yankee: The Old South and American National Character* (New York: Harper & Bros., 1957).

54. Daniel Webster, "The Constitution and the Union," in *The Great Speeches and Orations of Daniel Webster*, ed. Edwin P. Whipple (Boston: Little, Brown & Co., 1879), p. 605.

55. Hartz, *The Founding of New Societies*, p. 60.

56. See Webster's "The Constitution and the Union" (Seventh of March Speech, 1850), in Whipple, pp. 604, 605–19, 623, and "Exclusion of Slavery from the Territories," in Whipple, p. 573.

57. Richard H. Sewell, *Ballots for Freedom: Antislavery Politics in the United States, 1837–1860* (Oxford: Oxford University Press, 1976), p. 72.

58. Hartz, *The Liberal Tradition*, pt. III. For a general discussion of the tolerant Democratic amd Whig views on slavery, see Van Deusen, pp. 132–36; Avery Craven, *The Coming of the Civil War* (Chicago: University of Chicago Press, 1957), p. 309; and Welter, pp. 339 ff.

59. Elizur Wright, Jr., "Immediate Emancipation," in *Slavery Attacked: The Abolitionist Crusade*, ed. John L. Thomas (Englewood Cliffs, N.J.: Prentice-Hall, Inc., 1965), p. 11, and "The American Anti-Slavery Society Sends Instruction to Theodore Weld," in ibid., p. 25.

60. Hartz, *The Liberal Tradition*, p. 186.

61. John L. Thomas, "Anti-Slavery and Utopia," in *The Anti-Slavery Vanguard*, ed. Martin Doberman (Princeton, N.J.: Princeton University Press), pp. 240–69.

62. Lee Benson, *The Concept of Jacksonian Democracy* (Princeton, N.J.: Princeton University Press, 1961), pp. 44 ff. See also Van Deusen, pp. 55–56; Martin Duberman, *Charles Francis Addams* (Boston: Houghton Mifflin & Co., 1961), chap. 6; James Brewer Stewart, *Joshua R. Giddings and the Tactics of Radical Politics* (Cleveland: Press of Case Western Reserve University, 1970), pp. 12–14. Gidding's conversion to Antimasonry was quite grudging. Other antislavery leaders with Antimasonry convictions included Myron Halley, Alvan Stewart, and Jerit Smith as well as other members of the Liberty Party (see Sewell, pp. 55–56, 83–84).

63. Hartz, *The Liberal Tradition*, p. 250.

64. Ibid., pp. 6 ff., 141.

65. On the general validity of the slave economy, see Robert Fogel and Stanley Engleman, *Time on the Cross* (Boston: Little, Brown & Co., 1974). For a different perspective, see Barrington Moore, *Social Origins of Dictatorship and Democracy* (Boston: Beacon Press, 1966), chap. 3. And for an early contribution, see Eugene Genovese, "The Significance of the Slave Plantation for Southern Economic Development," *Journal of Southern History* (1962), pp. 422–37.

66. Charles Taylor, "Neutrality in Political Science," in *The Philosophy of Social Explanation*, ed. Alan Ryan (Oxford: Oxford University Press, 1973), pp. 139–71.

67. Sacvan Bercovitch, *The Puritan Origins of the American Self* (New Haven, Conn.: Yale University Press, 1975).

68. John L. Thomas, "Anti-Slavery and Utopia."

69. Greenstone, "Dorothea Dix and Jane Addams" (n. 41 above), passim.

Two ★

The Conflictual Evolution of American Political Science: From Apologetic Pluralism to Trilateralism and Marxism

Mark Kesselman

merican pluralism—or group theory, as it has also been termed—is frequently taxed with being politically conservative and apologetic. But what does one make of the following observation by a pluralist theorist writing in the 1930s? "Influence is the possession of those who have established their supremacy in the invisible empires outside of what is ordinarily known as government. From this point of view, the function of pressure politics is to reconcile formal political democracy and economic autocracy."[1]

In a similar vein, another pluralist at the same time observed, "The working of our present democratic machinery is rigged in favor of those interests that happen to fit in with the economic system."[2]

Originally fashioned in the prewar period as an alternative to Marxism, pluralism did not become an apologia for prevailing American political arrangements until after the Second World War. Eileen Sullivan notes, "It is only with David Truman and with the pluralists of the 1950's that interest group theory is used to justify a presently existing American political system."[3] Pluralist scholars from the 1930s until the 1950s, including Stephen Bailey, E. Pendleton Herring, Peter Odegard, and E. E. Schattschneider, agreed that the internal organization of interest groups was undemocratic, group leaders did not represent the interests of the rank and file, groups were not equal in strength, and government policy favored the interests of economically powerful groups and slighted the weak and unorganized. Prior to the 1950s, Sulli-

This paper was first presented to the University of Paris–I in January 1980. I am grateful for suggestions by Amrita Basu, Samuel J. Bickel, Douglas Chalmers, J. David Greenstone, John Hammond, Ira Katznelson, and Katherine Yatrakas. The paper was completed with the help of a Rockefeller Foundation Humanities Fellowship.

van observes, "The critical conclusion of political scientists ... is that the American polity cannot be legitimated as a democracy because power is so unequally distributed among organized groups and between the organized and unorganized."[4]

The shift from critical pluralism, which stressed that interest groups promoted economic inequality, to an uncritical apologetic pluralism occurred in the 1950s. "Apologetic pluralism" refers to the myriad works on American interest groups, voting behavior, political parties, public opinion, and political culture that appeared during the 1950s.[5] The new approach was elaborated by the major American political scientists of the period. Scholarly journals and college textbooks reflected the apologetic pluralist approach.[6] Although scholars differed in terms of the specific problems studied, the level of analysis, or the weight accorded to various factors, their methodological, theoretical, and normative approaches were broadly similar.

In the 1950s, apologetic pluralists attempted to integrate the theory and practice of politics both in the United States and the Third World. For a brief period, apologetic pluralism was almost undisputed; it continues to be a major current in American political science, albeit in truncated form. (David Garson points out that, from a theory of politics, it became one research area—the study of pressure groups—among others.) By the 1960s, however, the theoretical flaws were already evident. As stability was disrupted by political authorities and dissident groups in the United States and abroad, apologetic pluralism was challenged by scholars whose critical outlook was reminiscent of the earlier period.

The failure to "export" the pluralist model of political development to the Third World was evidenced by what conservative scholars termed political disorder; they reacted by proposing a barely veiled authoritarianism. The approach was applied with a vengeance as the United States attempted to shape political change abroad by installing, financing, and arming repressive regimes. It culminated in the United States invasion of Indochina.

The failure of pluralism stimulated two other approaches to the issue of political change. One is "trilateralism," a more interventionist and authoritarian approach than pluralism, associated with the Trilateral Commission. In contrast to the political development model, which adapted pluralism to the Third World, trilateralism applies to the United States (and other industrialized capitalist nations) the antipluralist approach fashioned in the 1960s in an attempt to subdue the Third World. A second reaction to pluralist theory and practice has been a Marxist approach to the capitalist state and the world capitalist system which attempts to integrate theory and practice regarding developments within the United States and abroad in a progressive rather than repressive fashion.[7]

Background of Pluralism

Two sorts of groups appeared in the apologetic pluralist model elaborated after the Second World War: interest groups and political parties. The two were complementary modes of linking citizens to the polity—processes that Gabriel Almond called interest articulation and aggregation—and were inspired by different theoretical and research traditions.[8]

The theoretical rationale for interest groups derives from the liberal tradition, whose classical expression is the Federalist Papers.[9] Madison explains in the Tenth Federalist that the new constitution is designed to prevent the tyranny of faction, whose most durable source is the unequal distribution of property. He accepts the legitimacy of unequal distribution of property, on the grounds that people naturally possess unequal faculties for acquiring property. (He both overlooks Rousseau's observation that natural inequality is exacerbated by social institutions and he fails to explain why natural aptitudes are necessarily legitimate: e.g., is a natural aptitude for violence an acceptable rationale for murder?)

In a democratic regime, the majority faction, which Madison equates with the poor, is likely to gain power. Since all factions act from self-interest and contrary to justice, this amounts to tyranny. A way must be found, therefore, to maintain a rough equilibrium among factions (in other words, to preserve property differences). Madison thus argues that liberty and equality are incompatible and opts for the former. Ironically, he then seeks ways to restrict the liberty of the majority to achieve equality. The Federalist Papers propose several mechanisms to prevent the poor (and other majorities) from mobilizing. One is large geographic constituencies, which maximize the number of cross-cutting interests. Another is republican government, in which direct participation is "filtered" through the medium of representation, and multiple political institutions are created responsible to divergent constituencies.

For Madison, republican government is the antithesis of democratic government: the latter involves direct participation and majority rule and tends toward a leveling of property differences. Despite the implicitly inegalitarian tendency in the Federalist approach, the distinction between popular and democratic government was later eroded, and the American political regime, with remarkably few institutional modifications, has come to be accepted as democratic. A revised democratic theory, centering on political parties, put forward by Joseph Schumpeter, was in part responsible.

According to Richard Hofstadter, the prevalent view during the founding period was that political parties were "sores on the body politic."[10] A succession of observers held similar views, including Charles Dickens, Igor Ostrogorski, and James Bryce in the nineteenth century, and Progressive reformers in the twentieth century. Despite initial opposition to political parties, the party system became a fundamental feature of American politics. Yet it was not until well into the twentieth century that Joseph Schumpeter provided a theoretical defense of mass political parties and oligarchical leadership, the second major strand of apologetic pluralism.[11] In the process, he tried to convert Michels's "iron law of oligarchy" into a standard of democracy.

According to Schumpeter, technical obstacles to political participation and the fact that most citizens are uninformed and apathetic make direct participation impossible and/or undesirable. Fortunately, mass political parties, controlled by professional politicians, have arisen to relieve citizens of essential tasks, including structuring political choices, formulating positions on issues remote from citizens' concerns, and providing a mechanism for political leadership. By classical democratic standards, the new arrangements would be considered undemocratic, as would every existing polity. Rather than accept such a disquieting conclusion, however, Schumpeter weakens the standard of democracy. Henceforth, democracy will be considered to exist if political parties are free to compete and electoral procedures are honest. Democracy become the right of citizens to participate in the selection of their rulers.

Schumpeter extrapolates from existing practice as the basis for his revision of democratic theory. It therefore is hardly surprising that this practice emerges from his circular exercise as both realistic and desirable. For Schumpeter, the substantive content of policies is irrelevant to the issue of democracy: what counts is not the policies themselves but the procedures by which they are adopted.

Schumpeter's theory is a self-fulfilling prophecy, in that citizen incompetence is cited to justify social and political arrangements which in fact foster this incompetence. The theory accepts as inevitable that the political sphere will be distant from citizens' daily concerns and that citizens will lack sufficient leisure, information, and other resources to exercise responsible choices. Individual citizens, not the system, are irrational. Schumpeter describes citizens as they have become under the influence of depoliticizing economic, social, and political institutions, and he therefore overlooks the influence that institutions wield. Rather than proposing alternative arrangements to encourage a different outcome, he advocates diluting democratic standards. Just as, according to Marx, liberal political economy elevates the laws of estranged labor to universal laws without inquiring into their origins, so Schumpeter (and the apologetic pluralism that he inspired) elevates the laws of estranged political participation to universal laws.[12]

Elements of Apologetic Pluralism

Apologetic pluralist theory combined empirical description of U.S. politics, the attempt to develop quasi-universal laws of political behavior deriving from a distorted reading of the American experience, and a normative defense of the status quo. For about a decade, the theory was universally accepted within American political science, save for the roundly criticized power elite perspective of Floyd Hunter and C. Wright Mills.[13]

According to apologetic pluralism, politics typically consists of competition among self-seeking private interest groups as well as self-interested political party leaders. As in Madison's conception, the main source of conflicts was divergent material interests. In the American case, these were considered to be partial, limited interests rather than class interests. The framework of a capitalist political economy is taken for granted; conflicts involve groups attempting marginally to increase their share of resources generated by the market and state.

The historical juncture may have provided some basis for this approach. During the 1940s and 1950s, capitalist hegemony was unchallenged, and conflicts were confined within narrow boundaries: hot and cold war, as well as the McCarthyist movement, stifled political dissent. The militant labor challenge of the postwar years was overcome in 1947, and a semicorporatist accommodation was fashioned among corporations, industrial unions, and government.

Political scientists overwhelmingly supported the lib-lab coalition forged by Roosevelt. The vital center seemed the fount of virtue, and extremism of any variety was dangerous. Stalinism and Nazism illustrated the dangers that might result from extremism. The political arena came to be seen as coterminous with conflicts among interest groups and competition among prosystem political parties; most political research on American politics during this period focused on these two phenomena.

Along with the behavioral approach with which it was associated, pluralist theory minimized the importance of structure, both formal political institutions as well as structural inequalities in state and society. No pluralist during this period accepted the simplistic view of Arthur Bentley, for whom groups were the only political reality.[14] However, although more sophisticated versions grafted new concepts, in Ptolemaic fashion they failed to resolve the theory's basic inadequacies.

Consider David Truman's attempt to explain power differentials among various interests as well as political stability and change. A critical flaw in his treatment of the relationship between "interest" and "interest group." He suggests that the power of an interest group depends on its access to government, a product of three factors: the group's internal cohesion and leadership skill (both functions of the group's internal organization), the character of governmental institutions, and the group's "strategic position in the society."[15] As for the first factor, Truman implicitly admits its limited significance, despite the attention he accords it: the interests which "achieve effective access and guide [governmental] decisions . . . may not be represented by organized interests. Governmental decisions are the resultant of effective access by various interests, of which organized interests may be only a segment."[16] But Truman does not explain why interests have varying degrees of power. The last factor might imply some view of overall political structure, yet Truman reduces it to an attitudinal dimension: "the group's status or prestige in the society, affecting the ease with which it commands deference from those outside its bounds."[17]

Truman's concept of potential group is meant to encompass interests not represented by formally organized groups and to account for overall systemic stability and change. A potential group for Truman consists of people who share attitudes on a given issue but have not been sufficiently provoked to organize a formal group. As J. David Greenstone has suggested, however, this reduces interests to subjective attitudes and preferences.[18] There are as many unorganized or potential groups as the distribution of responses to questions asked in a public opinion poll. Truman fails to analyze the contingent relationship between subjective preferences and objective interests as well as the relationship between interests and organization. Furthermore, he does not discuss how structural factors may affect the ability of social forces to mobilize when their interests are threatened.

Because his theory lacks a conception of interests, Truman frequently reduces interests to organized groups and their observable activity. For example, he suggests that the concept of public interest is not valid or useful because, on every issue, no matter how basic (e.g., waging war), there will always be some disagreement among citizens. Unanimity is thus the criterion used to ascertain the public interest. Truman uses a similar standard to suggest the absence of a unified interest for a broad grouping like business, since business associations often conflict on a given policy issue.[19] By this standard, however, it would be difficult to find any group, no matter how small, with an interest. Michael Rogin has pointed out that Truman does not apply the demanding standard of unanimity to discern the interests of specific interest groups but reserves it for more inclusive groups.[20]

Truman's attempt to demonstrate that potential groups maintain overall political stability is also questionable. He suggests that extremist groups are deterred from challenging the status quo by the threat that the large unorganized group, consisting of the broad majority of citizens who adhere to the rules of the game, will mobilize. Yet he admits that the process by which such mobilization occurs is an unexplored area and gives no illustration of when it has occurred.[21]

In the introduction to the second edition of *The Governmental Process*, Truman abandons the attempt altogether. He concedes that popular support for the rules of the game is far weaker than he first believed. In his revised explanation of political stability, it is American political leaders who have an interest in safeguarding the political game. Although this approach avoids what Truman recognizes might have appeared to be a "mystical" explanation, it hardly seems adequate to account for American political stability. (For example, it fails to explain the greater cohesion among American political leaders than among political leaders in comparable nations.) In order to provide an adequate explanation, structural factors not easily integrated with a pluralist approach need to be introduced.[22]

Robert Dahl's *Who Governs?* attributes the stable, democratic character of New Haven politics to a rough equality among groups. Dahl begins his study of New Haven by recognizing that groups have unequal resources. However, in the course of his research he finds that these inequalities are dispersed rather than cumulative. Not even the most privileged group wins every political battle; not even the least privileged group loses every one. "Like other groups in the community, from Negroes on Dixwell Avenue to teachers in the public schools, sometimes the [Economic] Notables have their way and sometimes they do not."[23] Dahl concludes that economic inequalities do not nullify democracy in New Haven, but he does not consider whether the persistence of stable and extensive economic inequality does not in itself constitute a substantial victory for New Haven's economic notables.

The apologetic pluralist approach had a pessimistic side as a counterweight to its optimism. Pluralism helped to lower expectations, restrain an uninformed citizenry, and insulate politics from the demagogic appeals of extremists. William Kornhauser described the dangers of mass society, in which the restraints of intermediary associations were eroded and an irrational citizenry succumbed to the blandishments of mass movements.[24] Pluralism was useful because it diverted attention from broad public issues to narrow self-interest and kept citizens at their political and economic last. For this reason, apologetic pluralism implicitly accepts liberal democracy and a capitalist economy: politics becomes the pursuit of private interest by public means. The public marketplace of pluralism, where subjective interests are pursued and subjective preferences registered, parallels (or is an extension of) the private marketplace.

The system being described was so amorphous that, for pluralist theorists, it barely seemed a system at all. Faithful to Schumpeter's approach, pluralists considered the system to consist of procedures for regulating conflict; the substance of what was regulated is irrelevant. Nonetheless the system had sharply etched boundaries: it was stable and self-regulating. Apologetic pluralism had a voluntarist view of politics. Government was *primus inter pares*. The reproduction of the whole system was quite automatic and not dependent on extensive government intervention. Since the process rather than the substance of government was emphasized, it was unnecessary to question the overall direction of state intervention.

The shape of the system emerges more clearly when compared to the implicit alternative: a highly ideological society with few intermediary groups, polarized between warring classes. Although this situation had never existed in the United States, American political struggles of the 1930s as well as the examples of Weimar Germany and Fourth Republic France gave shape to the fear. Moreover, lurking in the wings was the ultimate antithesis of pluralism: fascist and communist forms of totalitarianism. The pluralist system became defined as the vital center, and any other alternative seemed dangerous. First defined as a set of procedures without substantive content, the system was reified such that any proposals for substantial change were considered disruptive. Apologetic pluralist theorists thus became another veto group opposing change.[25]

The relationship of pluralist theory to democracy is colored by a fear of extremist, ideological movements mobilizing intensely motivated followers. Following Madison and Schumpeter, apologetic pluralism views the appropriate modes of political participation as membership in interest groups and electioneering. During this period, extensive survey research amply corroborated Schumpeter's arguments about citizens' lack of motivation and capacity. Most citizens engaged in virtually no political activity beyond voting, and they made their electoral choice on the basis of candidates' personalities and their own inherited party identification rather than the parties' stands on issues. Voters were astonishingly ignorant about political issues and distorted candidates' stands to match their own preferences in order to decrease cognitive dissonance. They displayed little logical constraint or ideological coherence in their political thinking and had only a shallow attachment to civil liberties and procedural democracy.

By contrast, political activists—who generally had greater status, education, and income—ranked higher on all measures of informed and responsible participation. Given these findings, apologetic pluralists viewed the limited extent of mass participation as a positive virtue: democracy was too precious to be entrusted to the people.[26] Truman comments, "In the subtle politics of developing emergency the elites are, for all practical purposes, the people."[27] During normal times as well, the people voluntarily remained politically quiescent.

The critical link in apologetic pluralism between ostensibly value-neutral empirical description and normative defense of the status quo is the theory of procedural democracy, which defines democracy as the legal right to participate, yet ignores the conditions and institutions that make effective participation possible. Pluralists were aware that political participation varied with class membership. But, by a process of blaming the victim rather than the system, they ascribed responsibility for this situation to nonparticipants. Dahl observes, "By their propensity for political passivity the poor and uneducated disenfranchise themselves."[28]

Pluralism and the Third World

The apologetic pluralist approach discussed thus far centered on the United States. A second postwar pluralist thrust in American political science, concerning the newly independent nations of the Third World, differed in three major respects.[29] These differences stemmed from the fact that the United States was already pluralist whereas other nations were, presumably, only in the process of becoming pluralist. First, political development theorists were antagonistic toward tradition in the Third World, whereas apologetic pluralism praised American political culture for promoting pluralism. Tradition and culture in the Third World were parochial, infused with primordial sentiments, and insufficiently individualistic—precisely the opposite of what was required for a modern pluralist society.[30]

Second, pluralism assumed an activist stance when applied to the Third World. Rather than seeking to conserve an existing pluralism, political scientists sought to promote the desired pluralist outcome. In order for development to occur, gaps and obstacles had to be overcome, attitudes fundamentally changed, and a new social infrastructure installed. As Karl Deutsch pointed out in a different context, nation building required tearing down existing institutions and cultural patterns before new ones could take root.[31]

Third, political scientists were concerned with the issue of structural change in the Third World. In the United States, endless change occurred, but it remained within the confines of the pluralist framework. In the Third World, however, structural change was a fundamental feature of nascent political development.

Despite manifold differences between pluralist and political development theories, basic similarities united the two. Both were part of the behavioral revolution in political science that looked beyond the formal framework of governmental institutions. Both believed that American political patterns were the most stable and advanced in the world. In fact, one value in studying the new nations was that history seemed to be repeating itself in telescoped fashion. Unable to study the birth of the first new nation directly, American political scientists were present at the creation of others. The Wilsonian dream of a world safe for pluralist democracy seemed to be reenacted after another World War. Through a mixture of cultural diffusion, universal processes of modernization, and United States influence, these nations would travel the road to pluralism. As Robert Packenham has shown, the goals of both policymakers and political development theorists encompassed such divergent objectives as attaining political stability, overcoming radical threats, securing economic growth through the development of capitalist economies, and developing pro-American orientations.[32]

Studies in nation building took the United States as the model toward which new nations would eventually converge. Although there were many obstacles to political development, there seemed little space in the theory for outcomes other than pluralism. Events soon proved otherwise.

Challenge and
Response in the 1960s

Domestic and foreign political events in the 1960s, as well as newly published research, soon cast doubt in the relevance of pluralism for all nations. Within the United States the civil rights, new left, black power, women's and antiwar movements diverged from the descriptive, theoretical, and normative aspects of pluralism. These movements challenged the rules of the game by refusing to abide by established procedures, were passionately ideological, and demanded large-scale rather than incremental change.

Things were no better abroad. Political change in the Third World never conformed to the political development model. Rather than a steady movement toward pluralism, there were military coups, insurgent movements, and authoritarian regimes.

The lack of pluralism at home and abroad was most clearly manifest in Vietnam. The United States government totally ignored pluralist precepts by sponsoring a repressive puppet government in the South and pursuing a genocidal policy in Indochina. These actions spawned a mass opposition movement in the United States. During the 1960s, when many American cities were the site of militant protest, universities were the scene of recurrent turbulence, and the state itself proved the chief lawbreaker within the United States, and abroad the politics of pluralism was eclipsed by the politics of class, race, social movements, and war.

Within political science, there was widespread criticism of both the domestic and Third World variants of apologetic pluralism. Such criticism, however, was indirect testimony to the dominance of pluralism. The theoretical agenda of American political science remained confined to the strengths and deficiencies of pluralism. Most criticisms in the 1960s remained within the pluralist mode; they identified inconsistencies in pluralism and attempted to realize its promise rather than elaborating an alternative approach. Only in the 1970s did antipluralist approaches emerge.

Many critical pluralists documented the persistence of extensive economic inequalities in the United States.[33] Some explored how members of the underclass were rational in their political thinking and protest tactics in face of a system that ignored and suppressed their demands. Others focused on the links between American political leaders and the social and economic elite. Several critical pluralists demonstrated inconsistencies and biases in pluralist theory and practice as well as the decline of pluralist practice in the United States through the increasing concentration of political power. Among the most incisive theoretical and empirical critiques of apologetic pluralism was that of Grant McConnell.[34]

McConnell's analysis stands at the crossroads of a reaction to the inadequacies of pluralism. His analysis points to three possible future directions: a strengthening and democratizing of pluralism by giving greater voice to the poor and to widely shared but underrepresented consumer interests; or rejecting pluralism in either a left or right direction. In the 1970s Marxist analyses extended McConnell's analysis of how private interests subverted public authority and democracy. Conversely, a reactionary approach began from McConnell's defense of presidential power and state autonomy from private interests, in order to advocate reforms, diametrically opposed to his intent, which sought to insulate political decisions from democratic processes.

Private Power and American Democracy

In an early work, McConnell studied the transformation of American society through a case study of changes in agriculture. He showed how agrarian radicalism in the late nineteenth century turned conservative as farmers declined from a broad-based majority and became organized into the American Farm Bureau Federation (AFBF), a narrowly based pressure group seeking privilege for wealthy farmers. In contrast to many pluralist works, *The Decline of Agrarian Democracy* focused on structural change in the United States. It used an objective standard to judge interests, explored the relationship between interest and interest group, and emphasized inequalities and internal stratification within the AFBF. The book displayed a critical stance, exposing as shortcomings of American democracy what apologetic pluralists described as natural and desirable.

Private Power and American Democracy is a sweeping indictment of apologetic pluralist theory and practice. McConnell explores how the distrust of government and centralization within pluralist theory have legitimated political and economic inequality, the capture of government by private interests, and the systemic bias against consumers, the poor, and blacks. It displays a passionate yet reasoned concern for social justice.

McConnell traces inequalities of power in the United States to four interrelated factors. Three concern the organization of interests, the fourth the relationship of interests to government.

a) Breadth of constituency: the narrow constituency of most organized groups leads them to pursue selfish material interests, whereas groups with a broader constituency are forced to seek a genuine reconciliation of interests as well as broad nonmaterial goals.

b) The organization of interests: more narrow, organized interests prevail over more diffuse ones within American politics.

c) Internal stratification: inequalities within organized interests, deriving from divisions between group leaders and rank-and-file members, often reinforce the division between wealthy and less affluent members;

d) Fragmentation: a decentralized American political structure permits narrowly organized groups to appropriate segments of government, thereby obtaining public authority, legitimacy, and material benefits.

Political institutions responsive to broad interests, including the presidency and national parties, occupy a secondary position within the system.

McConnell studies how three major interests—organized agriculture, business, and labor—gained disproportionate power in the United States. He documents the process by which the organized segments of these interests gained autonomy and control vis-à-vis less powerful members of their constituency, unorganized interests, and government. Further, local political elites benefit from a privileged relationship with these interests and help to perpetuate the prevailing patterns. Elites not only exercise control within their organized constituencies; through a process of logrolling and mutual accommodation, they stabilize the political system and preserve inequalities of wealth and power. This pattern of dispersed yet concentrated private power perverts American democracy.

Apologetic pluralists praised the fragmentation of political conflict, decentralization, and the insulation of functional spheres. Gabriel Almond, for example, suggested that political development required proper boundary maintenance between the functions and institutions of interest articulation and aggregation. Ralf Dahrendorf described the advantages of insulating industrial and political conflict. Similarly, Seymour M. Lipset suggested that the institutionalization of class struggle consisted of separating industrial and political disputes.[35]

McConnell questions this general approach (although not the specific instances cited). He agrees that decentralizing power and fragmenting conflict obscure class polarization and reduce the risk of extremist challenges. But, while opposed to extensive class conflict and extremism, he estimates that they are unlikely to develop in the United States. However, he identifies a further consequence of decentralization: it enables groups to use government for their own narrow private ends at the expense of wider public interests. Broadening the effective political constituency and centralizing political power would encourage the emergence of hitherto suppressed political issues, mobilize nonparticipants, and reverse the conservative bias of pluralism.

McConnell reaches far in his analysis of inequality in the United States, but by retaining the pluralist framework (despite his rejection of apologetic pluralism) he stops short at important points. Although his analysis rests on a sharp theoretical and normative distinction between public and private interests, the distinction is not developed adequately; he does not analyze the substantive content of the public interest nor distinguish among the claims of contending private interests.

McConnell tends to overestimate the degree of harmony in American politics and to underestimate the degree of centralization. On the one hand, he exaggerates the degree to which conflict is muted among and within interests: Michels' iron law does not preclude conflict within groups, nor does logrolling among organized interests spell an end to the intergroup strife or militant protest. For example, the postwar corporatist accommodation reached between corporations and industrial unions did not end industrial conflict. Nor did it eliminate internal union conflict deriving from rank-and-file pressure on union leadership (expressed in wildcat strikes and insurgent movements challenging established leaders). And the militant protest movements occurring in the 1960s find no place in his analysis.

On the other hand, according to McConnell, the power of interest groups derives from their ability to control issues within their narrow domain. But this does not explain how overall cohesion occurs, why there are so few oppositionist groups in the United States, the apparent passivity of those who suffer from prevailing arrangements, and the low degree of class conflict. McConnell obscures the role of the state in repressing conflicts, both through its distribution of ideological and material benefits and its exercise of force.

Despite his trenchant critique of apologetic pluralism, McConnell consciously remains within the pluralist tradition. While he recognizes that power and benefits are unequally distributed—"a substantial part of government in the United States has come under the influence or control of narrowly based and largely autonomous elites"—he distinguishes his position from a Marxian ruling-class perspective or the power-elite approach of C. Wright Mills (p. 339). According to McConnell, no single interest dominates American society. The diverse interests which appropriate privilege are characterized by mutual isolation: standoffish accommodation is hardly equivalent to unified domination. Like Dahl, McConnell considers the power of elites as "noncumulative," for "they tend to pursue a policy of non-involvement in the large issues of statesmanship, save where such issues touch their own particular concerns" (p. 339). Further, "The multiplicity of these elites and their separation from each other in organization sharply distinguish the reality from Marx's perception" (p. 340).

Since public authority is parceled out to diverse interests, each of which has succeeded in dominating its "own" government agency, state power is not exerted in a coherent way on behalf of any one group. The fragmentation of the state parallels the pluralist fragmentation of interests. McConnell is hardly oblivious to the fact that such fragmentation confers unequal benefits: indeed, this is one of his central points. But he asserts that this situation is not equivalent to oligarchy or class inequality: it is the dispersion of power, not centralization, that facilitates privilege. McConnell advocates concentrating and centralizing power within the government, thereby forcing it to rely on a broad national constituency for support. His prescription, which predates the height of the Indochinese War and Watergate, ignores possible abuses of presidential power and the net impact of state power. However fragmented the state, however much particular segments fall under the control of private interests, one can discern an overall thrust of state activity—even if (as will be analyzed below) that thrust is itself contradictory.

The Problem of Corporate Power

Among the plethora of private interests in American society, one is an obvious candidate for a dominant position. McConnell asks whether business exerts a "massive influence on the quality of American life" (p. 248); if it did, he observes, the problem would "be without solution. Fortunately, evidence that this is the problem is insubstantial; it is far more probable that, given the character of American society, this elite is incapable of exercising political domination save in exceptional circumstances and for very limited objectives and very limited times" (p. 254). McConnell does not analyze how the character of American society prevents corporate domination. He asserts that corporations do not dominate because they compete with each other and disagree on specific government economic policies. And yet he does not believe that competition among firms in a given industry precludes their cooperating to appropriate a sector of government.

McConnell does point to a factor, in another context, that might explain how business interests manage to overcome their mutual antagonism: he suggests that government helps to reduce conflict among competitors. For example, the federal government played a key role in helping farmers to organize within the AFBF, commercial interests within the Chamber of Commerce, and industrial workers within labor unions.

McConnell recognizes that business interests have captured many government agencies, but views the process as identical to the capture of government agencies by other private interests. "Instead of a conquest of government as a whole, control of significant parts of it may be established by particular business interests. This, as has been seen, is the pattern appearing in other areas of government.... In this capture of public authority [by business] in *particular* areas lies the most important problem." (p. 254, italics added).

Emphasizing the formal parallel between business and other organized interests, however, tends to overlook the central role of the particular government agencies linked to business, for example, the Departments of the Treasury and Commerce as well as the Federal Reserve Board. The jurisdictions of these agencies embraces the entire American political economy.

McConnell does not distinguish the varying extent of power exercised by different organized interests and government agencies. Further, by confining attention to specific governmental and business decisions, he ignores the private and centralized control of production. Instead, he views the basic problem posed by corporate power as the "decline of formality" that "accompanies the destruction of the distinction between public and private" (p. 297). The conclusion follows that "the problem of the large corporation as government would not arise if there were definite and unchallengeable criteria for corporate managers to observe" (p. 297). However, he does not specify the criteria that would resolve the problem of corporate power.

McConnell recognizes that "farm migrant workers, Negroes, and the urban poor have not been included in the system of 'pluralist' representation so celebrated in recent years" (p. 349). He analyzes the conservative implications of the theory and practice of American-style pluralism. Yet he never considers whether a capitalist mode of production is not inherently undemocratic.

McConnell attempts to purify rather than replace the pluralist vision. He aims to create a more just and equalitarian pluralist system by increasing the representation of consumer interests and the poor. However, he can be questioned on the same grounds he questions others: at critical points he substitutes moral indignation at conspiratorial subversion of American democracy for a structural analysis of inequality in the United States.

A Revisionist Approach to
Political Parties and Elections

In the 1960s, critics of the apologetic pluralist conception of the American electorate argued that responsibility for the apparent irrationality and passivity of the mass electorate derived from features of the political system and its leaders. V. O. Key put forward "the perverse and unorthodox argument... that voters are not fools.... In the large, the electorate behaves about as rationally and responsibly as we should expect, given the clarity of the alternatives presented to it, and the character of the information available to it."[36] Key found that vote switching was far more extensive than aggregate statistics indicated and that both the voters who switched parties and those displaying consistent voting patterns cast ballots congruent with their policy preferences.

Walter Dean Burnham further challenged the apologetic pluralist explanation for the passivity of the electorate.[37] In implicit contrast to Schumpeter, he argued that citizen apathy was not natural or inevitable but the product of institutional manipulation. Burnham demonstrated that extensive political mobilization at the beginning of the twentieth century had been restricted by institutional reforms, including nonpartisan local elections, cumbersome registration procedures, and literacy requirements.

This critique of the political party and election arena paralleled McConnell's approach. By emphasizing the institutional constraints limiting pluralist competition, it implicitly advocated reforms which would facilitate a more equalitarian pluralism.

A Conservative Reaction to Pluralism

During the 1960s, conservative scholars openly praised the nondemocratic aspects of American pluralism. For example, Edward Banfield and James Q. Wilson defended the urban political machine as an effective instrument for controlling citizens and centralizing and insulating political power.[38] In their view, liberal reformers failed to appreciate the rationality of the machine and its responsiveness to the needs of its constituents. From a related perspective, Charles Lindblom praised the untidy process of "muddling through," and he attacked reformers who exaggerated the rationality of planning.[39]

The Decay of Pluralism Abroad

Although the response of American political scientists to political conflicts in the Third World had a right and left variant, rather similar to developments within the United States, the conservative reaction was predominant. Four kinds of conservative responses are evident. First, scholars like Edward Shils discovered that manifold gaps and obstacles rooted in the Third World might prevent political development in these regions.[40] Second, counterinsurgency literature sought ways to subdue guerilla movements.[41] Third, European and United States history were combed for clues concerning the roots of political stability, now universally recognized to be problematic.[42] Attention focused on the historical patterns by which state authority developed and citizens became incorporated within the polity.[43]

Fourth, the most influential response within political science ques-

tioned the primacy accorded in earlier literature to economic development and political democratization. S. N. Eisenstadt, Samuel Huntington, and Aristide Zolberg discounted the possibility of pluralist self-
regulation and argued that the threat to political order came not only
from traditional groups and insurgent forces but from all social forces,
for example, students, the armed forces, and government bureaucrats.[44] Their answer was to create strong political institutions capable
of restraining political participation and maintaining political order.

This approach was later extended by the trilateral position. At first,
during the 1960s, pluralism was considered inappropriate for the Third
World nations less fortunate than the United States. Their difficulties
could be allayed only by authoritarian political institutions whose purpose was to contain (i.e., repress) demands from mobilized social forces.
By the 1970s the antipluralist medicine initially elaborated for the Third
World was being prescribed for the United States.

An opposing left critique in the 1960s—the dependency approach—
focused on the disastrous consequences of imperialism and neocolonialism for Third World nations.[45] The West was seen not as a cultural,
political, and economic benefactor but as a self-interested hegemonic
power which extracted material benefits (e.g., raw materials at cheap
prices) from formerly colonial areas and kept them in a condition of
dependence and neocolonialism. What characterized political change in
Third World nations was not political development but the "development of underdevelopment." From the dependency perspective, what
prevented pluralism in these nations was not their political immaturity
but that the United States supported antipluralist, repressive client regimes.

The 1970s:
The Crisis of World Capitalism

In the 1960s there were specific challenges to stability. In the 1970s a
more generalized crisis of global dimensions emerged as a result of
changes in the world balance of forces established since the Second
World War. The major changes included:

a) The declining ability of the United States to exercise military force
throughout the world, as evidenced by its defeat in Indochina, domestic
opposition to United States interventionism, and growing Soviet military
strength.

b) The declining ability of the United States and other capitalist nations to commandeer adequate supplies of raw materials at cheap
prices, especially petroleum.

c) The declining ability of the United States to reconcile its roles as participant and guardian of an international capitalist system based on free circulation of capital and goods.

d) The declining ability of capitalist economies to sustain economic growth and raise standards of living. Within the United States the crisis has been compounded by a precipitous decline in the support accorded political authorities, divisions within the coalition of corporate capital and labor that ruled since the 1930s, atrophy of intermediate associations (notably political parties), and a severe fiscal crisis of the state.

The pervasive nature of this crisis has provided the theoretical and political impetus for new approaches. Although pluralism probably remains dominant, two antipluralist currents developed in the 1970s: trilateralism, a reactionary attempt to extend the antidemocratic tendency of pluralism; and Marxism, which radically extends the democratic tendency within the pluralist approach.

Trilateralism

Trilateralism is meant to apply both to a specific organization—the Trilateral Commision—and to a scholarly and political perspective.[46] The Trilateral Commission was created in 1973 at the initiative of David Rockefeller, based on a proposal by Zbigniew Brzezinski, who was to be its first Executive Secretary, in his *Between Two Ages: America in the Technetronic Era*.[47] Brzezinski praised the West (and Japan) as the most advanced regions in the world but warned that they were being damaged by internecine rivalry. He advocated the formation of a Community of Developed Nations among the three regions of North America, West Europe, and Japan. A further impetus derived from the divisive effects of Nixon's New Economic Policy of 1971, in which the United States brazenly violated the rules of international economic order that it had written after the Second World War.[48]

The Trilateral Commission was initially composed of approximately 120 members, including transnational bankers of corporate executives, academics, politicians, and a sprinkling of labor union officials and others. The commission is a response to the multifaceted global upheaval which erupted in the 1960s. It seeks to unite the ruling classes of the industrialized capitalist nations and to manage a transition toward a new capitalist world order, in which declining United States global hegemony is replaced by a consortium of major capitalist powers (particularly the United States, Germany, and Japan). Much of the commission's impact comes from reports and recommendations prepared by subcommissions. Reports have addressed energy, North-South relations, international monetary problems, and industrial relations within capitalist nations.

The precise extent of the commission's power is hard to determine. Some view it as a conspiracy manipulating governmental policies among the trilateral nations. Others see it as a vain attempt to achieve impossible objectives and note that the commission has failed to reduce class conflict and interimperialist conflict or to achieve a new world order. The most dramatic evidence of the commission's success was the election of Trilateral Commissioner Jimmy Carter to the presidency in 1976 and the subsequent accession to high positions in the Carter Administration of twenty-four among the original sixty-three American commissioners. Yet it is questionable to what extent the Carter Administration's policies directly or indirectly derived from trilateralism.

As used here, trilateralism reflects an approach broader than the specific institutional embodiment of the Trilateral Commission. Trilateralism can be considered a new wave in political science, loosely linked to policy studies, the fastest-growing subfield in the discipline in the 1970s. The distance traveled from pluralism to trilateralism is indicated by the fact that the trilateral approach sees pluralism as the problem, not the solution.

In the pluralist view, there is a natural harmony underlying the variegated conflicts among interests and political parties. This optimistic assumption was questioned by the 1960s and rejected by the 1970s. Trilateralism is a product of the crisis of United States hegemony abroad and political stability at home. Apologetic pluralism was rooted in postwar American political and economic expansion. The "politics of productivity" stressed efficiency and growth, in an attempt to mute class conflict within the United States and on a world scale.[49] Trilateralism is rooted in declining American political and economic power, efficiency, and growth and seeks new mechanisms to contain conflicts.

Apologetic pluralist scholars did not serve the state directly and could describe, interpret, and legitimate in a relatively detached way. Trilateral scholar activists can afford no such luxury; trilateralism seeks specific solutions to a host of specific and overarching problems. Trilateralism is less theoretical and more historically focused and problem oriented than pluralism. It aims to understand and control the specific historical juncture rather than to describe universal patterns of political behavior. Although pluralism had separate variants applied to the United States and the Third World, trilateralism seeks to integrate these regions (and others) into a unified world order.

The political development approach stressed nation building. Trilateralism is fearful of nationalism and inept or hostile governments, which represent a threat to a world open to the free flow of commodities, capital, and labor.

Richard Falk observes, "The Trilateral Commission can be conceived as a geoeconomic search for a managerial formula that will keep this concentration of wealth [constituted by the capitalist sector of the highly industrialized portion of the world] intact.... In a sense, the vistas of the Trilateral Commission can be understood as the ideological perspective representing the transnational outlook of the multinational corporation."[50]

One threat to world order comes from unreliable governments. Yet the Trilateral Commission cannot simply oppose strong government. Falk suggests, "To thrive in a Third World setting, the multinational corporation needs a repressive, exploitative governmental structure such as that of Brazil.... In other words, the multinational corporation solution is viable only in conjunction with the support of powerful governments that possess strong military capabilities."[51]

Similarly, within the advanced capitalist region, although trilateralism has opposed protectionism and other forms of "irrational nationalism," it seeks to bolster the power of the state to deal with internal and external opposition. It also seeks to reduce barriers between theorists and practitioners of corporate and state policymaking.

Two faces of the trilateral approach, both antipluralist, can be discerned: corporatist reform and repression.[52] Commission reports have recommended progressive reforms going beyond existing practice in many trilateral nations. For example, the report on industrial relations urges worker participation on the Swedish model.

The repressive aspect refers both to the overall trilateral attempt to preserve existing inequalities within and among nations and to specific reform proposals. The repressive side is evident in the trilateral analysis of the dangers that exist to world order. Among the myriad dangers that the Trilateral Commission discerns, perhaps the gravest originates within trilateral nations, exceeding the threat posed by the Soviet Union, the Third World, or intercapitalist conflict. Pluralist theorists either assumed that the United States was basically stable or identified challenges to stability as deriving from extremist movements. In the trilateral view, the primary danger within the industrialized capitalist nations derives from the escalation of demands on the state inherent in pluralist politics. The danger derives not from a handful of extremists but from middle America.

Borrowing from Marxist analyses of this issue, trilateralism identifies two kinds of excessive demands: economic and political. In the economic sphere, citizens demand that the state keep its Keynesian promise of guaranteed economic growth and prosperity. As this has proved impossible to attain in the current era, dissension has grown. In the political sphere, traditional forms of participation (notably voting) have languished while angry protest from diverse social forces has risen. That citizens have lost confidence in government is reflected in an unfortunate decline in the "legitimacy of hierarchy, coercion, discipline, secrecy, and deception [by government]."[53] Both problems can be alleviated, according to the trilateral report "The Crisis of Democracy," by "a greater degree of moderation in the practice of democracy" and "limits to the indefinite extension of political democracy."[54] It is here that the authoritarian, repressive side of trilateralism comes to the fore and the circle is closed: When American-style pluralism seemed excessively democratic for the Third World, trilateral theorists proposed repressive political institutions. When pluralism was unable to contain the latent tension between capitalism and procedural democracy in the West, due to lagging economic performance and rising political conflicts, the same solution was ready at hand.

The Trilateral Commission fears that economic stagnation and demands for equality may jeopardize capitalism. Its proposed solution: appropriate the legitimacy of democracy in order to shore up support for capitalism at the same time that it seeks to curtail democratic practice. "One of the things democracy is about is to enable people and groups to operate in what might be called market environment rather than an environment which is largely determined by directives coming from government and political institutions."[55] For pluralism and liberal democracy more generally, capitalism and democracy coexist in uneasy tension. The two represent parallel structural arrangements: the marketplace of commodities and the marketplace of political ideas, parties, and programs. And yet the two clash in fundamental respects. Although it circumscribes the political sphere by assuming private control over production, liberal democracy espouses the principle of public and democratic control. Major decisions affecting the society should be made on the basis of social need and the public interest. This conflicts with capitalist arrangements, based on private control of productive resources (and thereby power), in which the deployment of capital is based on the quest to maximize profit and control. Pluralism seeks to contain this tension. According to Samuel Bowles and Alan Wolfe, trilateralism may represent a parting of the ways of democracy and capitalism.[56] Whereas the Trilateral Commission responds to the increasing tension between capitalism and democracy by attempting to limit democracy, the Marxist response is to transcend capitalism.

Marxism

The crisis of American politics in the 1960s stimulated the renaissance
—or, possibly, the naissance—of American Marxist theory. Marxism integrates dialectical, holistic, historical, political-economic, and
critical elements neglected by other approaches in political science. A
Marxist approach stresses the structural characteristics of the capitalist
framework of American politics as well as specific features of class
relationships in the United States. Elements include class inequality,
the unusual extent of capitalist hegemony and working-class subordination, and the emerging crisis of American capitalism.

Truncated Politics in
Advanced Capitalism

In contrast to both a pluralist approach, in which the public sphere is an
extension of the private sphere, and a power elite perspective, which
sees a fusion among top powerholders in diverse spheres, most contemporary Marxists emphasize the relative separation of the political and
economic spheres within advanced capitalism.[57] Every capitalist state
has sought to reproduce the separation between the economy and polity,
which is equivalent to ratifying private (capitalist) control over production. Paradoxical as it appears, the capitalist state usually intervenes in
an attempt to preserve the separation between the political and economic spheres, to depoliticize relations of production, and thereby to
maintain a truncated form of politics. Anthony Giddens points out, "The
stability of capitalist society depends upon the maintenance of an insulation of economy and polity, such that questions of industrial organization appear as 'nonpolitical.' "[58]

However, this insulation is constantly challenged. Procedural democracy forces the capitalist state to adapt to electoral majorities, and there
is an ever-present, if usually slight, possibility that an anticapitalist
majority will seek to establish public control over production, thereby
ending the separation between the two spheres.[59] From an opposite
direction, capitalists constantly seek to bend the state of their will. If
they wholly succeed, the separation of state and economy would collapse. Typically, however, the state holds these contending forces at
bay and maintains a tense equilibrium between the economy and polity.
Although the specific character of this equilibrium varies among different capitalist states, so long long as this situation persists, capital pos-
sesses far-reaching power, both through its control of production and its
political influence.

Capital exercises its power in ways which deeply affect the whole society. On the microlevel, for example, capital organizes the labor process with the goal of fragmenting, weakening, and deskilling the work force—thereby maximizing capitalist control and minimizing wage costs. Although the results of this process are socially devastating, it is eminently rational from the viewpoint of capital.[60]

On the macrolevel, corporate capital—concentrated and centralized within several hundred corporations—has exercised a decisive influence within the United States. For example, the automobile-housing-highway-petroleum lobby played a critical role in the suburbanization of the United States after the Second World War. What from one perspective is private capital exercising its prerogative to seek attractive investment opportunities is, from another perspective, the exercise of power in ways that fundamentally transformed American society.

Political inequality is the most important by-product of the normal process of capitalist production. Capital decides what material goods and services will be produced, where, by what technological processes, by which workers, as well as other fundamental matters shaping social life. Of course, capital is not sovereign. Its power is limited by competition among capitalists, market forces, class struggle, consumers, and the state. But so long as control over production remains in private hands, those who control the productive apparatus exercise immense political power.

The separation of economy and polity within a capitalist mode of production means that the state is drastically limited in scope. This was especially true for the nineteenth-century night-watchman state. The twentieth-century interventionist state has come to exercise substantial influence over conditions of production, through the regulation of demand and, more recently, supply (notably energy); the promotion of technology and physical infrastructure; and programs to provide capital with a skilled, compliant, and inexpensive work force. Nonetheless, in capitalist democracies, state intervention generally ceases at the point of production, even in the extreme case of social democratic regimes like Sweden.

The hidden face of power is exercised not so much by the suppression of specific issues from the political agenda as by the exclusion of the most fundamental matters of public concern from the political sphere. To ignore the limited scope of public decision making and to consider political arrangements democratic under these conditions is akin to accepting that democracy exists in a fifth-grade classroom because the youngsters elect class officers.

State Autonomy:
Limits and Extent

The separation of economy and polity can be viewed as a complementary process. State autonomy is decisively limited by the requisites of capital accumulation, although the separation of the two spheres also means that the state is not directly controlled by capital but enjoys limited autonomy.

State autonomy from capital is also decisively limited because the state is dependent on a prosperous economy so that it can tax a portion of the surplus to sustain itself. The state enjoys increased political support during periods of economic growth. Further, since crossing the Keynesian divide, the state has come to be held responsible for preventing economic disaster. To pursue its own self-interest, the state is forced to give high priority to the needs of capital.

However, the cyclical nature of capitalist production and the class-divided nature of capitalist society hinder this quest. Despite enormous state intervention, no way has yet been found permanently to overcome the unstable character of capitalist production. Both short-term periods of inflation and recession and long waves of economic stagnation recur periodically. Part of the explanation is that crises "discipline" the working class and prune out inefficient capital, thereby establishing the basis for further expansion. This situation sets limits to state counter-cyclical policies, despite heavy social costs.

If the limits of capitalist state autonomy are set by the structural features of capitalism, these same features also provide the state with a measure of autonomy and may force it to oppose the demands of capital. The separation between economic and political spheres implies not only that the state does not directly control production but that capital does not directly control the state.

Since, even in a situation of oligopoly, units of capital are engaged in perpetual competition, this limits the capacity of capital to capture the state. Capital requires essential services from the state which it cannot provide for itself, because they are unprofitable or require state sanction. Examples include state coercion backed by legal-rational procedures (e.g., judicial enforcement of contracts, maintenance of law and order, and legal protection of private property) and state-sponsored provision of social and physical infrastructure to assist capital accumulation.

The state is not a blind captive of capital. At important points it has intervened to prevent capital from acting in a self-destructive manner. Examples include state-imposed measures limiting capital's freedom to exploit the working class (such as maximum hours and minimum wages legislation) as well as welfare state programs. Despite the bitter resistance of most capitalists, these reforms have historically served capitalist interests by weakening anticapitalist opposition. That such measures have often been initiated as a result of working-class pressure indicates how the state plays a mediating role to stabilize capitalism.

Since the state is not completely beholden to either of its two masters, it has a measure of autonomy in deciding how to reconcile their conflicting demands. This involves more than mechanical balancing; although there are limits to state autonomy, the specific manner in which the state attempts to reconcile conflicting class demands is not predetermined. One way to distinguish capitalist states is by the mix of policies they have adopted in face of these conflicting demands.[61]

The Expansion and Crisis of Advanced Capitalism

In the past several decades, there have been major changes in world capitalism. In broadest outline, within the advanced capitalist societies, capital (organized within the corporate form) has because enormously more concentrated, centralized, and technologically based. What from one viewpoint constitutes the oft-celebrated postwar economic boom is, from another viewpoint, the triumph of corporate (or monopoly) capitalism. In the process, precapitalist and early capitalist modes of production have been snuffed out, and most areas of social life have been incorporated within capitalist social relations. In the political sphere, there was a general trend within advanced capitalism toward a ruling social democratic alliance between large-scale capital and organized labor.

Accompanying the extension, concentration, and centralization of capital has been its internationalization, under the aegis of American-based multinational corporations. Given the increased mobility of capital, labor, and commodities, no nation is isolated from developments within the world capitalist system.[62] An additional change within the recent period has been a reversal of the long wave of capitalist expansion that began after the Second World War; the current era is characterized by instability and a transition toward an uncertain future.

These features provide the context for a Marxist approach to American politics. The exceptional character of American politics had much to do with shaping the capitalist world system of the past several decades.

United States Exceptionalism

Each advanced capitalist nation is unique in the particular ways that capital, labor, and the state interact. State actions cannot be understood without examining specific historical situations.

An understanding of the capitalist state in the United States begins from the exceptional degree to which the American working class historically has been politically divided and weak.[63] A minority of the working class (differentiated on a racial, ethnic, and sexual basis) has been linked to a dynamic, technologically innovative corporate capitalist sector which accentuated divisions in the American working class. In return for the relatively high wages it paid, large-scale capital obtained labor-union authorization to introduce labor-saving technology (so long as this did not displace existing workers) and to pass along increased labor costs to the rest of the working class in the form of higher prices. Large-scale capital purchased labor peace and productivity gains but imposed inflation, unemployment, and a lower standard of living on a majority of the working class.

The sharp divisions within the American working class considerably weakened its political position. In other capitalist nations, where workers achieved a greater degree of political cohesion and militance, they were more successful in obtaining state programs that benefited the whole working class (e.g., public housing and medical care). In most industrialized capitalist nations, socialist or social democratic parties participated in ruling coalitions; by contrast, the American working class has been underrepresented politically and has received fewer state benefits as a result. While workers in the corporate sector were paid sufficiently high wages (until recently) to enable them to achieve relative comfort, workers in the service and small business sectors were triply victimized by low wages, high unemployment, and the meager character of state welfare programs.

An unusual characteristic of American politics, which helped to foster an apolitical conservative politics, has been the extent to which the bureaucratic sphere and the political party system have been separated. Partly as a result of Progressive reforms, there has been a decoupling of administration and politics. In the administrative sphere, bureaucratic agencies wield great power and organize their own constituencies for political support. The result has been the fragmented, inegalitarian patterns described by McConnell. Meanwhile, the party system provides echoes of corporate liberal policies, not choices. Given the fact that political parties have so little to do, fail to offer a range of genuine alternatives, and exercise so little impact on the overall direction of executive action, it is not surprising that there has been a steady decline of citizen participation in the formal electoral arena and an atrophy of the party system. Consequently, the state cannot develop cohesive policies nor mobilize support when it does act.

In the past, state intervention was fairly successful in reducing class conflict and stabilizing capitalism. However, with the unraveling of the lib-lab alliance due to the emergence of a pervasive crisis of capitalism, state intervention has provoked a fiscal and legitimacy crisis and has jeopardized the separation between the political and economic spheres. The more the state has intervened in the recent past, the more this has raised questions about the rationale for the separation of the economy and polity and the legitimacy of private economic control. If Lockheed, Penn Central, and Chrysler deserve a public bailout, why not the myriad small business concerns that fail every year, not to speak of the more numerous members of the working class.

On the other hand, the high rate of state spending has come under renewed attack. Although conservatives criticize state welfare programs, cutting back welfare expenditures risks provoking social protest. However, reductions in expenditures geared to assisting capital accumulation antagonize capital, and cutting military spending weakens United States hegemony abroad. Yet a failure to reduce state expenditures intensifies the fiscal crisis. As a result, state intervention has begun to compound the wider crisis deriving from economic stagnation and the declining position of the United States internationally. The state intervened in the past to regulate crisis by absorbing activities inadequately performed by private groups (e.g., welfare) and undertaking new activities (e.g., worker training). However, such intervention eventually eroded the liberal distinction between the public and private spheres. Attempting to quell class conflict, state intervention has begun to exacerbate it; attempting to depoliticize conflicts, it has politicized them. Rather than providing a solution to the contradictions of capitalism, the state has crystallized contradictions and contributed to a crisis of major proportions.

It seems ironic for Marxists to wage class struggle in the pages of scholarly books and articles; indeed, there is a danger of Marxism becoming "elevated" to a subfield within the social sciences. Yet, although the university is clearly not the foremost arena in which repression is exercised or challenged in advanced capitalism, its legitimating role should not be minimized. During the postwar era, American political scientists were nearly unanimous in celebrating the virtues of the American political system. If political struggles were primarily responsible for breaking this conspiracy of silence, critical pluralists also contributed. The central feature of advanced capitalism continues to be class inequality—a situation ignored by pluralism and recognized yet defended by trilateralism. Only Marxism has as its central goal understanding and challenging class inequality.

Notes

1. E. E. Schattschneider, *Politics, Pressures and the Tariff* (New York: Prentice-Hall, Inc., 1935), p. 287, quoted in Eileen P. Sullivan, "Pluralism in American Political Science: Progressives, New Dealers, and the Cold War" (unpublished ms., Department of Political Science, Columbia University, 1979), p. 8. The first section is informed by Sullivan's subtle analysis.

2. E. Pendleton Herring, *Group Representation before Congress* (Baltimore: Johns Hopkins Press, 1929), p. 257, quoted in Sullivan (n. 1 above), p. 8.

3. Sullivan, p. 11.

4. Ibid., p. 10.

5. The literature by pluralist scholars during this period is enormous. Several of the major works include Robert A. Dahl, "A Critique of the Ruling Elite Model," *American Science Review* 52 (June 1958): 463–69, and *Who Governs?* (New Haven: Yale University Press, 1961); V. O. Key, Jr., *Politics, Parties and Pressure Groups* (New York: Thomas Y. Crowell Co., 1964); Wallace S. Sayre and Herbert Kaufman, *Governing New York City: Politics in the Metropolis* (New York: W. W. Norton & Co., 1965); and David B. Truman, *The Governmental Process,* rev. ed., (New York: Alfred A. Knopf, Inc., 1970). I am focusing here on interest-group activity and not enumerating or analyzing works from related areas. Some recent literature critically analyzing pluralist scholarship includes David Garson, *Group Theories of Politics* (Beverly Hills, Calif.: Sage Publications, 1978); J. David Greenstone, "Group Theories," in *Handbook of Political Science,* vol. 1, *Micropolitical Theory,* ed. Fred J. Greenstein and Nelson W. Polsky (Reading, Mass.: Addison-Wesley Publishing Co., 1975), 243–318; Michael T. Hayes, "The Semi-Sovereign Pressure Groups: A Critique of Current Theory and an Alternative Typology," *Journal of Politics* 40 (Fall 1978): 134–61; William Alton Kelso, *American Democratic Theory: Pluralism and Its Critics* (Westport, Conn.: Greenwood Press, 1978); C. B. Macpherson, *The Life and Times of Liberal Democracy* (Oxford: Oxford University Press, 1977); Sullivan; and George Von der Muhll, "Robert A. Dahl and the Study of Contemporary Democracy: A Review Essay," *American Political Science Review* 71 (December 1977): 1070–96. Unlike these detailed studies, I am not attempting to analyze divergences among various scholars within the apologetic pluralist tradition.

6. Triebwasser has found that American government textbooks reflect these trends. Until the 1940s and 1950s, textbooks studied the interplay of economic political power, tended to present classical democratic theory rather than pluralist theory, and were more apt to be critical of American history and politics. Triebwasser finds that "the generally less critical—and sometimes even platitudinous—approach to discussions of American government and political processes did not fully emerge until the Second World War and Cold War periods in many of the major American government texts" (Marc A. Triebwasser, "The Dream, the Myth, the Reality of American Government as Presented in Major College Texts 1900–1975" [paper delivered at the annual meeting of the American Political Science Association, Chicago, September 1976]).

7. This article deals quite selectively with the enormous volume of American political science literature since the 1950s, ignoring such major subfields as Soviet studies, Western European politics, and international relations.

8. Gabriel A. Almond, "Introduction: A Functional Approach to Comparative Politics," in *The Politics of the Developing Areas*, ed. Gabriel A. Almond and James S. Coleman (Princeton, N.J.: Princeton University Press, 1960), pp. 3–64.

9. Louis Hartz, *The Liberal Tradition in America* (New York: Harcourt, Brace & Co., 1955).

10. Richard Hofstadter, *The Idea of a Party System: The Rise of Legitimate Opposition in the United States, 1780–1840* (Berkeley: University of California Press, 1969), p. 2.

11. Joseph Schumpeter, *Capitalism, Socialism, and Democracy* (New York: Harper & Row, 1975). My analysis borrows from Peter Bachrach, *The Theory of Democratic Elitism* (Boston: Little, Brown & Co., 1977); and Carole Pateman, *Participation and Democratic Theory* (Cambridge: Cambridge University Press, 1970).

12. See Quentin Skinner, "The Theorists of Democracy and Their Critics: A Plague on Both Their Houses," *Political Theory* 1 (August 1973): 287–306; and Alan Wolfe, "New Directions in the Marxist Theory of Politics," *Politics and Society* 4 (Winter 1974): 131–60. (Wolfe's conception of alienated politics parallels my point here.)

13. Although the pluralists severely criticized the power elite position, the two shared important features: both perspectives were static and failed to deal with structural change; both saw a continuity between political and economic spheres (however, apologetic pluralism stressed the openness and fluidity in both, while the power elite approach emphasized the centralization of control in the two spheres); and both denied the relevance of a class analysis of the United States. See Floyd Hunter, *Community Power Structure: A Study of Decisionmakers* (Chapel Hill: University of North Carolina Press, 1953), and *Top Leadership U.S.A.* (Chapel Hill: University of North Carolina Press, 1959). and C. Wright Mills, *The Power Elite* (Oxford: Oxford University Press, 1956). For a comparison of these different approaches, see Robert Alford, "Paradigms of Relations between State and Society," in Leon Lindberg et al., *Stress and Contradiction in Modern Capitalism* (Lexington, Mass.: D. C. Heath & Co., 1975): 145–60.

14. Arthur Bentley, *The Process of Government* (Chicago: University of Chicago Press, 1908).

15. Truman (n. 5 above), p. 506. That Truman considers the relationship between interests and organization as problematic distinguishes his work from much subsequent research which ignores the issue altogether. See Isaac Balbus, "The Concept of Interest in Pluralist and Marxian Analysis," *Politics and Society* 2 (February 1971): 151–77.

16. Truman, p. 507.

17. Ibid., p. 506. Von der Muhll (n. 5 above), p. 1079, suggests that Dahl lacks a conception of power and that, in his work, "social structure often appears as little more than an aggregate of the traits of individual actors."

18. Greenstone (n. 5 above), pp. 262–67.

19. He recognizes that "so-called business groups may be highly unified on those rare occasions when the foundations of private property are openly attacked" (Truman, p. 182), but does not question why the foundations of private property are so rarely attacked. Critical pluralists writing in the 1960s suggested that groups might use their power to suppress controversy. But Truman does not deal with the process of public agenda setting.

20. Michael Rogin, "Nonparitsanship and the Group Interest," in *Power and Community: Dissenting Essays in Political Science*, ed. Philip Green and Sanford Levinson (New York: Vintage Books, 1970), 112–19.

21. Truman, p. xi.

22. This revised account also raises further questions about the character of American democracy, which resembles the bowdlerized variety described by Arend Lijphart, *The Politics of Accommodation* (Berkeley: University of California Press, 1975).

23. Dahl, *Who Governs?* p. 75. In recent work, Dahl has considerably revised his earlier views. E.g., in "On Removing Certain Impediments to Democracy in the United States," *Political Science Quarterly* 92 (Spring 1977): 1–20, he argues that democratic theory needs to specify the conditions under which participation can be effective. He further asserts that democratic theory must consider the antidemocratic implications of hierarchy in the micro- and macrolevels of economic life. In "Pluralism Revisited," *Comparative Politics* 10 (January 1978): 191–203, he now argues that class is one of the most significant elements, even in pluralist situations. Further, he notes, "It is now pretty widely held that in its effects on decision-making institutions, organizational pluralism in polyarchies often fails to meet reasonable criteria for equality and, partly but not wholly as a result, for a broader 'public' or general interest" (ibid., p. 199). In *Who Really Rules? New Haven and Community Power Reexamined* (New Brunswick, N.J.: Transaction Books, 1978), G. William Domhoff challenges Dahl's interpretation of New Haven politics. Domhoff finds that the New Haven business community was far more powerful and city government far less powerful than Dahl suggests, and that the overlap between social and economic notables there is substantial. See also G. William Domhoff, *Who Rules America?* (Englewood Cliffs, N.J.: Prentice-Hall, Inc., 1967), *The Higher Circles* (New York: Random House, 1970), and *The Powers That Be: Processes of Ruling Class Domination in America* (New York: Vintage Books, 1979).

24. William Kornhauser, *The Politics of Mass Society* (Glencoe, Ill.: Free Press, 1959).

25. The concept of veto group is discussed by David Riesman, *The Lonely Crowd* (New Haven, Conn.: Yale University Press, 1967), pp. 244–48.

26. A classic statement of the argument that, given the poor quality of the mass electorate, limited participation is a positive virtue appears in Bernard R. Berelson, Paul F. Lazarsfeld, and William N. McPhee, *Voting* (Chicago: University of Chicago Press, 1954), chap. 14.

27. Truman, p. xliv.

28. Robert A. Dahl, *A Preface to Democratic Theory* (Chicago: University of Chicago Press, 1956), p. 8.

29. The political development literature is vast. For the seminal work marking the new departure, see Almond and Coleman (n. 8 above). Among the most influential research reflecting the political development approach is the Series in Political Development, published by Princeton University Press under the aegis of the Committee on Political Development of the Social Science Research Council. Because of considerations of space, the political development approach will be covered briefly. See my "Order or Movement? The Literature of Political Development as Ideology," *World Politics* 26 (October 1973): 139–54.

30. Regional studies provide a related example here. See, for the case of Middle East studies, Edward W. Said, *Orientalism* (New York: Pantheon Books, 1978), pp. 284–328.

31. Karl Deutsch, "Social Mobilization and Political Development," *American Political Science Review* 60 (September 1961): 493–514.

32. Robert A. Packenham, *Liberal America and the Third World: Political Development Ideas in Foreign Aid and Social Science* (Princeton, N.J.: Princeton University Press, 1973).

33. Some of the major works are Peter Bachrach and Morton Baratz, "Two Faces of Power," *American Political Science Review* 56 (December 1962): 947–52; and their *Power and Poverty: Theory and Practice* (Oxford: Oxford University Press, 1970); William E. Connolly, ed., *The Bias of Pluralism* New York: Lieber-Atherton, 1969); Domhoff, books cited in n. 23 above); Green and Levinson, (n. 20 above); Henry Kariel, *The Decline of Pluralism* (Stanford, Calif.: Stanford University Press, 1961); Michael Lipsky, *Protest in*

City Politics (Chicago: Rand McNally & Co., 1960); Theodore Lowi, *The End of Liberalism* (New York: W. W. Norton & Co., 1969); Charles A. McCoy and John Playford, eds., *Apolitical Politics: A Critique of Behavioralism* (New York: Thomas Y. Crowell Co., 1967); Michael Paul Rogin, *The Intellectuals and McCarthy: The Radical Specter* (Cambridge, Mass.: M.I.T. Press, 1967); Stanley Rothman, "Systematic Political Theory: Observations on the Group Approach," *American Political Science Review* 54 (March 1960): 15–33; and Jack L. Walker, "The Elitist Theory of Democracy," *American Political Science Review* 60 (June 1966): 285–95.

34. McConnell's major works are *The Decline of Agrarian Democracy* (Berkeley: University of California Press, 1953), and *Private Power and American Democracy* (New York: Alfred A. Knopf, Inc., 1966). Henceforth, page numbers in parentheses in the text are from the latter.

35. Almond, in Almond and Coleman (n. 8 above); Ralf Dahrendorf, *Class and Class Conflict in Industrial Society* (Stanford: Stanford University Press, 1950); and Seymour M. Lipset, "The Changing Class Structure and Contemporary European Politics," in *A New Europe?* ed. Stephen Graubard (Boston: Houghton Mifflin Co., 1964), pp. 337–70.

36. V. O. Key, Jr., *The Responsible Electorate: Rationality in Presidential Voting, 1936–1960* (New York: Vintage Books, 1968), p. 7.

37. Walter Dean Burnham, *Critical Elections and the Mainsprings of American Politics* (New York: W. W. Norton & Co., 1970).

38. Edward Banfield, *Political Influence* (Glencoe, Ill.: Free Press, 1961); and Edward Banfield and James Q. Wilson, *City Politics* (Cambridge, Mass.: Harvard University Press, 1963).

39. Charles Lindblom, *The Intelligence of Democracy* (New York: Free Press, 1965).

40. Shils's writings are collected in Edward Shils, *Selected Papers of Edward Shils*, 2 vols. (Chicago: University of Chicago Press, 1972–1975).

41. See, e.g., Nathan Leites and Charles Wolf, Jr., *Rebellion and Authority* (Santa Monica, Calif.: RAND Corp., 1966).

42. See, e.g., Seymour M. Lipset, *The First New Nation: The United States in Historical and Comparative Perspective* (New York: Basic Books, 1961); and Leonard Binder et al., *Crises and Sequences in Political Development* (Princeton, N.J.: Princeton University Press, 1971).

43. J. Samuel Valenzuela, "Labor Movements and Politics: The Chilean and French Cases in Comparative Perspective" (Ph.D. diss., Department of Sociology, Columbia University, 1979).

44. S. N. Eisenstadt, "Breakdowns of Modernization," *Economic Development and Social Change*, vol. 12 (July 1964); Samuel P. Huntington, *Political Order in Changing Societies* (New Haven, Conn.: Yale University Press, 1968); and Aristide Zolberg, *Creating Political Order: The Party-States of West Africa* (Chicago: Rand McNally & Co., 1966).

45. André Gunder Frank, *Capitalism and Underdevelopment in Latin America* (New York: Monthly Review Press, 1969); André Gunder Frank, in James D. Cockcroft, André Gunder Frank, and Dale L. Johnson, *Dependence and Underdevelopment: Latin America's Political Economy* (Garden City, N.Y.: Doubleday & Co., Anchor Books, 1972). The dominant modernization approach is compared with dependency within Latin America by J. Samuel Valenzuela and Arturo Valenzuela, "Modernization and Dependency: Alternative Perspectives in the Study of Latin American Underdevelopment," *Comparative Politics* 10 (July 1978): 535–57. Corporatism provided an alternative approach, first developed in Latin American studies and later applied to Western Europe. See Frederick Pike and T. Stritch, eds., *The New Corporatism: Social-Political Structures in the Iberian World* (South Bend, Ind.: Notre Dame University Press, 1974); and Phillipe Schmitter,

ed., *Corporation and Policy-making in Contemporary Western Europe*, special issue of *Comparative Political Studies*, vol 10 (April 1977). Also note that some major relevant works which do not fit within the approaches analyzed here include Reinhard Bendix, *King or People: Power and the Mandate to Rule* (Berkeley: University of California Press, 1978); Franz Schurmann, *The Logic of World Power: An Inquiry into the Origins, Currents, and Contradictions of World Politics* (New York: Pantheon Books, 1974); and Theda Skocpol, *States and Social Revolutions: A Comparative Analysis of France, Russia, and China* (Cambridge: Cambridge University Press, 1979). For excellent reviews of dependency and other recent approaches to inequality within the international political economy, see Robert W. Cox, "Ideologies and the New International Economic Order: Reflections on Some Recent Literature," *International Organization* 33 (Spring 1979): 257–302; James Petras and Kent Trachte, "Liberal, Structural and Radical Approaches to Political Economy: An Assessment and an Alternative," *Contemporary Crises* 3, no. 2 (April 1979): 109–47.

46. The section on trilateralism is based on Holly Sklar, ed., *Trilateralism: The Trilateral Commission and Elite Planning for World Management* (Boston: South End Press, 1980). I am grateful to Ms. Sklar for her help with this section. Also see Cox, (n. 45 above); Richard Falk, "A New Paradigm for International Legal Studies: Prospects and Proposals," *Yale Law Journal* 84 (1975): 969–1021; and Richard H. Ullman, "Trilateralism: 'Partisanship' for What?" *Foreign Affairs* 55 (October 1976): 1–19.

47. Zbigniew Brzezinski, *Between Two Ages: America in the Technetronic Era* (New York: Viking Press, 1970).

48. Trilateralism can be distinguished from neoconservatism, an explicitly rightist approach to international and domestic politics. For analyses of the major neoconservative works, see Peter Steinfels, *The Neoconservatives: The Men Who Are Changing America's Politics* (New York: Simon & Schuster, 1979); Fouad Ajami, "The Global Logic of the Neoconservatives," *World Politics* 30 (April 1978): 450–68; and Sheldon Wolin, "The New Conservatives," *New York Review of Books* 23 (February 5, 1975): 6–11.

49. Charles S. Maier, "The Politics of Productivity: Foundations of American International Economic Policy after World War II," *International Organization* 31 (Autumn 1977):607–33.

50. Falk, p. 1005. The trilateral approach recalls corporate liberalism of the early twentieth century as described by James Weinstein, *The Corporate Ideal in the Liberal State, 1900–1918* (Boston: Beacon Press, 1968).

51. Falk, p. 1008.

52. See William K. Tabb, "Social Democracy and Authoritarianism: Two Faces of Trilateralism," in Sklar (n. 46 above).

53. Michel Crozier et al., *The Crisis of Democracy: Report on the Governability of Democracies to the Trilateral Commission* (New York: New York University Press, 1975), p. 93.

54. Ibid., pp. 113, 115.

55. Ibid., p. 188.

56. Samuel Bowles, "Have Capitalism and Democracy Come to a Parting of the Ways? *Progressive* (June 1977); Alan Wolfe, *The Limits of Legitimacy: Political Contradictions of Contemporary Capitalism* (New York: Free Press, 1977); and Wolfe's essays in Sklar.

57. The first comprehensive Marxist analysis of U.S. political economy was Paul Baran and Paul Sweezy, *Monopoly Capital* (New York: Monthly Review Press, 1966). The aim of this section is not to analyze the many divergences among contemporary Marxist approaches to advanced capitalism but to suggest some common themes. Leftist journals, in which different approaches are developed, include the *Insurgent Sociologist, Kapitali-*

state, New Left Review, Politics and Society, Review of Radical Political Economics, Science and Society, and *Socialist Review.* Some recent influential works include Ernest Mandel, *Late Capitalism* (London: New Left Books, 1976); Ralph Miliband, *Marxism and Politics* (Oxford: Oxford University Press, 1977); James O'Connor, *The Fiscal Crisis of The State* (New York: St. Martin's Press, 1973); Nicos Poulantzas, *State, Power, Socialism* (London: New Left Books, 1978); Wolfe, *The Limits of Legitimacy;* and Erik Olin Wright, *Class, Crisis and the State* (London: New Left Books, 1978). For a fuller analysis of recent Marxist approaches to politics, see my "Trends in Marxist Studies of Politics: Class Struggle, Class Compromise, and Socialist Transformation," in a forthcoming volume on Marxism in American social science, edited by Bertell Ollman and published by McGraw-Hill Book Co. Marxist scholarship has had a heavy impact on some non-Marxist authors. See, e.g., Charles Lindblom, *Politics and Markets: The World's Political-Economic Systems* (New York: Basic Books, 1977), and Colin Crouch, ed., *State and Economy in Contemporary Capitalism* (New York: St. Martin's Press, 1979).

58. Anthony Giddens, *The State and Class Struggle: Trends in Marxist Political Studies within the United States* (London: Hutchinson University Library, 1973), p. 114.

59. This possibility may have been illustrated by Eurocommunism. See my "Continuity and Change on the French Left: Revolutionary Transformation or Immobilism?" *Social Research* 47 (Spring 1980): 93–113.

60. Harry Braverman, *Labor and Monopoly Capital: The Degradation of Work in the Twentieth Century* (New York: Monthly Review Press, 1974). There has been a rich literature stimulated by Braverman's seminal work. See special issues of *Politics and Society,* vol. 8 (1974); and the *Insurgent Sociologist,* vol. 9 (Fall 1978); as well as Richard Edwards, *Contested Terrain: The Transformation of the Workplace in the Twentieth Century* (New York: Basic Books, 1979); and Michael Burawoy, *Manufacturing Consent: Changes in the Labor Process under Monopoly Capitalism* (Chicago: University of Chicago Press, 1979).

61. Any concrete society is far more complex than this abstract two-class model suggests. The state must attempt to conciliate other groups, including the middling strata as well as forces with interests forged in culture and community (e.g., racial and ethnic groups).

62. Capitalism has always transcended national boundaries at the same time that its development has been intertwined with the rise of nationalism. But the integration of capital on a world scale has accelerated recently, and the crisis of world capitalism has had further international repercussions. Several major works include Samir Amin, *Accumulation on a World Scale* (New York: Monthly Review Press, 1975), and his *Unequal Development: An Essay on the Social Formations of Peripheral Capitalism* (New York: Monthly Review Press, 1976); Celso Furtado, Theotonic Dos Santos, and Herbert Souza, *The Internationalization of Capital,* vol. 2, (Toronto: Latin American Research Unit Studies, 1978); Christian Palloix, *L'Economie mondiale capitaliste et les firmes multinationales* (Paris: Maspero, 1975); and Immanuel Wallerstein, *The Modern World System: Capitalist Agriculture and the Origins of the European World Economy in the Sixteenth Century* (New York: Academic Press, 1974).

63. This is not the place to explain why. See Stanley Aronowitz, "The Labor Movement and the Left," *Socialist Review* 9 (March–April 1979): 9–61; Ira Katznelson, "Considerations on Social Democracy in the United States," *Comparative Politics* 11 (October 1978): 77–99, and *City Trenches: Urban Politics and the Patterning of Class in the United States* (New York: Pantheon Books, 1981); and Mike Davis, "Why the U.S. Working Class Is Different," *New Left Review,* nos. 123–24 (September–October 1980, November–December 1980).

Part II

The American Executive

Three ★

The King's Two Bodies:
Lincoln, Wilson, Nixon, and
Presidential Self-Sacrifice

Michael Paul Rogin

I

"The king has in him two Bodies," wrote the Elizabethan jurist Edmund Plowden,

> viz, a Body natural, and a Body politic. His Body natural ... is a Body mortal, subject to all infirmities that come by Nature or Accident. But his Body politic is a Body that cannot be seen or handled ... and this Body is utterly void of Infancy, and old Age, and other natural Defects and Imbecilities.[1]

The doctrine of the king's two bodies pointed politics in two directions. On the one hand, it separated person from office and made the realm independent of the body mortal who governed it. The language of the king's two bodies identified a body politic subject not to royal prerogative but to rule of law. Having served this function, it disappeared from modern political discourse. From this perspective, such residues in our

An early version of "The King's Two Bodies" was presented as an illustrated lecture to the conference, "The American Hero: Myth and Media," at the Institute of the American West, Sun Valley, Idaho, June 1977. On that and subsequent occasions, there were many helpful contributions. I am particularly indebted to Fawn Brodie, Francis Carney, Kim Chernin, J. David Greenstone, Charles Hersch, Griel Marcus, Nad Permaul, Robert Rydell, and Nancy Shinabargar.

Paul Conrad's cartoons, "King Richard II" (1973), "Blessed Are Those..." (1973), and Richard Nixon crucifying himself (1977), copyright *Los Angeles Times*, reprinted by permission.

Stanislav Rembski's portrait of Woodrow Wilson published with permission of Mr. Rembski.

Parts of this chapter were originally published as "The King's Two Bodies: Lincoln, Nixon and Presidential Self-Sacrifice." Reprinted from *The Massachusetts Review*, vol. 20, no. 3. ©1979 The Massachusetts Review, Inc.

vocabulary as body politic and head of state seem merely vestigial, in a modern legalism which clearly distinguishes occupant from office, subordinates person to law, and addresses the contractual relations of separate, single individuals.

On the other hand, the image of the king's two bodies could take the chief executive in the opposite direction, not separating physical person from office but absorbing the realm into the officeholder's personal identity. Crowned, robed, and anointed, the king acquired a royal body (plate 1). Unlike other mortals, he had a "Body... utterly void of ... natural Defects and Imbecilities." Far from gaining independence from its occupant, the office gave transcendent importance to the person. It placed him above the law. It transformed rational, independent citizens into limbs of a body politic, governed by their head. Since the king's body politic was immortal, the king who lost his crown lost his immortal body. From this perspective, the doctrine of the king's two bodies offers us a language in which confusions between person, power, office, and state become accessible. It alerts us to how certain chief executives found problematic their bodies mortal, and the human families and dwelling places which housed them; how they sought transcendent authority and immortal identity in the White House, absorbing the body politic into themselves; how they committed massive violence against the political institutions of the fathers and the lives of the republic's sons; and how their own presidential death consummated or shattered their project.

The American Revolution freed the colonies from the king's royal body. Revolutionaries rejected the loyalist claim that the crown was "chief head, and the *subjects* . . . *the members*" of the "body politic." "In America," said Tom Paine, "*the law is king.*"[2] America celebrated its bicentennial by overthrowing a president who, promising a "second American revolution," cast himself as king. "When the President does it," Richard Nixon explained, "that means that it is not illegal."[3]

"In absolute governments," Paine had written, "the king is law." Nixon had, like George III, "a monarchical view of his powers," commented Daniel Ellsberg. Archibald Cox heard in Nixon's words the echo of Louis XIV's "I am the state." Nixon had, Cox implied, laid claim to the king's royal body and merged his personal identity with the body politic.[4]

Richard Nixon, who knew his enemies called him king, did not turn to Louis XIV in self-justification. He quoted Abraham Lincoln instead, and quoted him with fair accuracy: "Actions which would otherwise be unconstitutional, could become lawful if undertaken for the purpose of preserving the Constitution and the nation."[5] Lincoln was looking back, like Nixon, on a war presidency. He had presided, as Nixon told David Frost, over an unpopular war which had sowed civil strife at home. He had, personally and without congressional authorization, conscripted an army; suppressed opposition newspapers; suspended the writ of habeas corpus and supervised the arrests, without due process of law, of thousands of opponents of the war; and, in what Charles Beard called "the most stupendous act of sequestration in the history of Anglo-Saxon jurisprudence," expropriated (his word was "emancipated") millions of dollars of private property.[6]

Lincoln, as Nixon also knew, was reviled as "dictator" and "despot" for these acts. He was, worse yet, a king without kingly stature. He was called, in language Nixon also heard applied to himself, "a huckster in politics," "the most dishonest politician that ever disgraced an office in America."[7]

Nixon had long been interested in Lincoln. He read *Abraham Lincoln: Theologian of Religious Anguish*, in his own final, presidential days. As Nixon cloaked himself in Lincoln's mantle, as he appropriated Lincoln's suffering to dignify his own, he must also have sensed something else. Assassination, the act which punished Lincoln for his violations of law, raised him to historical greatness. Without punishment, no redemption. Nixon was in the habit, he told Frost, of visiting Lincoln's sitting room when he had important decisions to make. The night before his own, self-inflicted assassination (as he said to Frost, "I gave 'em the sword, and they stuck it in"), he took Henry Kissinger into Lincoln's White House sitting room. In tears "we knelt down in front of that table where Lincoln had signed the Emancipation Proclamation. Where I used to pray. And then we got up." The next day President Ford, celebrating our "government of laws and not of men," once quoted and once paraphrased Lincoln. He offered Nixon's sacrifice to "bind up the internal wounds of Watergate." In the Nixon/Ford political theater, Nixon played not King Richard but Abraham Lincoln.[8]

Lincoln's sacrifice, in the American mythology we shall address in a moment, made him our political Christ, and it is appropriate that the doctrine of the king's two bodies derived from the two bodies of Christ. The king augmented his human body with a royal body; he aggrandized his mortal person with the immortal body politic. Christ's human body also joined his corpus mysticum in a dual unity, two bodies in one. King and Christ both shattered old forms of law. But Christ appeared at the transformational moment when existing law no longer expressed communal spirit. His kingship freed the community from ossified legalism and gave it new life. Christ's transfiguration served transcedent vision, not personal identity. The proof lay in his sacrifice. Crowned with thorns, Christ sacrificed his body mortal (plate 2) and gave birth to his mystical body, the regenerate community. The living king absorbed the realm into himself; the reborn Christ gave birth to the community and was taken back into it.

"All true Christians are of one body in Christ," John Winthrop told the Puritans on board the *Arbella*. "Love is the fruite of the new birth," said Winthrop. It forms "the ligamentes... which knitt these parts together."[9] Ford's call for "brotherly love" after Nixon's resignation faintly echoed this founding document of American community. For Abraham Lincoln and Woodrow Wilson, "Calvinist saviors who failed,"[10] and for the president who modeled himself after them, the stakes were higher. All three imagined themselves as founders, radically transforming the constitutional basis of the nation. The founding instrument for each of them was war. The White House, for all three, turned body mortal into body spiritual and conferred the power to create and destroy. Would they, in punishment for their lawless ambition, die the unsanctified tyrant's death? Would they be stripped of their royal bodies, or, redemptively sacrificing their mortal lives, would they regenerate the body politic?

II

Lincoln characterized his presidency, Nixon reminded us, by the violations of law necessary to save the Union. But his speech to the Young Men's Christian Lyceum, at the outset of his political career, warned against the tyrant who would violate the law and destroy the Union.

Our "fathers," said Lincoln of the men who made the Revolution, founded a "temple of liberty." The sons, mere "legal inheritors of these fundamental blessings," had to maintain it. The great man, however, "*denies* that it is glory enough to serve under any chief." He will not be satisfied "supporting and maintaining an edifice that has been erected by others"; for him the temple of liberty is a prison.

> Towering genius disdains a beaten path.... It sees *no distinction* in adding story to story, upon the monuments of fame, erected to the memory of others.... it thirsts and burns for distinction; and, if possible, it will have it, whether at the expense of emancipating slaves, or enslaving free men.

The fathers fought for the liberating doctrines of the Declaration of Independence, said Lincoln; to protect the Union from "an Alexander, a Caesar, or a Napoleon," the sons must confine themselves within the constitution and the laws.

> Let each man remember that to violate the law is to trample on the blood of his father.... Let reverence for the laws... become the

political religion of the nation; and let [everyone] sacrifice un-
ceasingly upon its altars.[11]

The Lyceum speech, Edmund Wilson first suggested, was Lincoln's
warning against himself. The young Lincoln feared that a "Caesar"
would bring down the fathers' "political edifice... at the expense of
emancipating slaves." The threat of slave expansion, said Lincoln two
decades later, showed that the sons had inherited a "house divided"
from the fathers. Lincoln now appealed beyond constitutional legal machinery to the revolutionary Declaration of Independence. Its promise of
equality, "temple of liberty" notwithstanding, had still to be redeemed.[12]

As antislavery freed sons from the political edifice of the revolutionary fathers, so it opposed the tyranny of master over slave. The arguments of "kings," Lincoln charged, enslaved men to labor for others
forever. The principle of "equal privileges in the race of life" promised
that "every man can make himself." The Declatation of Independence
thus emancipated children from the houses of their human fathers. In a
nation of immigrants, Lincoln explained, descent from actual fathers
divided Americans. The Declaration of Independence, "father of all
moral principle," united them. An American did not have to "pull down
the house of another" to rise; he could "build one for himself." In "The
House that Jack Built" Republican campaign broadside of 1860, "the
rails that old Abe split" built the fence, that enclosed the field, through
which passed the road, on which traveled the team, drawn by the boy,
who would fill the White House. Lincoln was "living witness," he told an
Ohio regiment, that "any one of your children" may come "temporarily
to occupy this big White House... as my father's child has."[13]

House, like body, is dwelling place of spirit. Lincoln seems to move
from images of confinement and destruction to liberation and opportunity, arriving finally at the locus of the president's corpus mysticum, the
White House. "They have him in his prison house," Lincoln said of the
slave. "They have closed the heavy iron doors upon him... and now
they have him, as it were, bolted in with a lock of a hundred keys." The
hope of opening doors for the slave, however, shattered the house of the
fathers and brought Civil War. Lincoln imagined himself, in the Lyceum
speech, as a "sacrifice" on the "altars" of "the temple of liberty." He
replaced himself (in his Civil War words to a bereaved mother) with the
"sacrifice upon the altars of freedom" of hundreds of thousands of
America's "sons."

I dared [said Lincoln at the end of his life] to dream this vision of the
White House—I the humblest of the humble—born in a lowly
pioneer's cabin in the woods of Kentucky. My dream came true, and

where is its glory? Ashes and blood. I . . . have lived with aching heart through it all, and envied the dead their rest on the battle fields.[14]

Antislavery took Lincoln to the White House. No mere servant of personal ambition, his vision spoke to desires for liberation deeply embedded in the culture and in Lincoln himself. Lincoln embodied the wish to be free. But Lincoln's power, he seems to have felt, was a source of devastation. Restoring the father's freedom to the Union, he had covered the republic in ashes and blood. This voice of accusation imposes no judgment on Lincoln from the outside; it is the voice spoken by Lincoln himself. The president, not merely his critics, magnified his responsibility. As the nation approached and fought Civil War, Lincoln assumed the burden of its suffering.

American culture offered Lincoln two symbolisms with which to give meaning to his power, one classical, the other Christian. Since the Revolution, Americans had seen their fate prefigured in the decline of republics of antiquity; they feared, as had Lincoln, the rise of a presidential "Caesar or Napoleon." John Wilkes Booth, repeating Brutus's *"Sic Semper Tyrannis"* as he shot the king, paired himself with Lincoln in classical tragedy. But Booth imposed no meaning on Lincoln's life and death that the president did not share. Caesar, Lincoln said, had been created to be murdered by Brutus, Brutus to murder Caesar.[15] The actor, Booth, played Richard III during the war, and the lines on the playbill—"Let them not live to taste this land's increase, That would with treason wound this fair land's peace"—pointed to Lincoln. As if twinned with Booth, Lincoln recited to White House gatherings Richard III's soliloquy when he was, the president explained, "plotting the destruction of his brothers to make room for himself." Unable to sleep, Lincoln took long walks at night against the advice of those concerned about his safety. On those walks he carried *Macbeth*. Returning from Richmond after the confederate surrender, Lincoln recited Macbeth's speech ending,

Duncan is in his grave;
After life's fitful fever he sleeps well;
Treason has done his worst: . . . nothing
Can touch him further.

The president who envied the dead their rest on the battle fields quoted the tyrant who could "sleep no more" and who envied the sleep of the murdered king.[16]

Sacrificing fathers' constitution and sons' lives to gain the White House, was Lincoln, he seems to have asked himself, anymore than a classical tyrant? Booth killed Lincoln as king, justly laid to rest for his insatiable, murderous ambition. On that classical reading, the killing of the king restored law and punished transgression. But although Nixon may be remembered as King Richard, Lincoln is not. Classical drama consigned Lincoln to a life full of sound and fury, signifying nothing. But Lincoln could also draw upon a Christian interpretation of the war, which rescued the nation from so bleak a tragedy and gave redemptive meaning to its suffering.

"Neither party expected for the war the magnitude, or the duration, which it has already attained," Lincoln said in his Second Inaugural.

> The Almighty has His own purposes. "Woe unto the world because of offenses... but woe to that man by whom the offense cometh!"... If God wills that [this terrible war] continue, until all the wealth piled by the bondman's two hundred and fifty years of unrequited toil shall be sunk, and until every drop of blood drawn with the lash, shall be paid by another drawn with the sword, as was said three thousand years ago, so still it must be said, "the judgments of the Lord, are true and righteous altogether."[17]

Lincoln made the war God's judgment on America for the sin of slavery. Such a reading, however, did not free Lincoln from responsibility; it magnified it. He had become the instrument of God's vengeance.

"We are coming, Father Abraham," shouted the crowds greeting Lincoln at the dedication of the Gettysburg cemetery. They chanted the words of the Union recruiting song (sung to the tune of "The Battle Hymn of the Republic"), "We are coming, Father Abraham, 300,000 more... to lay us down for freedom's sake, our brother's bones beside." Secretary of War Edwin Stanton, after the assassination, called the Gettysburg Address the "voice of God speaking through the lips of ... Father Abraham." This sanctimony should not obscure the meaning of the song, the chant, the name. Father Abraham was an Old Testament patriarch, "tramping out the vineyards where the grapes of wrath are stored." The chanting soldiers were willing Isaacs, offering themselves for sacrifice.[18]

God removed the biblical Isaac from the altar and substituted a ram. An Old Testament reading, moreover, as Dwight Anderson has pointed out, could not account for the death of Father Abraham himself. God's sacrifice of his son, Jesus, prefigured in the story of Abraham and Isaac, washed white human sins in the blood of the lamb and brought forth a new birth. "The fruite of the new birth" (Winthrop) was the corpus mysticum, the regenerate community. Lincoln's first speech against slave expansion, in 1854, began to prepare such an understanding of Civil War. Shifting from classical to Christian imagery, Lincoln warned, "Our republican robe is soiled, and trailed in the dust. Let us repurify it. Let us turn and wash it white, in the spirit, if not the blood, of the revolution." The Emancipation Proclamation—issued in "the year of our Lord one thousand and eight hundred and sixty-three, and of the independence of America the eighty-seventh"—fulfilled the revolutionary "spirit." Gettysburg offered the nation "a new birth of freedom."[19]

Sins are washed white in the blood, not the spirit, of the lamb, however, and Gettysburg was no mere spiritual purification. The "blood of the revolution," Lincoln claimed in the Lyceum speech, created a "living history" in every family—"in the form of a husband, a father, a son, or a brother . . . a history bearing the indubitable testimonies of its own authenticity, in the limbs mangled, in the scars of wounds received." As the revolutionary heroes disappeared, those "giant oaks," said Lincoln, must be replaced as "the pillars of the temple of liberty" by "other pillars, hewn from the solid quarry of sober reason."[20] This legal, passionless, bloodless political religion failed to reach into the hearts of men; it failed to hold the union together. The sacrifice on the altars of the fathers for which Lincoln had called was the sacrifice of passion; the ritual over which he presided was blood sacrifice. The "ligamentes . . . which knitt together" were the "limbs mangled" at Gettysburg and the other battlefields of war.

Lincoln shifted in the last paragraph of the Second Inaugural from the God of wrath to the New Testament God of love. He urged "charity." He wanted to "bind up the nation's wounds." (He had told Stanton he would end the war on the "Christian principle of forgiveness on terms of repentance.") Assassinating "the forgiver" (Melville), Booth completed Lincoln's Christian reading of the war. On Good Friday, April 14, 1865, the "parricides" (Melville) who killed Father Abraham transformed him into Christ. "It is no blasphemy against the son of God," asserted a Connecticut parson, "that we declare the fitness of the slaying of the second Father of our Republic on the anniversary of the day on which He was slain."[21]

The Lyceum speech ended with an appeal that Americans not "desecrate his resting place" until "the last trump[et] shall awaken our WASHINGTON." Lincoln's attack on slavery, Democrats charged, betrayed "our fathers who framed the government under which we live." Lincoln felt the force of that charge; denying it, he repeated it over and over again. He left Springfield for his Washington inaugural, he acknowledged, not merely as inheritor and maintainer of the edifice of the fathers but "with a task before me greater than that which rested upon Washington." That task, he explained at Independence Hall, was to preserve the fathers' Union while also reaffirming the fathers' moral commitment against slavery. Lincoln had to save the "mother land" without sacrificing the principle of the Declaration of Independence "that in due time the weights should be lifted from the shoulders of all men, and that *all* should have an equal chance." In the Lyceum speech the weight of the edifice lay on the sons as the price of Union; now Union and freedom must live or die together. Lincoln continued, "If this country cannot be saved without giving up that principle—I was about to say that I would rather be assassinated on this spot than to surrender it."[22]

That "wholly unprepared speech," as Dwight Anderson discovered, prefigured not only Lincoln's assassination but the meaning the nation would give it. Refusing to sacrifice Union or principle, he imagined sacrificing himself instead. Lincoln appeared in the 1860 cartoon, "When Washington Was the Sole Standard," as one of four small combatants at the feet of parentally disapproving Washington and the Goddess of Liberty. "Lincoln's Apotheosis," the carte de visite found in some version in nearly every American home album after the assassination,[23] shows Liberty's daughters carrying her son heavenward to his final "resting place" at Washington's bosom. The open arms of Washington the father (plate 3) also form the cross which has crucified the son (plates 3 and 4). Lincoln did not achieve "distinction" by overthrowing Washington, as the Lyceum speech feared. The sacrificed son atoned for his transgressions. Caesar's laurel halo and Christ's crown of thorns merge together (plate 4) as the father of his country welcomes Lincoln into heaven.

"The Federal Phoenix," an anti-Lincoln cartoon, pictured Lincoln rising from the ashes of the Declaration and the Constitution. Far from being destroyed, however, the "home of freedom" as Lincoln promised rose "disenthralled, regenerated, enlarged, and perpetuated" from the "ashes and blood" of Civil War. Lincoln presided over *The Birth of a Nation*. He was, in D. W. Griffith's words, "the savior, if not the real creator of the American Union." "The mystic chords of memory stretching from every battlefield," Lincoln's First Inaugural announced, "will yet swell the chorus of the Union." The prophecy alluded to the battlefields of Revolution; it was fulfilled in the battlefields of civil war. Lincoln was the war's climactic casualty. His own "limbs mangled" at Ford's theater "knitt...together" the corpus mysticum. His own bleeding body bound up that nation's wounds. Carried slowly by train for twelve days on a funeral procession through the North, Lincoln's body merged with the mystic body of the Union—the "great body of the republic," as Lincoln had called the American land, where "one generation passeth away, and another generation cometh, but the earth abideth forever." Alexander Stephens, Confederate vice-president, said, "With Lincoln, the Union rose to the sublimity of religious mysticism."[24]

This reborn, mystically sanctified Union was not the fathers' contractual association, however. Lincoln transformed that Union in order to save it. The heroine of *Birth of a Nation*, Elsie Stoneman, "began to understand why the war, which had seemed to her a wicked, cruel, and senseless rebellion, was the one inevitable thing in our growth from a loose group of sovereign states to a united nation." For Woodrow Wilson, with whose words Griffith introduced and supported his film, Lincoln helped move America from a divided, self-interested contractual association to a unified, spiritual, organic state.[25] He located in the presidency unprecedented power over life and death and over due process of law.

Lincoln believed in his youth there were "no miracles outside the law." But mere obedience to law provided America neither with unifying redemptive purpose nor with transcendent political hero. "The epic that Lincoln lived and directed and wrote" offered another pattern.[26] Rebirth required violent transgression, transgression called forth guilt, and guilt generated atonement. The great man, inspired by a vision of human freedom, shattered the political edifice of the fathers, personified the nation's guilt, and became its sacrifice. America rose from sanctified deaths to a new birth of freedom, the hero to political immortality. The obscure pioneer had risen from splitting the "giant oaks . . . under which his youth had been passed"[27] to his own stone temple and a place "greater than . . . Washington." What would Lincoln's model mean for Woodrow Wilson, the man Nixon called the greatest president of the twentieth century?

III

Richard Nixon said Woodrow Wilson was his "patron saint." He worked at Wilson's desk while he was vice-president; once elected president, he had Lyndon Johnson's desk moved out of the oval office and Wilson's moved in.[28] Nixon prepared his presidential death at Lincoln's desk; he lived his presidential life at Wilson's.

Wilson was the greatest president of the twentieth century, Nixon told Garry Wills, because of his vision of America's world role. Over that vision, Dwight Anderson has shown, Lincoln cast his shadow. As Lincoln had revived revolutionary principles by emancipating slaves during the Civil War, Wilson led, during World War I, "the attempt to emancipate the world." As the revolutionary fathers founded a union of American states, Wilson would found an international League of Nations. "As we once served ourselves in the great day of our Declaration of Independence," said Wilson, we would now "serve mankind."[29]

Wilson first projected America into world leadership in 1901, in a

speech defending the bloody suppression of the Philippine independence movement. Speaking on the 125th anniversary of the battle of
Trenton, Wilson recalled the revolutionary "dreams of our youth" for
the coming century of American "maturity." "The battle of Trenton was
not more significant than the battle of Manila," Wilson insisted.
America's emergence as a world power, transforming "a confederacy"
into "a nation," constituted a "new revolution." "A new age is before
us," Wilson wrote a friend, "in which, it would seem, we must lead the
world."[30]

America suppressed the Philippine struggle for colonial independence in the name of its own revolution. This paradox was not lost on
Wilson. "Liberty is the privilege of maturity, of self-control, of self-
mastery," he explained. "Some peoples may have it, therefore, and
other may not. . . . Training under the kings of England" prepared the
American colonies for self-government; we would now do for the Philip-
pinos what the kings of England had done for us; "they are children and
we are men in these great matters of government and justice."[31]

American leadership meant presidential leadership. The vision of
America's world role for which Nixon was indebted to Wilson was a
vision of presidential power. Presidential control over foreign policy was
"absolute," wrote Wilson. The central importance of foreign policy
would return the president to the preeminence from which congressional government had displaced him. Presidential power, moreover, would not be confined to foreign affairs. The Philippino "children"
required leadership because they were not "knit together" into a
"community of life." But America, too, was torn apart by class and
ethnic conflict. "The masters of strikes and the masters of caucuses"
placed petty, selfish interests over "civic duty." A president who rose to
authority in world leadership would weld America into an "organic"
nation at home.[32]

The revolution Wilson imagined in the name of the fathers, like the
one Lincoln consummated, transformed the constitutional basis of the
nation. The founders, wrote Wilson in *Constitutional Government*,
created a "mechanical" government of checks and balances. But "governments are living things and operate as organic wholes. . . . No living
thing can have its organs offset against each other as checks, and live."
Wilson rejected the contractual legalism of the constitutional fathers.
The Whigs, pointing to Andrew Jackson's violations of law, had labeled
him King Andrew I. Jackson, refusing to enforce a Supreme Court
decision, understood, in Wilson's words, that "the constitution of the
United States is not a mere lawyer's document; it is a vehicle of life." As
a living thing, the state required a single agent of direction. "Leadership
and control must be lodged somewhere," wrote Wilson, and they are

lodged in the president. The convention picks him out "from the body of the nation." Transforming a mechanical government of checks and balances into an organic unity, the president won the nation's applause, for "its instinct is for action, and it craves a single leader." Wilson imagined the president as the head of a living body politic. His chief executive did not bargain with other citizens and officeholders. Instead, he controlled the limbs of the presidential body, acquiring authority problematic in the unsanctified world of separate, self-interested individuals. Wilson was proposing a modern version of the doctrine of the king's two bodies.[33]

Wilson the political scientist made extravagant claims for presidential leadership over "children" abroad and citizens at home. These claims transformed the founders' constitutional "machine" into a body politic brought to life by its head. Wilson the presidential candidate seemed to sense the dangerous self-inflation such a doctrine implied. He was no "guardian," he said, treating Americans as "children" or "wards" and claiming to know what was best for them; rather, "we need some man who has not been associated with the governing classes to stand up and speak for us." Wilson was not, he insisted, a "political savior" from the "governing classes." He modeled himself instead on "a leader who understood and represented the thought of the whole people, ... that tall gaunt figure rising in Illinois, ... the immortal figure of the great Lincoln."[34]

Who but a "political savior" would imitate the "immortal... Lincoln?" Wilson's hubris seemed to worry him. Immediately after boasting that he had emancipated New Jersey from "slavery" to political bosses, he delivered a warning against the great orator reminiscent of Lincoln's warning against himself in the Lyceum speech.

> Don't you know [admonished Wilson] that some man with eloquent tongue could put this whole country into a flame? Don't you know that this country from one end to the other believes that something is wrong? What an opportunity for some man without conscience to spring up and say: "This is the way. Follow me."—and lead in the paths of destruction![35]

Wilson followed his warning, as had Lincoln, with an appeal to "reason rather than passion." He promised, as had Lincoln, "not a bloody revolution... but a silent revolution." These echoes are reminders not of the reason and spirit for which Lincoln and Wilson wished but of the passion and bloodshed of war. Like Lincoln, Wilson sensed destructive danger deep within himself, inseparable from his transforming public vision. "I am carrying a volcano about with me," he had once written.

How would Lincoln's example save such a man, soon to lead the country into war, from fulfilling his own prophecy of conflagration?[36]

In 1916 President Wilson dedicated a Lincoln memorial at the site of the log cabin where Lincoln was born. Much as had Lincoln himself, Wilson celebrated not the log cabin home but Lincoln's ability to escape it. "Every door is open," Lincoln's life showed, "for the ruler to emerge when he will and claim his leadership in the free life."[37] This celebration of Lincoln's "race of life" quickly turned, however, into a mournful evocation of homelessness. "Lincoln was as much at home in the White House as he was here," said Wilson. "Do you share with me the feeling, I wonder, that he was permanently at home nowhere?" Disembodied from any particular place—"the question *where* he was, was of little importance"—Lincoln was not "a man," Wilson would "rather say," but "a spirit." The price he paid was loneliness.

> That brooding spirit had no real familiars. I get the impression that it never spoke out in complete self-revelation, and that it could not reveal itself completely to anyone. It was a very lonely spirit that looked out from underneath those shaggy brows.[38]

Wilson had already written of the "extraordinary isolation" our system imposed upon the president. His evocation of Lincoln brought person and office together. "There is a very holy and very terrible isolation," said Wilson, "for the conscience of every man who seeks to read the destiny in affairs for others as well as for himself, for a nation as well as for individuals." Loyal to no particular friend, place, or body, Lincoln became in his melancholy isolation the embodiment of the people as a whole. Loyal to no interested self, he did not sacrifice the nation to personal ambition.[39]

America was unique among nations, Wilson explained to a group of newly naturalized immigrants. In other nations one's loyalty was to "the place where you were born." In a nation of migrants and immigrants, loyalty must be to "the place where you go." Other nations were, like families, partial to their own members. But while the American may remember "with reverence his mother and his father," his "purpose is for the future." Americans melted their differentiating, familial loyalties into universal ideals. Wilson knew this from his own experience. Though "born and bred in the South," he paid tribute "with all my heart to the men who saved the union." Giving up his "home" for his "heart," Wilson embodied the American people.[40]

In his early, traditionally conservative language, Wilson had given leaders authority over "children" and "wards"; he had spoken of slow, organic growth to maturity, and quoted Edmund Burke.[41] As he approached and occupied the White House, the president's organic metaphors shifted. Instead of evoking tradition and familial authority, Wilson absorbed the people into his own mystic body, himself into the spiritual body of the nation. This merging of self into communal body reached its climax after World War I, in Wilson's struggle to found a new world order. Speaking in defense of his League of Nations he explained, "When I speak the ideal purposes of history I know that I am speaking the voice of America, because I have saturated myself since I was a boy in the records of that spirit. . . . When I read my own heart . . . I feel confident it is a sample American heart." Wilson toasted George V of England as the equal of kings—"You and I, sir—I temporarily—embody the spirit of two great nations." But, like Lincoln's occupancy of the White House, Wilson's embodiment was temporary; "and whatever strength I have, and whatever authority, I possess only so long and so far as I express the spirit and purpose of the American people."[42]

There is, as Wilson had said of Lincoln, a "holy and terrible isolation" in the claim to read the destiny for others in oneself. Wilson needed, as he had told the immigrants in 1915, "to come and stand in the presence of a great body of my fellow-citizens . . . and drink, as it were, out of the common fountains with them." He told the Boston crowd greeting him on his first return from Europe how "very lonely [he has] been. . . . It warms my heart to see a great body of my fellow citizens again." Domestic opposition to the league threatened to isolate Wilson and call his motives into question. Traveling around the country to "drink . . . of the common fountains" with the people, Wilson insisted that the league "has nothing to do with my personal fortune—my personal ambition." He told the Pueblo, Colorado, audience how "very lonely" he would have felt in Paris if "I thought I was expounding my own ideas. . . . Don't you remember that we laid down fourteen points. . . . They were not my points." Wilson dissolved his identity into America, he implied, to counteract feelings of "personal pride." These feelings isolated him from "the body of my fellow citizens," engendering a loneliness that only fusion with American crowds could cure.[43]

The leader was lonely, Wilson said of Lincoln, because he could not share his deepest feelings. Public communion provided reassurance that those feelings were admirable, not violent and self-aggrandizing. Should Wilson lose public support, his "terrible isolation" would expose him in all his fatal pride. He would fulfill his own prophecy of the man "with eloquent tongue, . . . without conscience" leading "in the paths of destruction."

"This strange child of the cabin," as Wilson imaged Lincoln, "kept company with invisible things, was born into no intimacy save that of its own . . . thoughts."[44] Counterposing "invisible" spirit to self-interest, place of birth, and physical "intimacy," Wilson's "Body that cannot be seen or handled" (Plowden) soared above the world. As if invoking "that tall, gaunt figure rising in Illinois," a cartoon response to Wilson's invasion of Mexico in 1914 pictured the spectral "professor" rising above the blood-red ink he spilt on the map of Mexico. (plate 5).

The cartoon which criticized Wilson's imperial vision resembled his own self-image. Stanislav Rembski's portrait of the president hung in the library of the home to which Wilson retired from the White House (plate 6). It superimposed Wilson on a map of Europe, and his long, skeletal fingers accentuate his ghostly presence. Wilson looks more like a specter haunting Europe than like its liberator.

Disembodied spirits, after all, have real consequences, and Wilson counted on it. He knew that Americans had selfish interests which set them against one another. Soon after he was inaugurated, he called on the people to repudiate them. "The days of sacrifice and cleansing are at hand," Wilson proclaimed on July 4, 1913, in a speech at Gettysburg commemorating the fiftieth anniversary of the battle. The national tasks there consecrated were yet to be completed, Wilson announced. He spoke, not of American ends but of the means of war.

War fitted us for action, and action never ceases.

I have been chosen leader of the nation. . . . Whom do I command? The ghostly hosts who fought upon these battle fields long ago? . . . I have in mind another host. . . . That host is the people themselves. . . . The recruits are the little children crowding in. . . . Come let us be comrades and soldiers yet to serve our fellow men.[45]

War was a metaphor in this call for domestic reform. "The dictate of patriotism to sacrifice yourself" spoke to the subordination of self-interest. But the new freedom at home failed to overcome selfishness. It failed to make people "drunk with the spirit of self-sacrifice." Within a few years the "brothers and comrades" evoked at Gettysburg became "comrades and brothers" in war. The "little children crowding in" went as "recruits" to real deaths in France. The president, in "command" of that "host," had, like Lincoln before him, to come to terms with his battlefield dead.

Again and again, my fellow citizens [Wilson told the crowd at Pueblo] mothers who have lost their sons in France have come to me and, taking my hand, have not only shed tears upon it but they have added, "God bless you, Mr. President!" Why, my fellow citizens, should they pray God to bless me? I ordered their sons overseas. I consented to their sons being put in the most difficult parts of the battle line, where death was certain. . . . Because they believe that their boys . . . saved the liberty of the world.[46]

"This sacrifice," Wilson said again and again, required the establishment of a new world order. The boys who died in France merged with "the children" they died to save. Children in their mothers' arms brought tears to Wilson's eyes, "because I feel my mission is to save them." Wilson woke at night, he said, to hear "the cry, the inarticulate cry of mothers all over the world." These were at once the mothers who had lost their sons and those whose sons would die unless the league was born.[47]

Invoking dead and unborn children in his last speeches, Wilson transcended the physical world. He did not "command," he had said at Gettysburg, "the ghostly hosts who fought upon those battlefields long ago." World War I gave Wilson command over his own spectral army, "those dear ghosts that still deploy upon the fields of France. . . . Coming across sea in spirit of crusaders," the American boys were disembodied before their died. "Possessed by something they could only call religious fervor," they were "fighting in dream."[48]

Wilson did not invent the image of ghostly crusaders in battle. He saw it in his favorite movie, the first shown at the White House, the movie he described as "writing history with lighting." Wilson's *History of the American People* had sympathetically described the "ghostly visitors" whose "invisible Empire" restored racial order to the south. The "silent visitations" of this "mysterious brotherhood" materialized on the screen in *The Birth of a Nation*. Donning white masks, robes, and black crosses, the Knights of Christ transfigured bodies natural into holy unanimity. Wilson's "crusaders" subliminally invoked the midnight rides of the Ku Klux Klan[49] (plate 7).

Civil war did not, in Griffith's movie, bring forth the birth of the nation. Lincoln was the martyred hero of the first half of the movie. But assassination aborted, in Wilson's words, "Lincoln's idea of a spiritual as well as a physical restoration of the union." America was reborn in the triumphant ride of the Ku Klux Klan against the threatening dark bodies of the black race. The movie's closing title, celebrating Union, paid homage to this achievement of the Klan. Griffith quoted Daniel Webster's "immortal" words, as Wilson had called them, words which "almost create the thoughts they speak," and "called a nation into being: 'Liberty and Union, now and forever, one and inseparable." *Birth of a Nation* provided Griffith and Wilson a bridge from Southern, parochial loyalties to nationalism and—by way of the Philippines and the war to end war—internationalism.[50]

Birth of a Nation, called *The Klansman* when first released, should remind us of Wilson's violence, of his antipathy to Slavic immigrants and people of color, and of the attack on subversives and hyphenated-Americans which climaxed his holy war. The "hyphen," said Wilson in his speeches for the league, was "the most un-American thing in the world." Symbol of the immigrant's loyalty to his home instead of the American heart, it "looked to us like a snake. . . . Any man who carries a hyphen about with him carries a dagger that he is ready to plunge into the vitals of the Republic."[51]

Birth should remind us, however, of Wilson's dream of peace as well as of his Red Scare. Released in 1915 and seen by millions before Wilson took America into the war to end all wars, the movie's penultimate title asks "Dare we dream of a golden day when bestial war shall rule no more? But instead—the gentle Prince in the hall of Brotherly love in the city of Peace." Following these words, the god of war on a raging beast fades into a white-robed Christ, hovering over paradise. "The American people," Wilson promised in the last words he spoke to them, "have accepted the truth of justice and of liberty and of peace. We have accepted that truth, and we are going to be led by it, and it is going to lead us, and through us the world, into pastures of quietness and peace such as the world never dreamed of before." Wilson then reboarded the train taking him through the west, and collapsed of a stroke.[52]

Lincoln, "at home nowhere," entered the hearts of his countrymen on the funeral train carrying him through "the great body of the republic." Wilson, seeking renewed communion with the people of his own train journey, underwent a self-inflicted passion. Christ had failed to make his ideals practical, Wilson told the Versailles peace conference. "That is why I am proposing a practical scheme to carry out his aims." This imitation of Christ became an imitation of atonement. Brought to tears by children in their mother's arms, dreaming of the mothers' inarticulate cries, Wilson was not simply the savior of children; he identified himself with the children he had sacrificed. Finally to demonstrate he served not his own ambition but his "clients . . . the children," Wilson was willing to sacrifice himself. "If I felt that I personally stood in the way of the settlement," he promised, "I would be glad to die that it might be consummated." Doctors advised Wilson that the train journey endangered his health, but he insisted on continuing. "Even though in my condition it might mean the giving up of my life," he explained, "I would gladly make the sacrifice to save the treaty."[53]

In Wilson's earliest childhood memory, he stood at the gate of his father's house; he heard that Lincoln had been elected president and that there would be war. Wilson proudly remembered his father's Confederate loyalties. But Lincoln freed Wilson from his father's "home" and showed him the path to the American "heart." Now, in grand self-abnegation, Wilson reached the climax of his imitation of Lincoln. Freeing the creative self from the house of the fathers, Wilson and Lincoln seemed to fear, mobilized tremendous destructive power; its objective correlative was war. "Salvation" for the "volcano" within him, Wilson had written his fiancee, lay "in being loved." But violence separated the war president from his country's love. Wilson feared that his aggression had threatened the republic and sent its sons to their graves; but violence became redemptive if it consumed the self as well. Rejoining weeping mothers and sons, Wilson would not challenge the father's place. Merging with the bleeding body of the nation, he would atone for the untold battlefield dead. Violence sanctified the new order when a leader of sufficient greatness sacrificed himself. If the living Wilson could not take America into "pastures of quietness and peace," he would lead there in death: "We desired to offer ourselves as a sacrifice to humanity. And that is what we shall do."[54]

Wilson had evoked American pastures of plenty before, in the campaign of 1912, as he envisioned Columbus coming on the New World. "The hemisphere lay waiting to be touched with life," he imagined. "Life cleansed of defilement . . . so as to be fit for the virgin purity of a new bride." Immigrants coming to our shores, Wilson continued, also dreamed of an "earthly paradise," a land where they would be "rid of kings" and of "all those bonds which had kept men depressed and helpless."[55]

Columbus's dream, the immigrant's, Lincoln's, suited an agrarian, individualistic America. In the complex, corporate, industrial age, Wilson continued, life was not so simple. "Freedom has become a somewhat different matter."

> I have long had an image in my mind of what constitutes liberty. Suppose that I were building a great piece of powerful machinery . . . Liberty for the several parts would consist in the best possible assembling and adjustment of them all, would it not? If you want the piston of the engine to run with absolute freedom, give it absolutely perfect alignment and adjustment with the other parts of the machine, so that it is free, not because it is alone or isolated, but because it has been associated most skillfully and carefully with the other parts of the great structure.[56]

Government was not a dead machine, Wilson had said, and here he brought the machine to life. The pastoral promise at America's birth would be redeemed in technological utopia. The dynamo and the "virgin ... bride" were one. Wilson's body politic absorbed lonely, competing individuals into an organized machine. The president was not "alone or isolated" if he embodied the people; a piston was not along or isolated if it was part of the engine. "The locomotive runs free," Wilson explained, only when adjusted "to the forces she must obey and cannot defy." The new freedom was the freedom to rise with corporate, mechanical power.[57]

Now, near the end of his life, Wilson's "locomotive" failed to transport him into "pastures of quietness and peace." The son who had lost his mother, Wilson was not taken back into the virgin bride. Unlike Lincoln, he offered Nixon the model of failed sacrifice. Wilson's body royal died in 1919, unable to carry out the duties of office. But his human body lived on four more years, dreaming the people would turn to him again, "living witness" (Lincoln) to the failure of presidential self-sacrifice to give birth to the league and "emancipate the world."

Responding to a query about his health the month before he died, Wilson repeated the words of another aging ex-president: "John Quincy Adams is all right, but the home he lives in is dilapidated, and it looks as if he would soon have to move out." Driven from his "Body politic," the White House, the ex-president retained (Plowden) the "natural Defects and Imbecilities" of his "Body mortal." Wilson died in a replica of Lincoln's bed. His last words were, "I am a broken piece of machinery. When the machinery is broken—I am ready."[58]

IV

Young Richard Nixon's "earliest ambition" was to be a "railroad engineer." "At night I would lie in bed and hear the whistle of that train and think of all the places that it went." That "child" who "hears the train go by at night and dreams of faraway places," Nixon told the 1968 Republican convention, "tonight ... stands before you—nominated for President of the United States. You can see why I believe so deeply in the American Dream. For most of us the American Revolution has been won, the American Dream has come true."[59]

"I was born in a house that my father built," is the first sentence of Nixon's memoirs. But for Nixon, as for Lincoln, the journey from home to White House signified our revolutionary "birthright." Son of a streetcar conductor and, like Lincoln, descendent of wanderers, Nixon lacked defining loyalties to a particular, local place. Like Wilson's ideal American, he was "at home nowhere." (It was appropriate, as Anthony Lukas pointed out, that the major Watergate encounters which did not take place inside the White House occurred not in homes but in places of transit—motels, hotels, restaurants, and airport lounges.)[60]

The "spirit" that is at home nowhere, said Wilson of Lincoln, is "very lonely." It cannot "reveal itself completely to anyone." Vice-President Nixon, in words echoing Wilson's, once remarked, "A major public figure is a lonely man—the President very much more so, of course. You can't enjoy the luxury of intimate personal friendships. You can't confide absolutely in anyone."[61] Nixon spoke, like Wilson, to more than the president's office; he spoke to his own character. But while Lincoln, losing his body mortal, shared his corpus mysticum with the nation; and while Wilson tried to rise above the body natural in spiritual apotheosis; Nixon trapped himself inside his exposed human corpus and so was expelled from the King's royal body.

Like Wilson, Nixon saw foreign policy as the path to presidential greatness. "I have always thought this country could run itself domestically without a President," he said in 1971. "You need a President for foreign policy." Wilsonian internationalism generated a Red Scare after World War I, and Nixon owed his political career to the post–World War II Red Scare. "Today the issue is still slavery," he explained in a 1950 Lincoln birthday speech; only now slavery posed a threat not just to America but to the entire free world. As late as 1969, Nixon defended America's role in Vietnam on the Wilsonian grounds of self-determination; we were guaranteeing, he explained, "the free choice of the South Vietnamese people themselves."[62]

But Nixon did not accept Wilson as his model uncritically. Wilson's "eloquent tongue" transformed unshareable, private secrets into public oratory. He demanded open covenants, openly arrived at. Wilson's desire for open diplomacy, Nixon told Garry Wills in 1968, was his one mistake. He did not understand the need for secrecy.[63] Thanks both to the exhaustion of convincing public purposes for the war in Vietnam, and to his own personal character, Nixon did.

Lincoln made public the human injustice of slavery and the human devastation of war. Perhaps because the wish to be free still spoke to authentic possibilities in a society of small property holders, his rhetoric embedded the American dream in homely, lived reference. Lincoln retained connection to personal and social body. Condemned by press and politicians, he greeted White House throngs daily; he claimed these "public opinion baths" connected him to the popular will.[64] Wilson, soaring above the industrial capitalist age, retained a transcendent vision. His vision embodied only spirit, however. It separated state from society, political language from personal and social life. Wilson took "communion" with the people, not low-church, full-immersion, baptismal "baths." As if to compensate for the thinness of his dream of freedom, Wilson universalized it to the world.

Vision, used and embodied by Lincoln, attenuated and failed for Wilson, was exploited and absent in Nixon. Nixon completed the separation between public rhetoric and personal and social reality. Sleepless after the Kent and Jackson State killings, Nixon was drawn first to the Lincoln sitting room and then to the Lincoln Memorial. Once at the memorial, however, he spoke to the students there of football. Nixon's aides planned, as Griel Marcus discovered, to build his Second Inaugural around readings from Lincoln's. They had to abandon that plan when they read Lincoln's actual words. Lincoln's language had awakened the tangible senses—touch, sight, even taste and smell. Wilson retained only the voice. Nixon embodied "the great Silent Majority of my fellow Americans."[65]

Nixon represented the silent partly because he presided over a war requiring political silence. There was a chasm throughout the 1960s between America's stated goals and practice in Vietnam and our actual policies. By the time Nixon assumed office the war could not be justified in public terms at all; it had to continue as a secret. Secretly bombing Laos and Cambodia, while claiming he had a secret plan to end the war, Nixon planned to replace American troops with American technology and devastate Southeast Asia forever.

Secrets are vulnerable to exposure. Daniel Ellsberg's release of the Pentagon Papers, like the discoveries of the Cambodian bombings and the secret war in Laos, revealed the actual policies hidden behind the facade. Exposure brought home the human realities of the war. It revealed, in Ellsberg's words, the "real men and women" who made up the "killing machine." It also revealed the real casualties of battle. Instead of fighting Lincoln's war of punishment and redemption to free slaves from their time on the cross, the country which took its identity from "the bleeding heart of Christ," in Norman Mailer's words, was "killing Christ in Vietnam."[66]

To protect his foreign policy secrets from exposure, Nixon brought the war home. Defending "national security" against leaks, he accelerated the domestic spying and disruption begun by his predecessors. To win reelection while continuing an unpopular war, he initiated what John Mitchell was to call "the White House horrors." The "second American revolution" Nixon promised in 1971 would emancipate the boy for whom "the American revolution has been won" from the need to justify his policies. As Solicitor-General (now Supreme Court Justice) William Rehnquist argued, the president could claim executive privilege, or gather information by any means, in any area of his constitutional responsibility; he need explain his purpose to no one.[67] The president was constructing a hidden government within the Executive Branch. Nixon's revolution, reversing that of the Declaration, would end the need for authority to justify itself. Unlike Lincoln and Wilson, Nixon embarked on a founding in secret.

This secret founding radically differentiated politics and personality in the Nixon White House from its models. Larger purpose no longer sanctified executive expansion. Language provided Nixon with no mediation between private nightmare and legitimate public vision. The techniques of manufacturing celebrities, moreover, which propelled the Southern Californian to the top, widened the chasm between presidential image and ordinary mortal capacities. Exposure of "real men and women" was not merely politically dangerous, it endangered the president personally as well. Nixon's body royal and his body mortal were fatally at odds. That division forces us to examine a private language in which, unlike Wilson's, images of the natural body are present, but present, unlike Lincoln's, in forcefully unsublimated forms.

Wilson relied on the transcendent power of rhetoric. Nixon ferreted out the private conversations of others and secretly recorded his own. Wilson orated his important words in public; Nixon spoke his in private and recorded them on the White House tapes. The conviction that the language of bodies public concealed the secrets of bodies natural placed electronic surveillance at the center of the Nixon presidency.

"We have," wrote Edmund Wilson, "accepted the epic that Lincoln directed and lived and wrote."[68] Lincoln, in this poetic overstatement, imposed the private meaning of his political life on America. As impeachment resolved itself into a battle for possession of the tapes, Nixon, in spite of himself, imposed his. Without the tapes, Nixon would have remained president. If the tapes cost him the presidency, however, they did so on his own terms. The model of Lincoln was much on Nixon's mind as he rose and fell. But there was a major difference between Lincoln's epic and Nixon's epic. While Lincoln found legitimate public form for his interior life, Nixon had to keep his interior secret from the prying eyes of the world. The president, who could not "really let my hair down with anyone . . . not even with my family," was forced progressively, as he put it, to "undress" in front of everyone.[69] Recording and losing the White House tapes, Nixon visited his private hell on the nation.

It might be a tape recording, right? [says Norman Mailer's D.J., in *Why Are We in Vietman?*] Did you ever know the seat of electricity? It's the asshole. . . . I mean, just think of the good Lord, Amen, and all the while we're sleeping and talking and eating and walking and pissing and fucking...why there's that Lord, slipping right into us, making an *operation* in the bowels of Creation so there's a tiny little transistorized tape recorder...and it takes it all down, it makes all the mountainous files of the FBI look like paper cuttings in a cat shit box, and so there is the good Lord...there *He* is getting a total tape record of each last one of us...and now face your consequence, the Lord hears...the total of all of you, good and bad...and...one of his angels passes you on. To here or to there.[70]

The bug is seated in the anus, as D.J.'s mother's psychiatrist might explain, because it records shameful secrets. It collects one's contaminated inner body contents and exposes them to authority. Mailer borrowed his excremental vision of the last judgment from late medieval images; Flemish painters like Bosch and the van Eycks show the devil defecating sinners into hell (plate 8). "The whole world is possessed by Satan," said Martin Luther. "I am the ripe shard and the world is the gaping anus." The tape recorder is the modern, mechanical descendent of Satan's body.[71]

"What was Watergate?" Nixon asked in one recorded conversation. "A little bugging." The bugger—the word's two meanings are iconologically identical—invades one's private, physical space. Violating the most intimate, physical privacy, he inserts his device into office, home, symbolic body. The language of the White House tapes, over and over again, connected bugging and exposure to filthy inner body contents. Nixon and his official family concerned themselves obsessively with leaks, plumbers, dirty tricks, laundered money, with what Nixon called "espionage, sabotage, shit." Exposure meant (Nixon), "Sloan starts pissing on Magruder and then Magruder starts pissing on who, even Haldeman." "Once the toothpaste is out of the tube," in Haldeman's version, "it's hard to get it back in." Nixon called "the upper intellectual types...ass-holes, you know, the soft heads, soft." As the cover-up unraveled, everyone tried (Dean) to "cover his own ass." Fear meant inability to control the bowels: when Haig revealed to the White House staff a tape dangerous to Nixon, he could "hear the assholes tightening all over the room." Clark McGregor, remarked Dean Burch, "broke out into assholes and shit himself to death." In White House iconology, weak men—medium-grade ass-holes, D.J. called them—lost control of their bodies, exposed themselves, and invited invasion and domination.[72]

Bugging others gave the president power over their dirty secrets. In the White House view of the world, however (Nixon), "Everybody bugs everybody else." If Nixon bugged Dean, then perhaps Dean had bugged him. Where on his body could Dean have carried a concealed recording device, the president wanted to know. If CREEP bugged Democratic National Headquarters, then "obviously I was concerned about whether the other side was . . . bugging us." The public discovery of the tapes brought the nightmare of exposure home to the White House and turned Nixon's weapon against himself. Arthur Burns, as if echoing Mailer's D.J. and Tex Hyde, said when he read the tapes, "Here is a Doctor Jekyll. A split personality. What does it all mean? Does Nixon lead a double life?"[73] Arthur Burns had discovered Satan's body. In so doing he alluded to another body, the one the tapes were meant to protect. That was the king's royal body into which, to cover his nakedness, Nixon had crawled.

Nixon longed to replace (Plowden) "the Body natural . . . subject to all infirmities" with "the Body politic . . . utterly devoid of natural Defects and Imbecilities." The White House provided for the spirit a home to replace the human body.

"This house for example," Nixon told his staff the morning after he resigned.

> I was comparing it to some of the great houses of the world that I have been in. This isn't the biggest house. . . . This isn't the finest house. . . . But this is the best house. It is the best house because it has something far more important than numbers of people who serve, far more important than numbers of rooms or how big it is, far more important than numbers of magnificent pieces of art. This house has a great heart.[74]

Like Wilson, Nixon gave up his home for the White House heart. The heart was the heart of the king's royal body.

The taping system aimed to gain Nixon secure possession of the king's royal body. Secret Service electronics specialists embedded five microphones in Wilson's oval office desk. They bugged Lincoln's sitting room. Control over the tapes would make Nixon into Mailer's "Lord," passing judgment on others. He could leak their secrets and protect his own. He could transform his "Body mortal [Plowden] into a Body that cannot be seen or handled." In control of his own "record," to paraphrase William Safire, he would not be vulnerable to the judgment of history.[75]

"The Lord hears" your tape "and passes you on," said D.J., "unless you can put false material into the tape recorder. Think of that." "Why can't we make a new Dictabelt?" the president asked one of his lawyers, to replace one recorded months before. Backdated like the deed Ralph Newman, the Lincoln scholar, had affixed to Nixon's vice-presidential papers, the "false material" would pass a manufactured history off as a human one.[76]

Nixon not only proposed creating new tapes to protect his royal body but also destroying old ones which exposed his mortality. Suspecting that John Ehrlichman knew about the tapes, Nixon told H. R. Haldeman to claim "we only taped the national security, uh, information . . . all other information is scrapped, never transcribed." Nixon taped "national security"; it could not be said "the President . . . taped somebody."[77]

"Some sinister force," in Alexander Haig's words, did destroy part of one tape; it probably destroyed several others. It did not destroy them all. Instead, Nixon himself listened to tapes for days, deleted the most incriminating material, and released them. The censored tapes, incriminating enough, fed the demand for more. Nixon buried himself in the Lincoln sitting room to listen to tapes the week before he resigned. There he and his two lawyers, Fred Buzhardt and James St. Clair, heard together the June 23 tape which sealed Nixon's doom. Woodrow Wilson had rhetorically elevated himself above the body and approached the gates of paradise. As human body and royal body disastrously converged, Nixon flew fitfully from one house to another, from the White House to San Clemente and Key Biscayne. He had, notwithstanding, trapped himself inside.[78] Created to replace the president's body with the body of the presidency, the tapes exposed Satan's body and brought Nixon down.

Had Nixon early destroyed the tapes, he would have remained in office. But he would have acknowledged also the failure of his project. Retaining the tapes, Nixon retained the sources and symbols of his body royal; destroying them would have reduced him to mortality. As Nixon discovered, however, he could not retain his body politic without exposing his body mortal. Indeed, there was probably an impulse to disclosure at work. Nixon had made a political career from exposures. The microfilmed Pumpkin papers which the young congressman held before news cameras revealed Alger Hiss's secret Communist past. Hiss's discomfiture, wrote Nixon in Six Crises, showed the Communist conspiracy in action, "twisting and turning and squirming . . . evading and avoiding." Nixon had first exposed the secrets of those in authority. Then he saved his career by turning the weapon against himself. His own secret fund revealed in 1952, the vice-presidential candidate "bared his soul" to a mass television public and proved he was "clean." Exposing some secrets, he seems to have thought twenty years later, would save him from having to reveal all.[79]

In imitation of the Lincoln about whom he read, Nixon capitalized on his "anguish." He knew that Lincoln's ordeal finally silenced the many who questioned his motives, and Nixon had long made the display of his suffering a sign of his virtue. The redemptive value of self-punishment was a powerful theme in Nixon's presidential models and in the Protestant tradition he shared with them. Who could blame a sufferer for the violence he visited on others? But success so linked to masochism easily slid into failure. Nixon's self-punishing impulse broke free from its role as the servant of ambition to attack the prurient man at the top—now not Hiss but Nixon himself.

Nixon "destroyed" Hiss, he wrote in *Six Crises*. "I imagined myself in his place, and wondered how he would feel when his family and friends learned the true story." Nixon, as he wrote, was twinned with Hiss from the beginning of his career. At its end, on the tapes, he compared himself to Hiss over and over again. "We got the Pumpkin papers," the president reminisced to John Dean. "Nixon ran the Hiss case the right way," he wanted Dean to tell Senator Sam Ervin. "We really just got the facts and tore him to pieces." Nixon wanted Dean to admonish the Senate Watergate committee to follow his own example and, the implication was, do to Nixon what Nixon had done to Hiss. The president called down on himself the judgment he had passed on Hiss. In the drama he imagined and secretly recorded, the tapes would become his Pumpkin papers. Was the man drawn to filthy secrets in others driven in self-loathing to expose his own?[80]

Nixon collaborated in the exposure and destruction of the mortal hidden in the king's royal body. Persecution of his "enemies," he acknowledged to David Frost, provoked retaliation. Recognizing his complicity in his own downfall, Nixon called himself "paranoiac."[81] This self-analysis must be taken further. The man who located bad motives outside the self had a stake not only in creating enemies but also in losing to them. Defeat confirmed the victim's vision of the sinister, omnipotent forces arrayed against him; it proved their malevolence and his own innocence. From one point of view, innocence protected against self-loathing; but the two merged, finally, in their validation by punishment.

Nixon blamed himself not for self-loathing after his fall but for a form of (self) love. "I'm not a very lovable man," he admitted to Frost.[82] But his guilt, as he understood it, lay not in hating his body natural but in loving the members of his body politic.

Wilson's new freedom offered the liberty of a well-functioning engine; Nixon had compared his mind to a "machine"; it was safe to take it "out of gear once in a while" to "recharge," but it should never be shut off. Nixon had, Garry Wills wrote, conducted a search-and-destroy mission against his interior. He had constructed a mechanical false self-system to protect Satan's body from disclosure. Like Wilson, Nixon retreated from family and mutual interrelations into self. But this project, which required replacing the human self with the mechanical body of the state, contained a contradiction at its core. Generated by the danger of emotional ties, it bound the president to his royal body; it invested the love of the White House "heart" with overpowering significance. Nixon had not made "mistakes . . . of the head," he told Frost. His mind was not faulty in itself, but it had failed to "rule his heart." Nixon's remaining libidinal attachments made him vulnerable, as Nixon dramatized his fall, deserving of punishment and forgiveness.[83]

The tapes, Nixon explained, revealed "mistakes of the heart." They were like "love letters," Pat Nixon said, and should have been destroyed. Nixon had remarked years before, "I can't really let my hair down with anyone . . . not even with my own family." Nixon let his hair down with his official family. The tapes, said presidential lawyer Charles Alan Wright, "showed what the president of the United States is like when he has his hair down." Nixon retained the tapes, one psychoanalyst surmises, because for once, on them, he expressed what he really felt. They were, in the Nixons' imagery, love letters to the White House heart. The tapes were evidence of Nixon's love affair with the King's royal body.[84]

Nixon tried to "contain" Watergate politically, he told Frost. Because his "motive" was not "criminal," he broke no law. How could political motives be "mistakes of the heart"? The heart that has political motives, Nixon explained, was the heart too emotionally tied to members of the White House staff. Eisenhowever only cared if you were "clean," complained Nixon, remembering the general's humiliation of him over the secret fund exposure. Eisenhower was "cruel" to fire his old friend Sherman Adams, and to send Nixon to do it. He didn't care that Adams was, like Nixon's own aides, "innocent in his heart." "But I don't look at it that way," the president told John Mitchell. "We're going to protect our people."[85]

Nixon could not protect Haldeman and Ehrlichman. Flanked by a bust of Lincoln and a picture of his own family,[86] he publicly accepted their resignations. After that, he told Frost, "there wasn't a happy time in the White House except in a personal sense." Nixon distinguished happy moments with his family—"in the personal sense"—from White House happiness. He had forced himself to be a "good butcher" and fire his two closest aides. "I cut off one arm, and then cut off the other arm."[87] These were the limbs of the king's royal body.

Nixon insisted on the fusion of his own person with the presidential office. His lawyers claimed that executive privilege covered everyone working in the White House because "members of his staff . . . are extensions of the Presidency." This usage of "members" turned members as individuals into members as limbs of a body politic. Alternatively, Nixon made the limbs of his body natural into symbols of spiritual power. "If you cut the legs off the President America is going to lose," he warned.[88]

Of course it was self-serving for Nixon to confuse his own survival with the survival of the presidency, and to claim as "mistakes of the heart" actions he took to keep his official family under control. Of course he gained concrete financial rewards from charging improvements on his Key Biscayne and San Clemente houses to the White House, and from ordering the General Services Administration to "perform housekeeping duties at the Nixons' private home."[89] Nevertheless, Nixon's language betrayed the identity confusions deeply at stake. Unable to acknowledge his self-interested purposes, they gained, as Wilson's had, overwhelming power. Boundaries between self and environment broke down. On one hand, absorbing office into self, threats to the man were "so damn—so damn dangerous to the Presidency." On the other, radically separating man from office, Nixon sacrificed "personal" feelings to the presidency. Although "sometimes . . . I'd like to resign," he told Henry Petersen in 1973, "you have got to maintain the Presidency out of this." Two years later "he put the interests of America" before "every instinct in my body" and resigned.[90] Hypocritical though these claims of self-denial are, they faithfully reflect Nixon's failure redemptively to join the instincts of his body mortal to his body politic. Consider, in this light, how Nixon experienced his presidential death.

Nixon had at the end, one White House aide observed, "the look of a man who knew he was going to die." His meeting with his remaining congressional supporters the night he resigned, said a participant, "was a kind of death tableau." Death was surely on Nixon's mind the next morning. "My mother was a saint," he told his staff. "And I think of her, two boys dying of tuberculosis, nursing four others . . . and seeing each of them die, and when they died, it was like one of her own." Nixon had taped one of his living brothers, but he was no longer, in Lincoln's description of Richard III, "plotting the destruction of his brothers to make room for himself." Plots ended, he seems to have recalled his dead brothers in identification.[91]

Thomas Nast's immensely popular cartoon, after Lincoln's assassination, showed Columbia weeping at Lincoln's bier (plate 9). The image symbolized the transfiguration of Lincoln's body into the mystic body of the union. Wilson, sensitive to the same image, evoked mothers who had lost their sons as he neared his apotheosis. Nixon's mother had mourned not only his dead brothers but even four strange boys. There would be no pieta for him.[92]

The president turned from his mother and brothers to a quote he "found as I was reading, my last night in the White House." He recited to his staff Theodore Roosevelt's grief for the death of his wife:

> As a flower she grew and as a fair young flower she died.... When she had just become a mother, and when her life seemed to be just begun and when the years seemed so bright before her, then by a strange and terrible fate death came to her. And when my heart's dearest died, the light went from my life forever.[93]

The death of Nixon's "heart's dearest" was the death of his royal body. The "great heart" of the White House no longer beat for him.

Nixon, like Wilson, flirted with natural death. Wilson, who replenished his presidential body from communion with the people, traveled by train through the West; Nixon, who sustained his royal body in the company of other rulers, traveled by plane through the world. He traveled with phlebitis in one leg; "the President has a death wish," his doctor warned.[94] But the man who feared cutting the legs off the presidency did not lose his own. He died as king, not as Christ.

Christ's death united his human body (now to be present in communion) with his corpus mysticum. The crowned king, unlike the crowned Christ, retained two, separate bodies. Coronation merely supplanted the human body with the realm (plate 1). Stripped of its robe and crown, the king's royal body died; left with his natural body, the deposed king was "nothing." Conrad's cartoon, "The King is Dead," shows only an overturned royal hat. The king Richard whom Nixon played at the end was not Richard III but Richard II. Had Nixon, like Shakespeare's King Richard, gained royal stature as he lost his crown, he might have found the language to say:

> Therefore, no no, for I resign to thee.
> Now mark me, how I will undo myself;—
> I give this heavy weight from off my head.
> And this unwieldy sceptre from my hand,
> The pride of kingly sway from out my heart;
> With mine own tears I wash away my balm.
> With mine own tongue deny my sacred state,
> With mine own breath release all duty's rites:
> All pomp and majesty I do foreswear.

Stripped of his royal adornments, Richard II stared unbelievingly at his reflection in the mirror and asked,

> Was this the face
> That like the sun did make beholders wink?
>
> ... Thus play I in one person many people,
> And none contented. Sometimes am I king;
> Then treason makes me wish myself a beggar...
> Than am I king again...
> and by and by
> Think that I am unkinged, by Bolingbroke,
> And straight am nothing.[95]

"No one can know how it feels to resign the Presidency of the United States," Richard Nixon said. "I felt that resignation meant that I would be in a position of not having anything to live for." In the lines Conrad put under his cartoon of Nixon as Richard II (plate 10)

> O... that I could forget what I have been!
> Or not remember what I must be now.

Stripped of his royal body, King Richard (plate 1) was nothing.[96]

Nixon dressed the White House police in royal uniforms. He surrounded the White House with the trappings of royalty; Lincoln did not. Yet Lincoln assumed his own robe of office immediately after his election. He grew a beard. The wrath of the Calvinist avenger marked Lincoln's naked, cadaverous face (plate 11). Deep-set eyes, skeletal cheek-bones, tight lips, and jutting, aggressive chin compose a physiognomy of judgment. Commenting on the early, bearded portraits (plate 12), Hamilton and Ostendorf write, "The heavy beard softens the lines in his face, and makes him less gaunt. His eyes are lifted, giving the features a benign, almost saintly expression. He is now the man whom tens of thousands of Union soldiers will shortly know as 'Father Abraham!'" Saintly Father Abraham "will shortly" send many times "tens of thousands of Union soldiers" to their death; the beard is a mask hiding Jehovah's retribution.[97]

Early in 1863, after signing the Emancipation Proclamation, Lincoln began to clip his beard. In the pictures taken a few days before his death, the beard is hardly there at all (plate 13). As Hamilton and Ostendorf say, "The mask hiding Lincoln's intense emotions has fallen away and revealed a man at peace with himself."[98] We falsely remember Lincoln with full beard because he has absorbed its softness into the lines on his face. Taking the suffering of the Isaacs on himself, Father Abraham looks ready for his sacrifice.

Nixon could not strip off the robe of office or, to use his own metaphor, let his hair down. "It's something like wearing clothing—if you let down your hair, you feel too naked." Lincoln, his face marked by experience, seems in his last photos peacefully to accept responsibility for his tragically inevitable fate. Secluded in San Clemente as the end neared, Nixon read *Abraham Lincoln: Theologian of American Anguish;* it was too late to learn the part. Like a bad actor too preoccupied with his audience, Nixon imitated only the external signs of the character he had chosen to play. He could not play the role from within. That is why Nixon seemed at once self-consciously to manipulate his appearances before others and at the same time to be driven by irrational forces ("the heart") beyond his control.[99]

Lincoln may have dreamed of death, courted assassination, and provided the script to interpret its meaning; yet, because he embodied his passion, there seems nothing willful in his sacrifice. "I have impeached myself," Nixon told Frost. "I brought myself down. I gave 'em the sword. And they stuck it in, and they twisted it with relish."[100] Conrad shows Nixon busily nailing himself to the cross (plate 14).

Nixon's mother was a devout Quaker. At his father's Sunday school classes, young Richard learned about "the blood of the lamb." The children looked for the political significance of Christ's sacrifice, his cousin, Jessamyn West, has recalled, in hopes "that the blood had not been shed in vain."[101] (Her words echo the Gettysburg address echoing the New Testament.) Republican Congressman Edward Biester worried as Nixon's impeachment drew near. He feared that America was killing another king "to bring about a reunification and rebirth of the people." It was, Biester thought, a bloody, never-ending process. Christ, said Biester, was the last king to be killed, and his sacrifice signified that men could stop the cycle of killing kings and reenact it symbolically in the mass. Biester had a picture of Lincoln in his office. He hoped America would be guided by Lincoln's "forgiving humility" and spare Nixon.[102]

Biester associated Christ with Lincoln's forgiveness, kingship with human sacrifice. In the American political imagination, however, Lincoln's teaching is inseparable from his sacrifice. The Revolution's symbolic killing of the king did give birth to the new nation.[103] But America achieved "reunification and rebirth" in Lincoln's blood sacrifice. His sins washed white in the blood of the lamb, Lincoln rose to political immortality.

Biester finally supported impeachment. American presidents, he realized, were not kings, and impeachment showed they were not "above the law."[104] As Biester implied, Nixon's demise renewed American faith in a battered, constitutional system. It did so because Nixon, placing himself above the law, cast himself as king in American revolutionary symbolism.

Yet Biester's original suspicion of the sacrifice of kings should give us pause. Lincoln achieved a martyr's death; Nixon fell as tyrant. Nixon's rise and fall parodied Lincoln's, to be sure, but the victim of black comedy also has his social function. Nixon imagined he was protecting America from knowledge of the means he and his predecessors required to prosecute foreign war and preserve order at home. The constitutional system, in turn, loaded its sins upon Nixon to isolate him from normal politics and restore confidence in a government of laws. Nixon sank under a burden the nation did not wish to share. Lincoln's sacrifice gained the country's love; he became its lamb of God. Nixon drew upon himself the country's hate; he was its scapegoat. The separation of man from office did not merely expose the body mortal; it reaffirmed the office as well.

Nevertheless, Saint Nixon, his halo a tape recorder spool in one of Conrad's cartoons (plate 15), achieved his own crucifixion and apotheosis. As the president entered the helicopter bearing him from the White House for the last time, he turned and raised his arms in the familiar V sign. Eisenhower had his arms raised high above his head when Nixon first saw him, and Nixon adopted the gesture as his own. This time, so it seemed, Nixon could not lift his limbs much above his body. Arms outstretched, propeller halo overhead, he looks crucified to the helicopter (cf. plates 2 and 16).[105]

Earlier, at the height of Nixon's power, Dwight Chapin saw the pope "clearly blessing" Nixon's helicopter as it lifted from Saint Peter's Square. Now the helicopter, symbol of the Vietnam War and of the mechanical new freedom Nixon had failed to attain, raised him above the White House. (Cf. plates 3 and 16.) This "dynamo" was not a "virgin bride" reclaiming her sacrificed son. Transferred to *Air Force One* and alone in his private compartment, Nixon flew to his "pastures and quietness and peace," the estate he had renamed "Casa Pacifica" (House of Peace) in San Clemente. The House of Peace was no paradise for Nixon. Like Theodore Roosevelt, he wanted "to be in the arena." He had called "pitiful" "those who have nothing to do . . . just lying around at Palm Beach." Now he was one of them. Others might envy a life in the sun. For Nixon it signified perpetual motion, no exit, and no place to go. It was hell. There were only "the very nice house," "golf," "nice parties . . . good clothes and shoes, et cetera, et cetera, et

cetera. Or [said the boy who heard the train go by at night] travel if you
want to."[106]

Notes

1. Ernst H. Kantorowicz, *The King's Two Bodies* (Princeton, N.J., 1957), p. 7.

2. Joseph Galloway, "A Candid Examination of the Mutual Claims of Great Britain and
the Colonies," in *Tracts of the American Revolution, 1763–1776*, ed. Merrill Jensen (Indianapolis, 1967), p. 354; Tom Paine, "Common Sense," in *Common Sense and Other
Political Writings*, ed. Nelson F. Adkins (Indianapolis, 1953), p. 32.

3. Richard Nixon, quoted in Thomas C. Blaisdell, Jr., et al., *The American Presidency
in Political Cartoons: 1776–1976* (Salt Lake City, 1976), p. 252; Richard Nixon, interview
with David Frost, *New York Times* (May 20, 1977), p. 16 (cited hereafter as Frost, *NYT*).

4. Paine, p. 32; *San Francisco Chronicle* (May 21, 1977), p. 8.

5. Frost, *NYT* (May 20, 1977), p. 16. Lincoln actually wrote, "I felt that measures,
otherwise unconstitutional, might become lawful, by becoming indispensable to the preservation of the constitution, through the preservation of the nation" (Abraham Lincoln to
Albert G. Hodges, April 4, 1864, in *Abraham Lincoln, Collected Works*, ed. Roy P. Basler,
9 vols. (Springfield, Ill., 1953–55), 7:281.

6. See David Donald, *Lincoln Reconsidered* (New York, 1961), pp. 188–91; Griel Marcus, "Lincoln and Nixon: Strange Bedfellows?" *Newsday* (February 1, 1973), pp. 20–21.
Marcus and Garry Wills were the first to explore Nixon's effort to model himself on
Lincoln. See Garry Wills, *Nixon Agonistes* (New York, 1971), pp. 23–24, 42, 83, 105,
117–18, 140, 156–57.

7. Donald, pp. 3–4, 61–63.

8. Wills, p. 82; Anthony Lukas, *Nightmare: The Underside of the Nixon Years* (New
York, 1976), p. 635; Frost, *NYT* (May 5, 1977), p. 33; (May 26, 1977), p. 40; Gerald Ford,
August 9, 1974, in *Congressional Quarterly, Historic Documents of 1974* (Washington,
D.C., 1975), pp. 697–99.

9. Kantorowicz, pp. 15–17, 42–48, 61–78, 90–93, 194–206, 268; Erik H. Erikson,
Young Man Luther (New York, 1958), pp. 140–43; John Winthrop, "A Model of Christian
Charity," in *Puritan Political Ideas*, ed. Edmund P. Morgan (Indianapolis, 1965), pp.
84–92.

10. Wills, p. 83. Wills convincingly demonstrates Wilson's importance to Nixon. See
pp. 30–31, 42, 386, 392–97, 419, 422–27, 429–33.

11. Abraham Lincoln, "Address before the Young Men's Lyceum of Springfield, Ill.,"
January 27, 1838, in Basler (n. 5 above), 1:108–15. Edmund Wilson was the first to suggest
the personal importance of this speech for Lincoln's future career. See "Abraham Lin-
coln: The Union as Religious Mysticism," in *Eight Essays* (Garden City, N.Y., 1954). My
sketch of Lincoln derives from this essay, from Norman Jacobson, "Lincoln's Abraham,"
Helderberg Review 1 (Spring 1971): 14–19; and, most important, from Dwight Anderson,
"The Quest for Immortality: Abraham Lincoln and the Founding of Political Authority in
America" (Ph.D. diss., University of California, Berkeley, 1972).

12. Abraham Lincoln, speech at Springfield, Ill., June 16, 1858, in Basler, 2:461;
E. Wilson, pp. 190–91.

13. Abraham Lincoln, speech at Kalamazoo, Mich., August 27, 1856; speech at
Chicago, July 10, 1858; reply to N.Y. Workingmen's Democratic Republican Association,
March 21, 1864; speech to the 166th Ohio Regiment, August 22, 1864; all in Basler,
2:364, 2:499, 7:259–60, 7:512; Carl Sandburg, *Lincoln Collector* (New York, 1949), p. 162.

14. Abraham Lincoln, speech at Springfield, Ill., June 26, 1857; to Mrs. Lydia Bixby, November 21, 1864; in Basler, 2:404, 8:117; see also George W. Wilson, "A Prophetic Dream Reported by Abraham Lincoln," *American Imago* 1 (June 1940): 48.

15. Donald, p. 5; E. Wilson, p. 202; Jacobson, p. 18.

16. Sandburg, p. 219; E. Wilson, pp. 201–2; Anderson, pp. 211–16; Jacobson, pp. 17–18; William Shakespeare, *Macbeth*, act 3, scene 2.

17. Abraham Lincoln, Second Inaugural Address, March 4, 1865, in Basler, 8:333.

18. Charles Hamilton and Lloyd Ostendorf, *Lincoln in Photographs* (Norman, Okla., 1963), p. 153. Elliot Gorn's important, unpublished seminar paper, "Glory, Glory Halleluiah" (University of California, Berkeley, 1974), discusses the genesis and meaning of the "Battle Hymn of the Republic" and its variants. On Father Abraham, see pp. 30–32. Stanton is quoted in Donald, p. 8. Lincoln had compared Negro slaves to the "children of Israel" held in "Egyptian bondange" (speech at Springfield, Ill., June 26, 1857), in Basler, 2:409. On the Civil War as Calvinist retribution, see Edmund Wilson, *Patriotic Gore* (New York, 1962), pp. 3–106.

19. Abraham Lincoln, speech at Peoria, Ill., October 16, 1854; Emancipation Proclamation, January 1, 1863; Gettysburg Address, November 19, 1863; in Basler, 2:276, 6:30, 7:17–19. See Anderson, pp. 185–220.

20. Basler, 2:115.

21. Ibid., 8:333; Donald, pp. 139, 148–49, 153; Herman Melville, "The Martyr," *Battle-Pieces and Aspects of the War* (University of Massachusetts Press, 1962), pp. 141–42 (originally published 1866).

22. Abraham Lincoln, address at Cooper Institute, New York City, February 11, 1861; speech in Independence Hall, Philadelphia, February 22, 1861; in Basler, 3:522, 3:535–38, 4:190, 4:240. Also see Anderson, pp. 132–35.

23. Henry Louis Stephens, in *Vanity Fair*, July 7, 1860, reprinted in Rufus Rockwell Wilson, *Lincoln in Caricature* (Elmira, N.Y., 1945), p. 13; Hamilton and Ostendorf, p. 242.

24. Sir John Tenniel, in *Punch*, December 3, 1864, reprinted in Blaisdell (n. 3 above), p. 101; Abraham Lincoln, annual message to Congress, December 8, 1863; First Inaugural Address, March 4, 1861; annual message to Congress, December 1, 1862; in Basler, 7:53, 4:271, 5:527–28; see also Edward Charles Wagenknecht, *The Films of D. W. Griffith* (New York, 1975), pp. 59–61; Donald, p. 5; E. Wilson, "Abraham Lincoln," (n. 11 above), p. 197. Griffith's words quoted in the text are echoed in the book on Lincoln that Nixon read in his final days. See D. Elton Trueblood, *Abraham Lincoln: Theologian of American Anguish* (New York, 1973), pp. 5–6.

25. Wagenknecht, p. 60. Griffith uses Woodrow Wilson, *The History of the American People*, 5 vols. (New York, 1908); and see below nn. 33 and 34.

26. E. Wilson, "Abraham Lincoln," pp. 192, 197.

27. Marquis de Chambrun, *Impressions of Lincoln and the Civil War,* quoted in E. Wilson, "Abraham Lincoln," p. 186.

28. Wills, p. 395. Fawn Brodie informs me that the desk Nixon thought was Woodrow Wilson's in fact belonged to Vice-President Henry Wilson, the antislavery politician. Grant's Vice-President, Wilson, died in office in 1875.

29. Wills, pp. 30–31, 386; Anderson, pp. 227–30; Woodrow Wilson, speech at Boston, Mass., February 24, 1919; Thanksgiving Proclamation, November 7, 1917, in *The Messages and Papers of Woodrow Wilson*, 2 vols. (New York, 1924), 1:433, 2:645.

30. Woodrow Wilson, "The Ideals of America," *Atlantic Monthly* 90 (December 1902): 721–23, 726; see my "Max Weber and Woodrow Wilson: The Iron Cage in Germany and America," *Polity* 3 (Summer 1971): 566.

31. W. Wilson, "The Ideals of America," pp. 728–31; Rogin, p. 567.

32. W. Wilson, "The Ideals of America," pp. 732–34; Woodrow Wilson, *Constitutional Government in the United States* (New York, 1908), pp. 54, 59, 77. See also his *Congressional Government* (Boston, 1885).

33. W. Wilson, *Constitutional Government*, pp. 54–57, 60, 65, 68–69. I share Alan Seltzer's view that Wilson placed spiritual values above economic interests. But while Seltzer ties Wilson's political vision to a decentralized economic order, I emphasize his infatuation with presidential leadership in an organic state. A fuller account of Wilson's thought would have to address his political economy; such an account would show, I believe, that Seltzer's approach complements the one offered here. In distinguishing large corporations from trusts, Wilson showed a sympathy with technological organization which bridged the apparent gap between his nineteenth-century "man on the make" and the twentieth century corporate giant. Nevertheless, Wilson's commitment both to Seltzer's new freedom and to mine pulled him in contradictory directions and helped drive him above the social order into political messianism.

34. Woodrow Wilson, *The New Freedom* (Englewood Cliffs, N.J., 1961), pp. 49–53 (originally published 1913).

35. Ibid., pp. 30–31.

36. Ibid., pp. 30–33; Alexander and Juliette George, *Woodrow Wilson and Colonel House* (New York, 1959), p. 21.

37. Woodrow Wilson, address on Lincoln, September 4, 1916, *Messages and Papers*, 1:320.

38. Ibid., 1:321–22.

39. W. Wilson, *Constitutional Government*, p. 69; *Messages and Papers*, 1:322.

40. Woodrow Wilson, address at Philadelphia, May 10, 1915, in *Messages and Papers* 1:114–17; address at St. Paul, Minn., September 4, 1919, in ibid., 2:846–47, 850, 853.

41. W. Wilson, "The Ideals of America," pp. 724, 728–30.

42. Woodrow Wilson, address at Sioux Falls, S.D., September 8, 1919; address at St. Paul, Minn., September 9, 1919; response to King George V at Buckingham Palace, December 27, 1918; in *Messages and Papers*, 2:823, 855, 581.

43. Woodrow Wilson, address at Philadelphia, May 10, 1915, address at Boston, February 24, 1919; address at Pueblo, Colo., September 25, 1919; address at St. Paul, Minn., September 9, 1919; in *Messages and Papers*, 2:118, 638–39, 1113, 1124, 855–56. See George and George, pp. 117–18, 320–22.

44. Woodrow Wilson, address on Lincoln, September 4, 1916, in *Messages and Papers*, 1:322.

45. Woodrow Wilson, address at Gettysburg, July 4, 1913, in *Messages and Papers*, 1:15–17.

46. Woodrow Wilson, address at Independence Hall, Philadelphia, July 4, 1914; address at Gettysburg, July 4, 1913; message to the National Army, September 3, 1917; in *Messages and Papers*, 1:14, 426; Wills, p. 430; Woodrow Wilson, address at Pueblo, Colo., September 25, 1919, in *Messages and Papers*, 2:1127.

47. Woodrow Wilson address at Pueblo, Colo., September 25, 1919, in *Messages and Papers*, 2:1127; Woodrow Wilson, speech at Sioux Falls, S.D., September 8, 1919, in ibid., 2:825; George and George, pp. 292–93.

48. Woodrow Wilson, address at Pueblo, Colo., September 25, 1919; address at Boston, February 24, 1919; in *Messages and Papers*, 2:1120, 642–13.

49. See W. Wilson, *History* (n. 25 above), 5:58–64; Everett Carter, "Cultural History Written with Lightning: The Significance of *The Birth of a Nation*," *American Quarterly* 12 (Fall 1960): 347.

50. Woodrow Wilson, *Division and Reunion* (New York, 1893), p. 294; and *Constitutional Government*, p. 49.

51. Wagenknecht, p. 59; Carter, p. 347; Woodrow Wilson, address at St. Paul, Minn., September 9, 1919; address at Pueblo, Colo., September 25, 1919; in *Messages and Papers*, 2:846, 1114; W. Wilson, *History*, 5:212–13. *Birth of a Nation* was based on the racist novel by Thomas Dixon, *The Klansman* (New York, 1905).

52. Carter, p. 347; Paul O'Dell, *Griffith and the Rise of Hollywood* (New York, 1970), p. 35; Woodrow Wilson, address at Pueblo, Colo., September 25, 1919, in *Messages and Papers*, 2:1130.

53. George and George, pp. 21, 230, 292–94.

54. John Morton Blum, *Woodrow Wilson and the Politics of Morality* (Boston, 1956), pp. 3–4; George and George, p. vi; Sigmund Freud and William C. Bullitt, *Thomas Woodrow Wilson* (Boston, 1967), p. 289.

55. W. Wilson, *New Freedom*, pp. 161–62.

56. Ibid., pp. 162–63.

57. Ibid., pp. 163–64.

58. George and George, pp. 314–15; Blum, p. 3; Jacobson, p. 21.

59. Quoted in David Abrahamsen, *Nixon vs. Nixon* (New York, 1977), pp. 78–79.

60. Richard Nixon, *RN: The Memoirs of Richard Nixon* (New York, 1978), p. 9; Lukas (n. 8 above), p. 556.

61. Quoted in Abrahamsen, p. 172.

62. Nixon quoted in Abrahamsen, p. 214; in Michael Rogin and John Lottier, "The Inner History of Richard Milhous Nixon," *Transaction* 9 (November–December 1971): 24; and in Wills, p. 393.

63. Wills, pp. 30–31.

64. Donald, p. 64.

65. Abrahamsen, pp. 185–86; Marcus, p. 21.

66. Daniel Ellsberg, *Papers on the War* (New York, 1972), p. 41; Norman Mailer, *Armies of the Night* (New York, 1968), pp. 210–12, 239.

67. Nixon promised a second American revolution in his 1971 State of the Union address. He is quoted in Blaisdell, p. 252. On Rehnquist, see Pat Watters and Stephen Gillers, eds., *Investigating the FBI* (Garden City, N.Y., 1973), p. 445.

68. E. Wilson, "Abraham Lincoln," p. 197.

69. Nixon quoted in Abrahamsen, p. 173, and in Lukas, p. 630.

70. Norman Mailer, *Why Are We in Vietnam?* (New York, 1967), pp. 23–25.

71. See the panels of hell in the Jan and Hubert van Eyck dyptich of the crucifixion and last judgment, Metropolitan Museum, N.Y. (plate 8), and in the Hieronymous Bosch tryptich, "Garden of Earthly Delights," Prado, Madrid. The Luther quotes are from Norman O. Brown, *Life against Death* (New York, 1959), pp. 211, 226. Cf. pp. 202–33. For a psychoanalytic interpretation of Nixon's personality in terms of secrecy and anality, written well before the Watergate exposures, see Rogin and Lottier.

72. See Alan B. Rothenberg, "Why Nixon Taped Himself," *Psychoanalytic Review* 62 (Summer 1975): 202–23. The phrases quoted in the text come, in order, from the tapes of September 15, 1972 (quoted in Lukas, p. 333); March 17, 1973, and March 17, 1973 (both quoted in Rothenberg, p. 205); April 8, 1973, March 13, 1973, and March 19, 1973 (all quoted in Lukas, pp. 416, 394, 397); and from Bob Woodward and Carl Bernstein, *The Final Days* (New York, 1976), p. 369.

73. Richard Nixon to John Wilson and Frank Strickler, recorded conversation of April 19, 1973, quoted in Paul Conrad, *The King and Us* (Los Angeles, 1974), p. 190; Richard Nixon to H. R. Haldeman, recorded conversation of April 25, 1973, in Lukas, pp. 515–16; Frost, *NYT* (May 5, 1977), p. 32; Woodward and Bernstein, p. 168.

74. Richard Nixon, "Remarks to Members of the Cabinet and the White House Staff," in *Historic Documents*, p. 690. I am indebted to Nancy Shinabarger for calling my atten-

tion to this passage. See Richard Nixon to John Ehrlichman, recorded conversation of April 14, 1973, quoted in Conrad, p. 86.

75. Lukas, pp. 502, 507, 510.

76. Mailer, *Why Are We in Vietnam?* p. 25; Woodward and Bernstein, pp. 25–27; Lukas, pp. 609, 486.

77. Lukas, p. 514.

78. Ibid., pp. 624, 737–39; Woodward and Bernstein, pp. 124–32.

79. Richard Nixon, *Six Crises* (New York, 1962), pp. 36–37, 70; Lillian Hellman, *Scoundrel Time* (New York, 1977), pp. 80–81; Rogin and Lottier, pp. 24–25; Wills, *Nixon Agonistes* (n. 6 above), pp. 93–114, 155–56.

80. Nixon, *Six Crises*, p. 35; Garry Wills, "The Hiss Connection through Nixon's Life," *New York Times Magazine* (August 25, 1974), pp. 76–77, 87–89; *San Francisco Chronicle*, "Nixon Relives the Hiss Case" (May 3, 1974), p. 5; Lukas, pp. 391–92; Rothenberg, pp. 219–20. See Conrad's cartoon, "The Pumpkin Tapes," *The King and Us*, p. 61.

81. *New York Times* (May 20, 1977), p. 16.

82. *San Francisco Examiner* (September 4, 1977), p. 11.

83. Rogin and Lottier, pp. 21–22; Wills, *Nixon Agonistes*, pp. 373–74; Frost, *NYT* (May 5, 1977), p. 33.

84. Frost, *NYT* (May 5, 1977), p. 33; Woodward and Bernstein, p. 166; Abrahamsen, pp. 173, 220; Lukas, p. 581.

85. Frost, *NYT* (May 5, 1977), pp. 32, 33; Richard Nixon to John Mitchell, recorded conversation, March 22, 1973, quoted in Lukas, p. 408.

86. Lukas, p. 459. "Your parents have the strength of Lincoln," a Nixon speechwriter told Julie Nixon. See Woodward and Bernstein, p. 304.

87. Frost, *NYT* (May 5, 1977), p. 33.

88. *New York Times* (November 15, 1973), p. 1; Lukas, p. 392; Rothenberg, p. 210; cf. Wills, pp. 394–95.

89. Lukas, pp. 474–84.

90. Lukas, p. 452; Richard Nixon to Henry Petersen, recorded conversation of April 27, 1973, *Submission of Recorded Presidential Conversations to the Committee on the Judiciary of the House of Representatives by President Richard Nixon, N.Y. Times,* ed., (New York, 1974), p. 783; President Nixon's resignation speech, August 8, 1974, *Historical Documents,* p. 685.

91. Lukas, p. 730; Abrahamsen, pp. 244–45; Nixon, "Remarks to Members of the Cabinet and the White House Staff," *Historical Documents,* p. 691.

92. Blaisdell, et al., p. 102; Hamilton and Ostendorf, p. 279.

93. Nixon, *Historical Documents,* pp. 691–92.

94. Woodward and Bernstein, p. 214.

95. Conrad, p. 215; William Shakespeare, *Richard II,* act 4, scene 1. See also Kantorowicz, pp. 24–41.

96. Frost, *NYT* (May 26, 1977), p .40; Conrad, p. 75.

97. Abrahamsen, p. 215; Hamilton and Ostendorf, pp. 70, 230.

98. Ibid., pp. 229–371.

99. Abrahamsen, p. 172; Lukas, pp. 634–35. For the understanding of Nixon as a bad actor, I am indebted to a good actor, Michael Lerner.

100. Frost, *NYT* (May 5, 1977), p. 33.

101. Abrahamsen, p. 67.

102. Lukas, pp. 752–53.

103. See Winthrop Jordan, "Familial Politics: Thomas Paine and the Killing of the King, 1776," *Journal of American History* 60 (September 1973), pp. 294–308.

104. Lukas, p. 754.

105. Conrad, p. 181; Nixon, *RN*, p. 80.

106. Wills, p. 28; Lukas, pp. 206, 479, 481; Abrahamsen, pp. 245–48; Frost, *NYT* (May 26, 1977), p. 40.

Four

Ambivalent Leviathan: Herbert Hoover and the Positive State

Peri E. Arnold

I t is a curious feature of the American political system that, unlike other industrialized systems, it did not quickly or fully evolve a highly centralized, expansive government charged with the maintenance of economic and social stability.[1] Throughout the world the positive state is correlative with advanced industrialization, but the traditional verities of American political culture created an obstinate barrier to the positive state. Americans are inculcated with values of localism, direct democracy, ruralism, individualism, and autonomy, which are objectively contrary to the character of the positive state.

Yet, to be sure, American government did expand in response to rapid economic change. But while this expansion greatly increased the scope and functions of the state, it failed to increase substantially the national government's capacity to plan or its ability to reallocate valued goods in the society. As Grant McConnell observes, a notable characteristic of modern American government "is the conquest of segments of formal state power by private groups and associations."[2] In the American context, government expanded in service to particular minoritarian interests.

Although this minoritarian interpretation persuasively accounts for the most regular patterns that characterize American national politics, there are certain exceptional periods when majoritarian politics has flourished, where the state has acted cohesively and decisively to plan and reallocate. This paper attempts to provide a consistent interpreta-

I am grateful to the American Council of Learned Societies for a grant-in-aid which supported part of the research reported herein.

tion for the rise of the positive state which recognizes both the typical pattern and these sporadic interludes—as well as the reasons why these interludes remain limited and exceptional. In what follows I will suggest the importance of certain conceptual commitments (and their evolution) in the American political tradition which altered the capacities and potential of the American state.

The minoritarian political base of expanding government in America defused much of the vigor of the old antistate argument in American political life. In this century businessmen, the most likely recruits to that argument, were far more likely to support the expansion of the state's role in the economy than attack its growth. While the antistate argument achieved prominence on several occasions in this century, it lost the bulk of its adherents when businessmen learned that the state could serve their interests.

A third argument about the state has become common since the 1940s. Rejecting both the antistate and the minoritarian arguments, a number of Americans who might be styled social democrats argue that the state must routinely place for socioeconomic change and the redistribution of valued goods. This vision of the positive state differs from the minoritarian model of the expansive state in that it is presumed to be responsive to majoritarian politics. But paradoxically, while the ends of the minoritarian and majoritarian arguments are opposed, the sporadic capacity of the positive state to plan and redistribute in response to majoritarian demands owes much to the growth of the minoritarian state. For it is the minoritarian justification for the positive state which facilitated the development of public instrumentalities which rendered government sporadically capable of responding to majoritarian political claims when they arise in the polity. In a sense, as I shall show, when Americans learned to accept the minoritarian positive state they began a process of conceptual change in regard to their relationship to government which undermined the power of the old, antistate argument and made them more apt to rely on state power for solutions to societal problems. Yet, because most Americans have not squarely accepted the majoritarian positive state argument, national government often wields great power without a sense of the public ends or larger purposes of public policy. Such a purpose can only come from the people, and Americans are caught in an ambivalence toward government which entails the acceptance of the expansive state at the same time that it includes fears about the power and ends of the state.

The Foundation of the
Positive State in America

The Founding period and the Constitution itself provided fertile soil for
values which are hostile to the development of the positive state. As the
Founders resolved their ambivalence between fear of government and
the necessity for governmental competency, they created a mechan-
ically disjointed government, thinking that safety lay in the necessity for
all the independent parts to cooperate before government could act.
What their creation also made possible was the development of a fragmented regime within which sectionalism and then narrow but powerful
economic interests would find well-placed leverage points within government.

In this century, as American national government expanded and increased its involvement in the life of the society, the preexisting barriers
to expansive government shaped the character of America's positive
state. It is fragmented, cannot plan, and is uneven and inconsistent in
its responses to societal demands. But it has the basic, systematic
characteristics of the positive state. American national government is
enmeshed in the economic and societal processes of the nation. Its
officers are held politically responsible for the vitality and health of the
economy. It is even viewed by many Americans as primarily responsible
for managing the complex social problems of an advanced industrial
society[3]—although the weaknesses of American national government
often result in its inability to fulfill these expectations.

How did this state of affairs come about? How, in the face of great
opposition from within the American political tradition, did the positive
state develop in this country? A satisfactory answer to this question will
take the form of an explanation of elements within this political system
which mitigate its antigovernmental biases. Two very different kinds of
answers seem likely: one, based on interest-group, political-pressure
model, would stress changes in socioeconomic relations which have
made possible insistent demands for increased governmental action.
Thus, the economically based processes within contemporary society
might be shown to negate the strongest impact of its political tradition.
To be satisfactory, this answer would identify those groups and relations
which have changed and explain their increased political activity and
strength. A second explanation would stress the dynamic character of
American political traditions and attribute the growth of the positive
state at least in part to some new conception which arose within the
existing patterns of political relationships and served to short-circuit the
established biases against expansive, centralized government. To be

satisfactory, this kind of answer would have to show how a new conception of the state functioned to defuse biases against government.

Only the first of these two potential routes to an explanation for the rise of the positive state has been vigorously pursued. Leading scholars of American politics have identified the change in relations between economic interest groups and government as the operative condition for the rise of the positive state.[4] With the rapid growth of the economy, these scholars hold, groups that formerly opposed expansive central government found public authority to be a necessary stabilizing factor in the maturing, growing market economy. Yet, these groups would only accept an expanded governmental presence if it was controlled with private groups. As Grant McConnell shows, expanded public authority was continually tied to narrow political constituencies with the growth of the state in America.[5] On this minoritarian interpretation, then, while government expanded, its primary responsibility was keyed to narrow and privileged sectors of this society.

This account of the rise of the positive state is persuasive but incomplete. There are instances in American political history when political movements afforded presidents the opportunity to overcome the limits of the fragmented regime in a way that the authors of this minoritarian account often endorse.[6] Lincoln in the Civil War, Roosevelt during the Great Depression, and Johnson embracing civil rights as his own cause, all attest to this fact. It must be stressed, of course, that these attempts to breach the barriers to unified government, while often of great importance, are always short-lived. Although a Jefferson or a Roosevelt might temporarily solidify their parties and rule as though they were prime ministers, unhampered by the separation of powers, presidents learn that they cannot rely continually on support from their parties in Congress. While unusual circumstances may disrupt it, the equilibrium in the American political system reinforces political fragmentation. Nevertheless, the exceptional episodes make clear that, while the minoritarian view sheds light on the peculiar American relationship between minoritarian politics and expansive government, it does not account for the centralized aspects of the modern state which, if only sporadically, are amenable to majoritarian politics.

How did the positive state, if it was the product of minoritarian demands, develop this occasional yet crucial capacity for responding to majoritarian demands? Critics of minoritarian politics point particularly to the presidency as a redeeming majoritarian force in American politics.[7] The expansion of the president's power and organizational capacity is the most dramatic institutional change in twentieth-century American government. It is this enlarged capacity in the office, the expanded ability to control government as well as lead the nation, that makes the presidency the most sensitive receptor of majoritarian demands in the governmental system. But why did a regime in which governmental expansion depended upon narrow interest–group assent and checks develop an expanding capacity for centralized, executive leadership?

One might want to argue that in this century majorities, based on increasingly coherent group interests, embraced the presidency and fought to reinforce that office. Yet an argument of this sort seems untenable in the face of the fragility of American political parties, the lack of consistent redistributive issues in American politics, and the degree to which American political processes muddle the possibilities of dramatic political cleavages.[8] Consequently, the alternative approach which employs conceptual change as a key condition for political change would seem a more promising way of dealing with the increase of centralized executive power in the face of minoritarian politics.

But how can one inquire into the relationship between conceptual and political change in a society? The approach used here will focus on a paradigmatic case of a political actor who attempted to resolve the tensions in American politics between antigovernmental values and the alluring efficacy of the positive state. Such an approach to the problem, while admittedly both tentative and limited because it offers no access to large-scale conceptualization of action in the polity, still has the virtue of allowing some access to the immediate relationship between idea and action in individual behavior. And it provides a closer connection between thought and action than is obtainable by examing multiple actors. In particular, this approach can be especially illuminating where the individual is both typically American and historically significant.

Herbert Hoover and the Positive State

More than any other prominent American politician of his time, Herbert Hoover's career constituted an attempt to span the fissure between traditional American political values and the positive state. He is little understood and widely caricatured as the last of the laissez faire Old Guard.[9] Yet, at various times, Hoover exhibits all three American views of the state. At a key point in his political career he was instrumental in shaping the development of the minoritarian positive state. Then and later he was an influential spokesman for strengthening the presidency within the national government. Nevertheless, Hoover feared public power and its inherent coerciveness and at two dramatic points became a fierce spokesman for the antistate argument. Much of Hoover's public life constituted a search for a resolution between the fear of government and the functionally necessary expansion of government. His ambivalence toward the positive state was characteristically American, as was his resolution of that ambivalence.

The widely held caricature of Hoover stems from his vitriolic attacks on Franklin Roosevelt, big government, and the New Deal. But, in fact, these matters were not major substantive themes in his political career. Two great policy concerns, rationalizing the marketplace and reorganizing the executive branch, dominated Hoover's attentions during the greater period of his public service. During his tenure as secretary of commerce, 1921–27, Hoover extended his department's activities to achieve greater market stability in the economy. He attempted to use the Department of Commerce as a catalyst to rationalize the economy. The other concern, executive reorganization, drew his attention through the 1920s and into the 1930s and again in the late 1940s and 1950s. Here Hoover was a major influence in formulating proposals which were meant to increase the president's capacity for managerial control and the executive branch's centralization.

Hoover's work in economic management led him first to adopt the minoritarian argument for the positive state. Then his deep interest and work in executive reorganization led him beyond that, and he urged the strengthening of centralized executive authority which became, in turn, the focus and instrument of the majoritarian positive state argument. But Hoover's stance toward the positive state was always instrumental. Through much of his career he was in search of instrumental changes within government which would render government better able to perform desirable functions efficiently.

During the 1930s Hoover took on the role of an antistatist ideologue. His attack on "big government" belied his activities in the 1920s and was at odds with his reorganization work in the late 1940s. But the sting of his political defeat in 1932, combined with the expansiveness of Roosevelt's rhetoric, engaged Hoover's most basic values, for he remained a man of the American political tradition. The antistate argument came easily and believably to his lips, even if it did not provide the principles upon which the largest part of his political life was conducted.

How did Hoover reconcile his political values with his recognition that the maturing American economy required an expanded public role and a government capable of performing new tasks? An examination of Hoover's work in the Department of Commerce and in government reorganization will help answer this question. And an understanding of Hoover, in turn, may provide some insight into this society's tension between its political values and its acceptance of the positive state.

The Visible Hand:
Commerce's Role in the Marketplace

From the time he contemplated entering the cabinet in the Harding administration, Hoover thought that government's most pressing task was to aid business to stabilize the marketplace and overcome "wasteful" gyrations in the business cycle.[10] As secretary of commerce he attempted to use his department to achieve economic stability that could not be attained solely through private economic activities. It was clear to him that the private sector could no longer, by itself, guarantee a stable, healthy economic life for the nation.

Secretary Hoover attempted to provide a solution to this problem through indirect government intervention in business. If the problem was that individual businessmen acted "irrationally" when behaving competitively, then the relations of businessmen must be restructured to provide each of them with the capacity to recognize the relationship between their individual decisions and the price stability (and profitability) of the whole industry.[11]

Hoover understood that the trade association, which had been increasingly touted by its supporters as the answer to economic disorganization, could serve as the instrument of stabilization.[12] But, he realized, it would only fulfill this function if the great preponderance of the members of an industry were also members of the association. This had been the single largest problem for the associations; as wholly private organizations they had too little appeal to encompass the total membership of an industry. But, Hoover reasoned, if trade associations are the most promising instrument of economic stability, then all government activities aimed at serving business ought to be funneled through them. This would strengthen their activities, give them the appearance of authoritative status, and make membership in them appealing.[13] Thus, he reformed the Department of Commerce to make possible an alliance between government and the trade associations.

Under Hoover, the Department of Commerce provided aid to trade associations in three distinct ways. One, it aided them to organize statistical programs whereby they could collect and distribute data to their members concerning production, sales, and supplies. Two, the department was reorganized into commodity divisions to supply specialized trade information and guidance to trade associations. Three, it worked to create trade associations in industries which, heretofore, had been disorganized.

Shortly after taking office, Secretary Hoover spoke to the annual convention of the United States Chamber of Commerce about the need for reliable statistical information available within an industry: "Various industries have tried time and time again to secure such data informally, but it is essential to success that it should be collected and presented to the whole of the commercial community, buyer, seller, and banker, by some department of the Government which approached the whole problem in a purely objective way, which will hold the individual's return absolutely confidential."[14] But in December 1921, the U.S. Supreme Court struck a sharp blow at the whole enterprise of trade association informational services. The Court, in the so-called hardwood lumber case, declared "open-price" trade associations in violation of the Sherman Act.[15] Narrowly read, this decision ruled that trade associations could no longer collect and exchange information concerning the selling price of products within their industry, organize meetings of members to coordinate response to statistical information, and openly urge the limitation of production. But the business community, with Secretary Hoover in the lead, read the Hardwood decision as a grave threat to the existence of trade associations and any form of useful statistical program.[16]

Secretary Hoover took on the mission of saving trade-association statistical programs from the ravages of the Justice Department and the Supreme Court. He began an inconclusive negotiation with Attorney General Daugherty, attempting to gain advance approval for a scheme whereby the Department of Commerce would become the collector and distributor of statistics (but no price information). The department's role would, at one and the same time, insure that the anonymity of individual firms would be preserved and that statistical information would be wisely distributed, not only among the industry but to the public as well.[17]

The attorney general was unwilling to promise that all activities undertaken under Hoover's plan would be consistent with the Sherman Act. Hoover, nevertheless, launched his program. His position was made more tenable by the Supreme Court ruling on trade-association statistical programs in *Maple Flooring Manufacturer's Association* v. *U.S.*[18]

Thus, Secretary Hoover used the Department of Commerce to protect trade associations from the threat of antitrust actions by the Department of Justice. Hoover reasoned that the Department of Commerce's role in collecting and distributing statistics removed the threat that an association's statistical program would be treated as a conspiracy to violate the Sherman Act. But there is no doubt that Hoover understood the role of associations to be the restraint of trade. He called that role an "abridgement of competition which did not violate the laws."[19] That it might be contrary to at least the spirit of the antitrust

laws did not trouble Hoover in the least. He valued the goal of cooperation for mutual benefits among businessmen far more highly than le-
gality. As Grant McConnell observes, "Hoover had a distaste for the use
of law. Law implied compulsion; . . . it was formal and . . . inflexible."[20]

The second means through which Hoover's Department of Commerce accommodated trade associations was through the development
of the commodity divisions of the Bureau of Foreign and Domestic
Commerce, and a similar administrative entity, the Division of Simplification of the Bureau of Standards. Hoover's intent was simple: if the
department was going to serve trade associations, then there ought to be
a new kind of administrative unit which would link the department and
the associations. Hoover felt that the Bureau of Foreign and Domestic
Commerce could be made far more useful to business if it was able to
deliver particular services to them and, in turn, deal with their particular statistical and informational needs in implementing the program
heretofore described. By the end of 1922, Hoover had established seventeen commodity divisions.

Hoover intended the commodity divisions to be representative
agencies. If they were supposed to serve specific industries, he thought
it natural that they should also represent those industries. At a practical
level, this meant that the activities of the divisions should be guided by
the businessmen who benefit from the activities. But Hoover's conception of functional representation performed another service; it tied expanded government to the private sector and appeared to defuse the
coercive possibilities of public power.

Secretary Hoover insured the representativeness of the commodity
divisions by virtually granting the power of appointment of heads of the
divisions to trade associations in their respective industries. For example, the first division chief to be appointed was P. L. Palmerston who
had previously managed the Foreign Trade Bureau of the Rubber Association of America.[21] As the director of the Bureau of Foreign and
Domestic Commerce, Dr. Julius Klein, proudly announced in his report
for 1922, the men who headed the divisions "have been selected, in
most instances, with the desires and recommendations of the interested
industries in the most direct and acceptable manner that could be de-
vised."[22]

Neither Hoover nor any of his minions ever questioned the limits of
their scheme of functional representation. The business firm which remained outside a trade association or, worse, the consuming public,
were not constituents that Hoover sought to account for in his scheme of
representation. As I will show below, he did attempt to expand the
representative system, but only by encouraging the formation of trade
associations in heretofore unorganized industries. Thus, Hoover's sys-

tem of representation at the Department of Commerce neatly fit over the probable biases of power in American industries. The more organized industries, these firms with a greater sense of the utility of business organization, and those firms already aligned into coherent groupings were given particular advantage, access, and voice in government. As for the rest, the disorganized, it seemed they did not need a voice.[23]

Assistant Secretary of Commerce J. Walter Drake provided detailed evidence of the relationship between appointive practices and representation in his 1925 testimony to the House Appropriations Committee. Drake gave to the committee a list of thirty-five names of employees of the Bureau of Foreign and Domestic Commerce who had been nominated by trade associations.[24] This list included the heads of every commodity division with three exceptions: coal, petroleum, and specialties. Drake's list is interesting not only because it gives evidence of the extent of private sector domination of the department but also because it revealed the consequences of the department's not having established alliances with organizations in several industries.

The coal, specialties, and petroleum divisions were not allied to their respective industries because these industries either lacked adequate industry-wide organization or had such organization which was already allied with other governmental agencies (as in the case of the petroleum industry's ties to the Departments of State and the Interior). As can be seen by examining the heads of the commodity divisions over time (see table 1), the organizational stability of an industry was a significant factor in achieving stability in the leadership of the commodity divisions. Of the seventeen divisions created in late 1921 and 1922, seven required replacement of chiefs in 1923. Among these seven were coal, specialties, and petroleum. The four others were automobiles, textiles, lumber, and machinery. In automobiles and lumber changes were made in response to trade association needs. The automobile industry was dissatisfied with M. H. Hoepli, its first appointment, and forced him out of the division. In the lumber industry the post was simply alternated between two persons, both approved by the dominant industry associations. Textiles, on the other hand, was an internally conflictual industry and was unable to maintain steady relations with the Department of Commerce.

In 1924 four divisions again required new chiefs. Of these, the changes in the lumber and machinery divisions represented switches back to former heads. In the coal division, the changes represented still another failure by a head who had been appointed by the department without unified industry nomination. In 1925 the specialties division again required a new chief, with the department's choice in that industry failing again.

Table 1
Changes in Chiefs of the Commodity Divisions (1922–1925)

Divisions and Chiefs – 1922 (original Appointees)

Agricultural implements	George Bell
Automotive	M. H. Hoepli
Chemical	Charles C. Concannon
Coal	Francis R. Wadleigh
Electrical equipment	R. A. Lundquist
Foodstuffs	E. G. Montgomery
Hides and leather	Wilburn J. Paige
Iron and Steel	Luther Becker
Lumber	Axel Oxholm
Machinery	Walter H. Rastall
Paper	John Matthews, Jr.
Petroleum	Henry C. Morris
Rubber	P. L. Palmerton
Shoes and leather mfg.	Arthur Butman
Specialties	Henry H. Morse
Textiles	Edw. T. Pickard
Transportation	Eugene S. Gregg

Changes – 1923

Automobile	Percy Owen
Coal	Francis M. Shore
Lumber	Jesse C. Nellis
Machinery	Ronald H. Allen
Petroleum	Homer S. Fox
Specialties	Warren L. Hoagland
Textiles	William R. Meadows

Changes – 1924

Coal	Charles P. White
Lumber	Axel Oxholm
Machinery	Walter Rastall
Minerals (new)	Guy C. Riddell
Paper	O. M. Butler

Changes – 1925

Automobile	Irving H. Taylor
Electric equipment	D. S. Wegg
Lumber	J. C. Nellis
Rubber	Everett G. Holt
Specialties	Eric T. King

Source: Drawn from J. Walter Drake's testimony, U.S. Congress, House, Committee on Appropriations, *Hearings: Department of Commerce Appropriations Bill, 1925,* 68th Cong., 2d sess.

This record suggests two related conclusions. One, divisions in which the department took the initiative in appointment were less likely to maintain continuity of leadership. Two, those industries that were internally divisive were less likely to maintain stable relations with the department's commodity divisions, with leadership tenure as a measure of stability.

The commodity divisions demonstrate Hoover's reliance on the trade associations as a legitimating and checking factor on the expansion of government. These divisions, as Hoover intended, were inextricably tied to the industries they served. They were therefore dependent upon the stability of their industry to maintain their own continuity and capacity for work. Here, as in the already described case of the collection and distribution of statistical information, Hoover assured the consistency of the expansion of government functions with the canons of the American tradition by vesting public authority in private hands.

Hoover's statistical information service and the commodity divisions best served those industries with established trade associations. But what could be done for industries that lacked effective organization? This was the largest challenge facing Hoover in his war against the business cycle.

Secretary Hoover used the department to encourage industry-wide organization. He expected his subordinates to aid businessmen in their quest for organization. This was particularly the case with the Division of Simplification in the Bureau of Standards. This agency gathered leading representatives of an industry, paving bricks, for example, and helped them agree to reduce their product to a specified range of standardized items. Those industries which already had strong trade associations usually had already instituted a program of standardization and simplification. The process of simplification could be justified as a case of rationalization which made the entire product line more understandable to the consumer. But the reduction in numbers of models and the creation of standard sizes are also prerequisites for the possibility of the trade association stabilizing the market. Nonprice competition had to be reduced before price competition could be regularized. The Division of Simplification worked largely with unorganized industries and was exceptionally successful in introducing organization into preexisting commercial chaos. By late 1927 the division had fully promulgated recommendations for simplification that were adopted by 4,986 firms in sixty different industries.[25]

The encouragement and guidance of organization building in business invariably thrust the Department of Commerce, with its authority and stature, into the private sector. While the department worked with well-organized industries, it was able to subordinate its functions to available private sector associations. But to build new organization in business Hoover and Commerce had to lead in ways that could threaten to unveil the enlarged potential coerciveness of expanded government which, partly because of his own fear of state power, Hoover was working so hard to conceal.

This problem is best seen in Hoover's efforts to organize the construction industry. He thought that the construction industry needed a self-coordinating mechanism whereby it could adjust to sharply varying seasonal demands for its product. Hoover also thought that the industry needed to generate nationwide standards of quality and a code of industrial ethics.

Secretary Hoover called a conference in Washington during May 1922, to which he invited representatives from all areas of the construction industry. Out of this meeting came the American Construction Council, which was to be the umbrella federation for the myriad number of specialized and local associations in the industry. The council was to have a dual role. It would formulate industry standards of practice which it would also fight against any attempts to legislate public regulations for the industry.

Hoover thought that the head of the American Construction Council should be a prestigious figure. Therefore, he invited Franklin Roosevelt, who had run for vice-president on the Democratic ticket in 1920, to become "Czar" of the building industry. Roosevelt happily accepted the job. As James M. Burns observed, "Roosevelt served as a respectable figurehead; more than that, he took a keen interest in gathering data and in long-range planning to iron out sharp seasonal fluctuations in the industry.[26]

Hoover and Roosevelt agreed on the necessary course of action for the industry. On the occasion of the public announcement of Roosevelt's designation as head of the council, both he and Hoover spoke of the necessity of curing the evils of the industry through cooperation rather than government regulation. What the building trade needed, they agreed, was concentrated action by the great majority of the members of the industry to guarantee sound trade standards and good business ethics.[27] Over the next year, Hoover and Roosevelt developed a program of industrial cooperation for the construction industry, focusing particularly on the collection and dissemination of useful statistics. Roosevelt particularly desired to work closely with the Department of Commerce on the matter of statistical information, and Hoover was willing to oblige the man, who from all appearances, was acting as his protege on matters of government leadership of business.[28]

But an issue appeared which divided Hoover and Roosevelt and which exemplified the consequence of government organizing leadership for business. Roosevelt turned to Hoover for aid, or muscle, in forcing cooperation with the council. In mid-June 1923, Roosevelt urged Hoover to forcefully intervene with the heads of two major construction firms who had proven obstinate in dealing with the council. He thought that pressure from Hoover would force the recalcitrants into line.[29]

Roosevelt's request presented a choice to Hoover which he had attempted to avoid in all of his expansionist activities at Commerce. He operated on the assumption that government could be used to encourage business growth and self-regulation while at the same time not threatening business with coercion. This was easily managed in the commodity divisions where governmental entities were simply placed in the hands of already organized business. But when the Department of Commerce took a leadership role in business, then the question naturally arose concerning what government would do about those individuals who refused to follow the leader. Roosevelt presented this dilemma to the Secretary of Commerce, and Hoover absolutely rejected the suggestion that he apply coercion in support of the council's programs.[30] Hoover was unwilling to use public authority coercively to nurture his own creation.

While using the Department of Commerce to seek economic stability, Hoover attempted to resolve the tension between the antigovernmental values of the American tradition and the desirable efficacy of the positive state by allowing private associations to guide new governmental functions and organizations. But this solution was inadequate because it obscured rather than eliminated the problem. Trade-association domination of the commodity divisions did not entail a political alchemy through which the coercive potential of government was abolished. Rather, such domination did enable private interests to harness some of the possibilities of public power (and its coerciveness) for their own purposes. Thus, while the subordination of public agencies to private associations served to mask the problem of coercion, that problem refused to remain hidden.

Hoover's strategy for overcoming the dichotomy between private values and public government depended on the existence of already stable private assocations. Where industry lacked organization, the specter of coercion reappeared to be dealt with anew. For without stable private associations, there was not arrangement whereby the coercive threat of expanding government could be veiled. In instances such as this, exemplified by the creation and guidance of the American Construction Council, Hoover and the department had either to provide overt pressure on businessmen or surrender the possibilities of real and effective leadership of business. Under these conditions Hoover was incapable of using government to further his purposes because he could not overcome his fear of public authority openly used to shape the actions of the businessman. In the end, Hoover was not able to effectively resolve his personal dialectic between a fear of government and a recognition of the necessity for expanded governmental activity in the war against the business cycle.

The Efficient State:
Administrative Order and Public Power

Throughout his public career, Herbert Hoover was inordinately interested in the effective management of public organizations. From his single-handed organization of the Committee for Belgium Relief in 1914, through his rebuilding of the Department of Commerce in the 1920s, to his direction of the Hoover Commissions in the post–Second World War period, Hoover was preeminently a man dedicated to the improvement of large organizations. It is of more than passing interest that these public concerns were rooted in his earlier education and private professional life. He was educated as a mining engineer and, at the high point of his professional life, created one of the leading international consulting firms in the mining industry.[31]

Hoover's actions in regard to the management of public organizations strongly suggest that he understood organizational efficiency to be a value of greater importance than those entailed in the notion of limited government. While he never expressed his view of the relationship between governmental efficacy and public power, his actions give clear indication that he would prefer government strength to weakness and centralization to decentralization if those were the conditions for establishing efficient government. Yet there is no indication that he was conscious of these trade-offs.

In Hoover's long involvement with public management, one theme stands out in immediate contrast to his general espousal of antigovernmental values. In two of the three instances of his major involvement with executive reorganization, Hoover espoused recommendations for strengthening the president's role in regard to administration and centralizing the executive branch. How could Hoover favor these proposals while fearing the role of centralized government and effective public power in American society? An examination of Hoover's three major reorganization efforts will reveal that his concern with governmental efficiency, under certain conditions, could effectively displace his sensitivity to public power.

Hoover participated in three episodes of executive reorganization between the 1920s and the 1950s: the Joint Committee on Reorganization and the first and second commissions on the Organization of the Executive Branch (Hoover Commissions). In the first two of these, he favored recommendations for administrative reform which would quicken and strengthen the centralizing tendency of the positive state and, consequently, its ability to respond to majoritarian politics. But in the last of these reorganization efforts, the second Hoover Commission, he adopted a position that was almost diametrically opposite his earlier views and used reorganization recommendations as the medium for an argument against the positive state.

What markedly distinguished the second Hoover Commission from Hoover's earlier reorganization activities was that the second commission's statutory mandate clearly specified that it should consider whether the national government should perform the functions then entrusted to it. Unlike the earlier reorganization episodes, this one was directed to give substantive policy its greatest attention. In Public Law 108, the 83d Congress specified that the first purpose of the commission should be to recommend "methods and procedures for reducing expenditures to the lowest amount consistent with the efficient performance of essential services, activities and functions."[32] The law further stated that the commission should, among its other purposes, eliminate "activities which are competitive with private enterprise."[33] The openly political mandate of the second commission encouraged Hoover to focus his attention on the national government's policies and not on its organization. At the same time, the statutory mandate of the commission appeared to be consistent with the aims and character of the new Eisenhower administration so that there was little external resistance to the commission's engaging in a diatribe against the positive state.

The contrast between Hoover's views as expressed in the second commission and his work in the two other reorganization efforts with which he worked is striking. In 1920 Congress created the Joint Committee on Reorganization to make recommendations for change in executive branch organization.[34] The Republican-dominated Congress sought to pare back the war-bloated government left after the end of World War I. But whatever antistate and antipresidential biases underlay the Congress's intention became secondary once Warren G. Harding took office. As soon as Harding was safely in the presidency, Congress empowered him to appoint a representative to the Joint Committee. Informally, the members of the Joint Committee agreed to elect the president's representative to be their chairman.[35] The president appointed Walter F. Brown to the Committee, and, henceforth, it operated as if it were a presidentially directed reorganization effort. Instead of creating its own reorganization plan, the Joint Committee requested that the president create such a plan in consultation with the officers of his

administration. Henceforth, Walter Brown acted as Harding's assistant
for reorganization planning, instructed the president on how to deal with
the committee's members, and worked with the individual cabinet
members in shaping reorganization plans in regard to their departments.[36]

Hoover, who Harding had appointed as secretary of commerce, took
the opportunity presented by this request to recommend expansion of
his department. He recommended, and actively sought implementation
of, a plan to add a number of agencies from Agriculture, Interior, Labor,
Navy, Treasury, and War to Commerce.[37] But, for Hoover, this reorganization episode necessitated more than just a bureaucratic struggle
for the expansion of his department. He began to see that the existing
administrative organization of the national government, along with its
dispersal of authority and responsibility, violated his understanding of
the principles of good organization. Hoover, consequently, began to
urge that reorganization lead to the reform of the capacity of the presidency along with changes in the basic relationships between Congress
and the executive branch. In short, he became a spokesman for centralization in the national government.

Two fundamental principles of administration shaped Hoover's
thoughts on reorganization. One, he argued that all federal administrative agencies should be ordered on the principle of organization by like
purpose.[38] Throughout the executive branch, departments were grab
bags of different functions and purposes. Two, Hoover thought that all
responsibility for an organization ought to rest at its pinnacle; good
organizations maintained the rule of hierarchy. But Congress, adhering
to the traditional and minoritarian belief in the fragmentation of public
power, had often placed major discretion over agency operations in the
hands of bureau chiefs. Department heads, not to speak of the president, were left powerless over functions which they should control.

During the 1920s, and into his presidency, Hoover argued for these
principles and, furthermore, insisted that Congress grant reorganization
powers to the president. In the Joint Commission on Reorganization's
hearings, early in 1924, he testified that even department secretaries
could not be trusted to abide by the principles of good administration.
"Cabinet heads," he stated, "necessarily take color from their subordinates and subordinates are, from the nature of things, bound to be in
opposition to serious change."[39] Thus, the task of properly ordering the
administrative organization falls on the president and Congress. But can
Congress be trusted to act responsibly in regard to the integrity of
administrative organization? At best, Hoover argued, Congress will be
confused; at worst, they will consciously violate the principles of good
administration. Therefore, Hoover continued, proper reorganization de-

pends on a higher perspective. Only the presidency offers the perspective necessary to bring order and good administration to government. He therefore recommended that the president be granted the authority to "make such changes within the limits of certain defined principles as may be recommended to him by an independent commission to be created by Congress."[40]

Hoover's proposal fell on deaf ears, but in 1929, as president, he proposed a similar plan. He urged that Congress grant to the president the power to reorganize the executive branch with the advice of a joint congressional committee, or subject to congressional veto.[41] Congress eventually responded with the Economy Act of 1932. But this act hedged the new reorganization powers given to the president by enabling either house of Congress to veto his action.[42] On December 9, 1932, Hoover issued a reorganization plan, but it was promptly vetoed. He responded to the veto with sharp and telling language: "Either Congress must keep its hands off now or they must give to my successor much larger powers of independent action than given to any president if there is ever to be reorganization. And that authority to be free of the limitations of the law passed last year which gives Congress the veto power, which prevents the abolition of functions, which prevents the rearrangement of major Department."[43] Put simply, Hoover was saying that administrative efficiency demands presidential power.

To fully understand the logic of Hoover's concept of reorganization, it must be stressed that for him "efficiency" by no means meant government's capacity to save money. The concept, in other words, was not another way of talking about minimizing the size, cost, and activities of government. On the contrary, when Hoover spoke of efficiency he meant the capacity of government to effect its programs. This is exemplified during the fall of 1923, in Hoover's response to a cut in the Department of Commerce's budget by the Bureau of the Budget. Secretary Hoover appealed to President Coolidge, arguing that expenditures for "reproductive" programs are beneficial in that they aid growth in the economy. He stated, "I cannot but believe that the country would welcome a statement from you that in these matters reduction is the worst sort of national economy and that real economy lies in building up our national assets."[44] Furthermore, in later testifying to the Joint Committee on Reorganization, Hoover observed that whatever the monetary savings that may result from reorganization, they are not as important as the increase "in the ability of Congress to handle certain types of expenditures with better comprehension and long view policies."[45] For Hoover, reorganization was a means to achieve greater centralized coordination in government for the purpose of increasing the capacity of government to act effectively.

Hoover's second experience with reorganization came not so much because of his work in the 1920s but because of his hostility to the New Deal and his attacks on Roosevelt. The first Hoover Commission was created in 1947 by a Republican-dominated Congress to recommend the dismantlement of the "bloated" (and Democratic) federal establishment.[46] Republicans expected the commission to serve as a transition mechanism in preparation for the Republican president who would take office in January 1949.[47] Congress specified that the commission was to have twelve members, with four each appointed by the president, the majority leader of the Senate, and the Speaker of the House. In each case, two of the appointees were to be Democrats and two Republicans. Hoover was appointed by Joe Martin (R.-Ind.), Speaker of the House, only after it was prearranged that he would serve as chairman of the commission.[48]

But, of course, the first Hoover Commission did not become an instrument of Republican revenge. The reports of the commission, particularly in regard to the organization of the presidential office, are totally concerned with increasing the capacity of the chief executive to generate policy and manage an expanded executive branch.[49] The work of the commission was divided into major areas and assigned to task forces composed of members of the commission along with outside experts. Only the analysis of the presidency was handled differently. The part of the commission's *Report* dealing with the presidency was formulated and drafted by Hoover with the help of one aide, Don K. Price. Herbert Hoover "constituted himself the task force for the treatment of the Presidency."[50]

As Hoover confronted the problems of the executive office and observed its growth in capacity for organizational leadership in the wake of Roosevelt's reforms (particularly resulting from the Brownlow Committee *Report* and the Reorganization of 1939), his ideological opposition to big government so prominent in the 1930s vanished.[51] Instead, he began to view the presidency and the executive branch through the same conceptual apparatus he had used during his struggles for reorganization in the 1920s. Rather than recommending the destruction of expanded national government, he led the first Hoover Commission to recommend means for making expanded government function more efficiently. In the introduction to the part of the Commission *Report* titled "General Management of the Executive Branch," Hoover wrote: "Responsibility and accountability are impossible without authority— the power to direct. The exercise of authority is impossible without a clear line of command from the top to the bottom, and a return line of responsibility and accountability from the bottom to the top."[52]

Hoover's contribution to the Commission's *Report*, and his view of the presidency, seems perfectly consistent with the views of the President's Committee on Administrative Management (Brownlow) during the New Deal and its heralded call for greater presidential authority over the executive branch.[53] But it is instructive to compare the apparent motivation for the recommendations of the President's Committee and Hoover's later assessment of the presidency and the executive branch. The committee's view was shaped primarily by profound political considerations. Europe in the 1930s seemed to herald the decline of democracy, and the members of the President's Committee, Louis Brownlow, Charles Merriam, and Luther Gulick, viewed the strong, Democratic executive as America's most effective bastion against the threat of extremist disorder.[54] Hoover's view of the presidency, while consistent with that of the President's Committee, was founded on a wholly apolitical basis. He embraced the necessity for increased presidential power and control only because it seemed a prerequisite for increasing government's efficiency. Had the only issue been the essentially political concerns of the members of the President's Committee, Hoover would most certainly have been led to the opposite conclusions. But left to deal with the president's role in terms solely of organizational order and efficiency, he developed recommendations which were consistent with the work of the President's Committee.

A brief review of Hoover's key recommendations in regard to the presidency will show how he managed to espouse centralization and increased power in the chief executive office without abandoning his attachment to antigovernmental values. Hoover saw three means for strengthening the position of the president in the executive branch. One, he recommended the removal of all barriers to hierarchical authority within the executive branch. In particular, the commission report urged that no major discretionary authority be vested in any officer below department secretary. By placing responsibility for all programs on department heads, ultimate responsibility was vested in the presidency.[55] Two, Hoover and his commission recommended the reorganization of the departments of the executive branch "as nearly as possible by major purposes in order to give a coherent mission to each department."[56] Three, Hoover urged that the president be given added staff support along with absolute freedom over how he would appoint, organize, and use such personnel.[57] If implemented, Hoover stated, these reforms would go far to overcome the basic problems of the executive office, which are unclear authority, weak lines of communication, and the lack of presidential tools for formulating and overseeing policy.[58]

Through the medium of the Commission on the Organization of the Executive Branch, Herbert Hoover ultimately proved to be a friend of the strong presidency and the sort of coherent central authority required by the majoritarian positive state. The 1948 presidential election, which made it clear that the commission's eventual report would not serve as the transition documents for a new, Republican administration, clarified the purpose of executive reorganization for Hoover and the commission.

While President Truman had treated Hoover cordially and required his administration to cooperate with the commission's study, he naturally regarded it as an instrument of the opposition. Some of his advisors recommended that he use the occasion of his stunning victory over Dewey to attack the commission for bias and refuse further cooperation.[59] But Budget Director James Webb, who was Truman's main liaison to the commission, showed much greater perception of its direction and likely recommendations. He understood that Hoover was capable of issuing a report that would be eminently favorable to the conception of the presidency which had guided Democratic administrations since 1933. Webb wrote the following to Truman the day after the electoral victory: "I believe there is now a possibility of getting the last Republican President to urge you to accept an implementation of and organization for executive responsibility that the Republican party has historically denied to Presidents. If that can be managed, you will undoubtedly be able to achieve—with at least a show of bipartisan agreement—a new level of Presidential leadership and effectively discharged responsibility for administration unknown in our history."[60] Truman restrained his tendency to lash out at opponents. Instead, he followed Webb's advice with the extraordinary results that Webb predicted. The last Republican president joined in a celebration of the expansive, modern presidency.

Through his career, from the 1920s through the late 1940s, Herbert Hoover's activities in executive reorganization reflected a consistent view of public organization and its needs. In both periods, he urged reforms that would strengthen and centralize the national government. In his reorganization work, he gave no indication that he feared government's strength. In fact, as James Webb understood, Hoover's views on reorganization were distinct from his political values and views which opposed the growth of the public sector. These views concerning organization rested wholly on his views of the principles of good administration. Hoover understood reorganization to be a process of rectification whereby the administrative organization of government could be made coherent and subordinated to executive leadership. In applying his principles of good administration for the purpose of improving administration, Hoover seemed to operate as if there were no germane differences between public and private organization; all organizations ought to be efficient, he thought, and the principles by which organizations achieved efficiency were the same for both public and private organizations.[61]

Herbert Hoover's perception of the principles of good administration allowed him to skirt effectively the tension between his political values and his attraction to the apparent efficacy of the positive state. He had not been able to banish the specter of coercive public power in his policies for economic stabilization in the 1920s, but concepts of good administration allowed him to separate government from notions of power and politics. Hoover, of course, did not thus resolve the dialectical tension at the heart of American politics between the traditional verities of the political culture and the functional necessity for the positive state. Rather, he found a conceptual means for dealing with key aspects of government, its scope and capacity, without engaging his antistatist political values that so dominated both his rhetoric of the 1930s and his direction of the second Hoover Commission. But as the second Hoover Commission exemplified, this separation of organizational matters from politics was fragile. When the mandate of executive reorganization included an investigation of governmental policy as well as organization, Hoover was not adequately able to maintain the separation he needed to conceptualize the national government in terms of instrumental efficacy.

Conclusion

Herbert Hoover's political career teaches that it is possible for Americans to formulate justifications for the positive state while retaining strong antigovernmental values. This case also suggests that a prerequisite for such a justification is that the functions of the state be understood in apolitical terms. Within the context of reorganizations seeking greater governmental efficiency, Herbert Hoover understood the state not as a system for distributing scarce resources where different groups have competing interests but as a massive machine in need of fine tuning. At its greatest efficiency, he conceived of the machine as capable of increasing benefits for all.

How much insight into American politics can Hoover's example offer? The problem of any analysis generalizing from a single case is that it is unlikely that one can fully demonstrate the appropriateness of the case as a basis for generalization. The thought of a single individual, obviously, cannot capture the whole American experience with the positive state. Yet, one need look no farther than American political science to see that Hoover's translation of the state into apolitical terms

1
The King's Two Bodies:
Coronation Portrait of Richard II

1

2

2
Christ's Body:
Matthias Grunewald, Crucifixion

3
"Washington and Lincoln
(Apotheosis)," 1865

4
"Washington and Lincoln
(Apotheosis)," 1865

3

4

5
Olaf Gülbransson, "Jetzt ist Amerika schon in der Tinte!" *Simplicissimus*, May 11, 1914

6
Stanislav Rembski, Woodrow Wilson

6

7

7
The Ride of the Ku Klux Klan,
Birth of a Nation, 1915

8
Satan's Body: Hubert and Jan
van Eyck, Crucifixion and Last
Judgment

8

9

10

9
Thomas Nast, "Columbia Grieving at Lincoln's Bier," *Harper's Weekly* (April 29, 1865)

10
Conrad, Richard Nixon as Richard II

11
Abraham Lincoln, August 26, 1858

11

12
Abraham Lincoln, February 24,
1861

13
Abraham Lincoln, April 10, 1865

14
Conrad, Richard Nixon as Christ

12

13

14

15
Conrad, "Blessed are Those..."

16
Richard Nixon leaves the White
House for the last time

15

16

has a parallel in one of this society's main attempts at political self-understanding.

In the last several decades, first through pluralism and more recently through public policy evaluation, political science's dominant approaches to the study of American politics have deemphasized government and its authority. Those political scientists who have worked within the mainstream of their discipline have focused their attentions on the role of private groups, the behavior of individual political actors, and the economic efficiency of discreet governmental activities. In those approaches to the study of American politics which have been most fashionable over the last three decades, there has been little room for research on the state per se. American political science has taught us much about group politics, individual voting behavior, the formation of political attitudes, and the career patterns of individual politicians (or at least we "know" of these things within the frame of reference of the theories which have guided mainstream political science). But research has taught Americans much less about the changes in structure and authority in the national government during this century. Similarly, concerns such as the capacity of the national government to identify and react to demands for the redistribution of societal resources, or the relationship between the developing positive state and nonpublic centers of power, have received very little attention by researchers. It is noteworthy that most of the scholarship which stands in exception to the above generalization originates from outside the mainstream of political science, history, and economics.[62]

Pluralism and policy evaluation within political science both tend to ultimately reduce politics to the nonpolitical. For these approaches, the state is a dependent variable. In exactly the same period that the American positive state was reaching its adolescence, political scientists devoted a massive amount of their energies to the task of reducing the phenomena of politics into prepolitical phenomena amenable to methods and terms borrowed from sociology, psychology, or economics. In a manner reminiscent of Herbert Hoover's displacement of public power with efficiency, American political science displaced politics and the state with apolitical categories drawn from other disciplines, so that the study of public policy occurs within a framework where its actual impact on social life is largely obscured. American political science offers at least one indication of the utility of the case analyzed in the paper.

To the degree that Hoover's career provides an acceptably paradigmatic case of the American political experience into mid-century, there is cause for concern about the health of this polity. Hoover's logic, in regard to the growth of the state, necessitated discarding *both* the virtues of the American antigovernment tradition and the potential virtues of the positive state. As he exhibited in his strategy as secretary of commerce for dispersing public authority to private interests, Hoover surrendered the possibility of private sector values as real checks upon the potential tyrannical uses of public authority. He subverted this possibility by placing public authority in hands of private industrial groups which were beyond the checks of public responsibility. By doing this he did not further protect Americans from the misuse of public power; he only assured that it would be private and not public agents which misused that power. While Hoover further undermined the effective power of antipublic sector values with his defense of the positive state in the 1940s, his couching of that defense only in terms of efficiency, and without respect to the substantive goals the state should seek, left the state impaired from coherently responding to majoritarian values and demands if they should be mobilized in American politics.

Herbert Hoover wrestled with a problem that is characteristically American. Like him, this society is caught between the poles of its conflict between private regarding values and the positive state. And like Hoover, American's have not wholly resolved this conflict. Current tax protests and widespread criticism of governmental regulation are only symptoms of deep-seated discomfort with large government in America. Americans have yet to learn to live comfortably with the positive state.

This discomfort with extensive government is more than a quaint characteristic of American society. It is a symptom of the impoverishment of our political values. The failure to resolve, in a coherent and consistent fashion, the conflict between antigovernmental values and the positive state results in immobility. Americans are neither adequately protected from the state nor are they capable fully of using the state to address fundamental societal problems. In this sense, the American political system is backward and American government underdeveloped. But this backwardness and underdevelopment are not so much immediate characteristics of American political institutions as they are features of the ways Americans conceptualize their politics.

Notes

1. The complex of issues which underlie the nexus between economic growth and governmental functions is examined in Charles E. Lindblom, *Politics and Markets* (New York: Basic Books, 1977). Many observers note the relationship between economic and political development. Important representative examples are Max Weber, *The Theory of Social and Economic Organization*, ed Talcott Parsons (New York: Free Press, 1964), pp. 337–41; and S. M. Lipset, *Political Man* (New York: Doubleday & Co., Anchor Books,

1963), chap. 2. Speaking from their particular perspectives, several scholars have noted the importance of inquiring into the apparent incongruity between the robust American economy and the curiously less well-developed American polity. See Samuel Huntington, *Political Order in Changing Societies* (New Haven, Conn.: Yale University Press, 1968), pp. 93–139; Grant McConnell, *Private Power and American Democracy* (New York: Alfred A. Knopf, Inc., 1967), pp. 367–68; Louis Hartz, *The Liberal Tradition in America* (New York: Harcourt, Brace & World, 1955), pp. 211–19; and Walter Dean Burnham, *Critical Elections and the Mainsprings of American Politics* (New York: W. W. Norton & Co., 1970), chap. 7.

2. McConnell, p. 162.

3. For a discussion of the failure of repeated attempts to add a planning component to expanding American government, see Otis Graham, *Towards a Planned Society* (Oxford: Oxford University Press, 1976).

4. The so-called revisionist historians have undertaken research demonstrating fascinating relations between private economic interests and new governmental policies during the early years of this century. For leading examples, see James Weinstein, *The Corporate Ideal in the Liberal State* (Boston: Beacon Press, 1968); and Gabriel Kolko, *The Triumph of Conservatism* (New York: Free Press, 1963). The two political scientists who most articulately argue the character and consequences of a private interest-group foundation for the positive state are McConnell in *Private Power and American Democracy*, and Theodore J. Lowi, *The End of Liberalism* (New York: W. W. Norton & Co., 1969).

5. McConnell, esp. chaps. 6–8.

6. E.g., see E. E. Schattschneider, *The Semisovereign People* (Hinsdale, Ill.: Dryden Press, 1960), chaps. 7, 8; McConnell, chap. 10; and Lowi, esp. chap. 10.

7. See McConnell, pp. 366–68. For a more extensive discussion of the majoritarian implications of the presidency, see McConnell, *The Modern Presidency*, 2d ed. (New York: St. Martin's Press, 1976), esp. chap. 6. Also see Louis Koenig, *The Chief Executive*, 3d ed. (New York: Harcourt, Brace Jovanovich, 1975), pp. 9, 10.

8. See Walter Dean Burnham, particularly chaps. 5–7.

9. See Richard Hofstadter, *The American Political Tradition* (New York: Alfred A. Knopf, Inc., 1951), chap. 11.

10. Herbert Hoover, *Memoirs*, vol. 2, *The Cabinet and the Presidency* (New York: Macmillan Publishing Co., 1952), pp. 36, 61–62, 167–76.

11. Secretary Hoover implicitly seemed to understand a problem of group organization and cohesiveness that has been treated extensively by Mancur Olson, Jr., *The Logic of Collective Action* (New York: Schocken Books, 1968).

12. On the role and status of trade associations in the first two decades of the century, see Benjamin Kirsch, *Trade Associations* (New York: Central Book Co., 1928).

13. Note the discussion of the incentives for group membership in Olson, chaps. 1, 2.

14. Speech published in *New York Times* (April 29, 1921).

15. *American Column and Lumber* v. *U.S.*, 257 U.S. 377 (1921). The origin of this case was in the Department of Justice's challenge to the practices of the American Hardwood Manufacturers' Association.

16. George E. Lamb and Carrington Shields, *Trade Association Law and Practice* (Boston: Little, Brown & Co., 1971), p. 8. For the reaction of trade associations to the Hardwood decision, see *Nation's Business* 19 (February 1922): 34–36.

17. Correspondence, Hoover and Daughtery, Trade Associations: 1922–24, Official Files, Commerce Papers, Herbert Hoover Presidential Library. Hoover's formal plan for the collection and distribution of statistics is presented in the memo "Cooperation for Distribution of Trade Statistics," January 10, 1924, Trade Associations: 1922–24, Official Files, Commerce Papers, Herbert Hoover Presidential Library (henceforth, O.F., C.P., H.H.P.L.), West Branch, Iowa.

18. 268 U.S. 563 (1924).

19. Herbert Hoover, *Memoirs*, 2:168.

20. McConnell, *Private Power*, p. 67.

21. *New York Times* (August 17, 1921).

22. U.S. Department of Commerce, *Annual Report: 1922* (Washington, D.C.: Government Printing Office, 1922), p. 96.

23. McConnell, *Private Power*, p. 161.

24. U.S. Congress, House of Representatives, Committee on Appropriations, *Hearings: Department of Commerce Appropriations Bill*, 68th Cong., 2d sess., 1925, pp. 2–3.

25. U.S. Department of Commerce, *Trade Association Activities* (Washington, D.C.: Government Printing Office, 1927), p. 75.

26. James MacGregor Burns, *Roosevelt: The Lion and the Fox* (New York: Harcourt, Brace & World, 1956), p. 85.

27. *New York Times* (May 15, 1922).

28. E.g., letter, Hoover to Roosevelt, May 24, 1923, Construction, O.F, C.P., H.H.P.L.

29. Telegram, Roosevelt to Hoover, June 7, 1923, Construction, O.F., C.P., H.H.P.L.

30. Letter, Hoover to Roosevelt, June 12, 1923, Construction, O.F., C.P., H.H.P.L.

31. Herbert Hoover, *Memoirs*, vol.1, *Years of Adventure* (New York: Macmillan Publishing Co., 1952), p. 102.

32. Quoted in U.S. Commission on the Executive Branch, *Final Report to Congress* (Washington, D.C.: Government Printing Office, 1955), p. 1.

33. Ibid.

34. Public Res. no. 54, 66th Cong. On the Joint Committee, see P. E. Arnold, "Executive Reorganization and Administrative Theory: The Origins of the Managerial Presidency" (paper presented to the 1976 annual meeting of the American Political Science Association; and Ronald C. Moe, *Executive Branch Reorganization: An Overview* (Washington, D.C.: Library of Congress, Congressional Research Service 1977), pp. 13–16 (file no. 77-246G).

35. Letter, Reed Smoot to Harding, April 15, 1921, Harding Papers, file 303-1, Ohio Historical Society, Columbus, Ohio (microfilm edition, reel no. 196).

36. E.g., letters Brown to Harding, June 13, 1921, and May 26, 1922, and Harding to Brown, May 27, 1922, Harding Papers, files 303-1 and 303-3 (microfilm edition, reel no. 196).

37. Letter, Hoover to Walter Brown, October 21, 1921, file 80553/4, RG 40, National Archives, Washington, D.C.; letter, Hoover to Elliot Goodwin, May 16, 1921, U.S. Chamber of Commerce, O.F., C.P., H.H.P.L.

38. Letter, Hoover to Rep. W. W. Chalmers, April 6, 1922, House of Rep. Chalmers, O.F., C.P., H.H.P.L. See Leonard White, *Introduction to Public Administration* (New York: Macmillan Publishing Co., 1926), p. 66. White bases his discussion on the principles of departmentalization on a quote from Hoover concerning organization by "major purpose."

39. U.S. Congress, Joint Committee on the Reorganization of the Administrative Branch of the Government, *Hearings* (Washington, D.C.: Government Printing Office, 1924), testimony of January 22, 1924.

40. Ibid. It is probable that Hoover's inspiration for this recommendation lay in section 12 of the act of 1903 which established the Department of Commerce. That section gave the president unlimited powers to transfer agencies performing statistical services to the Department of Commerce.

41. W. Brooke Graves, *Basic Information on the Reorganization of the Executive Branch: 1912–1948* (Washington, D.C.: Library of Congress, Legislative Reference Service, 1949), p. 372.

42. 47 Stat. L. 413–15 (1932).

43. Quoted in Ray L. Wilbur and Arthur M. Hyde, *The Hoover Policies* (New York: Charles Scribner's Sons, 1937), p. 575.

44. Letter, Hoover to Coolidge, November 5, 1923, president, O.F., C.P., H.H.P.L.

45. U.S. Congress, Joint Committee on the Reorganization of the Administrative Branch of the Government, *Hearings*, testimony of Januray 22, 1924.

46. 61 Stat. L. 246 (1947). On the first Hoover Commission, see Herbert Emmerich, *Federal Organization and Administrative Management* (University: University of Alabama Press, 1971), chap. 5; and P. E. Arnold, "The First Hoover Commission and the Managerial Presidency," *Journal of Politics*, vol. 38 (February 1976).

47. Letter, Klein to Hoover, July 18, 1947, 1st HC, General Management of the Executive Branch, Correspondence—Klein, H.H.P.L.

48. Telegrams, Klein to Hoover, Hoover to Klein, July 18, 1947, and letters, Klein to Hoover, July 21 and 24, 1947, 1st HC, General Management of the Executive Branch, Correspondence—Klein, H.H.P.L.

49. Commission on Organization of the Executive Branch of the Government, *Report to Congress* (Washington, D.C.: Government Printing Office, 1949), esp. see the first section, "General Management of the Executive Branch."

50. Emmerich, p. 86.

51. Don K. Price observes that Hoover "had great sympathy for the basic outline of the changes that had been made in the reorganization of 1939 following the Brownlow Report" (Price, "Oral History Interview," H.H.P.L., p. 14).

52. Commission on Organization of the Executive Branch of the Government, *Report to Congress* (n. 49 above), p. 1.

53. The Brownlow Committee (formally the President's Committee on Administrative Management) was created by Franklin Roosevelt to advise him on necessary reform to increase the president's capacity to control the formulation and implementation of policy within the executive branch. It was chaired by Louis Brownlow, and Charles Merriam and Luther Gulick were its other members. See the President's Committee on Administrative Management, *Report* (Washington, D.C.: Government Printing Office, 1937); and Richard D. Polenberg, *Reorganizing Roosevelt's Government* (Cambridge, Mass.: Harvard University Press, 1966).

54. See the discussion of the Brownlow Committe members' motivations in Barry D. Karl, *Executive Reorganization and Reform in the New Deal* (Cambridge, Mass.: Harvard University Press, 1963).

55. Commission on Organization of the Executive Branch, *Report to Congress*, pp. 29–51.

56. Ibid., p. 34.

57. Ibid., pp. 11–28.

58. Ibid., pp. 3–5.

59. Coates related that Dean Acheson, a Truman appointee to the commission, advised the president to disown the whole enterprise after the November victory (see Charles B. Coates, "Oral History Interview," Herbert Hoover Presidential Library).

60. Memo, Webb to Truman, November 5, 1948, Papers of James Webb, Harry Truman Library, Independence, Mo.

61. On the status of the public-private distinction in orthodox administrative theory and in particular regard to Herbert Hoover as a proponent of that theoretical stance in regard to administration, see Harold Seidman, *Politics, Position and Power* (Oxford: Oxford University Press, 1970), chap. 1.

62. In political science, until the late 1960s, such work was the product of a small group of scholars usually identified as antipluralists, or at least nonpluralists. Leading examples of this group include V. O. Key, E. E. Schattschneider, Grant McConnell,

Walter Dean Burnham, and Theodore J. Lowi. In other social science disciplines and history, work of this character had been labeled as "revisionist" or "radical." Certainly until the 1970s, and still true to some extent, labels such as "antipluralist" or "revisionist" serve to indicate a niche or ghetto for the scholarship and scholar in question. Such labels have been symptoms of the cognitive influence of the mainstream of these disciplines in delineating alternative approaches as idiosyncratic.

Part III

★

Interest Groups

Five ★

Political Change in America: Highway Politics and Reactive Policymaking

Ronald C. Kahn

Introduction

S cholars have traditionally used the size and make-up of the constituencies of American political institutions to explain political change in America. The work of Grant McConnell offers the most comprehensive and subtle interpretation of the relationship between the constituencies of political institutions and the nature of policymaking processes and public policy itself.[1] Building on this legacy, we shall compare the role of presidents and Congresses since 1955 in highway politics and policymaking. The major question for analysis is, To what degree does the differences in the size and make-up of the constituencies of the presidency and Congress influence the type of politics that occurs, the interests that are represented in those politics, and policy outcomes?

A major component of this analysis is a comparison of McConnell's work with that of Gary Orfield.[2] Like McConnell, Orfield emphasizes the importance of systematically comparing the presidency, the House, and the Senate with regard to their receptiveness to the public will and their roles as policy innovators in the American political system. However, McConnell and Orfield differ fundamentally in their conclusions. McConnell emphasizes that, because the House and the Senate have far narrower constituencies than the presidency, they allow primarily narrow economic interests to prevail in policymaking, and they establish

I would like to thank Oberlin College for supporting my research during Fall 1978 at Northwestern University's Transportation Center Library, the staff of that library for their assistance, and J. David Greenstone for his careful and insightful reading of earlier drafts of this paper. Most of all I would like to thank Grant McConnell for his brilliance and subtlety as a teacher and scholar and his humanity as an individual. Of course, any errors in judgment and fact are my own.

institutional arrangements that favor private interest groups. This makes it extremely difficult for electoral politics to be a forum to counter the power of private, primarily economic interests. McConnell stresses that the presidency, in part because of its far wider constituency, is the usual source of innovation and of public policies that emphasize values of equality and fairness that protect wider publics than those usually represented in the interest group structure. In contrast, Orfield argues that at crucial times our national legislatures have been major sources of innovation and have protected the interests of wider publics while the president has failed to do so. Differences in size and heterogeneity between legislative and presidential constituencies and the particular institutional arrangements in the House and Senate (committee system, seniority, rules, etc.) do not always, or even most of the time, lead to liberal presidential policies and conservative House and Senate actions, according to Orfield.

Our findings suggest that McConnell's approach offers a far more useful explanation of highway politics since 1956 than does Orfield's. However, Orfield's approach offers a somewhat better explanation of highway politics during 1955–56, the "founding" period for modern highway policymaking, when the massive Interstate Highway Program was established. For in 1955–56, on such important issues as highway taxation and truck weight and size limits, it was the House Public Works Committee, not the president, which sought to protect the interests of noncommercial highway users and other citizens who were poorly represented in the highway policymaking arena. However, in this founding period, McConnell's approach is substantiated in several extremely important ways. As is predicted by McConnell's theory, logrolling among private road construction interest groups, public highway officials, and commercial highway users resulted in institutional arrangements and policies (such as the highway trust fund, the defeat of a cabinet level Highway Board to oversee the Interstate Highway Program, and the taxation schedule) which placed future highway policymaking into narrow, privativistic interest-regarding hands. That is, while there was an important shift in 1955–56 in the highway policymaking arena from its past domination by rural and farm interests to one incorporating the needs of highway users in both rural and urban areas, this newly widened policy arena was reabsorbed into a narrow interest-group system. This resulted in a highway politics and policymaking since 1956 that conforms to McConnell's constituency analysis. For all presidents since 1956 (even though they substantially differed ideologically) have been the sources of innovation in the highway program. They consistently have sought to protect the interests of citizens, such as urban residents, who have been poorly represented in the highway policymaking arena, and have sought to change institutional arrangements so that values other than narrowly economic ones predominated. In issues areas such as highway beautification, relocation assistance to citizens forced out of their homes by highway construction, the encouragement of transportation planning as distinct from the more narrow highway planning, and the funding of urban mass transit options from the highway trust fund, it was the president who sought innovation. And as McConnell predicted, the House, made up of narrow constituencies, opposed these innovations while the Senate, consisting of more heterogeneous, wider constituencies, supported the president at crucial times. Because of fundamental inequities in the formal and informal institutional arrangements for highway policymaking which was established in this founding period, and because of basic constituency differences and institutional arrangements in the House and Senate, the highway policymaking process since 1956 can best be characterized by the term "reactive policymaking." Electoral and interest-group politics since 1956 have not been able to correct the fundamental transportation and urban problems caused by crucial decisions made in 1955–56 about the process of highway policymaking for the nation.

The "Political Logic" of Grant McConnell[3]

Basic Theory

McConnell's principal concern in American politics is the lack of a clear demarcation between public and private power. He argues that this is largely due to two factors: first, American government is dominated by hundreds of small decision-making arenas; second, there is an orthodoxy in American political theory, which political actors accept, that favors both small constituency policymaking and private interests. As McConnell points out: "Much that is central to the major issues of American politics turns upon the character of the constituency, particularly upon the size and shape of the political unit within which decisions must be made.... Within what boundaries and to which unit shall an issue of substance be referred? To ask this in effect is to ask, Who shall rule? It is also to ask, What kind of policy shall be followed, and for whose benefit?"[4]

One of McConnell's major theoretical contributions in his critique of small constituency politics. As we move decision-making arenas from the presidency (the largest constituency) to the most local decentralized decision-making unit (such as a local grazing board made up of cattle owners, established under the Taylor Act), McConnell identifies several negative consequences for the democratic character and quality of decision making: (1) the smaller the decision-making arena, the greater the chance that social and economic power will prevail; (2) the more informal the style of decision making, the greater the chance that more narrow, primarily economic interests will prevail, the less chance issues can become politicized, and the weaker the distinction between private and public values; (3) the greater the autonomy of the decisionmakers from outside control, the less diverse the interests represented in the decision-making arena, and the less chance that wider publics who lack a direct economic interest in the policy will influence that policy.[5]

In McConnell's view, the boundaries of American political institutions are the best predictor of the type of decisions that will be made in them. When decision making moves to political institutions consisting of wider constituencies, open conflict between interests, the visibility of issues, and the concern for the interests of wider publics all increase. For the most part, however, McConnell sees the American polity primarily as a myriad of small geographically and functionally defined decision-making arenas which make policy for all citizens but are representative of a much smaller section of the populace. Consequently, McConnell does not believe that narrowness or political power in one decision-making arena will usually be cross-checked by actors and interests in other decision-making arenas. Rather, the power of private interest groups, and more local interests, usually of a material nature, prevail. The cross-checking of interests is limited since opposition from within the narrow decision-making arenas is limited by elites within. Rather than true compromise, that is, a real clash of interests, logrolling between leaders within different narrow constituencies becomes the rule, producing wasteful policies which consider only narrowly defined concerns. Most important, the public interest, that is, the interest of wider publics (since for McConnell there is not *one* public interest) is disregarded. In sum, the basic reality of American politics is small constituency politics.

Decentralization of authority in the federal system and the fragmentation of Congress into more narrow functional units make it difficult for unorganized or less powerful groups to gain enough political influence to produce a redistribution of values and goods. In comparison to Dahl and Truman, McConnell emphasizes the cumulative effects on public policy of our decentralized political system and the oligarchy of power within private interest groups. Many narrow public decision-making arenas place severe constraints on political change which perpetuate social inequality, and result in conformity of values within these narrow constituencies and thus in the making of public policy itself.[6]

Finally, McConnell argues that there is an "orthodoxy" in American politics whose values support small constituency politics. The orthodoxy opposed coercive government, underestimates the dangers of private power, and legitimates small constituency politics through a myth of grass roots democracy. Its effect was reinforced by the Progressive movement which reduced the formal power of political authorities while at the same time causing political power itself to be viewed in pejorative terms. However, it is primarily the small constituency structures themselves and not the orthodoxy that cause for McConnell the most serious problems in American government.

Presidential, Senate, and House Action:
Implications for Political Change

McConnell's constituency analysis has decisive implications for explaining the role of the president, Senate, and House in policymaking and political change. Because the president represents the widest of constituencies, as compared with the Senate and House, McConnell expects that he will advocate fundamentally different types of policies, consult with a much wider set of interests, and focus on the effects of policy decisions on wider publics. The president will be less concerned with more narrow economic and material interests than the House and Senate, and will have somewhat less incentive to logroll between interests, given the wider set of pressures on him. Most important, only the president is able to see the effects on public policy of the fact that decision making in other parts of the political system is controlled by more narrow interests.[7] Issues of equality, liberty, and fairness are more apparent to the president, given his constituency, than to Congress, which consists of representatives from geographical districts with more narrow interests. Recruitment to functionally based committees insures that specific policy is made by legislators who do not represent the interests of citizens from the more heterogeneous nation. Therefore, McConnell argues it is more likely that presidents, rather than congressmen or senators, will favor innovations in public policy, will seek to change the make-up of decision-making arenas to allow for the inclusion of wider sets of values, and will be most sensitive to inequalities of political power and policy outcomes.

Congress, made up of representatives from many smaller constituencies, looks at issues much more narrowly. The committee system with its functional specialization is even less representative of national interests than is the House and the Senate as a whole. McConnell argues that the problem is not just one of factions, that is, lobbyists and the special interest groups, exerting pressure:

> The real problem is quite different. Whether pressure is effective or not, it is usually unnecessary. Each congressman (and, to a lesser extent, each senator) is chosen by and represents a constituency that is smaller than the president's. Necessarily, the congressman's constituency has less diversity than the president's. In some areas, it includes little more than a single predominant economic interest—a particular farm commodity or industry. In such a constituency or in one with a few interests, there is little point in applying pressure on the elected representative; he will be keenly aware of the situation and may be relied upon to seek advice from the interest in question. Such a congressman is not a true lobbyist, though he is more effective than most lobbyists in accomplishing his ends. As a consequence, the producers of cotton, oil, apples, airplanes, and many other products have especially good representation in Congress. In a national context, however, the voices of individual interests are much less resounding, and often their echoes are drowned out in the competing clamor of the others.[8]

The power of private interest groups is significantly increased by the fragmented system of governance in Congress, the thousands of functionally organized bureaucratic agencies, and the need of these agencies for the support of private interest groups when seeking support from Congress or the president.[9] Interest groups and bureaucrats as well as the most interested congressmen/senators on the committees with oversight functions will all fight to maintain autonomy over their particular area of public policy. Since the boundary of the decision-making arena is important to all these interests, we would expect that the greatest amount of mutual support (which I would argue is a form of logrolling) will occur when there is an attempt to widen the decision-making arena. Each actor will fight to protect narrow jurisdictions over public policy.[10] In such a system, McConnell argues, there are inherent limitations on the effectiveness of environmental or civil rights policy, that is, any policy that requires many small constituencies, who are involved in more narrow economic policies and programs, to alter their basic policy concerns in order to meet wider public values in our society. The president, rather than more narrow functional committees in Congress, will be expected to be concerned about these wider issues. Also, if McConnell's thesis is correct, then we would expect that the Senate, made up of members who represent larger more diverse constituencies than in the House, will be somewhat more amenable to the needs of wider publics.

An Alternative Interpretation of
American Politics: Gary Orfield

Gary Orfield presents a very different view on the role of the presidency and Congress in political change. Orfield argues that there is no inherent liberal bias in the presidency or conservative bias in the Congress. While he agrees that the power of the president is limited by our fragmented political system, he does not support McConnell's major premise that the structure of Congress, made up of representatives from smaller constituencies, leads to policies that are necessarily more conservative, less progressive, or less in the public interest; nor does he stress the negative aspects of narrow functional committees.

Rather, Orfield argues, both the presidency and Congress reflect the electoral politics of the day; electoral politics reflect public opinion and the interests of citizens. He argues that too many liberal scholars (like McConnell) have incorrectly assumed that there is a progressive liberal majority that is not able to work its will only because of structural defects in the political system.[11] Orfield argues that opposition to programs and difficulties in passing progressive legislation simply mirrors ambivalence toward these policies in the wider general population and that political institutions reflect this ambivalence in the electoral majority. Orfield does admit that chairmen of congressional committees may reflect earlier electoral majorities and therefore may be out of line with more recent public opinion.

When a progressive majority exists, as occurred in the Johnson landslide of 1964, Orfield argues, legislation in line with that majority will be passed by Congress regardless of structural factors in Congress, such as the seniority rules, the committee system, localism, and other small constituency attributes.[12] In contrast to McConnell's approach, Orfield analyzes civil rights and education policy in the Nixon years to show that there is no inherent progressive bias in the large constituency presidency.[13] Indeed, in his account the mutual cross-checking between committees, progressive House and Senate leadership, and "the floor" are structural elements that counter the conservatism (or really narrowness) of small constituency policymaking arenas in these legislative bodies. At least, in the 1960s and 1970s House and Senate rules were neutral, helping both liberals and conservatives seek their objectives. As a result Congress, not the president, at important times is likely to be progressive and innovative.

Thus, where McConnell emphasizes the degree of narrowness or breadth of the constituency of the political structure which frames public policy, Orfield stresses the size of the liberal and conservative majorities in the House and Senate and political values of politicians, including the president, who win or lose power. For McConnell, policy outcomes and the possibility of political change depend less on an increase in the number of liberals on the Agriculture Committee in the House (as happened in 1964) than on the fact that both the liberals and conservatives from farm districts dominate the Agriculture Committee. For McConnell, while elected officials may come and go and the proportion of liberals and conservatives change at the margins over time, the most important point is the continuity in the subsystems of power, the informal, yet significant coalitions between the functional congressional committees, agencies which implement the policy, and private interest groups.

Given these fundamental differences, McConnell and Orfield disagree on the means to achieve political change. McConnell argues that we should reduce the power of small constituencies by giving more power to the president and other political institutions with wider constituencies and reduce the decentralization of power within the federal system. Orfield argues that we should reduce the incumbent bias in election laws so individuals with new ideas that are representative of more recent public opinion can achieve positions of political power.[14] It is the faith in electoral politics by Orfield and McConnell's skepticism about the usefulness of elections to secure political change, especially in the House and Senate, that help explain their contrasting views about the power of private interest groups in America. For McConnell stresses that private interest groups have far too much power in American government, while Orfield emphasizes that private interest groups are not significant antidemocratic forces in our nation.

Of course, neither McConnell nor Orfield has written on highway politics. My findings settle matters between them only as they apply to this one-issue area. However, analysis of even this one-issue area does allow one to explore the validity of their two very different positions about the receptivity of the presidency and the House/Senate to political change and to the needs of wider publics and about the power of private interest groups in American politics.

Expected Findings

If Grant McConnell's "political logic" is correct, then we would expect that there will be significant differences in the highway policies advocated by the president and those advocated by the House and Senate. There also should be somewhat less significant, but clear, differences between the policies advocated by the Senate and the House. With its larger, more diverse, districts the Senate should advocate policies closer to those of the president than will the House. Also, if McConnell is correct, these differences between the type of highway policies advocated by the president and Congress should be consistent over many administrations. That is, presidents of different parties and ideologies should advocate policies that not only resemble each other but differ in systematic ways from those favored by Congresses, and these differences in turn should reflect on the differences in the size and make-up of members' constituencies in those bodies.

The major committees involved in highway policymaking in the House and Senate are the Public Works Committees and the Subcommittees on Roads within these committees. The Bureau of Public Roads (BPR), now called the Federal Highway Administration (FHA), is the federal agency responsible for the highway program. Many significant policy decisions are made by state highway departments who are represented before Congress by the American Association of State Highway Officials (AASHO). The major lobbying umbrella for private interests groups involved in highway politics is the National Highway Users Conference (NHUC) which more recently (1973) has changed its name to the Highway Users Federation for Safety and Mobility (HUFSM). This is a coalition of auto and tire manufacturers, road user groups, and bus operators. It represents more than six hundred industries that use highways. The most important more narrow purpose interest groups are the American Trucking Association (ATA), the American Automobile Association (AAA), the American Road Builders Associations (ARBA), plus various organizations of governors, mayors, and county officials.

We would expect, if McConnell's theory is correct, that the nature of the policymaking arena itself will be an important issue, and when it comes up all actors, whether in the public or private sector, will support the traditional federal-state relations in highway policymaking. Logrolling, in other words, will function to protect the economic needs of different interest groups and will occur among private groups and public highway officials. In the case of highway policymaking, this means that the traditional decentralization of authority over highway policy to the states will continue. More important, if McConnell's argument is valid, nonhighway interests and nonhighway users will continue to have limited influence over public policy. All highway interests will attempt to keep "outsiders" from the highway policymaking arena, whether these be the president, mass transportation interests, or city dwellers. When we talk of outsiders, who are not part of the highway policymaking arena or the needs of wider publics, we are referring to citizens, groups, or public officials who are not primarily highway users or concerned about highway construction but whose lives or official responsibilities are affected by the building of roads. These might include government officials authorized to enforce civil rights laws in government contracts, auto safety laws, anti-inflation policy, urban development, and mass transit policy or citizens and groups advocating such policy. Traditionally, such outsiders from the highway policy process have advocated the use of trust fund moneys for such purposes as highway beautification, management of the economy, mass transit development, highway safety programs, home building for citizens forced out of their homes by highway construction, and integrated highway, transportation, and overall urban planning. Commercial highway users, highway construction interests, public highway officials, and groups representing car owners have opposed both the use of trust fund moneys for these purposes and the establishment of institutional arrangements that would give power over highway planning to public officials and groups advocating a wider use of trust fund moneys for purposes other than road construction, narrowly defined. If any change in the breadth of the highway policymaking arena occurs we would expect, if McConnell is correct, that such changes will be advocated by the president. Also, if a wider definition of what constitutes a road cost is sought, we would expect that the president, representing a wider constituency than the House, Senate, or the Bureau of Public Roads or state highway departments, will advocate such changes. For state and public highway officials to do otherwise, McConnell argues, would be to forsake the support of private road users and economic interests who benefit from a decentralized policymaking arena.

If Orfield is correct, the legislative system will be quite *permeable* to demands and will respond to electoral pressures over time. Moreover, we should find that there will be far fewer systematic differences between the president and the House/Senate with regard to highway policymaking. In other words, presidents will differ more among themselves than they will disagree with congressional committees and the House and Senate. If Orfield is correct, and if any consistent patterns can be identified, they should not be based on the nature of the constituency of the different parts of the highway policymaking arena, as McConnell predicts.

Both McConnell's and Orfield's interpretations of American politics, of course, offer only a probalistic account of the relationship between the constituency of political institutions, the nature of politics within them, and the public policy that results. In statistical terms McConnell is concerned only with central tendencies, not in saying that *at all times* the president will protect the interests of wider publics than Congress or that *at all times* the Senate protects wider interests than the House. Therefore, to test the validity of McConnell's and Orfield's interpretations of American politics even in the single area of highway politics, we must consider an extended time period. In this case we look at highway politics from 1955 to 1976, a period when the Interstate Highway Program was established and implemented. In this period we had three Republican presidents (Eisenhower, Nixon, and Ford) and two Democratic presidents (Kennedy and Johnson). The fact that these presidents differed so fundamentally in ideology makes a comparison of their actions on highway policy an extremely good test of McConnell's constituency analysis. For if all these presidents, given their ideological differences, sought policies to protect wider publics and the House/Senate did not, then a substantial confirmation of McConnell's thesis is offered in the area of highway politics and policymaking.

It is important to give special emphasis to the legislative period during which major decisions are made about the nature of the political arena for future policymaking. In these founding periods the power of the various constituencies are set into law, and more informal expectations are established about the influence and activities of both public officials and private interest groups. Therefore, we shall first look at the founding period for the Interstate Highway Program, and then in a briefer section of the paper explore the politics of its implementation.

Highway Politics in 1955–56

Highway politics in 1955–56 confirms Orfield's view that Congress can be more innovative in public policy and protect wider publics than can the president. For on the question of taxation policy and weight and size limits for trucks, the House Public Works Committee, not President Eisenhower, was most supportive of the needs of noncommercial road users. However, on the question of the allocation formula for interstate road money, McConnell's constituency analysis was confirmed. Also, McConnell's emphasis on the relationship between the constituencies of congressional committees and the type of politics that occurs within them is confirmed by the radically different way in which the House Ways and Means Committee in 1956 handled highway tax issues compared to the 1955 effort by the House Public Works Committee to write highway tax legislation.

Most significantly, McConnell's major premise—that logrolling rather than sincere conflicts between diverse interest groups, or between public officials and private interests, dominates American politics—is supported by our analysis of highway politics in 1955–56. As McConnell predicted, one is impressed by the similarity of views on policy by Bureau of Public Roads officials, state highway officials, road user groups, and highway builders. This is especially obvious in issues such as the allocation formula, the trust fund, federal truck weight and size limits, differentials on taxes for trucks and cars, and most important, issues that would produce changes in the traditional state rather than federal control of highway policy.

The Allocation Formula

Consistent with his wide constituency, President Eisenhower initiated an interstate road program which shifted from concentrating federal support on farm to market roads to roads linking the whole nation. Moreover, he sought a *needs formula* that would allocate to each state the funds needed to complete its part of the interstate system irrespective of cost, so that states could complete the same percentage of their sections of the interstate network with each passing year. This constituted a major shift in highway policy since highway money in the past was allocated to states on the basis of existing rural post roads, land area, and population. Gary Schwartz has established that Eisenhower was most interested in linking up all the major population and business areas. He was less concerned about building roads *within* metropolitan areas to help solve intrametropolitan area traffic problems.[15] The Bureau of Public Roads, supported by the American Association of State Highway Officials, not the president, advocated extra urban freeways in order to secure the widest support in Congress for interstates.

Constituency analysis also helps explain the differences in position by the House and Senate Public Works Committee. Since the House Public Works Committee (and its Subcommittee on Roads), including Chairman George Fallon (D.-Md.) consisted of congressmen from primarily urban and suburban districts, it supported the needs formula. By contrast the Senate Public Works Committee (and its Subcommittee on Roads) consisted of Senators from primarily rural states, especially Western states, which traditionally benefited under the old formula. The highway bill supported by Senator Gore, chairman of the subcommittee on Roads, favored continuation of the formula that took land area and rural post roads into consideration. The relationship between the two proposals and how the states of the different legislators would benefit is shown in tables 1 and 2. These tables suggest that under the Gore formula constituencies which were represented by members of the Senate Public Works Committee would do far better than those represented by members of the House Subcommittee on Roads of the House Public Works Committee. Members of the Senate Public Works Committee were assured that a mean of 144.6 percent of the interstate highways would be authorized for their states over the expected ten-year

Table 1
**Allocation of Highway Funds, under the Formula Favored by
Senator Gore, to the States Having Members on the Senate
Committee on Public Works**

Members of Senate Committee on Public Works	Urban %	Under Gore Favored 1954 Allocation Formula: % of Interstate Highway Completion over 10-Year Program[a]
Dennis Chavez (Ch.)(D.-N.Mex.)[b]	65.7	120
Robert S. Kerr (ranking Dem.) (D.-Okla.)[b]	64.9	110
Albert Gore[a] (Ch. Sub-com. on Roads) (D.-Tenn.)[b]	52.3	131
Pat McNamara (D.-Mich.)[b]	73.4	65
Richard Neuberger, (D.-Oreg.)[b]	62.2	99
Edward Martin (ranking Rep.), (R.-Pa.)[b]	71.6	164
Frances Case (R.-S.Dak.)[b]	39.3	283
Prescott Bush (D.-Conn.)[b]	78.3	40
Stuart Symington (D.-Mo.)[b]	66.6	105
Strom Thurmond (D.-S.C.)[b]	41.2	171
Thomas Kuchel (R.-Calif.)	86.4	57
Roman Hruska (R.-Nebr.)	54.3	315
Norris Cotton (R.-N.H.)	58.3	220

[a] $\bar{x} = 144.6$.
[b] Members of Subcommittee on Roads.

life of the program. In the states of members of the House Subcommittee on Roads a mean of only 113.9 percent of the interstate
program would be authorized. Most important, under the Gore formula
specific states such as Maryland, Ohio, Michigan, California, Delaware,
New Jersey, and Florida would be authorized substantially less than 100

Table 2
Allocation of Highway Funds, under the Formula Favored by Senator Gore, to the States Having Representatives on the House Subcommittee on Roads[a]

Members of the House Subcommittee on Roads	Congressional District: Urban %	Under Gore Favored 1954 Allocation Formula: % Interstate Highway Completed Over 10-Year Program in Home State[b]
George Fallon(Ch.) (D.-Md.)	100	64
John J. Dempsey (D.-N.Mex.)	At large (65.7)	120
Frank E. Smith (D.-Miss.)	53.8	150
John C. Kluczynski (D.-Ill.)	100	103
Tom Steed (D.-Okla.)	53.7	110
Clifford Davis (D.-Tenn.)	87.8	131
John A. Blatnick (D.-Minn.)	51.8	108
Robert E. Jones, Jr. (D.-Ala.)	55	129
Brady Gentry (D.-Tex.)	48	153
Frank M. Clark (D.-Pa.)	55.2	164
J. Harry McGregor (R.-Ohio)	50	73
George A. Dondaro (R.-Mich.)	88.2	65
Myron V. George (R.-Kans.)	N.A.	204
Gordon H. Scherer (R.-Ohio)	96.1	73
William C. Cramer (R.-Fla.)	57.6	80
John F. Baldwin (R.-Calif.)	81.1	57
Bruce Alger (R.-Tex.)	97.5	153

[a] Many more House members' districts both on the Public Works Committee and in the full House would lose significant interstate funds if the Gore formula was enacted into law.
[b] $\bar{x}$ = 113.9.

percent of their interstate program during the ten years. The two committees also differed with regard to the percentage of their membership from states which would fare poorly under the Gore formula. A comparison of the House Public Works Committee in the Eighty-fourth Congress (1955–56) with the membership on that committee in earlier Congresses shows that states which would fare poorly under the Gore formula increased their seats from eight in the Eighty-first Congress (1949–50) to ten in the Eighty-fourth Congress. This constituted approximately one-third of the Public Works Committee and six of the seventeen seats on its Subcommittee on Roads. Only three of the thirteen members (23%) of the Senate Public Works Committee come from these states. As McConnell predicted, constituency differences in the House and the Senate (and the presidency) resulted in quite different positions on public policy. Constituency differences such as were found in these House and Senate committees and which were magnified when the full House and Senate had to vote on highway legislation helped explain why they differed on the allocation formula.

However, numbers which show a greater percentage of congressmen from urban constituencies on the House Public Works Committee than senators on the Senate Public Works Committee do not tell the full story of why the Public Works Committee rejected the Gore formula, especially when we see that five of the seven congressmen who were from states which fared poorly under the Gore formula were Republicans, three of whom were recently elected. Of greater significance for understanding the rejection of the Gore formula by the House Public Works Committee was the fact that all the Congressmen who were in leadership positions on the House Public Works Committee came from urban states. George Fallon, the chairman of the Subcommittee on Roads and the second-ranking Democrat on the Public Works Committee, came from Maryland. Both the ranking Republican on the roads subcommittee (McGregor) and the ranking Republican on the Public Works Committee (Dondaro) came from Michigan. Maryland and Michigan would fare poorly under the Gore formula. Finally, Charles Buckley of New York, who took over the chairmanship of the Public Works Committee in 1949 (from William Whittington of Miss.), was concerned that construction of urban interstate roads not be delayed, even though New York would not do as poorly under the Gore formula as other populated urban states. These findings show the significance of seniority and leadership in highway decision making and support one of Orfield's major conclusions about congressional power: that the seniority system, committee structure, and the power of chairmen can result not only in conservative but also in liberal policies. However, in the

Senate Public Works Committee all leadership positions were held by senators from states that would fare well under the Gore formula.

The result was a classic distributive compromise. In the legislation that passed in 1956, spending for rural and primary state roads under the old Gore formula was increased, and the Gore formula was used for the first three years of the interstate program. This gave rural states a head start in the interstate program. But the major consequence of the 1956 Highway Act was to expand the constituency for highway legislation from primarily farm interests to business, wider road uses, and urban interests. Consistent with McConnell's view, the president led in this shift in the highway policymaking arena. The response of the House and Senate was related to the character of the constituencies they represented, but the House supported the president more than the Senate.

Taxation Policy

The major issue in the area of taxation policy was whether truckers should pay higher rates of taxation than car owners. Truckers favored across-the-board taxation; that is, they were willing to pay more per gallon as long as the same increase was applied to car owners. Across-the-board taxation does not take into account the fact that interstate roads cost more to build because trucks must be serviced by additional lanes, thicker road beds, higher overpasses, and wider lanes. In other words, across-the-board taxation ignores *ton*-miles as a measure of road use. Only with tax differentials can road use measured in ton-mile terms, which is a better indicator of road use, be incorporated into the tax structure. Without differentials the car owner pays the cost of constructing roads for truck use.

On this question the House Subcommittee on Roads and its parent Public Works Committee favored tax differentials since Chairman Fallon wanted to insure that trucks would pay a proportionate part of the cost of interstates. But the Eisenhower Administration did not support Fallon. The position of the president against protecting the wider public as compared with the position of the House Committee on Public Works indicates that on this issue Orfield's and not McConnell's position is confirmed. Experienced with building roads, the House Public Works Committee knew that road costs would be greatly increased by truck use and rationally had advocated a tax program to pay for that use. The Senate Public Works Committee, althought it did not formally deal with the tax writing section, had a similar view to that of the Fallon Committee. These efforts at equity, however, ran afoul of the power of the trucking industry.[16]

There was a massive lobbying campaign by the American Trucking

Association, supported by tire and truck manufacturers, against the 1955 highway legislation because it included the dreaded tax differentials for car and truck owners. House leaders Rayburn and McCormack specifically mentioned that this lobbying effort was the cause of the defeat of highway legislation in 1955. Here McConnell's concept of an orthodoxy which favors traditional committee jurisdictions in legislation, that is, the reluctance of many congressmen to permit any outsiders, including other congressional committees, to tamper with *their* committee's jurisdiction becomes important. Specifically, it was argued by the trucker's lobby that it was *unfair* to allow the Public Works Committee to write tax provisions. Although a Subcommittee of the Ways and Means Committee sat in on the tax writing sessions and hearings of the Fallon Committee in 1955, and the House leadership (Rayburn and McCormack) had given the Fallon Committee the task of writing the highway tax bill, the American Trucking Association effectively used as one of its major arguments against the higher taxes that this arrangement was unfair since the Fallon Committee did not "understand" all the taxation issues.

Indeed, the political debate changed dramatically when tax writing in 1956 was shifted to the Ways and Means Committee, the traditional tax writing committee in the House. Experienced with building roads, the House Public Works Committee has stressed that highway costs would be greatly increased by truck use and rationally advocated a tax program to pay for that use; by contrast, the Ways and Means Committee's constituency was the business community and was most concerned about the "equitable" treatment of the business community. Most significantly, the very different reception to the policy of tax differentials by the House Ways and Means Committee as contrasted to that of the House Public Works Committee confirms McConnell's position that the constituencies of political decision-making arenas dictate both the type of political process that occurs and the content of the policy itself. In particular, Congressman Hale Boggs, one of the most influential members of the Ways and Means Committee, was very sympathetic to the trucking industry and saw tax differentials as a form of "regulation" rather than taxation.[17] Notwithstanding detailed information from the American Association of Railroads on the subsidy given to truckers by across-the-board taxation, Boggs felt that if tax differentials were to be enacted they would have to be established by the House Interstate and Foreign Commerce Committee and the Interstate Commerce Commission. In effect, the Ways and Means Committee was more concerned about the competitive relations between forms of transportation than about the fairness of the tax schedule between car and truck owners. In the end, the Ways and Means Committee prevailed. Rather than the wide differentials of the Fallon bill, the final bill in 1956 placed a modest tax of $1.50 per 1,000 pounds of weight for trucks over 26,000 pounds.

The conflict over tax differentials also shows the importance of McConnell's views about collusion between public officials and private interest groups. The AASHO refused to take a position on differentials in 1955 on the relation of road costs to truck use even when peppered by the House Public Works Committee. However, at its December 1955 national meeting after the defeat of highway legislation, AASHO passed a resolution calling for only reasonable increases in taxes on gas and tires, the use of both bonds and direct user taxes to pay for roads, and no federal weight and size limits on roads. It *publicly* opposed tax differentials.[18]

McConnell's major premise that private interest groups logroll among themselves also is supported by highway politics in 1955–56. The American Automobile Association, although it supported modest tax differentials, did not effectively advocate them. Interviews with AAA lobbyists and committee staff people suggest that the AAA lobbyists were overawed by ATA efforts to oppose differentials.[19] The AAA unsuccessfully tried to get reimbursement for states who constructed toll roads to stop future double taxation of car owners. The American Association of Railroads (AAR) was also not effective in its efforts to get tax differentials to keep trains more competitive with trucks. The Ways and Means Committee discounted railroad views, given the obvious bias of their position. The AAA and AAR were no match against the actions of the AASHO, road building groups, and the NHUC. The American Federation of Labor also supported differentials. Yet clearly their major lobbying efforts were concentrated on a successful attempt to secure prevailing wage legislation in the highway bill and thus keep contractors from importing cheap labor into high-wage areas. As McConnell predicted, each interest group was most successful in the issue area most *economically* crucial to them. They lobbied less for secondary economic interests and were less successful at achieving them. Few private interest groups lobbied for the needs of wider publics.

Of great significance with regard to testing the validity of McConnell's constituency analysis is the fact that in contrast to McConnell's expectations President Eisenhower, who represented a far wider constituency than members of the House and Senate, refused to support tax differentials, the innovation in tax policy which had been advocated initially by the Fallon Committee. The president refused to support a policy that would protect noncommercial highway users and set into law a principle of taxation that would secure greater equity as to who finances highways. The House Committee on Public Works, with a narrower constit-

uency than that of the president, sought to protect wider publics. This
position by the Eisenhower Administration is evidenced by the fact that
in 1955 it refused to lobby for the Fallon proposal. Also, after the defeat
of the highway bill late in 1955, because it included the Fallon tax
program, the Eisenhower Administration came out forcefully against tax
differentials. The secretary of commerce told the Business Advisory
Council that the Eisenhower administration will do anything reasonable
to pass the highway bill, and highway user and builder groups were
invited to the White House.[20] After the meeting of the Business Advisory Council, *Transport Topics* ran a headline which read, "Across the
Board Highway Tax Boosts OK'd by Eisenhower."[21] Although stripped
of its tax writing authority, the Fallon Committee still sought in
1956 to secure tax differentials on the floor of the House. To aid in this
effort during the 1956 hearings on the highway bill, it sought data from
the Eisenhower administration on the relationship between truck use of
the interstates and the expected construction and maintenance costs for
the new roads and to equate such costs to questions of highway taxation.
The Eisenhower administration refused to admit that there was a
relationsip between road costs and truck size or to give the Fallon Committee data on such a relationship for purposes of devising a tax
schedule. On the important question of highway taxation, committees in
the House and Senate, not the president, supported the interests of
wider publics. Therefore, we see a confirmation of Orfield's position, not
that of McConnell, on the relationship between the constituencies of
presidents and congressmen and the positions they take on public issues.
However, on other aspects, such as the role of logrolling in American
politics and the significance of the relationship between the constituencies of congressional committees and their positions on public policy,
McConnell's views are confirmed through our analysis of highway taxation politics in 1955–56.

Maintenance of
Federal-State Relations

State and federal highway builders and private user interest groups also
agreed on continuing the traditional federal-state relations in the highway policy arena in which the states have traditionally built the roads.
They decide the routes, what type of highways to build, and standards
for construction within ranges set by the Bureau of Public Roads. The
American Association of State Highway Officials writes model policies
or codes, such as that for the weight and size of trucks. However, each
state has the final say as to its specific policy. State control of highway

policymaking favors local economic interests which, as McConnell predicts, have more influence at the state level than at the national level of policymaking.

Public highway officials and private interest groups first publicly joined forces to protect this traditional highway policymaking arena when they defeated an Eisenhower Administration proposal to establish a Federal Highway Corporation, whose board would include the secretaries of the treasury, interior, agriculture, and commerce. Under the original Eisenhower plan, this board would finance the roads by selling bonds. More important, the board would have the authority to settle any disputes between federal and state highway officials, that is, between the Bureau of Public Roads and the state highway departments. Outsiders would thus have had a major say in highway policymaking. The Bureau of Public Roads, the American Association of State Highway Officials, the American Automobile Association, the American Trucking Association, and members of both the House and the Senate Public Works Committees all opposed the board. Indeed, the board would have diluted their influence over highway policy by providing a forum in the highway policy process for the concerns of cities, nonhighway users, and evern critics of highways who advocated more comprehensive transportion planning and a far more "liberal" definition of highway costs. Indeed, presidents could have used the board as a vehicle to adjust highway tax and spending levels in order to control the economy.

Even more significant toward protecting traditional federal-state relations in highway policymaking was the establishment of the highway trust fund, an issue not debated in 1955–56. As staff members of the Public Works Committee in the House and Senate emphasized in interviews, the establishment of the trust fund was the single most significant decision made in the founding period. The trust fund first helped secure passage of this massive highway bill since highway users were assured that any money that they were taxed would go for roads. Even more significant was its importance to future highway politics. On one side, highway funds would not have to go through the normal appropriations process, so that congressmen, other than those in the Public Works Committee in the House and Senate and the House Ways and Means Committee, would not review the highway program and user tax schedule. Highway spending would not be weighed against other national needs. Waste could not easily be found. On the other side, establishment of the trust fund united the coalition of public officials and private interest groups which supported highway construction. Road user groups all could argue that *as a matter of right* they should have the veto power over highway policy because *they* are paying for the roads. Public highway officials and private road construction groups could support the trust fund for it assured continued financing of roads without the need to justify them to politicians outside the coalition. Most important, the trust fund made highway officials even more solicitous of the needs of highway users rather than wider publics because wider publics were not paying the bill. All these user and highway building groups had an interest in keeping trust fund moneys from being diverted into groups outside the highway coalition. Highway politics after 1956 displayed this process in action.

Truck Weight-and-Size Limits

The one area in which traditional federal-state relationships in the highway area were modified was the adoption of a federal standard for truck weight-and-size limits. Before 1955, states had established truck weight-and-size limits. The AASHO periodically made a model truck weight-and-size law, which the states could *voluntarily* adopt. The AASHO would raise the recommended axle weights and size every five to ten years to meet new higher standards, which state trucking associations had gotten passed in some state legislatures. But the federal limitation that was finally passed in 1956 was very generous. It called for the withholding of federal highway funds from any state which allowed vehicles with axle weights over 18,000 pounds on one axle and 32,000 pounds on a tandem axle, or an overall gross weight in excess of 73,280 pounds or width in excess of ninety-six inches, or the corresponding maximum weights or widths permitted for vehicles under laws and regulations in effect July 1, 1956, whichever is greater.[22] This law was acceptable to the American Trucking Association, but it certainly was not as stringent as some congressmen wanted. No rollbacks in states with higher weight-and-size limits were called for. The new law increased weight-and-size limits in a substantial number of states. More important, enforcement of the limits and implementation of special permits for larger trucks were still in state hands.

The Eisenhower administration wanted to support traditional federal-state relations in highway policymaking and not place limits on the productivity of trucks. It opposed federal weight-and-size standards. The AAA, not wanting to oppose the stronger ATA, took no lead in this matter. The AASHO and private interest groups favoring more roads did not want this issue to stall the building of more roads. Therefore, in contrast to the expectation of McConnell, it was a congressional committee, not the president, which sought to protect the safety and economic interests of wider publics, in this case car owners, who would be forced to pay the costs of larger, heavier trucks and incur increased risks to their safety.[23]

The Founding: Partial Confirmation of the McConnell and the Orfield Approach

The period during which the Interstate Highway Program was established provides confirmation of important aspects of both McConnell's and Orfield's approaches. On the question of the allocation formula, McConnell's approach is confirmed. The president, representing a wider constituency than the rural dominated Senate and even the House, advocated a major shift in the highway program from farm roads to roads important to national transportation links. Also, McConnell's major thesis on how small constituency politics leads to the presence of entrenched private interest groups, logrolling between private interest groups, and the lack of conflict between the goals and legislative tactics of private interest groups and public highway officials is well supported by our findings on the founding period. We also see support for McConnell's constituency analysis in the differences in highway taxation politics before the House Public Works Committee in 1955 and the Ways and Means Committee in 1956.

However, on other major issues, the intrests of wider publics than state and federal highway officials, commercial road users, and private road builders were *not* articulated by the president as McConnell would predict, but rather, in most cases, by the Public Works Committee in the House. This was the case on the question of tax differentials, changes in traditional federal-state highway policymaking (as seen in truck weight-and-size limits), and other issues. Also, the increased urban emphasis in the highway program was the result of BPR, not presidential initiatives. The BPR, supported by the AASHO, sought wider political support in Congress for roads.[24] This pattern, in which policy initiatives and the interests of wider publics are fostered by congressional committees and government agencies rather than the president, shows the significance of general shifts in public opinion to policy change, a finding consistent with Orfield's analysis. We see a partial breakdown of McConnell's constituency analysis. However, a fairer test of McConnell's thesis requires a longer time perspective. Presidents, congressional committees, private interest groups, and highway officials must be studied over several administrations before we can see whether or not the consistencies in behavior predicted by McConnell occurred.

Highway Politics since 1956

Highway politics since 1956 confirms McConnell's major thesis about the relationship among constituency size, characteristic political processes within political institutions, and resulting public policy. An analysis of major issues of highway politics shows a consistent pattern, particularly since 1960. Presidents Kennedy, Johnson, Nixon, and Ford sought to protect car owners rather than commercial highway users, and individuals affected by highway construction rather than highway users in general. Also, as McConnell predicted, on most issues the Senate took positions closer to those of the president than the House. Highway user interest groups like the ATA, AASHO, American Road Builders Association (ARBA), and the AAA opposed many of the innovations sought by the president. Specifically between 1960 and 1976, presidents, usually with Senate support and House opposition, have sought comprehensive transportation planning rather than more narrow highway planning, a Department of Transportation under a strong secretary, and lower highway spending. They also have sought to use highway funds to help manage the economy; to divert highway trust funds to pay for special bus lanes, perimeter parking, and other mass transit uses in cities; and to *substitute* mass transit for urban sections of the interstate system.

Comprehensive Planning

Since the Eisenhower years, presidents have sought to change the emphasis in transportation planning from that of road building to more coordinated transportation planning. In 1962, Kennedy secured legislation that called for comprehensive transportation planning in cities over 50,000 by July 1965. However, the language of the 1962 legislation was not precise enough to force such planning and overcome the tendency of state highway departments to build roads at the lowest cost in engineering terms and to stress economic growth rather than other values in highway planning.

To help overcome the nation's transportation problems, President Johnson led the successful fight in 1966 to establish the Department of Transportation and sought, unsuccessfully, to give its secretary the power to do wider planning and force states and localities to at least ask the question whether more highways or more mass transit or a combination of both was best for their urban areas.[25]

The politics surrounding the establishment of the Department of Transportation illustrate McConnell's basic claims about American politics. Each separate area of transportation (highways, waterways, etc.) engaged in logrolling to keep outsiders, like a strong secretary of transportation, from influencing policy in its own transportation area. Moreover, chairmen of the relevant committees in Congress that handled the particular transportation legislation supported separate agency (and interest group) efforts to keep their autonomy. Congressman Fallon's House Public Works Committee was particularly successful in limiting the power of the secretary of transportation to little more than that of making studies. Highway, airport, and other agencies that would be included in the department successfully shaped the final bill to make sure, first, that any specific project would be decided on by the appropriate congressional committee and, second, that the agencies in the department would not have to compete with each other for the secretary's approval when securing funds.[26]

In 1969, the Nixon administration established the Office of Environment and Urban Systems at the assistant secretary level in the Department of Transportation. Its mission was to achieve a balance between human, environmental, and engineering values in the development of comprehensive transportation systems. That office, which oversees the compliance of the Department of Transportation with the National Environmental Policy Act, especially with regard to writing environmental impact statements, has had success in stopping or fundamentally altering plans for highly publicized projects such as the Miami Airport in South Florida, the Riverfront Expressway in New Orleans, and expressways in the San Antonio area. However, it has been less successful overseeing the ongoing daily highway planning in our nation. Mertins reports that transportation planning continues to be heavily dominated by highway construction, with an emphasis on more narrow engineering and economic values rather than a stress on comprehensive transportation planning which is integrated with overall urban planning.[27]

"Diverting" Highway Trust Funds

It is on the issue of diverting of highway trust funds to pay for road costs more broadly defined (than in the 1956 legislation) that we see the most consistent differences in the behavior of presidents, the Senate, House, federal and state highway officials, and private road user and builder groups. The term "diversion" itself of course indicates the initial narrow focus of the highway policymaking arena since it assumes that political actors already have a very restricted idea of what constitutes road costs suggests that spending on any other even closely related activities is illegitimate. This structuring of political debate places proponents of beautification, relocation assistance, mass transit, and comprehensive planning on the defensive.

Highway Beautification

The first serious effort to secure diversion of trust fund money occurred in the area of billboard control. In 1957 President Eisenhower supported billboard control and advocated that states which limit billboards along the interstates be given a .5 percent bonus on federal funds. The Senate supported extra funds for this purpose. The House took no action. In 1958 a voluntary program of billboard control was passed. It remained law through 1965. States received 90.5 percent of federal funding rather than 90 percent. By 1965, only twenty-five states had signed an agreement to remove billboards. Only ten states actually had removed billboards and had received the bonuses. Billboards on only 209.2 miles of highways in the 41,000-mile interstate system were controlled by 1965. In 1958 states also were authorized to spend up to 3 percent of their highway funds for buying strips of land beyond the normal right-of-ways to allow scenic views. By 1965 only three states used such funds. The secretary of commerce said states evidently emphasized funds for highway construction rather than beauty.[28] Once money was appropriated, state highway departments were pressured to use highway money just to build roads and therefore did not emphasize these supplemental programs. As McConnell's approach predicted decentralization of authority from national institutions to states or to localities on matters of regulation, local economic interests would be allowed to prevail politically, given the smaller, less heterogeneous constituencies (in state legislatures, agencies, or city councils) in which they must operate.

In 1965, President and Mrs. Johnson used their personal influence to secure highway beautification by seeking more stringent laws for billboard control and junkyard screening near interstate roads. President Johnson sought a 100 percent fund cutoff. Congress gave the BPR the authority to cut off 10 percent of all federal road funds in states which refused to comply. Yet, even with the 1965 legislation, states still did not move on billboard control. By 1969 only 1.9 million dollars were spent on billboard removal. Most of these funds were for a sign inventory. In 1969 the Senate supported a 15 million dollar appropriation for a *pilot* project to try to remove all billboards on interstate roads in a few states. The House opposed this program. In 1970, after highway beautification legislation failed in 1969, the House and the Senate finally agreed to the Nixon Administration program to spend 108 million over three years, 1971–73, for billboard and junkyard control. Thus, fourteen years after the passage of the massive interstate highway program in 1956, Congress approved a highway beautification program of some scale. During these years, in confirmation with McConnell's constituency analysis, the Senate supported highway beautification while the House usually opposed an effective program. In 1974, 65 million dollars per year were allocated for fiscal years 1974–76.[29]

Presidents, however, have not only had problems getting Congress to declare highway beautification as a goal for the nation, they have had even greater difficulty getting Congress to approve moneys *from the trust fund* for beautification. When President Johnson in 1965 sought to use moneys in the highway trust fund for billboard control, safety, and highway beautification programs, state highway officials, road building groups, and highway user organizations blocked these efforts. They opposed what they saw as the unnecessary diversion of highway funds awary from road construction. To gain support for the 1965 legislation, President Johnson agreed to earmark tax revenues to these purposes from 2 percent of the excise tax on new cars, tax revenues that were not then assigned to the highway trust fund and would ordinarily have gone into the general treasury. In 1971, President Nixon also tried to secure money from the highway trust fund for beautification and safety programs. Again the House opposed the president while the Senate supported the use of trust fund moneys for these purposes. The House view against diversion again prevailed. Today, funds for highway beautification, junkyard control, and road construction on public lands come from the general treasury, not the highway trust fund. Road user taxes do not pay for these programs, thereby increasing the already large subsidy to commercial and noncommercial highway users inherent in the highway tax system.

Relocation Assistance

Relocation assistance reveals a similar pattern. In 1956, Robert Moses of New York asked that relocation assistance for citizens and firms be part of the definition of highway construction costs. The House Public Works Committee, which had an urban orientation at the time, supported it. Yet the Senate Public Works Committee opposed the provision. The House committee dropped the provision during the markup of the bill in the conference committee and Senator Lehman's attempt to reinstate it on the Senate floor failed. Schwartz reports that there were no strong groups lobbying for it is in 1956.[30] Yet in the same year public utilities did get federal highway funds for moving utility lines.

Since 1956 presidents have sought to use money from the highway trust fund for paying relocation costs to citizens, for helping citizens to find decent replacement housing, and (in more recent years) for the actual building of replacement housing. In 1962, President Kennedy with Senate support sought to pay relocation costs to citizens. But the House rejected the plan although it did allow that at their discretion state highway departments could provide advisory assistance and information to relocatees. In 1966, after hundreds of thousands of people had already been moved out to permit highway construction, the Congress authorized a study of the problems facing relocatees. In 1968, payments to relocatees for moving costs were authorized by Congress. In 1969, although no highway legislation made its way through both branches of Congress, the Senate passed and the House rejected Nixon administration initiatives to have replacement housing for relocatees considered part of the cost of road construction. In that same year, the Senate supported and the House rejected Department of Transportation legislation requiring the states to have housing plans for relocatees in place *before* specific highway projects are approved by the Department of Transportation. The House was supporting the view held by George Fallon of the Public Works Committee and highway construction interests that such a policy would delay road construction. In 1970, the House did approve the use of federal highway moneys for constructing housing for relocatees. However, the language of the law specified that such payments were to be made only where no other housing was available. I have not found any instances where trust fund moneys have been used for this purpose. Clearly, no sizable expenditures for home construction have been authorized from the trust fund for the thousands of people moved out of their homes and businesses by highway construction since this provision was passed.

In this period, the middle and late 1960s through the 1970s, many interstate highways were being delayed and several blocked because of opposition from urban citizens. The president, usually supported by state highway officials and the Senate, most of whose members had inner city areas within their states, sought to spend highway funds to respond to causes of this opposition. The House, where a majority represented rural and suburban areas rather than inner city districts, opposed these efforts, The ATA, the AAA, and other road user groups also opposed this diversion of funds. They opposed any attempt to use trust fund moneys for any purposes other than what they considered were the *direct* costs of road construction. Wider publics had very limited influence over highway policy, especially in the House, even when the president and the Senate supported their efforts. What aid did come it was too late to meet the problem for which it was appropriated. The roads had been built. The people had been forced out of their homes. As McConnell's constituency analysis predicts, in the policy areas of highway beautification, relocation assistance, and on the question of whether trust fund moneys should be used for such programs, we see a consistent pattern of presidents advocating the policy needs for wider policies then highway users with the Senate supporting and House opposing them.

Mass Transit

During the middle and late 1960s the Johnson and Nixon administrations concluded that the only way to achieve comprehensive transportation goals and planning for large cities was either to abolish the highway trust fund or divert moneys from it to pay for other forms of transportation, such as mass transit. In 1970, Secretary of Transporation Volpe and President Nixon publicly advocated replacing the highway trust fund with a transportation trust fund.[31] In 1975, President Ford advocated that a transportation trust fund be established and that two cents of the four cents per gallon of gas taxes earmarked for interstate roads be designated for other urban roads than interstates, for mass transit, and even for nontransportation needs.[32] In general, rather than tranform the trust fund as a legal entity, presidents have favored diversion of trust fund moneys to pay for mass transit in cities and the replacement with mass transit of designated sections of the interstate system before construction. Finally, presidents have sought "pass-through" provisions which would allow city and regional transportation authorities to have greater influence over transportation planning and the approval of highway mass transit in their locales, thus reducing the power of state highway departments over urban transportation planning. Highway politics since 1956 shows a consistent pattern in which presidents, supported by the Senate, sought laws to allow cities to spend highway funds for uses that were opposed by the House. Also, we see the House consistently favoring the highest appropriations for road spending and new highway construction programs to make sure that moneys flowing into the trust fund would be spend for roads as the interstate program winds down. This position, moreover, has been supported by private road user groups and state and federal highway officials who have opposed the creation of a transportation trust fund and reduced spending on highways, a position strengthened by the need to involve six different legislative committees in any effort to transform the highway trust fund.[33]

The first response by Congress to growing opposition in major cities to interstate highway building was to protect the existing policy pattern by passing legislation opposing the impounding of funds by the president, prohibiting the use of highway trust funds by an agency other than the Federal Highway Administration, and raising the percentage of federal payment on urban highways, other than interstates, from 50 to 70 percent. The House even passed legislation to try to force the District of Columbia to build some sections of the interstate system which it and citizen groups had blocked through actions in Federal Court. The Senate and the president opposed this attempt to force Washington, D.C., to build roads it did not want.

President Nixon achieved a limited diversion from the highway trust fund in 1971 by persuading the House approve highway trust fund spending for special bus lanes and perimeter parking lots on the interstates, although one-third of the funds for these projects were to come from the general treasury.

After deadlock over the diversion of highway trust funds resulted in the failure of the House and Senate to agree on a highway bill in 1972, private interest groups and highway officials began to fear that the highway program would be brought to a halt. As a result of these fears, and after a long struggle in conference committee in 1973, Nixon secured the first diversion of highway trust funds for mass transit. The 1973 act allowed states to replace segments of their proposed interstate systems with subways and other forms of mass transit and authorized cities to use highway funds to buy commuter trains. In a complex compromise this diversion of funds for mass transit was phased in over the fiscal years 1974, 1975, and 1976. During that time money would come from the general treasury in equal amounts to the diverted funds, thereby preserving gas tax proceeds for highway construction. However, by 1976, mass transit would be paid for by highway trust fund moneys. During the long struggle to divert highway trust funds to mass transit projects, the president was consistently supported by the Senate and opposed by the House.

In 1975–76, Congress considered pass-through provisions which reduce the influence of state highway departments over transportation planning by allowing greater influence over transportation planning for local officials, transfers between regular urban and interstate categories in the highway trust fund, and shifting highway funds to mass transit needs. In 1976, these pass-through laws were passed with the support of the governors and the opposition of AASHO. With the replacement of state highway departments by transportation departments with wide planning resources, we see the slow movement toward transportation planning and the allocation of transportation funds based on wider interests than those of only road users. In 1976, a two-year extension of the trust fund was passed incorporating these provisions. Completion of the interstate system was put off until 1990.

Since 1956, constituency differences between the president, Senate, and House have conformed to McConnell's analyses. Presidents since

Eisenhower, together with the Senate, had supported diversion to aid wider publics than highway users and builders. The House consistently opposed these pass-through provisions, comprehensive planning, mass transit diversions, and local option innovation. At the same time, these efforts to expand the definition of transportation from one of highways to mixed systems have had limited results, thereby confirming McConnell's pessimism about the power of private interests.

Even with pass-through provisions and more local options; the Department of Transportation estimated in 1975 that by 1990 only 6.2 percent of federal transportation funds will be spent on mass transit. The figure is up from 5.2 percent in 1971.[34] By 1975, only four cities had used provisions to allow the transfer of interstate funds to local urban roads. Use of trust funds for busways has been minimal. By 1977, 90 percent of the 42,000-mile interstate system was opened to traffic, with most of the uncompleted mileage in cities. Movement toward more comprehensive and mixed highway planning cannot be attributed only to the power of the president but also to local opposition to roads, the use of federal courts to stop road construction, and to environmental legislation which gives local citizens the means to intervene in the highway construction process. Those actions structured the politics of roads since 1956.

It may appear that the highway lobby *lost* in 1973–76. The trust fund has been opened up. Yet in reality they have lost little. They merely are paying a surcharge of less than 5 percent to mass transit to continue to allow highway interests to have a built-in advantage in securing funds for road construction.

Conclusion

In the founding period of the Interstate Highway Program we find only a partial confirmation of McConnell's interpretation of American politics. In most cases it was the House Public Works Committee, not the president, which tried to protect the interests of wider publics than road builders and commercial road users. The House Public Works Committee advocated weight-and-size limits for trucks and tax differentials. On these matters Orfield's stress on the significance of the current distribution of political opinion for explaining legislative outcomes certainly fares at least as well as McConnell's. Only on the question of the allocation formula do we see the president, House, and Senate clearly reflecting constituency interests in the way McConnell describes.

Perhaps of greater significance for understanding highway policymaking and policy in 1955–56 is the realization that McConnell's view, that small constituency politics results in logrolling between officials and private interest groups and among private interest groups themselves, is substantiated by our analysis of highway politics in this founding period. The failure to establish a national transportation policy and to meet the changing needs of our cities for mixed transportation systems is one of the consequences of actions taken in 1955–56 to set up a trust fund and to allow the continuation of traditional federal-state relations in highway politics. There also is evidence that politics during that period showed a desire by all actors, both public officials and private interest groups, to maintain traditional federal-state relations in highway policymaking and to place into law, through the trust fund arrangement and other decisions, a protection for the autonomy of the highway policymaking arena from outside interference in future years. Finally, highway politics in 1955–56 indicate that major interest groups tended to achieve their *most important* economic goals. Truckers achieved across-the-board taxation, and labor secured prevailing wage legislation. However, groups representing wider publics, such as the AAA, did not fare as well. Utilities received aid to relocate their facilities to allow highway construction. Citizens did not.

Highway politics since 1956, in contrast to the period of the founding of the Interstate Highway Program, suggests that we must come to a very different conclusion as to the importance of McConnell's constituency analysis for understanding highway politics in America. In all issue areas, except truck weight-and-size limits, presidents since Eisenhower have been supportive of the needs of wider publics than the House or Senate.[35] We see this in the areas of highway/transportation planning, highway beautification, relocation assistance, diversion of highway trust funds for mass transit, and on the issue of allowing local option to encourage mixed transportation development. Presidents consistently have advocated positions that favored the needs of individuals and groups other than highway users and builders. As McConnell asserts, the Senate tends to support presidents on these questions. The House consistently has been most protective of the needs of highway users and builders.

Highway politics since 1956 also suggests the importance of decisions made in the founding period of the Interstate Highway Program. The creation of the trust fund and the establishment of other formal *and informal* relations between public highway officials and private interest groups had led to logrolling between these groups. This has blurred distinctions between public and private power. Coordinated efforts by public highway officials and private road user and building groups to sustain the autonomy of the highway policymaking arena has made it very difficult to transform the process of highway planning into one of transportation planning, so that decisions can be made with the needs of wider publics in mind.

As a result the American political system on this issue has not been as permeable as Orfield suggests. Electoral politics, even Johnson's landslide in 1964, had little effect on highway policymaking. Structural elements, the constituencies of the presidency, House, and Senate and political institutions within the highway policymaking arena, are much more useful for explaining highway politics. In the system of reactive policymaking that we have in America, political advantages inherent within the structure of specific policymaking arenas cannot easily be overcome by electoral and legislative politics.

Notes

1. See Grant McConnell, *Private Power and American Democracy* (New York: Alfred A. Knopf, Inc., 1966), for the major statement of his interpretation of American politics. Other important contributions by McConnell include *The Modern Presidency*, 2d ed. (New York: St. Martin's Press, 1976); *The Decline of Agrarian Democracy* (Berkeley: University of California Press, 1953); and "The Spirit of Private Government," *American Political Science Review* 52, no. 3 (September 1958): 754–70.

2. See Gary Orfield, *Congressional Power: Congress and Social Change* (New York: Harcourt Brace Jovanovich, Inc., 1975), for the major statement of his interpretation of American politics. Another important contribution of Orfield is *The Reconstruction of Southern Education: The Schools and the 1964 Civil Rights Act* (New York: John Wiley & Sons, 1969).

3. McConnell has defined an American "orthodoxy" which has "a political logic that has important consequences in the development of American Democracy." See McConnell, *Private Power*, chap. 3, for an explanation of this "orthodoxy." I believe McConnell's interpretation of American politics also has a "political logic" that helps improve our understanding of specific political institutions and the complexities of the American political system.

4. McConnell, *Private Power*, p. 91.

5. McConnell also uses this type of argument to explain why democracy *within* private interest groups is limited. However, I will limit the analysis of highway politics to decision making within public arenas. See McConnell, *Private Power*, chap. 5, for a statement of why governance within private associations is not usually democratic. McConnell has a very different view on the question than David Truman, *The Governmental Process* (New York: Alfred A. Knopf, Inc., 1964), chap. 16. For an excellent analysis of the McConnell, Dahl, Lowi, and Truman approaches to group politics, see J. David Greenstone, "Group Theories," in *Handbook of Political Science*, vol. 2, *Micropolitical Theory*, ed. Fred I. Greenstein and Nelson W. Polsby (Reading, Mass.: Addison-Wesley Publishing Co., 1975), chap. 4, pp. 243–319.

6. See Greenstone, pp. 262–78.

7. See McConnell, *The Modern Presidency*, esp. chap. 3, for his statement about the differences between the constituency of presidents and congressmen.

8. Ibid., p. 55.

9. See Marver Bernstein, *Regulating Business by Independent Commission*

(Princeton, N.J.: Princeton University Press, 1955), for the most complete statement of this argument with regard to regulatory agency politics.

10. When the interests of all participants in a narrow policymaking arena are evident, formal logrolling does not have to occur. The results are the same.

11. See Orfield, *Congressional Power*, p. 6. Although Orfield does not specifically name McConnell as one of these liberal scholars, McConnell does offer the most sophisticated theory of why presidents will tend to be more progressive than Congress in the way they look at public policy. It is not clear to me that to say that presidents will shape policies with wider publics in mind than in the House or Senate is equivalent to asserting that presidents will be more *liberal* in ideological terms. The example of Nixon, one Orfield uses, suggests that, even though he was ideologically conservative, he still shaped the question of bussing in terms of wider publics and changing the constituencies within the American system that could deal with an issue. In this case, he wanted to reduce the power of the Supreme Court, a political institution with a wide constituency base.

12. Ibid., pp. 18–19.

13. Ibid., chaps. 5–9.

14. Ibid., chap. 13.

15. See Gary T. Schwartz, "Urban Freeways and the Interstate System," *Transportation Law Journal* 8, nos. 1 and 2 (1976):167–264, for an excellent article on the relationship between the Interstate Highway Program, the increase in the urban expressways, and the effects of these roads on the cities.

16. See Ronald Kahn, "The Politics of Roads: National Highway Legislation in 1955–1956" (master's diss., Department of Political Science, University of Chicago, 1967), chaps. 5 and 6, for a description and analysis of highway tax politics in the House and Senate in 1955–56. See ibid., pp. 262–63, for a discussion of one of the most pitiful appearances before any congressional committee in 1955–56. A highway official from Ohio, not representing the American Association of State Highway Officials, begged the Ways and Means Committee to support tax differentials in order to set an example for the states. His state was under attack by state trucking associations using their influence in neighboring states to bring sanctions against Ohio truckers because it was one of a few states that had a tax law with major differentials.

17. Ibid., p. 234.

18. *Transport Topics* (December 12, 1955), p. 1 (official paper of the American Trucking Association).

19. Kahn, pp. 171–73.

20. *Transport Topics* (October 24, 1956), p. 6.

21. Ibid (October 31, 1955), p. 1.

22. 70 Stat. 381:108(j) (1956), 23 U.S.C.A.:158(j) (1957)

23. See Kahn, pp. 120–23, 253–63.

24. Schwartz, pp. 196–204.

25. See Herman Mertins, Jr., *National Transportation Policy in Transition* (Lexington, Mass.: D. C. Heath & Co., 1972), pp. 77–107, for the most detailed and sophisticated analysis of the politics involved in the creation of the Department of Transportation. Mertins also argues that, since the inception of the agency, it has not been able to do comprehensive transportation planning and policymaking.

26. Ibid.

27. Ibid., pp. 175–95.

28. *Congressional Quarterly Almanac* (1965), p. 727.

29. Ibid. (1969), p. 665, and (1974), p. 705.

30. Schwartz, p. 237.

31. *National Journal Reports* (June 6, 1970), p. 1198.

32. Ibid. (July 12, 1975), p. 1032.
33. Ibid. (April 26, 1975), p. 614.
34. Ibid., p. 617.
35. See *Congressional Quarterly Almanac* (1968), pp. 519–21, and (1974), pp. 703–8, for a discussion of truck-weight and size limit politics. In 1968, the Senate Public Works Committee advocated higher truck-weight limits on interstate roads and secured passage of a bill that increased truck-weight limits to over 105,000 pounds on some trucks. It never was called up on the House floor. American Trucking Association lobbyists admitted privately that such legislation could not pass in an election year. In 1974 a more modest truck-weight limit passed the Senate. It increased weight limits for trucks using the interstate highways from 73,280 pounds to 80,000 pounds and would increase truck-weight limits in about half the states. The reason the Senate initiated this action was because Western state senators said that it was in the interest of "equity" that Western states have weight limits similar to those in the East. The 1956 legislation had grandfathered in weight and size limits in *excess* of 73,280 pounds in some (mostly Eastern) states while setting weight limits *at* 73,280 pounds in states which in 1956 were at or below that limit. Similar "equity" arguments have been used within states by the American Trucking Association before 1956 when states determined all weight and size limits. The Nixon administration supported, but did not actively lobby for this increase, which was more modest than the increase attempted in 1968. It argued that the new 55-mph speed limit on interstates and recently enacted higher tire and brake standards for large trucks would reduce safety hazards from heavier trucks on interstate roads. The House Public Works Committee deleted the Senate-passed truck-weight limits in committee but refused to support on the House floor specific language in the House bill that would direct its conferees to oppose the Senate-backed higher truck-weight limits. As in truck weight and size limit and tax legislation in 1955–56, we find that McConnell's constituency analysis is not confirmed by truck-weight and size-limit politics since 1956. For the president chose not to support the needs of wider publics, car owners, and people living near highways who oppose larger trucks. However, McConnell's constituency analysis is confirmed when we compare the actions of the Senate and the House. The Senate, whose constituencies better represent Western states took the lead on this matter. However, this is the only issue area in which we see McConnell's constituency analysis not conformed with regard to presidential and House/Senate actions. Since 1956 on the question of tax differentials between car and truck owners, a policy area we do not detail in this paper, we see presidents consistently advocating tax differentials of a far higher magnitude than those supported by the House Ways and Means Committee.

Six

★

Liberalism, Money, and the Situation of Organized Labor

Karen Orren

One of the obstacles of studying the politics of a liberal regime is precisely the permissive relations between state and society. Even in the relentless policymaking of the last half century or so, there are major institutions that are best perceived in the shadows they cast over the origins and prospects of otherwise diverse government interventions. Such an institution is organized labor.

This may seem an odd claim considering that organized labor maintains one of the most active lobbies in Washington. But an inventory of its projects ranging from public health insurance to energy to common situs picketing only heightens the sensation that this substance is less revealing than the shadows. Certainly there is nothing to suggest that labor lobbyists represent the emblematic associations of a modern liberal society, whose economic tactics regularly extend to the outer limits of tolerable collective action. This allusiveness may in part explain the extraordinary scarcity of studies of labor politics and the fact that the best of what has been written is preoccupied with the problems of why it is that American labor does not conform to some other pattern.[1]

The following essay is an attempt to politically *situate* organized labor in the United States. Its first premise is that the political significance of labor unions must be understood in the context of the changing international monetary order. The monetary system is linked to the growth of unionism by the issue of the wage level, and to union politics as the changing requirements of managing the currency modify constraints on public policy. The argument below builds on the idea that the international gold standard at once disciplined government and society and kept them at arm's distance from each other; as such, it constituted the mainspring of liberalism.[2] When the gold standard broke down, the new expandable currency enabled a patching together of a system of social privileges and compensations over which the government presided rather than ruled: thus, "interest-group liberalism." Within this general picture, organized labor may be identified as a prominent feature. Under the gold standard, the unions emerged as the most stable and effective resistance to the strictures of the monetary system; in the post–World War II period, the monetary system has been able only with great difficulty to resist the strictures of union power.

Another theme of the essay is that unions have been historically a kind of antibody to the capitalist cure: by maintaining wages above the level at which they would otherwise clear the market for labor, they interfere with the adjustment of costs necessary for the regeneration of production after a cyclical downswing. To the extent that this may have been masked by inflation, in recent years it has taken on renewed importance under foreign economic pressures. The argument may be distinguished from Marxist-influenced studies that offer an underground history of American labor, where those fragments of the working class following the logic of a social response are repeatedly overwhelmed by this or that ruling class stratagem. In this sense, also, there is a sterility to discussions about the "conservatism" of American labor. Recalling McConnell's appraisal of dollars-and-cents politics in the liberal orthodoxy, one may observe that American unions, with no political ideology or fixed alliances and little interest in codetermination of industry, cannot but be considered more "radical" than some of their European counterparts.[3]

The third perspective of the essay is shaped by the first two. The question of how the government might obey both deflationary monetary rules and tolerate self-determined labor unions was deferred for almost three decades by the grace of an international economic and political imbalance favoring the United States. The answer is found, I believe, in the relationship of labor organization to the organized action of other social groups. Except perhaps for the desultory interest in coalitions, this topic ranks high with labor on a scale of scholarly neglect—despite endless talk of systems and the fact that these relationships strikingly illustrate a practical unity in liberalism to complement the ideological. The analysis below will show that labor unions have been reconcilable with the monetary discipline they aimed to resist only under certain organizational conditions, conditions unencumbered by the interventionist state; and that unions have been reconcilable with state-administered interest-group liberalism only under changed and relaxed monetary conditions.

A last introductory remark: virtually every step of the argument is riddled with professional controversy—the causes of union growth, the role of foreign events in American depressions, the influence of unions on the structure of wages, and so on. Where possible, I have tried to avoid these disputes in order to clear some new ground that may then be open to cultivation and refinement.

I

The importance of the monetary system in the development of American labor organization over the past century is indicated on a graph plotting union membership by year: sharply up from the depression that began in 1893, sharply down after the depression of 1920–21, sharply up again during the depression of the 1930s; at no other points are there changes of comparable magnitude.[4] Each of the economic downturns was influenced by international as well as—and arguably more than—domestic forces, transmitted through the mechanism of the international gold standard.

The inexorable workings of the gold standard shaped the character of the unions: the flight abroad of gold, the contraction of domestic credit, wage reductions and unemployment; then, with lower prices for American goods, more exports, a renewed influx of gold, and business expansion. The dominant objective was the protection of wages through a strategy of organization, strikes, and collective bargaining. Although more broadly based and ideological strategies were attempted, they were, along with other drawbacks, tactically and organizationally unsuited to the rigors of deflation; in an economic system that demanded that wages go down, they were on that account not more "radical."

With the gold standard securely enshrined after the election of 1896, the monetary system determined labor politics. Under the gold standard government could and did promote business enterprise, regulate monopolies, suppress, legalize, or arbitrate strikes, and improve working conditions; the latter two, usually the domain of the states, were the subjects of labor pressure-group activity. Federal laws influenced the relative price of American goods and labor by tariffs and immigration statutes, and in these areas also labor took an active legislative role.[5] But the government could do virtually nothing to interfere with the deflationary spiral. The Federal Reserve System was designed primarily to relieve currency crises such as had occurred in the so-called Bankers' Panic of 1907; true, in 1919 it delayed tightening credit to protect agriculture and in 1920 delayed relaxing credit until wages had fallen further; but this discretion rested on the fact that most of America's trading partners had yet to restore their currencies to the gold standard following World War I. In short, since the unions' *raison d'être* was resisting and restoring wage cuts, and since by 1900 even the farmers had given up on bimetallism, the limited politics of the unions complemented their industrial strategy.

The depression of 1893 illustrates the overbearing pressures of international finance.[6] Given that the United States had a fixed exchange rate of $20.67 per ounce of gold, the fall in world gold prices during the 1890s would itself probably have forced down American prices. But as it happened, there was doubt abroad whether in the wake of the political agitation of the 1880s the government could withstand efforts to abandon the gold standard; only a poor European crop that increased the demand for dollars to buy American food stemmed the massive outflow of gold provoked in 1890 by the Sherman Silver Purchase Act and Congress's provision for higher military pensions and public works. When in the next session a bill was passed for the free coinage of silver, the outflow resumed, and frantic measures by the Treasury and private banks to acquire gold only heightened misgivings. In May 1893, after several months of depressed stock prices, the market collapsed, and runs on banks and public hoarding of currency followed one another in a panic, reinforcing the deflationary effects of the continuing gold drain; in August, New York banks suspended cash payments to their depositors. By fall, business loans were down 15 percent from their annual peak. For the next three and a half years labor was forced to play its part. At the time of the banking panic there were already over one million or about one-sixth of the labor force unemployed; in the next year lower wages were paid to almost every group on which there are historical records—transportation, bituminous coal, the building trades, unskilled and farm workers, manufacturing workers except printers, and federal employees except postal workers.[7]

All of the major strikes of the period attempted to roll back wage reductions: Cripple Creek (1893), Great Northern Railway (1894), bituminous coal (1894), Pullman (1894), meat packers (1894), and Leadville silver mines (1896). Union membership figures give little indication of the dimensions of resistance: for example, the United Mine Workers had less than 20,000 members in 1894 when 125,000 men struck the mines. But what is even more significant is that the crisis honed a finer point to labor's weapons. Certainly wage cutting had been a cause of numerous and important strikes before; but earlier it had mingled with ideas of socialism, anarchism, producers' cooperatives; and there had been a stronger emphasis on legislative action. Now, whatever was left of these doctrines by the 1890s was sloughed off: fraternal elements that had survived the Knights of Labor, for example, the end to secrecy and ritualism in the Industrial Association of Machinists; the defeat of the political program within the American Federation of Labor, isolating the Socialists from the main body of the labor movement; the latter event mirrored in specific industries, for example, the end of the Marxist Hebrew Trades as an important influence in the garment centers. Appeals for sympathy strikes were turned aside by labor leaders; the Pullman disaster in particular was interpreted as a stunning lesson in the pitfalls of the general strike and "One Big Union," as well as in the inherent hostility of government.

Institutional changes accompanied and reproduced labor's preoccupation with protecting wages. The first was the growing domination of the AFL: by 1897 the AFL comprised 60 percent of all union members, and with the return of prosperity and recruitment of new workers this figure was 80 percent of 1904. Another 10 percent was claimed by the equally wage-conscious railway brotherhoods.[8] Second was the establishment of permanent structures of labor-management bargaining across a given trade or industry. This system had been tried in the stove-molding industry in 1891, where unions and trade associations set up machinery to handle grievances and enforce rules of strike conduct, but it had not covered wages paid at individual work sites. This last, in a detailed schedule of rates to level competitive conditions among mines in different locations and terrains, was the achievement of the Interstate Agreement in bituminous coal mining, negotiated as a result of the strike in 1897 when the industry's wages hit their historical bottom, and generally considered to be the greatest labor victory of the decade.

The social implications of the trade agreement were seen in the bitter anthracite strikes of 1902, when the bituminous miners kept their contract and did not strike in sympathy. As if in final repudiation of the class solidarity rhetoric of the previous decade, there was the founding in 1893 of the Chicago Civic Federation, composed of leading labor and business leaders, which intervened in a number of strikes and wage disputes; this later grew to a national organization led by Mark Hanna and Samuel Gompers, chairman and vice-chairman, which both repudiated the "open shop" position of the National Association of Manufacturers and defended the virtues of business monopolies that were growing apace with unions as a result of the depression.[9]

The depression of 1920–21 proved the effectiveness of labor's strategy of protecting wages and its liabilities in a time of falling prices. As in 1893, the downturn was a kind of accidental overdose of medicine prescribed anyway, this time because of grossly inflated wartime prices and the post-Armistice repatriation of foreign gold.[10] But the Federal Reserve Board, insecure in the face of its first test at monetary stabilization since its creation in 1913, pressured by the Treasury to maintain the value of government bonds and solicitous of a financially overextended agricultural sector that had many friends in a Congress still armed with the Overman Act, kept its loans below market rates, fueling rather than dampening the inflation. Not until the end of 1919, when gold had been withdrawn to a level perilously near the minimum reserved required by law, were discount rates raised but then very steeply. By August, the downward snap in prices could be compared only with the contractions following the War of 1812 and the Civil War. Unemployment climbed to over 15 percent in 1921, in 1922 to 27 percent in construction and 54 percent in mining. Wages fell, the largest monthly drop on record, 7 percent in January 1921, and kept declining until they had reached a 20 percent decrease one year later.

Strikes in coal mining, textiles, printing, clothing manufacturing, railway shops, and parts of the construction industry successfully opposed wage reductions. In general, workers in industries with significant union membership suffered less wage deflation than nonunion industries. Comparing hourly wages—that is, not taking into account the fact that businesses often reduced payrolls by cutting hours or laying off workers, always the union preferences—union scales remained virtually flat, whereas workers in nonunion industries experienced a 17 percent cut. This last was more than the drop in consumer prices, constituting a loss of real earnings of 3 percent, while the union groups actually gained. Moreover, the fact that nonunion wages plus fringe benefits rose more rapidly with the return of prosperity and the onset of the era of "welfare capitalism" suggests that the *sole* economic benefit of union membership during these years was as a cushion against deflationary shocks.[11]

These successes, however, could not conceal the hazards of labor's present tack in the face of changed circumstances. Due to the great increases in productivity brought about by World War I and by the technologies of electricity and combustion engines, prices had fallen and real wages were rising. Not only did this further hamper organizing efforts in an atmosphere suffused with anti-Bolshevism and a surplus of labor from the depressed farm regions but also in 1920–21 arbitrators' awards frequently used a cost-of-living standard to scale down union demands.[12] In 1921, the Executive Council of the AFL called at the convention for a "well-considered theory capable of real service in the practical problem of determining wages."

The dilemma, which was to plague organized labor throughout the decade, was in part a consequence of the institution of the Federal Reserve System and its substitution of government control for the reflexes of private bankers. As already explained, the System was fairly helpless in the situation of a gold outflow. But since there was no legal *maximum* of gold backing to the currency, when gold flowed into the country in enormous quantities in the 1920s to purchase inexpensive goods and securities, the New York Federal Reserve Bank "sterilized" it; in other words, it did not allow the gold to proportionately expand the currency and cause a rise in prices, as would have happened automatically under the pre-1913 monetary regime. This was done because in the opinion of Bank Governor Strong and others expansion would have destabilizing effects on booming American industry; and the System countered agriculture's demand for more currency by low-interest rates and by gold certificates that at once built a public constituency for gold and ended up back in the safety deposit boxes at the banks.[13]

The question might be raised whether labor's support of the 1924 La Follette campaign, calling among other things for legislative measures to stop the Federal Reserve's "deflation," did not reflect labor's organizational frustrations in the midst of industrial prosperity; more likely the endorsement was because of the farmer-labor plank against the Esch-Cummins Transportation Act, under which the railroad workers had recently received a wage cut, and the party's opposition to the labor injunction; most likely of all, it was simply because the Democrats had nominated the conservative John W. Davis. But the campaign aside, the general reticence of Gompers and other labor leaders on the money question was entirely appropriate to a movement both dedicated to the welfare of existing trade unionists and dependent on worsening economic conditions in order to gain new recruits.

In any case, the AFL was ready with its revised strategy at the convention of 1925. Workers must continue to "oppose all wage reductions," but now the accent would be shifted from the distribution side of the economic process to the production side. Wages were above all necessary to stabilize the purchasing power of labor; and so that selling prices be lower and wages higher the AFL recommended union-management cooperation with the goal of increasing efficiency. By efficiency the AFL did not mean more labor-saving machinery but rather scientific management techniques, toward which it relinquished its previous sarcastic opposition, and the elimination of "waste." As it had in the war, labor would participate on production committees in return for collective bargaining.[14]

The organizational thrust of such a position might be described as "boring from above," and that was the tactic adopted by the AFL in the campaigns to unionize the auto assembly plants and southern textiles. In the first, letters were sent to officials of General Motors and Henry Ford offering to "mobilize the creative ability of workers"; in textiles, local strikers were assisted by the distribution of cooperation propaganda and AFL staff speeches before church groups and Chambers of

Commerce. These campaigns failed for a variety of reasons besides their apparent innocence, one of them being the organizers' inability to answer the question of why an outside union, and not a company union, was needed to participate in increasing productivity. Where union-management cooperation had its strongest appeal was for aging companies or those in declining industries already locked into collective bargaining agreements, whose competitors could take advantage of low costs in purchasing plant and equipment.[15]

The adverse course charted for unions against other nonmanagement groups is indicated in a pamphlet the AFL issued to explain the new wage policy. "Higher productivity without corresponding increase of real wages means that the social position of the wage earner in relation to other consumers becomes worse," and in 1927 the *Federationist* began to publish monthly indexes of labor's share in production and consumption, along with studies of individual industries to show the variance of labor's portion of value-added by manufacture; unions finding their portion dropping due to "unjustifiable" increases in other factors were urged to press for increases in wages. But if organized labor now traded the Knights' vision of a phalanx of the middle classes for going it alone with management in productivity conferences, the unions picked up new allies among intellectuals and academics: John Dewey wrote in the *New Republic* that the AFL was "no longer cursed as revolutionary and subversive but blessed as constructive, safe, and patriotic"; economics professors praised labor's new wage-and-production theories because they were similar to their own.[16] Persons such as these had never fancied the dreamy Knights, and their power was on the rise.

Some scholars friendly to the New Deal have ridiculed the idea that the great depression of the 1930s was in any important respect caused by events abroad.[17] Insofar as they refer only to the stock market crash of 1929, they are on reasonable ground; although here, too, one might counter that the excess of speculation can be traced straight to the Federal Reserve's policy in the mid-1920s of keeping interest rates in New York lower than those in London in order to ease Britain's climb back onto gold. More significant is that the crash and subsequent bank failures and gold outflow in 1930 did not resolve itself through the cycle of banking suspensions, rise in interest rates, return of gold, and business revival as happened in the Panic of 1907. There is evidence of this familiar sequence (minus the suspensions) and an upturn in economic conditions in the first months of 1931; it is at this point, the economy's failure to continue upward, that foreign events become the critical factor.[18]

In May 1931, Austria's largest private bank, the Kreditanstalt, was forced to close, followed in July by the closing of banks in Germany and the freezing of foreign assets, especially assets of Britain and the United States. This provoked a run on the pound sterling by France and Holland, all climaxing on September 2 when Britain abandoned the gold standard. Anticipating the same action by the American government, public and private holders of dollars abroad and of securities on deposit in this country began to rapidly convert them to gold. By mid-October the gold stock had declined so drastically as to have offset all of the net influx of the previous two years. In response to the outflow, the New York Federal Reserve Bank raised its discount rate from 1½ ro 2½ to 3½ percent in the passage of a single week. While this unprecedentedly severe step slowed the drain temporarily, it also created a dramatic increase in bank failures and currency hoarding. By January 1932, money available for business activity was 30 percent lower than when Britain left gold.

Only with this wrenching contraction did wages give way to the deepening crisis. Because prices had declined steadily after the stock market crash—wholesale prices fell by 10 percent in 1930 and 15 percent in 1931—real wages of workers who remained employed had actually increased. Business and government leaders, as well as the unions themselves, kept to the doctrine of the 1920s that wages must be maintained for purchasing power, and the large corporations in particular resisted reducing wages until fall 1931, even though by that time there were over eight million unemployed. Then, shortly after Britain abandoned gold, U.S. Steel, Bethlehem, and General Motors led the way for the others. Wages went careening downward until in March 1933 weekly earnings were only 49 percent of what they had been in 1929; accounting for the drop in the cost of living, real earnings had dropped 29 percent.

A careful study of the years 1929–33 finds that once again unions succeeded in protecting their own: classed according to their previous wage levels and trends, industry groups with a high degree of unionization showed wage declines of 10, 8, 12, and 6 percent, compared with nonunion cuts in each group of 36, 17, 17, and 17 percent, respectively—permitting as a conservative conclusion that union wages were approximately 30 percent higher than nonunion wages in 1933. Moreover, the workers in the process of becoming organized enjoyed greater immunity from reductions than those already organized, suggesting attempts by employers to ward off unionization; where the union was weakening, wages dropped to the level of unorganized workers.[19]

It would be satisfying to round out this section with the argument that unions had brought about the end of the gold standard whose deflationary discipline they had organized to resist. Several leading economists in the 1920s and 1930s in effect made this claim, that the rigidity of wages prolonged and intensified the necessary painful readjustments or caused such a volume of unemployment as to make recovery a near impossibility.[20] I shall abide by the resolve, however, to skirt economic controversy and conclude only with the observation that "wages are sticky downward" would be an axiom of monetary policy from now on. And, of course, the United States did not finally abandon gold for another thirty-eight years.

II

The New Deal is the link between the gold standard era and the monetary system of the postwar period. It is difficult to conceive how the gold standard might have been reinstated internationally without dismantling the social and political structures wrought by the domestic policies of the 1930s. One thinks perhaps of the deficit spending and consequent inflation necessary to lubricate the vast machinery of subsidies, public works, and regulatory price fixing that would later be known under the rubric of "interest-group liberalism." But inflation as such was not incompatible with the gold standard, provided that gold supplies are ample and that all trading partners are bent on an expansionary economic policy, which, after the disaster of the depression and the buoyancy of wartime production, the Allies all were. The more difficult issue, and the one that the Bretton Woods planners papered over rather than spoil the mood of collaboration, is the downward adjustment of prices and incomes within nations when trade imbalances inevitably occur.[21] The deflationary prescription of the gold standard had provoked disruptive, sometimes violent, and above all successful resistance when the labor movement was small. Given the scope of organization at the close of the decade and the specific strength of unions within the major export industries, the likelihood of worker acquiescence and the political will to secure it seem to have been at best remote.

What had caused the impasse? It is generally taken for granted that the New Deal changed and strengthened labor unions, but in a manner that has been imperfectly understood. Apart from the scholarly neglect of the specific relevance of the international dimension, there are other confusing elements. One is the prominent role of labor in the Roosevelt coalition after 1936. Insofar as this is seen as an electoral and legislative buttress to labor's changed industrial position and the enlarged role of the federal government in fighting depression, and not as some change of heart from a perversely apolitical past, it is an important factor.[22] However, the suggestion that it represented a serious deviation from unionism "pure-and-simple" is misleading: organized labor emerged from the depression and, for that matter, from World War II as wage conscious as before and, as both Roosevelt and Truman learned to their chagrin, without the slightest indication of having taken on compromising alliances.

The more complex issue is the extent to which the upsurge of labor militancy and organization was in response to New Deal labor policies—in particular the National Recovery Act and the Wagner Act—as part of a vague design for a corporatist state. Schlesinger writes that "the NRA and Section 7(b) came to Minneapolis" and "the NRA came to San Francisco"; but these phrases preface narratives of strikes ended in the old-fashioned way of state militia and arbitration, except that in San Francisco Hugh Johnson, head of the NRA, did arrive to denounce the strikers as a threat and a menace.[23] Certainly the NRA was a "historic moment," as John L. Lewis said, but whether it was a historic moment different from, say, the 1918 Armistice which signaled an even more widespread series of strikes is difficult to determine; in important defeats such as in autos, textiles, at the Weirton steel works and elsewhere, the moment arrived too soon. More important, there is the question of whether the speculative boom in industrial production in spring and summer 1933, providing the first favorable conditions in many years for workers to recoup their losses, might not itself have triggered the union activity.

Within the scheme of the NRA, moreover, labor unions were superfluous. The primary goal of the NRA, to stimulate production through higher wages and prices, was accomplished through the minimum-wage and maximum-hour provisions of the industry codes established by businessmen among themselves; of the over seven hundred code-making procedures, labor was represented with voting privileges in twenty-three and without voting privileges in twenty-seven.[24] Anything that might disturb the stability of these cartels was contrary to the logic of the act, and the National Labor Board worked vigorously to avoid strikes.

The Wagner Act proved far more favorable to labor's aims, but probably least so in stimulating union organization. The important breakthroughs in the mass-production industries and the split in the AFL were already underway at the time of its passage. Again, most of the activity, as well as its ebb, can be explained by the strategically favorable business upturn of 1935 and the recession of 1937. The major union campaigns of the 1930s were marked by the company espionage and pitched battles that characterized earlier struggles in labor history; the difference between victory and defeat in a major strike still often hinged, as before, on the intervention of the state governor. The delaying tactics of business—refusal to bargain, refusal to sign a written contract—were effectively eliminated only after 1938 when the most dramatic gains had already been registered.[25]

None of this is to argue that the National Recovery Act and the National Labor Relations Board did not play an important part in union tactics, but rather that independent elements of economic conditions and worker and company strength are sufficient to account for what happened. It is interesting in this regard to compare 1933–38 with 1898–1904. Both periods are characterized by steady growth in manufacturing following severe depressions, each with a year of downturn at the end (1937 being more severe) and milder fluctuations (1900, 1902, 1934) midway. From 1898 to 1904 unions quadrupled their membership from a half-million to over two million or 6.5 percent of the civilian labor force; in the second period unions increased from around 6 percent or three million members to over seven million or 13.4 percent of the work force. Considering that in 1900 twice as many workers were engaged in agriculture and that the attitude of government was often not only not neutral but actively hostile; and considering that the depression of the 1930s began with an already established labor movement with seasoned leaders, well entrenched in many industries (construction, clothing, railroads, anthracite coal, printing) and with embryonic organizations elsewhere, the contribution of New Deal labor policies appear to be less than decisive.

If this interpretation is correct, the particular accomplishments of the New Deal period may be observed best *after* the depression, in the years immediately following World War II, when union membership continued to grow. The impetus to the rash of postwar strikes was a reduction in real wages administered by the government's Little Steel formula and by layoffs and reduced hours, while prices moved upward with the lifting of controls. In that sense, the circumstances were not unlike those that spurred worker militancy following the Civil War and World War I. Again, comparison with these earlier episodes is instructive, for they point to the fact that the Roosevelt years modified what historically had been certain social limits to labor union growth. Put somewhat differently, the policies of the New Deal may be said to have neutralized inherent capacities for organization of different social groups and to have changed the system of checks among them. In doing so, they at once undermined what had been the pliant social base of the gold standard and laid the labor bedrock of postwar money.

One important check on union growth was agriculture. Because food has always claimed a large portion of a worker's income, a period of declining prices for agricultural products relative to industrial prices has usually meant an increase in real wages. Insofar as a primary benefit of union membership is the protection of the worker's income, such an automatic increase is a disincentive to union membership. Thus the decade of the 1920s liberally extended credit during the war and paid unprecedented prices for their products; farmers had spent much of their windfall on land speculation and breeding animals. The delay of the Federal Reserve in contracting credit to correspond to the outflow of gold was especially catastrophic in this respect, for the most frantic speculation took place in the immediate postwar boom. When the tightening finally came it caused a collapse, first in real estate, then in small-town banking. More important, the ending of wartime credits to foreign governments meant a steady loss of the European markets. After the trough of the depression in the summer of 1921, industrial prices began to rise again, but agriculture did not share in the recovery. Since an average of 40 percent of a worker's paycheck went for food, even as money wages were being cut real wages rose: they recovered to 90 percent of their 1920 level by 1923. Farm prices, however, dropped to only 53 percent of their 1920 level and recovered more slowly over the decade.[26]

The 1870s, despite the usual characterization as a depression era, shows a similar pattern. Although there was a recession in 1872 and a financial panic in 1873, the number of railway track miles and the output of coal, pig iron, and copper doubled during the decade; manufacturing claimed 30 percent more workers in 1879 than in 1869.[27] During the Civil War wages had risen, and even though they lagged considerably behind the rise in prices, in 1869 they stood 40 percent above prewar levels. Agricultural prices, on the other hand, had doubled during the war but dropped abruptly afterward; with land in cultivation greatly expanded by the Homestead Act, prices continued to decline until the panic of 1873, when they leveled off for the rest of the 1870s at roughly prewar levels. As with World War I, the Civil War was followed by a spurt of trade union activity, only to have members fall away with the break in business conditions and fail to return to the rolls with the recovery.

The two major waves of farm organization correspond to these periods of severely depressed prices. Beginning in the 1870s, there were several primitive attempts to cooperatively purchase equipment and supplies, and the Farmer Union and the Farmers' Equity tried to fix the prices of cotton and wheat, respectively, through systems of crop withholding and cooperative marketing. The most successful operations of this type were the cooperative grain elevators and the unusually businesslike California Fruit Growers exchange; but in general these ventures were doomed by the sheer number and diversity of farmers involved. The fragmentary strength of farm groups was more effectively spent as a protest against the organizational advantages of big business, especially railroads, and they initiated a long series of legislative acts against price fixing, discriminatory rates, and the consolidation of parallel lines. In the 1920s there were new attempts to raise the price of farm products through producers' cooperatives and the so-called Sapiro plan for "orderly marketing"; but again, organizational rivalries and regional and commodity differences were more easily submerged in obtaining changes in the antitrust laws to permit cooperative than they were in actual commerce, and almost all of the plans failed. Nor was the Hoover Farm Board more successful when it tried to stop avalanching prices by organizing existing and new cooperatives into a number of marketing corporations along commodity lines and supported by government loans.

The New Deal cut the Gordian knot: voluntary programs to limit production, marketing agreements with food processors, and, later, a system of marketing-quota procedures; in other words, the favorite techniques of monopolies and cartels, but now the government paid the farmers for their participation with acreage rentals, allotment benefits, and price supports. When World War II required that farmers produce more of certain commodities at controlled prices, their further cooperation was sweetened by the promise of price supports based on parity for two years after the hostilities ended; then, in order that agricultural markets not be permitted to collapse as they had following the Civil War and World War I, price supports became a permanent fixture of public policy. It has been estimated that in any given year between 1948 and 1972 farm prices were on the average 40 percent higher than they would have been without price supports; translated into food costs, that is, allowing for varying cost of marketing, prices to consumers would have been roughly half that saving or an average of 20 percent.[28] Moreover, the overall stabilization of prices removed the episodes of rapid decline in the cost of living which contributed to the weakening of laboring organization.

A second social limit to union growth had been the capacity of businessmen to organize to resist and reverse union encroachment on what they considered their domain. One type of this organization is, of course, the corporation itself, which historically had as one motive for forming a more effective defense against employee militancy; with their extensive resources corporations were best able to utilize the full range of antilabor methods, from the sticks of blacklisting and private police to the carrots of welfare capitalism.[29] Also, however, small and medium-sized businesses commonly grouped together for offensive combat against trade union. While these groupings first became a regular part of the industrial scene in the 1880s when they successfully aimed against the Knights of Labor, they appear in their most aggressive and imaginative forms in the years following labor victories, in the late 1890s and early 1900s, and in 1920–21. They were a great variety: trade associations within industries that, among other things, organized labor bureaus to bypass union business agents; coalitions of local businessmen that paid workers not to strike and employers to hold out against employees; "citizen alliances," local groups led by the National Association of Manufacturers that called for boycott of union-made goods; the massive postwar drive known as the "American Plan," made up of literally hundreds of open-shop groups across the country.

Most of the preferred tactics of both corporations and trade groups were proscribed as unfair labor practices in the Wagner Act; in the postwar period employer animus has been diverted to legislative arenas where the requirements of political compromise and the vagaries of administration have blunted antiunion attacks.[30] Moreover, there are several subtle ways in which the NLRB had hindered business combination against business in determining the appropriateness of the bargaining unit, where the inclusion of several firms in a multiemployer unit may increase the employers' strength in a competitive industry. For example, if a group of employers seeks to form such a unit along with one union that has organized the majority of employees, it will not be done over the protest of another union that has organized the majority of employees in a single company unless there is a clear bargaining history to support the larger unit. Also, until Taft-Hartley made it illegal, the NLRB always recognized the smaller unit where the larger would mean that the majority of employees would vote not to be represented by a union; after 1947, although the board took the position that all categories of employees would be included in a multiemployer unit where that was the established pattern, single units were approved if it could be shown that the larger unit would impede union organization. Analogously, these rulings apply to multiplant units within a large corporation, weakening the employer's ability to exploit the advantages of size and diversity against union organizing.[31]

Second is the use of the lockout as a weapon to contest union demands in collective bargaining. Until the early 1960s, lockouts were permitted to multiplant units only in the face of unusual economic or operational difficulties that would result from a threatened strike, and not as a means of bringing pressure on one group of employees by locking out another. In the multiemployer unit, the question has turned on whether one member company can lock out his employees to protect himself against a "whipsaw" or selective strike against another member. Until 1954, the NLRB said no, seriously undercutting the employers' interest in group bargaining; until 1965, such defensive multiemployer lockouts were permitted only if no temporary replacements were used for the locked-out workers. And the idea that one employer might lock out employees to support a fellow employer in some other bargaining unit has been dismissed as "an invitation to industrial chaos."[32] Although under the Wagner Act neither the lockout or bargaining unit structure may be used offensively to destroy unions per se, and in any case could not be expected to have the dramatic effects of blacklisting and espionage, the restrictions on companies' collective defenses in bargaining may be an important aspect of the relative advantages of union membership.

The monetary circumstances in which these changes occurred illustrate the transitional nature of the New Deal, were fundamental to its achievements, and may be stated concisely. Most important, the success of the agricultural price supports and the Wagner Act were entirely dependent on the absence of international economic discipline. The higher prices for goods and labor would under normal conditions have cause an outflow of gold and either a decline in prices or an increase in unemployment; both of these results were incompatible with the aims of recovery in general and the protection of union privileges in particular. But by the early 1930s the organization of international bankers and governments that had managed the gold standard was in shambles, and, after an initial jump in gold imports following the dollar devaluation that accompanied the Agricultural Adjustment Act in 1934, gold continued to flow to the United States as a result of political instability in Europe, especially France.

On the other hand, the fact that an expansionary domestic policy could be pursued *without* actually abandoning the gold standard had, I believe, certain long-range effects on the future position of organized labor. In the first place, at a minimum the break with gold, had it occurred, almost certainly would have meant greater White House receptiveness to proposals by Federal Reserve Board Chairman Eccles for a closer integration of monetary and fiscal policy. Second, abandoning gold and thus explicitly acknowledging the nation's economic independence might have strengthened the "planner" faction within the administration, especially the group active after the NRA debacle—Ezekiel, Means, Chase, Loeb, and others. Any of their various schemes for government-directed business expansion would have been incompatible with the usual process of collective bargaining without regard for productivity or overall utilization of resources.[33] Finally, the continued promise to buy gold at $35 an ounce had by the end of World War II attracted three-quarters of the world's gold to the United States, and this abundance was an important reason for American opposition at Bretton Woods to Keynes's plan for an international clearinghouse without gold. Without building speculation, suffice to say that had the plan been implemented the postwar system in which organized labor would play so prominent a role would have been vastly different.

III

If the New Deal changed organized labor's *quantitative* position, so to speak, the monetary system instituted after World War II made the critical *qualitative* difference. From the situation of being the major group resistance to the discipline of the gold standard, unions became a primary determinant of society's money supply, the level of prices, and the value of the currency in circulation. This is not to say that labor leaders perceive their power in this way instead of in terms of their bargaining strength or that, at least until very recently, they would attribute it to the Federal Reserve as well as, say, the Wagner Act; indeed, at the point of individual union behavior the objective remains the same: of protecting wages, now against inflation and the cost of living rather than deflation. But for organized labor as a bloc or unified interest, the monetary system has shaped its relations with government; it may partly explain also the union's passivity in organizing new members.

This shift in labor's position is based on a reversal in the postwar system of the relationship between the price of gold and all other prices—including the price of labor or wages—which prevailed under the gold standard. When the government promised to exchange an ounce of gold for $20.67, there could be no more money in circulation than there was gold to cover the obligation (or, really, that part of existing dollars that might reasonably be expected to be presented for exchange). Government policy could try to improve the country's gold position by tariffs or interest rates to attract capital from abroad; but within these bounds, all other prices represented a competition for shares of available currency. Thus, higher wages for some workers could mean lower profits, or unemployment and lower wages for other workers. In either case, that was secondary to the setting of the gold price.[34]

The Bretton Woods agreements also provided that America would fix a gold price, which it did at $35. But since the vast portion of the world's gold was buried at Fort Knox and America's trading partners fixed their currencies to the dollar, the gold price was no longer an effective constraint on how many dollars could be placed in circulation. Instead, the Employment Act of 1946, which was actually the confirmation of policies followed since 1940, directed the monetary authorities to seek "maximum employment, production, and purchasing power." Almost two decades and several skirmishes with the concept of full employment later, the Federal Reserve described its mission as follows: "Monetary policy focuses on the volume and availability of bank reserves in relation to the credit demand being generated by current economic forces, and assesses whether the volume of such demands, given the share being satisfied by bank credit and monetary.expansion, is making for inflationary or deflationary tendencies."[35] In other words, assessments aside, the number of dollars, that is, their value, is established in response to economic forces, including the force or price of labor rather than the other way around.

This reversal did not determine that unions would take on the role that they did, but it created the definite possibility. When a wage bargain is struck it generally creates a need by the employer for more dollars from his banker. If the employer raises his prices, this will ordinarily increase the need for dollars by the company's customers, whether other companies or final consumers. The Federal Reserve, watching the tugs on the credit lines from the banks, must make a decision whether to accommodate the demand for more dollars; or to allow the new price to compete for available purchasing power and, should the price hold, reduce the demand for other goods and cause temporary unemployment with the aim of bringing the economy back into adjustment through a reallocation of resources. Should the Federal Reserve decide to accommodate a rise in wages greater or lower than an equivalent rise in production—a fortuitous result since productivity is not normally a subject in American collective bargaining—the process will have lowered or raised the value of dollars held by society as a whole.

There were, from the end of the war onward, several reasons why, just taking the union side into account, adjustment instead of accommodation would be difficult. First was the scope of collective bargaining itself, extending over the basic industries—transportation, utilities, construction, manufacturing; and the union's practiced ability, proven repeatedly over the decades to come, to protect wages in a time of slackening employment. Since "wages are sticky downward" was a premise accepted even by employers, the resistance to deceleration of wage increases became, in the expansion-minded postwar period, the equivalent to resisting wage cuts under the gold standard.[36] Second, contracts extending longer than the span of a year made their debut in the General Motors–United Auto Workers settlement of 1948 and spread to other industries in the 1950s, insulating union wages from monetary restraint and putting whatever pressure might be applied on the economy elsewhere. Third, wages in the highly organized and oligopolistic "heavy" industries rise together in patterns which, while not entirely unresponsive to employment and profits, are removed from the supply-and-demand conditions that determine the setting of wages in unorganized industries; this expands the impact of any given wages in settlement and makes any required adjustment that much more substantial.[37]

The Federal Reserve Board, for its part, would seem among the institutions directed by law to seek full employment the most likely candidate to resist union-wage pressures. In addition to its relative remove from politics, it has since the war taken the longer view, emphasizing the possibility of inflation causing a 1929-style depression; has tempered its unemployment estimates with such factors as age, sex, and skill level which it considers immune to monetary policy; and has consistently been concerned about the international position of the dollar. So it is interesting to observe the Federal Reserve's actions in the decade from 1955, when the *Minutes* of the Federal Open Market Committee report Chairman Martin's conclusion that the economy was suffering from "wage-cost-push-inflation," through 1964, just prior to the Vietnam buildup. The first characteristic of the *Minutes* is a regular attentiveness to collective bargaining developments, a fairly even-handed scorn by the chairman and others for both unions and management who expect the monetary authorities to "validate" their wage bargains, and a repeated warning that the System must not validate them because of inflationary tendencies which could lead to depression and the pricing of American goods out of the world market. The second characteristic is the constantly stated intention to "signal" the parties of the committee's determination on that score, combined with the failure for a variety of reasons to take any action.

One reason that appears most often is the coincidence of a wage hike with the Treasury's coming to market and the Federal Reserve System's duty to do nothing that might destabilize market conditions: that was the restraining influence, for example, after the increase in oil wages in 1959 and after the dock settlement of 1963. Foreign concerns intervened: the steel settlement of 1956, which Martin termed a "disaster," was reluctantly validated because the System's desire to support the British pound after the Middle East crisis; and the steel settlement of 1960, because the System must not appear to be trying to stifle the European boom underway. There was unwillingness to tighten during a recession, as with the auto and aircraft contracts of 1958; and when a recovery was weak and there was an overhang of unemployment, as with the trucking, electrical appliance, and auto settlements of 1964. Strikes were uniformly treated as times when no tightening action could be taken because of their effects on productivity. Similarly, although there was frequently the impulse to send a signal during contract negotiations, the committee's hand was stayed by the fear that if the settlement was still generous and inflation continued it would seem a futile gesture and create political problems for the System.[38]

This is not to say that there was never a tightening in response to wage increases: for example, there was after the workers in the copper and auto industries received automatic raises in June and July of 1956;

and earlier that year a general tightening was intended to "strengthen the backs" of businessmen in negotiations to come. But by August the committee followed the chairman's intuition that it was time to relax credit; he had seen help-wanted signs near the railroad station in Chicago even though it was summertime when there was ordinarily a low demand for labor, and there was "an important political decision [the presidential election] coming up in eight weeks." And, although the recession triggered by the Federal Reserve in 1957 was due to overexpansion in the capital goods sector, there are indications in the *Minutes* that the degree of tightening was partly due to regret over not having acted to stem inflationary wage increases the previous year. But again the stop-go pattern was the rule, and during 1958 the System embarked on an expansion.[39]

Moreover, after the recessions of 1957 and 1959 failed to slow wage increases and the high interest rates of 1966 spent their entire force against the housing industry, monetary authorities as well as other economic agencies in the government began to give up on the idea of resisting wage increases directly. In 1969, as money supply growth was reduced from 6.5 percent annual rate in 1968 to 2.8 percent, and negotiations continued to push wages upward—the construction workers gained their largest increases since 1951—the Nixon administration announced that it fully expected and would not blame unions and management if they raised wages and prices in their own interest and hoped only that the tightening of credit would break their inflationary outlook for the future.

Organized labor's ability to induce rather than conform to monetary policy has dominated its relations with the administrative branch of government since the 1950s. The emphasis on wage-price programs since the Vietnam War on slowing domestic inflation has raised the issue in its plainest form; in the second-term Eisenhower and Kennedy administration, attention was focused on the more benign question of the tendency of wages to advance ahead of productivity, thereby worsening the U.S. balance-of-payments and weakening the dollar abroad—without, however, as would have happened under the gold standard, bringing international pressures to adjust domestic industry. There can be no question that the recurrent White House concern with wage settlements reflected underlying political strain; but the description of government-labor relations by one Nixon price controller as a "continuing courtship" more accurately accounts for the details of the entire period.[40]

Characteristic of administration deference to group power generally, the recognition and enhancement of union leaders in both their industrial and power-broker roles was a bipartisan affair, the Democrats encouraged by political alliance and the Republicans by a philosophical reticence toward government intervention in the economy. It is worth noting that the most conservative of the postwar presidents, Eisenhower, had as his two most influential cabinet members Charles Wilson, who as vice-president of General Motors introduced the escalator clause into collective bargaining, and George Humphrey, who with Benjamin Fairless of U.S. Steel had negotiated the 1947 steel contract largely on John L. Lewis's terms. The cultivation of selected union leaders—Reuther and later Woodcock of the UAW, McDonald of the Steelworkers, and Meany of the AFL-CIO—corresponded to the economic theories held by successive councils on economic advisors about the importance of the "key" industries; and in return the administrations got help on miscellaneous labor disputes: McDonald's willingness to cooperate with Kennedy in the steel intervention in 1962, Reuther's public opposition to the 1967 New York subway strike, Meany's participation on the Nixon Pay Board, and so on. Indeed, it is arguable that no aspect of public policy has done more to legitimize the power of organized labor than the long sequence of administrative attempts to persuade them to control wages. Each, from Eisenhower's exhortations to the recent Carter voluntary guidelines, is based on the premise that labor leaders are insulated from market pressures and may take a statesmanlike attitude. Even the strategy of singling out a scapegoat as an example of the misuse of power—usually this has been the construction unions, given special denouncing by Johnson, placed under a freeze five months before everyone else and deprived of their privileges under the Davis-Bacon Act by the Nixon administration, and the object of the special wage-stabilization program under Ford—has suggested the justice of union wage-making activities as a whole. And the readiness with which each administration has withdrawn from the fray at the early signs of real battle is tacit, if grudging, acceptance of the industrial status quo.

With regard to the Congress, labor leaders have been able to trade a cooperative attitude toward wage controls for presidential support of priority legislation: in the case of the Kennedy guidelines, support for manpower training; for the 1966 guidelines, Johnson's reversal on the minimum-wage increase; for the Nixon Pay Board, concessions on bargaining rights for public employees; and since the wage programs were short-lived and/or not enforced, labor got the best of the bargain. The broader significance of the postwar monetary system for labor's legislative strategy is more complex. From one point of view, since the monetary system acts as context for unions rooted in the industrial sphere, no special legislative objectives are entailed beside labor's steady support for welfare and labor measures. At least, that was the case until recently.[41] But considered in light of the monetary context, these objectives themselves take on a different meaning. Three examples may be offered as working hypotheses. Consider the matter of expenditures for purposes such as defense, public works, medical insurance: apart from direct benefits to union members, deficit spending is the complement to monetary policy in an approach to full employment and stable prices by the manipulation of aggregate demand. As such it displaces other possible approaches, including direct governmental intervention in specific labor markets, which would intrude on union prerogatives. Also, there is the impact of deficits on monetary action, the degree to which those expenditures are financed by Federal Reserve purchases of government securities and results in more expansion than otherwise.[42]

Second is the issue of unemployment. Labor unions have historically been vulnerable to the charge that by restricting markets and maintaining wages at high levels they cause unemployment.[43] One of the major benefits of postwar economic policy has been to lift this stigma from the unions and place it on government; and in the late 1950s the doctrine of the Phillips curve had turned collectively bargained inflation into a kind of manpower program, a "trade-off" against more people out of work. The monetary system operated to make the *existence* of unemployment a foundation of union power, since the higher the unemployment rate the less likely the Federal Reserve would "invalidate" wage bargains. As the Marxists might put it, the reserve army reinforced the reserve level, inverting the laws of supply and demand in the process. Given the fact that the expanding and contracting pool of unemployed are either unskilled and unlikely to enter the unionized sector or at the lower end of wages and seniority within unions, fluctuating unemployment at moderate levels under an accommodating monetary regime may be more advantageous than nearly full employment. Nevertheless, unemployment, particularly with its racial composition, remains the domestic Achilles' heel of organized labor. The resulting ambiguity may be an important aspect of the labor–liberal–civil rights coalition; in fact, one might date its start and finish from the 1940s when unemployment was a volatile issue inside the Democratic Party—a favorite cause of the liberals and a main rationale for the Southern wing's plan for using the antitrust laws against unions—to the 1970s and its supersedence by the issue of inflation. If this is so, the War on Poverty, the manpower programs of the late 1960s and 1970s, the civil rights issue in general, and so on, had largely symbolic benefits for labor; by extension, the support of the minimum wage may stem also from the unions' problematic relations with the marginal worker.

Third, the accommodating monetary atmosphere may have contributed to the diminished urgency until recently of labor law reform, especially Section 14(b) of Taft-Hartley. Although this as well as other organizational issues have remained a staple on the legislative agenda, both Presidents Kennedy and Johnson backed away from promises of support to labor without having suffered noticeable retaliation. This deemphasis may complement the relative quiet on the organizing front during those years. Since management could pass wage increases along as higher prices validated by the Federal Reserve, the pressures exerted by lower-paid, unorganized workers was considerably lessened.

Labor's legislative activities, as well as the unions' relationship to government as a whole, takes on an entirely different dimension under mounting international pressures on the monetary system. In fact, the strain that has persisted over the last twenty years is attributable to those same pressures in milder form. The Kennedy guidelines, the first aggressive interventions into private collective bargaining since World War II were designed to strengthen the U.S. trade position in the wake of the run on gold that occurred when the Europeans in 1958 made their currencies externally convertible and found the dollar shortage was over. The Johnson forays into wage setting in steel, aluminum, and copper in 1965 were seen by the administration as the real goods side, along with the repeal of the gold cover on Federal Reserve deposits and capital controls, to slowing the deterioration in the balance of payments; the establishement of the Cabinet Committee on Price Stability in early 1968 was in large part a response to "Secretary [of the Treasury] Fowler's need for further assistance on the home front."[44] Although the Nixon wage-price freeze apparently was separable in that policymakers saw it to be justified on domestic grounds alone, the setting and timing of the new economic policy were influenced by international factors: the earliest sign that the "gradualism" policy had failed was the circumvention of monetary restraint by the banks' heavy borrowing of Eurodollars, which were of course themselves a creature of the balance-of-payments deficit; the controls were linked to the shutting of the gold window and the dollar devaluation and stunting its anticipated inflationary effects.

The growing importance of the international economy is evident in the *Minutes* of the Federal Open Market Committee. In October of 1960, when the official price of $35 was broken for the first time on the London gold market, the mention of the balance of payments was inserted in the directive to the account manager, and Chairman Martin began his decade-long series of commentaries on the balance of payments being "the most significant shadow in the domestic business picture," the cause of "the crisis approaching in the Western World," and the "shift in financial leadership from the U.S. to Europe." From now on, in assessing unemployment, the balance-of-payments was considered a major cause, and, for that reason as well as the internationalist bias of a solid minority of committee members, doubts about correct policy were "resolved in favor of less ease," causing one member to complain that the foreign tail was being permitted to wag the domestic dog. Over the next ten years the FOMC allowed foreign economic considerations to take precedence over domestic requirements perhaps fifteen or so times. The most controversial was a rise in the discount rate in December 1965, but with the inflation that accompanied the Vietnam War this action was soon vindicated as the right move for the wrong reasons—much as the war would continue to dull the distinction between international and domestic motives, for the duration and into the peace.[45]

A difference between these pressures and those from 1973 onward is that the former were publicly presented and often privately regarded as distractions from a predominantly domestic focus. Kennedy used wage-and-price guidelines as a kind of public relations campaign internationally to cover domestic expansion at home; the foreign actions taken in conjunction with Nixon's freeze were taken in an aggresive, almost punitive, posture against miscreants who would not fairly revalue their currencies and quit plundering American treasure; the Federal Reserve was careful to avoid "overt" action that would draw attention to its internationally inspired decisions.[46] But the "supply shocks" of 1973 worked to closely bind the domestic and international economies: the oil price discredited the notion that foreign trade played only a very small part in the U.S. GNP and could be safely subordinated; the food shortage joined in to dramatize the rate of inflation and create a broad constituency for monetary restraint. By the time he announced his wage-and-price program in 1978, on the day in November when the dollar hit its all-time low on the foreign exchange markets, President Carter abandoned the traditional Democratic position that inflation can be controlled without high interest at home, and he openly connected the 1 percent rise in the discount rate to the plight of the currency.

Since the shocks of 1973, and especially since the recession that resulted in 1974–75, organized labor has pressed for legislation to force the Federal Reserve to keep to an accommodationist course. There have been two points of attack, the first of them on actual operations. Beginning with an unsuccessful plan in 1975 sponsored by Congressman Reuss to mandate the expansion of the money supply at a rate determined by Congress, this approach has been watered down in legislation that requires Senate confirmation of the Federal Reserve chairman and his appearance on a regular basis before various congressional committees to announce and defend the System's monetary targets. Lobbied by labor, Congress, through resolutions on the floor and in committee reports, notably those of the Joint Economic Committee, has expressed its preference for lower interest rates and its explicit opposition to the use of monetary policy for international purposes.[47] A variation is the Humphrey-Hawkins Full Employment Act, which has at least as a secondary purpose the triggering of monetary expansion as a means of meeting employment objectives now that the Federal Reserve can no longer be expected to respond indefinitely by habit.

The second point is the structure of the Federal Reserve System. In February 1975, the AFL-CIO called for and has since sponsored bills providing for a four-year term for the chairman, coterminous with the president; for the abolition of the Federal Open Market Committee with its five rotating Federal Reserve bank presidents, and for its functions to be taken over by the presidentially appointed Board of Governors; and for extending representation on all committees and banks in the System to consumers and organized labor.[48] In other words, no longer certain of its future ability to induce accommodation as a "constituency" of an "independent" Federal Reserve, labor has tried to bring its electoral strength to bear through direct political channels.

One explanation competing with the priority of monetary affairs in labor's strategy is simply that the above initiatives are part of a traditional liberal or social issues program that is endangered by tight money and have nothing to do with collective bargaining. But at least two pieces of early evidence suggest the contrary. First is that, beginning in 1977, the AFL-CIO's COPE scorecard for congressmen began to tally votes separately on issues directly affecting labor and on social issues. Second, in 1977 the AFL-CIO convention set out the most ambitious agenda of labor legislation since 1935, including common-situs picketing, collective bargaining for public employees, and a comprehensive revision of the basic labor law; in 1978 Al Barkan, head lobbyist, made it known that these changes would take precedence over social issues.[49] Although some unions have publicly disagreed with this position, and there are other plausible reasons to explain it—declining membership, wildcat strikes, public parsimony—it is also consistent with labor's present need to shore up its political and organizational position in the face of a fundamental change in the monetary environment.

IV

By way of conclusion I might briefly consider some implications of the preceding analysis for liberal government and its study. As a starting point, it may be assumed that foreign pressures on the dollar will continue and that current wage-price policies will not be successful in pulling down the rate of inflation below that of America's major trading partners. Under these conditions, the "state" might be sufficiently "strong," as it were, to harden the money supply by adhering to a growth target roughly in line with expected productivity. Setting aside purely technical problems, this situation would be similar to the gold standard in that the government would set the price of money by determining its supply, and all other prices must adjust. Nor does the vaunted electoral power of labor, its alleged "veto" in Congress, appear as an insurmountable obstacle to such an event, considering the intense public support for fighting inflation and the poor record of labor on issues, such as labor law reform, when it has had to stand alone. It is not even out of the question that some unions in industries that would profit from increased exports might lend tacit support, particularly if protectionist strategies fail.

The hardening of monetary policy, however, would come up against unions in the industrial sphere to produce several destabilizing effects. The first is strikes. The rigidity of money could be expected finally to "stiffen the backs" of management against union demands, especially during the transition years to lower inflation. Strikes themselves could be expected to take on a different character in the changed monetary context, more prolonged and bitter than the sometimes almost conspiratorial strikes when they served mainly to roll the steam out of the membership prior to serious negotiations.[50] An increase in prolonged strikes would lower productivity and cause a worsening in the balance-of-payments. And the union's success in maintaining their own wages would cause disproportionate deflation elsewhere in the economy, with the likelihood of recession, increased unemployment, and social disruption. In short, the "strong" state confronted with well-entrenched, wage-conscious unions necessarily raises the specter of the "stronger" state capable of promulgating and enforcing a ban on strikes, freedom of assembly, and the rest. Again, the absence of established political bonds and apparatus of American labor might serve to raise rather than lower the probability of such extreme measures as compared to Britain, say, or even West Germany.

An alternative train of events would be a more gradual use of the monetary levers as government softens base of union power. Earlier, agricultural prices and the restraint of methods of opposition used by business were mentioned as the primarily social supports to labor strength after the depression of the 1930s and comments will be restricted to them, although there are certainly others. One may imagine any number of measures that would serve the desired end, but even moderate steps well within the range of political possibility would mean dismantling parts of the system of interest-group liberalism, which, for all its egregious and well-documented failings, has been the fulcrum of political stability for five decades. Consider agriculture: while govern-

ment is bound to continue some kind of program to even out farm prices
if for no other reason than the potentially disastrous effects of an upward
movement like that in 1973, there have been several proposals which
would achieve this result without the same pressure on food prices
produced by current programs. These vary from the government's entry
into the commodities futures market to direct cash payments to farmers
in periods of overproduction, but all prescribe a turning away from the
price supports, acreage set-asides, and a system of loans upon which
rests the political establishment of agriculture.[51]

As for strengthening the hand of business against the unions, this can
happen by means well short of using the antitrust laws against unions or
truly backward labor law reform: one way is simply to resist labor's own
recent legislative proposals for better NLRB enforcement and increased
access to members in organizing, as unions lose members in traditional
jurisdictions and must recoup in the terrains of right-to-work, and
sophisticated personnel management. Another is the appointment of
appropriately conservative members to agencies with labor-related
jurisdiction; thus, for example, the Nixon-Ford CAB ruled, over union
protest, that opening airlines might provide financial assistance from
their own fares to a fellow airline shut down by a strike. An indirect
approach, and one underway by the present administration, is deregulation, since unions as well as companies have benefited from the absence of competition in the regulated industries.

The problem with the "softening"' approach is that it must proceed
piecemeal through the Congress. Although unions probably do not have
veto power there, they do have considerable leverage over the administration in its endless quest for wage and price controls. For example, the
UAW president, Douglas Frazer, last year resigned from the Labor-
Management Group as a protest against the administration's backing
away from the common site picketing bill; more recently the Teamsters
have given notice that they will take into account President Carter's
actions to deregulate the trucking industry when they decide how
closely to abide by the voluntary wage guidelines.

Both interest-group liberalism and liberalism pure-and-simple, however, as well as the status quo in union-government relations, may receive bolstering from an unexpected quarter, namely, the conservative
forces which while they oppose inflation may also resist measures to
effectively contain it. The unions have already met with their increasing
strength in the taxpayer revolts in the states, and labor only narrowly
beat back a 1978 amendment to the Humphrey-Hawkins bill that would
have made the unemployment program contingent on a specified low
rate of inflation. But more recently, when President Carter asked for an
extension of the Council on Wage and Price Stability, this same group

attacked the wage and price guidelines, and, in particular, the use of government procurement to enforce compliance; it will no doubt continue to be prominent in the White House–Congress struggle for control of the Federal Reserve. The role of the anti-inflation conservatives is not unlike that of the Progressives as McConnell has described them in the consolidation of liberalism early in this century, advancing the interest of private power as they vigorously decry its effect.[52]

There are of course several other possible developments that could be discussed. One is the policy of direct government intervention on the supply side of selected export industries to increase productivity: this would raise the old question of the 1920s of whether an outside union or some other organization would be best suited to the task. Another solution is corporatism, which would go against the grain of localism in American labor but is consistent with balance-of-payments problems and with certain trends toward centralization in the labor bureaucracy.[53] There are many fermenting agents in the mixture, for example, the union pension funds, control of which might, as some union leaders hope, revitalize the labor movement and might, on the other hand, split older and younger members along productivity versus money-wage lines.

Although the foregoing discussion has been prompted by substantive and not methodological concerns, it does contain certain methodological implications that may occur to readers attentive to such issues. One of them is the question of whether there is not support here for the "other face of power" approach to studying American politics, even as that idea is defused ideologically by the discovery of a trade unionist staring out instead of a businessman. But this would be, I believe, a false lead. If there is any point to be made about power in the essay, let it be in its emphasis on the interrelations among groups, governmental and nongovernmental, as they impinge on one another's actions. Insofar as this suggests a theory of power, it is a transactional one rather than the domination-oriented formulation of Bachrach and Baratz.[54] In this respect, also, the recent ecumenical emphasis on the State, with its reassertion of the importance of authority relations when considered in the light of a transnational question such as the monetary order, is seen to be only an intermediate stage of analysis.

It is of course no coincidence that a diminished fascination with who governs in Milltown, U.S.A—and predictably, too, even in Washington, D.C.—corresponds to the declining hegemony of the American democratic system worldwide; and a movement away from what has been a profoundly nationalistic bias in studying American society and politics may be expected as a matter of professional survival. More than that, however, the essay has perhaps demonstrated the usefulness of an international perspective for analyzing configurations and institutions which, because they have appeared relatively stable, have been in important respects poorly discerned and their sources altogether invisible.

Another methodological implication of all this may be the reemergence of the normative elements of pluralist analysis from their latent—if often pejoratively exposed—position since the 1920s. In the era of interest-group liberalism, which fairly well parallels the development of political science as a discipline, the question has frequently been asked, Why no socialism in the United States?—and researchers have imposed a would-be grid of class relations on what appears to be a stubbornly pluralist polity. Similarly, as logjams among major interests and aspirations become more characteristic than their adjustment, pluralism may be expected to become the question, the grid, rather than the answer. One result of this may be the challenging of certain cliches. Consider, for example, the "decay of the status order," brought on by industrialization, accompanied by the rise of new groupings based on anxiety and acquisitiveness, and routinely offered as partial explanation for the current overload on political and economic institutions.[55] But a closer look at labor politics, at least in America over the span of the last century, suggests that overload was avoided not by status attachments but by a set of mutual checks and organizational disabilities among industrial and nonindustrial groups, circumstances surmounted only by the constructive measures of the administrative state.

A second result should be the reassessment of the problematic relations between pluralism, with its emphasis on the positive benefits of collective action, and other core values of liberalism—McConnell's great question. Nor is this merely a matter of theoretical interest as resistance to labor union demands becomes perhaps *the* most troubling domestic question of capitalist governments. Again, the above analysis suggests that there may be somewhat more of a game than the cacophony of alleged inner crises and contradictions would suggest.

In any case, the problem of organized labor will no doubt vex statesmen and intrigue political scientists until someone invents a substitute for gold and a substitute for oil and surely even then.

Notes

1. See, e.g., J. David Greenstone, *Labor in American Politics* (New York: Alfred A. Knopf, Inc., 1969), chap. 11. The classic statement of the problem is made by Selig Perlman in *A History of Trade Unionism in the United States* (New York: A. M. Kelley, 1969), pt. III. Also see C. Wright Mills, *New Men of Power* (New York: Harcourt Brace & Co., 1948); and Daniel Bell, *End of Ideology* (New York: Free Press, 1961), chaps. 10 and 12. Greenstone's study, based on data from three cities rather than from national politics,

is not only the most significant contemporary treatment but it is also the most recent.

2. The role of the gold standard as the central regulating institution of nineteenth-century society and economy is the thesis in Karl Polanyi, *The Great Transformation* (Boston: Beacon Press, 1957). It is interesting to note that even in the most systematic discussions of "interest-group liberalism" the precise position of organized labor in the scheme of the administrative state is obscured. See Theodore Lowi, *The End of Liberalism*, 2d ed. (New York: W. W. Norton & Co., 1979), pp. 77–91. Also, relatively little attention is paid to labor in Charles Maier, *Recasting Bourgeois Europe* (Princeton, N.J.: Princeton University Press, 1975), despite introductory remarks to the effect that the corporatist arrangements of post–World War I Europe rewarded labor leadership at the expense of the fragmented middle class (pp. 11 and 15).

3. Grant McConnell, *Private Power and American Democracy* (New York: Alfred A. Knopf, Inc., 1966), pp. 365 ff. and passim. On European unions, see Lloyd Ulman and Robert J. Flanagan, *Wage Restraint: A Study of Incomes Policies in Western Europe* (Berkeley: University of California Press, 1971); and John P. Windmuller, ed., "European Labor and Politics: A Symposium," *Industrial and Labor Relations Review* 28 (December 1974, and January 1975): 3–88, 203–81.

4. On membership figures and trends, see Irving Bernstein, "The Growth of American Unions," *American Economic Review* 44 (July–December 1954): 302–8; Leo Wolman, *Growth of American Trade Unions, 1880–1923* (New York: National Bureau of Economic Research, 1924); Leo Wolman, *Ebb and Flow of Trade Unionism* (New York: National Bureau of Economic Research, 1936). Also see Orley C. Ashenfelter and John J. Pencavel, "American Trade Union Growth," *Quarterly Journal of Economics* 83 (August 1969): 434–48. For the diversity of theories on the causes of union growth see Albert A. Blum, "Why Unions Grow," *Labor History* 9 (Winter 1968): 39–72.

5. At the 1893 convention, the American Federation of Labor endorsed bimetallism. On labor's role in legislation, see John R. Commons, ed., *History of Labor in the United States, 1896–1932*, vol. 3, by Don D. Lescohier and Elizabeth Brandeis (New York: Macmillan Co., 1935), pp. 554–57, 575–77; and Perlman, pp. 198–207. Also see John Morton Blum, *The Republican Roosevelt* (New York: Atheneum Pubs., 1971), pp. 112–13; and Arthur Link, *Wilson: The New Freedom* (Princeton, N.J.: Princeton University Press, 1956), pp. 264–76, 426–30.

6. See O. M. W. Sprague, *History of Crises under the National Banking System* (Washington, D.C.: Government Printing Office, 1910), pp. 127 ff. and 154 ff.; and Milton Friedman and Anna Jacobson Schwartz, *A Monetary History of the United States, 1867–1960* (Princeton, N.J.: Princeton University Press, 1963), pp. 104 ff. and 131–34.

7. Paul H. Douglas, *Real Wages in the United States, 1860–1926* (Boston: Houghton Mifflin Co., 1930), chaps. 6–11.

8. Wolman, *Growth of American Trade Unions*, pp. 118–19. In *Ebb and Flow in Trade Unionism*, pp. 84 ff., Wolman makes the further point that union membership was concentrated in the prewar years in transportation, building, printing, and coal mining; and in these industries strong unions compared favorably in influence with the most powerful union organizations in other countries.

9. See Marguerite Green, *The National Civic Federation and the Labor Movement* (Washington, D.C.: Catholic University of American Press, 1956). The essential labor history for 1896–1932 is John Commons, ed., *History of Labor in the United States*, vol. 4, by Selig Perlman and Philip Taft. On the trend of business incorporations, see Louis M. Hacker, *The Course of American Economic Growth and Development* (New York: John Wiley & Sons, 1970), pp. 244–49.

10. Friedman and Schwartz, pp. 221–39. Also see W. P. G. Harding, *The Formative Period of the Federal Reserve System* (Boston: Houghton Mifflin Co., 1925), pp. 148 ff. The

United States was still on the gold standard after 1913 to the extent that gold determined longer-term movements in the total stock of domestic money. But the Federal Reserve Act, to provide for elasticity, incorporated a "real bills" doctrine linking money supply to business transactions and thus gave considerable leeway in the shorter run. An interesting view of the significance of this change from the British perspective is in Roy Harrod, *The Dollar* (New York: Harcourt, Brace & World, 1963), chaps. 2, 3.

11. Douglas, pp. 562–64. On this period see also Daniel J. Ahearn, *The Wages of Farm and Factory Laborers, 1914–1944* (New York: Columbia University Press, 1945), chaps. 4, 5.

12. Irving Bernstein, *Arbitration of Wages* (Berkeley: University of California Press, 1954), p. 3.

13. Lester Chandler, *Benjamin Strong, Central Banker* (Washington, D.C.: Brookings Institution, 1958), pp. 199 ff. This fascinating book is of great interest with respect to the early Federal Reserve System, from its conception in 1907 until Strong's death in 1928.

14. Milton J. Nawordny, *Scientific Management and the Unions, 1900–1932* (Cambridge, Mass., 1955), pp. 1–121; and Jean Tripp McKelvey, *AFL Attitudes toward Production, 1900–1931* (Ithaca, N.Y.: Cornell University, 1952). It is during these years, in the face of extreme governmental hostility, that labor's management matches perfectly McConnell's description of the orthodoxy of "private government," pp. 79 ff. Consider the remarkable document, "Industry's Manifest Duty." "We feel the hour has struck for a pronouncement of the aims of labor that more nearly express the full implications of trade unionism than has yet been undertaken in these annual reports. . . . Henceforth the organization of workers into trade unions must mean the conscious organization of one of the most vital functional elements for enlightened participation in a democracy of industry whose purpose must be the extension of freedom, the enfranchisement of the producer as such, the rescue of industry from chaos, profiteering and purely individual whim . . . and the rescue of industry from incompetent political bodies. . . . It is not the mission of industrial groups to clash and struggle . . . the true role of industrial groups, however, is to come together and legislate in peace, to find the way forward in collaboration, to give of their best for the satisfaction of human needs" (*AFL Convention Proceedings* [1923], pp. 31–34).

15. See Sumner Slichter, *Union Policies and Industrial Management* (Washington, D.C.: Brookings Institution, 1941), chaps. 12–18. On labor organizing strategy in the 1920s, see James O. Morris, *Conflict within the AFL: A Study of Craft versus Industrial Unionism* (Ithaca, N.Y.: Cornell University, 1958), chap. 3.

16. John Dewey, "Labor Politics and Labor Education," *New Republic* (January 19, 1929), pp. 212–13; and Lyle W. Cooper, "The American Federation of Labor and the Intellectuals," *Political Science Quarterly* 43 (September 1928): 388–407. Also see Robert Dorfman, *Economic Mind in American Civilization*, vol. 5 (New York, 1959), chap. 18.

17. For examples, see John Kenneth Galbraith, *The Great Crash* (Boston: Houghton Mifflin Co., 1961), pp. 14–16; and Arthur M. Schelsinger, Jr., *Crisis of the Old Order* (Boston: Houghton Mifflin Co., 1957), pp. 233–34.

18. Friedman and Schwartz, chap. 7, esp. pp. 313–19, 359–62; and Irving Fisher, *Booms and Depressions*, (New York: Adelphi Co., 1932), pp. 92 ff.

19. Harold M. Levinson, *Unionism, Wage Trends and Income Distribution* (Ann Arbor, Mich.: Bureau of Business Research, School of Business Administration, University of Michigan, 1951), pp. 44 ff. Also see National Industrial Conference Board, *Salary and Wage Policy in the Depression*, (New York: National Industrial Conference Board, 1932), pp. 28–29.

20. E.g., A. C. Pigou, *The Theory of Unemployment* (London: Macmillan & Co., 1933), pp. 101–2, 252, 236–37; and Lionel Robbins, *The Great Depression* (London: Macmillan & Co., 1934), pp. 60–75, 160–72, 186–90. For historical evidence on the rigidity of wages

during depressions under the gold standard, see Robert R. France, "Wages, Unemployment, and Price in the United States, 1890–1932, 1947–1957," *Industrial and Labor Relations Review* 15 (January 1962): 171–90.

21. Richard N. Gardner, *Sterling-Dollar Diplomacy: Anglo-American Collaboration in the Reconstruction of Multilateral Trade* (Oxford: Clarendon Press, 1956), pp. 114–17, 290–91. See also Brian Johnson, *The Politics of Money* (London: J. Murray, 1970), chaps. 5, 6.

22. The change-of-heart argument is advanced most plausibly in Ruth L. Horowitz, *Political Ideologies of Organized Labor* (New Brunswick, N.J.: Transaction Books, 1978).

23. Arthur M. Schlesinger, Jr., *The Coming of the New Deal* (Boston: Houghton Mifflin, 1959), pp. 386, 390, 392.

24. The figures are from Murry Edelman, "New Deal Sensitivity to Labor Interests," in Milton Derber and Edwin Young, *Labor and the New Deal* (Madison, Wis.: University of Wisconsin Press, 1957), p. 166.

25. A good summary of the legal changes is in Irving Bernstein, *The Turbulent Years* (Boston: Houghton Mifflin Co., 1969), chap. 13. This book is indispensable for a detailed and colorful survey of labor developments during the period of the New Deal, as is its companion volume, *The Lean Years* (Boston: Houghton Mifflin Co., 1960), for 1920–33.

26. Murray R. Benedict, *Farm Policies of the United States 1790–1950* (New York: Twentieth Century Fund, 1953), pp. 168–69, 173.

27. Arthur F. Burns, *Production Trends in the United States Since 1870* (New York: National Bureau of Economic Research, 1934), pp. 288, 294.

28. Willard W. Cochrane and Mary E. Ryan, *American Farm Policy, 1948–1973* (Minneapolis: University of Minnesota Press, 1976), pp. 380–81.

29. On the antilabor purposes behind the founding of the NAM's National Industrial Council and trade associations generally, see Robert A. Brady, *Business as a System of Power* (New York: Columbia University Press, 1943), pp. 199 ff. Also see the comment in John Commons, ed., *History of Labor in the United States*, vol. 3, p. 297, on the fact that the centralization and consolidation of industry under the control of finance capitalists put decisions in the hands of men inaccessible and insensitive to workers in the factories; and, one might add, more sensitive to monetary developments. In this light, also, consider the long leadership of the antilabor forces by United States Steel and its close association with the Morgan bank.

30. Again, a full-dress study begs to be written. But for exemplary accounts see John Davenport, "Labor and the Law," *Fortune* 59 (May 1959): 142–43 ff., and "NLRB on the New Frontier," *Fortune* 66 (July 1962): 255–56 ff.

31. Rainbow Bread Co., 92 NLRB 181, 182 (1950); May Department Stores, 50 NLRB 669 (1943); Delaware Knitting Co., 75 NLRB 205 (1947); Joseph E. Seagram & Sons, 101 NLRB 101 (1952).

32. Morand Brothers Beverage Co., 99 NLRB 1448 (1952); Buffalo Linen Supply Co., 109 NLRB 447 (1954); *American Ship Building Co. v. NLRB*, 380 US 300 (1965); Friedland Painting Co., 158 NLRB 571 (1966).

33. See Marriner S. Eccles, *Beckoning Frontiers* (New York: Alfred A. Knopf, Inc., 1966), pp. 266–86 and passim; and Ellis W. Hawley, *The New Deal and the Problem of Monopoly* (Princeton, N.J.: Princeton University Press, 1966), pp. 44–45, and chap. 9.

34. See Fred Hirsch, *Money International* (London: Penguin, 1967), pp. 48–63; and John Hicks, "Economic Foundations of Wage Policy," *Economic Journal* 65 (September 1955): 389–404.

35. Quoted in Sherman Maisel, *Managing the Dollar* (New York: W. W. Norton & Co., 1973), p. 65.

36. Orley C. Ashenfelter, George E. Johnson, and John H. Pencavel, "Trade Unions

and the Rate of Change of Money Wages in United States Manufacturing Industries," *Review of Economic Statistics* 39 (January 1972): 27–54; and Marvin Kosters, Kenneth Fedor, and Albert Eckstein, "Collective Bargaining Settlements and the Wage Structure," *Labor Law Journal* (August 1973), pp. 517–25. Also see "The Effect of Union Strength on the U.S. Philips Curve, *American Economic Review* 58 (June 1968): pp. 456–67.

37. Otto Eckstein and Thomas A. Wilson, "Determination of Money Wages in American Industry," *Quarterly Journal of Economics* 86 (August 1962): 379–414. On the importance of multiyear contracts, see Robert J. Flanagan, "Wage Interdependence in Unionized Labor Markets," *Brookings Papers on Economic Activity*, no. 3 (1976), pp. 635–81.

38. U.S. Federal Open Market Committee, *Minutes*, January 27, 1959; January 29, 1963; December 10, 1956; January 12, 1960; May 6 and May 27, 1958; November 24, 1964; and (on strikes) July 22, 1952; June 28, 1959; and passim. The F.O.M.C. *Minutes* which, in the 1960s in a bargain with Congress were released for the period beginning 1936 and are no longer available for meetings after 1973, provide an extraordinary glimpse inside policymaking. Unfortunately, the yearly volumes are unindexed and the reader has no choice but to plow through the some 27,000 typescript pages.

39. Ibid. for August 7, 1956; March 15, 1956; September 25, 1956; March 5, 1957.

40. Arnold Weber, "The Continuing Courtship: Wage-Price Policy through Five Administrations," in Craufurd D. Goodwin, *Exhortation and Controls, The Search for a Wage-Price Policy, 1945–71* (Washington, D.C.: Brookings Institution, 1975). Labor's postwar governmental relations is yet another lacuna in the literature. Something of a picture may be patched together from Walt Whitman Rostow, *The Diffusion of Power* (New York: Macmillan Publishing Co., 1972), chaps. 15, 29; Vivian Vale, *Labour in American Politics* (London: Routledge & Kegan Paul, 1971); Frank Cormier and William J. Eaton, *Reuther* (Englewood Cliffs, N.J.: Prentice-Hall, Inc., 1970); Grant McConnell, *Steel and the Presidency* (New York: W. W. Norton & Co., 1963); David J. McDonald, *Union Man* (New York: E. P. Dutton, 1969); and Joseph C. Goulden, *Meany* (New York: Atheneum Pubs., 1972).

41. See the interpretation in Greenstone (n. 1 above), pp. 387 ff., in which labor represents a kind of vanguard of the "consumer class" allied in the Democratic party. The monetary analysis suggests that this alliance may have been conditional on a successful "producer class" alliance in the industrial sphere.

42. See table 8.1 and accompanying remarks in James M. Buchanan and Richard E. Wagner, *Democracy in Deficit: The Political Legacy of Lord Keynes* (New York: Academic Press, 1977), pp. 115, 116. On intervention in selected labor markets, see "Anti-Inflationary Demand Management in the United States: A Selective Industry Approach," *International Monetary Fund Staff Papers* 19 (July 1972): pp. 344–94.

43. A recent statement of the argument is in John A. Garraty, *Unemployment in History: Economic Thought and Public Policy* (New York: Harper & Row, 1978), pp. 188–96.

44. Quoted in James L. Cochrane, "The Johnson Administration: Moral Suasion Goes to War," in Goodwin (n. 40 above), p. 281.

45. U.S. Federal Open Market Committee, *Minutes*, October 25, 1960; February 12, 1963; November 14, 1961; October 24, 1961 (remarks by Governor Robertson); and passim. Also see Maisel pp. 222–24.

46. See Chairman Martin's remarks in U.S. Federal Open Market Committee, *Minutes*, October 25, 1960; October 24, 1961; March 6, 1962; May 7, 1963; December 12, 1964; and passim.

47. See, e.g., the testimony of Chairman G. William Miller, *Hearings*, Committee on

the Banking, Finance and Urban Affairs Committee, U.S. House of Representatives, 95th Cong., 2d sess., July 28 and August 7, 1978, pp. 4–73; and the *1978 Joint Economic Report*, 95th Cong., 2d sess., March 21, 1978, esp. pp. 30–37.

48. Statement by Andrew J. Biemiller, *Hearings*, Committee on Banking, Finance and Urban Affairs, U.S. House of Representatives, 95th Cong., 2d sess., July 18 and 26, 1977, pp. 42–52.

49. See Charles W. Hucker, "Organized Labor Takes a Hard Look at Whom It Will Support This Fall," *Congressional Quarterly Weekly Report* 36 (January 8, 1978): 193–98.

50. The best single account is in William Serrin, *The Company and the Union* (New York: Vintage Books, 1974). Also see Orley Ashenfelter and George E. Johnson, "Bargaining Theory, Trade Unions and Industrial Strike Activity," *American Economic Review* 59 (March 1969): 35–45.

51. For a discussion of these agricultural proposals, see Robert W. Crandall, "Federal Government Initiatives to Reduce the Price Level," *Brookings Papers on Economic Activity*, no. 2 (1978), pp. 407–17.

52. McConnell, *Private Power in American Democracy* (n. 3 above), chap. 2.

53. See Robert W. Cox, "Labor and Hegemony," *International Organization* 31 (Summer 1977): 385–424.

54. Peter Bachrach and Morton S. Baratz, *Power and Poverty* (New York: Oxford University Press, 1970), chaps. 1–3.

55. See, e.g., John H. Goldthorpe, "The Current Inflation: Towards a Sociological Account," in Fred Hirsch and John H. Goldthorpe, *The Political Economy of Inflation* (Cambridge, Mass.: Harvard University Press, 1978), pp. 197 ff; and similar arguments in Samuel Brittan, "The Economic Contradictions of Democracy," *British Journal of Political Science* 5 (April 1975): 129–59; and Michael J. Brenner, "Status Politics and the Emerging International System," *Social Science Information* 12 (December 1973): 103–28. These are, by the way, quite excellent articles.

Part IV

★

Cities in a Federal System

Seven ★

Urban Bureaucracy in Urban Politics: Notes toward a Developmental Theory

Matthew A. Crenson

A Comparative Perspective

In city politics, as in many other pursuits, bureaucracy grows more obtrusive. The particularistic business of trading in patronage and favors—once the mainstay of the urban polity—goes on still. But it is overshadowed now by the bigger business of rule-governed administration. A generation of wars between bosses and reformers separates the two ways of doing business, and it is the same great conflict that frequently seems to supply a frame of reference for interpreting city politics in its new, bureaucratic phase. In the rule of today's urban administrators, some analysts recognize the same forces that once challenged the rule of the urban machine; the bureaucratic regime of the contemporary city becomes an institutional expression of municipal reform triumphant, and its singular character may be revealed by its departures from the "private-regarding" code of the boss and his followers.[1]

The departures are not illusory. The bureaucratic way of doing business in cities is unquestionably different from the way of the bosses. But the contrasts that distinguish the two political styles should not obscure a certain family resemblance between the enterprises themselves. Perhaps the most important source of this affinity is the simple fact that both political enterprises are distinctively urban ones. Evidences of this common tie grow more significant as the historic struggles of bosses and reformers fade further into the past and give way to political divergences of a fundamentally different character. Today the most notable political distinctions in cities are not the ones between different brands of urban politics but between city politics as a whole and the politics of institutions that impinge increasingly on the municipal arena from the outside—national corporations, national labor unions, and national agencies. For most cities of the present day, the contrast between machine politics and reform politics is probably less immediate, acute, and momentous than the one between urban politics and national politics. And when the political ways of the city are set beside their national counterparts, what strikes an observer most is not the diversity that exists among the various strains of city politics but the underlying urbanism that they all have in common—a consistent pattern of organization and activity that distinguishes urban politics in general from politics beyond the city limits. Such family traits have led some observers, like Theodore Lowi, to recognize in today's municipal agencies and their agents the heirs of yesterday's municipal machines and their bosses.[2]

Political power is the most obvious mark of kinship, but city administrators are not related to city bosses simply because bureaucracies are powers-that-be in cities and machines are the powers-that-were. A most substantial sign of likeness is that the powers, past and present, seem to have grown from the same kinds of roots. Urban machines and bureaucracies alike have drawn their strength, as Lowi points out, from "their cohesiveness as small minorities in the midest of the vast dispersion of the multitude." It is a decidedly contextual kind of power. Only when set against the background of a "dispersed, permissive unmobilized society"[3]—an urban society—does it come to life. The same kind of power might achieve less prominence if it stood, not surrounded by an unmobilized multitude, but wedged within a compact mosaic of organized pressure groups.

In city politics, however, such pressure groups have seldom crowded the field. The "vague and latent conception of a corporate democracy of interest groups" seems to have made far less headway in urban than in national politics, where Grant McConnell has detected its influence in a host of political and administrative arrangements.[4] It is national politics, in fact, which provides a standard of comparison for recognizing what is distinctive about the politics of cities. The vast dispersion of the urban multitude becomes evident, perhaps, only by contrast with the more explicit groupings, the more structured conflicts and alliances of Washington pressure politics. The conception of interest group democracy which McConnell and others have used to interpret politics at the national level supplies a benchmark for surveying the very different contours of political and bureaucratic power in cities.

The distinctive nature of this urban power is reflected even in the successive waves of reform which have risen to attack it. When Lincoln Steffens scolded the municipal public for its passivity in the fact of political bosses and boodlers,[5] he was recognizing both the unmobilized character of the urban multitude and the extent to which it made possible the power of the city machine. A similar awareness seems to have become widespread among more recent reformers, who have called for the systematic encouragement of citizen participation and citizen organization in order to counteract the organized power and obstinacy of bureaucratic agencies that tower over a politically diffuse population. Some of the same reformers have also insisted that giant bureaucracies be cut down to size through decentralization, so that they might be just as dispersed as the multitude that they serve. Municipal bureaucracy, it seems, has inherited not only the power of the machine but also its status as the "urban problem" of its time. Questions of bureaucratic responsiveness, effectiveness, and service delivery hang almost as heavily over city politics today as complaints of bossism, graft, and governmental incompetence did in the days of the machine.

But even though the two institutions may be powerful and problematic in similar ways, city bureaucracy falls far short of its political predecessor in a third respect. The machine has not yet been superseded as an intellectual device for organizing our understanding of city politics. Among students of urban politics, it has provided a reference point, not only for the analysis of contemporary urban bureaucracy but also for the interpretation of municipal politics in general.[6] "Because the machine has played such a central role in the field," writes Martin Shefter, "prevailing conceptions in the literature of urban politics on a number of important issues—the political significance of ethnicity and social class, the relationship between elite and mass political behavior, the modes of centralizing political power in the city—have been influenced by the efforts of scholars to understand the emergence, character, and decay of the machine."[7]

In particular, the confrontation between machine bosses and their reform-minded antagonists has served the interpreters of urban political struggle and change as one of the chief landmarks from which to take their bearings. In the classic formulation by Edward Banfield and James Q. Wilson this encounter becomes the political embodiment of a broader collision between the "private-regarding" ethos of the lower-class immigrant and the "public-regarding" temperament of the native, middle-class Protestant. Behind the attackers and defenders of the machine, Banfield and Wilson have arrayed the "two fundamentally opposed conceptions of politics . . . to be found in cities."[8]

Although the machine itself may no longer stand at the heart of the urban polity, the idea of the machine continues to serve as a focal concept in the study of city politics. Urban bureaucracy cannot lay claim yet to such analytic centrality, even though many of the analysts seem ready to acknowledge the centrality of bureaucratic institutions in municipal government. City administrators, they suggest, "probably have greater influence in the policymaking process of large-city government than any other class of influentials,"[9] and several recent studies have concluded that urban bureaucracies and bureaucratic decision rules, more than anything else, determine the nature and distribution of the public benefits that result from the policymaking process.[10] Alongside such observations, however, there is also the confession that our understanding of these influential bureaucracies remains "curiously underdeveloped."[11] Although many bits of evidence suggest that city politics has taken on an increasingly bureaucratic cast, the significance of this transformation, the organization of the evidence, and the character of urban bureaucracy itself have yet to come into focus.

No theory of municipal bureaucracy has risen to replace the theory of the municipal machine. And this essay offers none. Instead, it suggests that a useful starting point for such a theory may be found in an analysis of the contrast between urban public bureaucracies and their national counterparts. It is sufficient for the present to indicate the nature of this contrast in rather general terms. Consider, for example, the description of municipal agencies as organized minorities in the midst of an unorganized multitude. Together with many other accounts which emphasize the insulation of city agencies from external influences and groups,[12] their autonomy,[13] and their isolation,[14] this observation might be used to construct a plausible and consistent bureaucratic character sketch. But the same character would be a glaring misfit outside the sphere of the urban polity. The terms used to describe municipal agencies, after all, are not the ones that typically appear in portrayals of national bureaucracies. In fact, one of the most frequently cited traits of the national agencies is precisely the extent to which they are surrounded, not by an unorganized multitude but by a multitude of organizations. Perhaps the main ingredient of their influence is their "ability to command the support of fervent and substantial clientele groups."[15] They are not free-standing islands of organized interests.[16]

What makes the domestic bureaucracy of national government a useful standard of comparison, of course, is not simply the fact that it is different from urban bureaucracy. The difference also holds a certain political and historical significance. At a time when the federal role in urban affairs grows increasingly evident, the contrast between the two species of bureaucratic institutions becomes a living presence in cities and not just a convenient device for political analysts. Like the earlier confrontation between the machine and its antagonists, the interplay of urban and national administration has helped to define the agenda of urban problems, the character of political conflict in cities, the content of urban policy, and the probable directions of institutional change. More than any other institution in city government, urban bureaucracy has provided a meeting place of encounters between urban and national interests, and municipal administration has been the chief object and agent of nationalizing tendencies in city politics—the channel through which federal regulations, federal funds, and federal power have been brought to bear on local problems.

City bureaucracy is the leading element in a movement that promises to make municipal government almost as much a national institution as a local one. It is not simply that urban governments grow more cosmopolitan but that in the process their distinctive "urbanism" becomes increasingly precarious. Municipal bureaucracies have typically operated as organized minorities surrounded by a politically diffuse urban multitude—public agencies in the midst of a public-at-large. But the proliferation of organized constituencies, clienteles, and private interest groups in city administration is one sign that the disparity between urban and national bureaucracy is diminishing.

The principal axis of variability and change in urban politics was once defined by the distance from machine politics to reform politics. Today it is more likely to be found in the gap that separates the bureaucratic politics of the city from its national counterpart. City politics is being "nationalized." The nature of the change cannot be seen clearly through a comparison of bosses and reformers, or even by contrasting pre-bureaucratic city machines with modern city agencies. In a bureaucratic age, the most important political variations are the ones that exist between different types of bureaucracies, not the differences between bureaucratic and pre-bureaucratic organizations. But the use of the machine as a standard of comparison tends to obscure such bureaucratic diversity, and by masking the differences that distinguish urban bureaucracies from bureaucracies elsewhere, it also conceals the continuing process of change by which city administration is being assimilated to the national pattern.

Even more important, the distinctively urban character of city politics may be lost from view when the urban machine serves as a vantage point. Looked at from the perspective of the machine, modern city agencies are distinctive primarily because they bureaucratic—a quality that hardly distinguishes them at all from a host of other public organizations that never come to roost within the limts of any municipality. In a society where almost every institution has been brushed by the forces of bureaucratization, the idea that city politics has become bureaucratic suggests only that it has become nearly indistinguishable from politics almost everywhere else. It has not—at least not yet. And the failure to recognize its distinctiveness may help to reduce its comprehensibility.

The understanding of city government and its problems, as Matthew Holden has pointed out, "implies more for political scientists than attention to the wheeling and dealing of politicians who happen to be located in cities. It requires some approach to the specifically urban within the generally political."[17] The aim of the present venture is to locate the "specifically urban" within the generally bureaucratic. In city administration, of course, what is specifically urban may be subject to erosion as national institutions come to dominate the conduct of urban affairs. This means that some aspects of city administration may not be "urban" at all, that bureaucracy may be more urban in some cities than in others, and that within a single city different public agencies may exhibit differing degrees of urbanism. In short, the forces of social and political change may create a range of bureaucratic variations between the urban and the national—in much the same way that urban polities themselves moved by degrees from the era of the boss to the age of the bureaucrat.

Form and Function in
Urban Bureaucracies

In big cities of the United States, the do-it-yourself era in municipal administration came to an end during the two generations that straddled the Civil War. Before this time, essential municipal services were provided most frequently by volunteers and part-time amateurs, or they were supported by voluntary subscription. Afterward, responsibility for delivering city services was parceled out among permanent, hierarchical agencies staffed by full-time public employees. The process of departmentalization followed different sequences in different cities, but many municipalities seem to have taken some of their first steps toward a bureaucratic mode of production where police services or public education were concerned. Boston organized its police department in the late 1830s; New York in the mid-1840s; the younger city of Milwaukee followed suit in 1855; and full-time police officers were patrolling the streets of Los Angeles by the 1880s.[18] The appearance of full-time public schoolteachers sometimes preceded the debut of the policemen (as in Boston and Los Angeles) and sometimes followed (as in New York and Milwaukee), and it was seldom very long after the emergence of police departments and public school systems that city governments created a range of other agencies devoted to fire protection, public health, and sanitation. In little more than half a century a fairly standard array of bureaucratic agencies had risen up in most of the large municipalities, each department organized around some function whose performance had become a governmental responsibility during the course of urbanization.

While the administrative offshoots of municipal government were still developing, fresh bureaucratic growth had also begun to appear at the national level. But it was growth of a distinct kind—different, not only from administrative developments in the municipalities but from most of the preexisting bureaucratic institutions in the federal government itself. Prior to 1861, almost all federal departments had been structured around specialized governmental functions, as were the emergent municipal agencies of the era. But after 1861, federal agencies began to break out of the functional mode and became instead the bureaucratic reflections of specific clientele groups and their demands. In the national government, according to Richard Schott, "the new departments of this period—Agriculture, Labor and Commerce—were devoted to the interests and aspirations of particular economic groups."[19] To an increasing extent, a central consideration in the shaping of national administrative agencies was not the nature of the service to be rendered but the identity of the clients who were to receive it.

Often the clientele took shape as a formal organization even before its patron agency did, and it was the pressure exerted by organizations of would-be clients that sometimes induced Congress to legislate bureaucratic agencies into being. The creation of the Department of Labor in 1913, for example, was the culmination of a fifty-year lobbying campaign led at first by the Knights of Labor and subsequently by the American Federation of Labor. The Department of Agriculture originated in the political efforts of the United States Agricultural Society during the decade before the Civil War.[20]

These were only two of the more obvious manifestations of a movement toward clientele-oriented administration, a bureaucratic tendency which later became much more elaborate and extensive, not only in the federal bureaucracy but in state government as well. The principal contribution of the states to the onward march of clientelism lay in the proliferation of occupational licensing agencies during the latter half of the nineteenth century, each organized around some trade or profession and usually controlled by its practitioners.[21] But city governments contributed almost nothing to the spread of this emergent bureaucratic regime. With the possible exception of local real estate commissions and some building inspection agencies, there was no counterpart in municipal government for the profusion of clientele-oriented agencies which had begun to overgrow the higher levels of government.

The difference between municipal and other governments in this respect has been a persistent one. In cities, the dominant administrative categories continue to be defined in functional terms—police protection, education, sewage disposal, fire fighting, and refuse collection, for example. But in the states, and especially in the national government, the functional grouping of administrative responsibilities is much more frequently interrupted by the intrusions of clientelism as a principle of organization. Different types of administrative functions may be drawn together under the jurisdiction of a single agency because they are all designed to benefit the same segment of the population. In other cases, a single type of service—collecting price information, for example—may be performed by several separate agencies, because several different clienteles have a need for it. When embodied in the formal structures of administrative agencies, clientelism means that bureaucratic subdivisions will correspond to population groupings and that bureaucracies will specialize not only in particular types of services but in the types of people served.[22]

In national government, the formal arrangements for clientele-oriented administration are embedded in a more general pattern of bureaucratic politics and policymaking. A bureaucratic regime that permits public agencies to specialize in serving particular clienteles is also one in which the private interests of clientele groups are likely to tinge the conduct of public business. This blending of public and private interests is encouraged less by the formal characteristics of administrative organization than by political expediency. Federal agencies characteristically enjoy a high degree of autonomy from presidential or party control. The price of this freedom, as Grant McConnell has observed, is that they also tend to be isolated from executive or partisan protection. Such isolation may leave an agency dangerously exposed to external assault and ready to seek security from these dangers in the embrace of a clientele group. "In return for special consideration of its interests," says McConnell, "the private group supports and defends the agency from attack and from demands that general executive policy be followed." From many such alliances, there emerges a pattern of bureaucratic politics whose chief characteristic is "the conquest of segments of formal state power by private groups and associations."[23] To endow these conquests with legitimacy, there is the ideology of "interest-group liberalism," in which it becomes "both necessary and good that the policy agenda and the public interest be defined in terms of the organized interests in society."[24]

By most accounts, clientelism is a characteristic feature of federal administration, but until recently the formal organization of municipal bureaucracy has carried hardly a trace of this tendency. An important part of the explanation may lie in the political histories of cities. Though a later generation of reformers would attempt to hold party politics at arm's length from urban administration, it cannot escape notice that municipal bureaucracies grew up in cities of the nineteenth century side by side with urban political machines. Machine politics, with its particularistic exchange relationships and its personalistic appeals, may seem an odd accompaniment for a city's first steps toward the rule-governed rationalism of bureaucratic administration. But beneath its inapposite operating style, the machine possessed another character which may have been more congenial to bureaucratic development. It was an instrument of political centralization. The function of the machine politician was to gather together the fragments of power that lay scattered through a municipality and, by subjecting them to central direction, to reduce the sometimes wild unpredictability of city politics.[25]

The concern for political predictability and central control was one that machine bosses shared with other municipal actors. Martin Shefter, in a persuasive account of political party consolidation in New York, concludes that the Tammany empire was founded upon a coalition between party politicians and members of the city's upper class—chiefly the representatives of established manufacturing and mercantile firms. The partners in this alliance had a common interest in the orderly management of a turbulent mass electorate, in taming the extortionate impulses of ward politicians through a reliable system of party discipline, and in reducing the opportunities for lesser businessmen to exercise influence by bribing low-level public officials.[26]

Where such interests flourished, there might be considerable resistance to the centrifugal pull of administrative clientelism, and the proponents of central control seem to have flourished more often than they failed. Writing almost fifty years after the consolidation of the Tammany forces, Frank Kent discerned a prevailing pattern of alliance between urban political bosses and "the big business interests," who turned to the boss as "a way of keeping things from running wild." Kent conceded that the businessmen might hate the necessity of relying on the boss, "but," he observed, "the necessity exists, and they would far rather have one boss with centralized power to deal with than a lot of little ones with influence over only a few votes."[27]

A political system in which the notion of "one boss with centralized power" had such forceful and durable appeal was an inauspicious setting for the proliferation of strong, organized administrative clienteles, and still less promising as a situation in which such groups might achieve formal bureaucratic recognition. Under the shadow of the machine, for example, one of the more plausible platforms for clientele organization—the urban neighborhood—appears to have been allowed few opportunities for the development of an independent organizational life.[28] If clients—the people who were beneficiaries or targets of an agency's services—could organize to influence the conduct of administration themselves, they would have little need, after all, for the mediating services and special favors of machine politicians.

The machine was the leading manifestation of centralizing tendencies that ran strong in city politics during the last third of the nineteenth century and persisted for some time afterward. A second sign of the times was the rise of municipal imperialism. Beginning before the Civil War, big cities grew bigger by absorbing politically independent communities on their outskirts. The purpose of the central city's "imperial dominion," according to Milton Kotler, was "to control the neighborhoods for the sake of the economic and political interest of the central business district, which had formerly been impaired by their political independence."[29] Its result was certainly to subject municipal affairs more firmly to central direction.

Municipal bureaucracy itself was a third element that contributed to the same trend. Urban services became more predictable and controllable when responsibility for them rested with the full-time employees of bureaucratic agencies and did not depend on volunteerism of philanthropy. Administration might be even further insulated from extraneous disturbances when it was organized around functions rather than clienteles. A municipal client confronting a functionally organized bureaucracy finds that he must look to several separate agencies in order to advance his interests as a consumer of urban services. The residents of a neighborhood, for example, must deal with one agency if they are worried about public health, another if their concern is refuse collection, and still a third if the problem is dilapidated housing. When the interests of a clientele group are disaggregated in this fashion across several different agencies, no particular agency is likely to feel the full force of its influence. Such administrative arrangements could inhibit even the formation of clientele organizations. For political machines, on the other hand, the full-time patronage jobs that become available in an expanding municipal bureaucracy may have provided an important stimulus to growth.

At a time when national administration was drifting toward clientelism, therefore, municipal bureaucracies were taking shape under the influence of political circumstances that made them relatively immune to the direct pressures of clientele groups and organizations. The urban administrative regime was nourished by centralizing tendencies of which political machines, municipal imperialism, and urban bureaucracy itself were all manifestations. In fact, the same centralizing trends that made city agencies resistant to clientelism may well have increased the susceptibility of national administration to these pressures. At least one turn-of-the-century political observer, Moise Ostrogorski, perceived a direct relationship between the rise of powerful local party machines and the decomposition of party organizations in national government.[30] Without unified national parties to provide political leadership, federal agencies were left to work out their own political destinies, and their destinies frequently included political alliances and understandings with the clientele groups most directly interested in agency business. A weak or fragmented national party structure, according to Norton Long, both permits and makes necessary such partnerships between national public agencies and private interest groups—"permits because it fails to protect administration from pressures and fails to provide adequate direction and support, makes necessary because it fails to develop a consensus on a leadership and a program that makes possible administration on the basis of shared decisional premises."[31]

In cities, however, the political conditions that accompanied the emergence of municipal bureaucracies made youthful public agencies less reliant on the support of clientele groups. Here, Ostrogorski found centralized political party organizations whose presence helped to keep organized interest groups from intruding directly upon government institutions and inhibited government's access to the interest groups. The local party boss, Ostrogorski observed, was like a broker or wholesale dealer in influence. As he centralized political power in his own hands, "he drove the 'lobby' into the background just as in commerce and industry the small shopkeepers or manufacturers retired before the large stores and factories."[32]

Although most of the machine politicians have since retired to the background themselves, contemporary assessments continue to place the "lobby" on the sidelines of city politics: "Interest groups are neither so well organized, extensive or effective in local political activity as they are in state or national politics."[33] In part, the peripheral role of private interest groups in municipal affairs today may reflect the continuing influence of the political and administrative arrangements laid down in the centralist era of the urban machine. But other factors have undoubtedly helped to keep alive the legacy of the city bosses—or at least that portion of its which has inhibited the emergence of organized clientele groups and retarded development of the bureaucratic clientelism that continues to distinguish national from municipal administration.

One significant consideration is that the political leaders who supplanted the boss and his partisans in many cities may have been no more hospitable to clientelism than their predecessors. Municipal reformers from the turn of the century onward usually equaled the bosses in their devotion to governmental centralism and surpassed them in their determination to resist "local and particularistic interests." Reform proposals for at-large elections, city-manager government, and other modifications of municipal structure "would concentrate political power by sharply centralizing the processes of decision-making rather than distribute it through more popular participation in public affairs."[34] The fact that both the urban machine and the municipal reform movement harbored such centralist inclinations may help to account for another similarity between them. The same kinds of upper-class allies who could be found among the backers of Tammany were also prominent among the supporters of urban reform, and they exhibited a similar concern for political predictability and central control. "The business, professional, and upper-class groups who dominated municipal reform movements," writes Samuel Hays, "were all involved in the rationalization and systematization of modern life. . . . The most important single feature of their perspective was the rapid expansion of the geographical scope of affairs which they wished to influence and manipulate, a scope which was no longer limited and narrow, no longer within the confines of pedestrian communities, but was now broad and city-wide, covering the whole range of activities of the metropolitan area."[35]

Such aspirations called for a degree of central coordination in city politics that easily matched anything of which a machine boss might be capable, but they also provided the foundations for a centralist ideology more explicit and complete than any of the boss's attempts at self-justification. By insisting on a city-wide arena for the conduct of public business, the municipal reformers helped to call into being a city-wide interest—an interest, they argued, "that pertained to the city 'as a whole' and that should always prevail over competing, partial (and usually private) interests."[36] Municipal government could realize its highest potential, the reformers thought, "when political leadership is exercised by men representing the public at large, rather than 'special interests.'"[37]

Viewed by itself, the reform ideology has the look of a self-evident and not especially insightful truth. Its claim to ideological distinction has usually rested less on its own intellectual content than on the contrast that it presented to the machine politician's way of doing business: reformers were public-regarding, presumably, while the boss was private regarding. The distinction, however, has proved to be an elusive one,[38] and in the effort to establish a clear difference between bosses and reformers an even more remarkable contrast has been almost completely overlooked. While the ideology of the municipal reformers elevated the general above the special interest, the developing orthodoxy in national politics seemed to do just the opposite. "Interest-group liberalism," whose influence in national administration has been described by Theodore Lowi,[39] rested its definition of the public interest on the same competing, partial, and private interests that the municipal reformers had refused to recognize. That two such different ruling ideologies should exist within a single political culture at approximately the same time is not merely a curiousity but an additional sign of a systematic difference between urban and national politics. Although the reformers' creed was forged to express a division within the urban polity, it may be even more revealing as a reflection of what is distinctive about city politics as a whole.

In addition to meeting the transient exigencies of the war against the machine, for instance, the reformers' collectivist principles may also have had some foundation in the character of municipal business itself. It was not merely that city administration tended to be organized around functions rather than clienteles; the nature of the functions themselves was also notable.

The responsibilities which had been thrust on municipal governments during the nineteenth century were by-products of urbanization.[40] In nonurban settings they seldom became matters of public policy, but when a large and heterogeneous population was densely packed together within a relatively small area, such things as trash disposal, policing, fire protection, and water supply soon became major items of public business. Urbanization had not only increased the magnitude of these problems. It changed their character. In a sparsely populated rural area a casual approach to garbage disposal might be a sign of personal slovenliness, but in a densely populated city it could become a public health and fire hazard whose costly consequences might be borne by thousands of one's fellow citizens. Most municipal agencies were organized around such problems; it was their responsibility to control the costs and hazards that the activities of some citizens imposed on others. The principal clientele for municipal services was therefore the "others"—an indefinite category of citizens whose membership could hardly ever be specified in advance. They were the anonymous public-at-large who reappeared in the municipal reformers' conception of the urban political community.

But they were unlikely to figure so prominently in the practical operations of public agencies. Where the identity of the clientele was uncertain, bureaucrats would not be powerfully drawn to clientelism, and the origins of some municipal services help to reveal just how diffuse the urban clientele might be. When police work emerged as a specialized bureaucratic function, for example, its focus was not the task of securing justice for the individual victims of robbery, burglary, or assault. Instead, it appears that the policeman's chief assignment was to deal with offenses against public order and public decency. Riot, drunkenness, unruly behavior, and lewd conduct were the crimes for which police departments were most urgently expected to provide remedies.[41] It was difficult to identify the individual victims of these offenses, not because they were victimless but because the victim was a generalized public-at-large whose moral sensibilities or standards of decorum had been threatened. This disembodied, collective victim seems to have been the policeman's chief and original client.

The purposes that lay behind the formation of police departments were remarkably similar to the ones that figured in the creation of public school systems. The economic and occupational advantages that individual pupils might secure through education were, as Carl Kaestle points out, a minor consideration in the design of public organizations for urban schooling. Far more important was the goal of "character-building"—the conversion of would-be street urchins, often tainted by the alien influences of immigrant parents, into "industrious, sober, punctual, God-fearing citizens."[42] Individual schoolchildren might conceivably realize material benefits from moral training of this sort—at least it could help them avoid trouble. But the proponents of public education obviously had other beneficiaries in mind. In a sense, the principal clients of the public school system were not its pupils but the members of a larger urban public who had to live with them. For this more widespread clientele, the civilizing influence of education might bring some relief from juvenile barbarism and from the more particular embarrassments of juvenile vagrancy, theft, intemperance, and prostitution.[43]

Where the intended beneficiaries of a public service were so broadly defined, the emergence of strong clientele organizations could be seriously impeded. The citizens who might enjoy the fruits of police work and public schooling did not even have a common point of contact in the policeman or the schoolteacher. One could benefit from the labors of these public servants without actually being the subject of their ministrations. Moreover, the benefits themselves were not the sort that could easily be captured by specific individuals. If municipal employees remove one citizen's garbage from the sidewalk with particular efficiency and dispatch, not only he but his neighbors as well may have reason to be grateful. What is true for such municipal goods as public sanitation is even more emphatically the case where benefits like public order, public health, or "character-building" are concerned. They are diffuse commodities which bear a limited resemblance to the economist's "public goods." If one city resident is to enjoy the advantages that come from these things, the same advantages must necessarily become accessible to many of his fellow citizens. Since it is difficult to restrict the distribution of these benefits to specific people, they would be relatively ineffective as membership incentives in the construction or maintenance of a bureaucracy's clientele organizations.[44]

The benefits of most municipal services, though not always the services themselves, tend to be indivisible.[45] A similar indivisibility may also be found, of course, in the products of a few national agencies—

most notably, the ones concerned with international defense or diplomacy. National security, in fact, is routinely cited as an example of an indivisible public good. But the national agencies that deal in this comprehensive commodity are, for that reason, a rather distinctive breed within the federal bureaucracy, and it is significant that one of the singular traits of their species is its relative independence from clientele organizations. "While bureaucratic policy-making in many fields has been primarily a reflection of a system of external group pressures," writes Francis Rourke, national defense is one "where the expertise and interests of bureaucratic organizations have themselves been controlling factors in the evolution of public policy."[46] Among national agencies, the bureaucratic characteristics associated with defense and diplomacy are distinctive ones, but what is distinctive in national administration is typical of its municipal counterpart.

Outside the field of national security, it is true that some other federal agencies also seem to exhibit a strong "municipal" character. The resemblance is especially pronounced in the case of federal regulatory agencies, created (like the urban bureaucracies) to protect the public-at-large against costly or dangerous consequences arising from the activities of particular classes of private citizens or business corporations. Yet, unlike the municipal bureaucracies, these national agencies have been notable as the roosting places for a large and varied flock of private interest groups—most of them representing industries subject to regulation and some of them powerful enough to capture the regulating agencies.[47] On the one hand, the case of the federal regulatory agencies suggests that services designed for the public-at-large may be no more typical of urban administration than they are of national administration. On the other hand, the federal example casts serious doubt on the proposition that such diffuse definitions of the bureaucratic clientele tend to inhibit the emergence of strong bureaucratic lobbies.

In fact, the apparent similarities between national regulatory agencies and municipal bureaucracies tend to fade away on close examination. Studies of the regulatory agencies indicate that many of them were brought into being not to protect the public at large against the abuses of business corporations but to protect the business corporations from one another and from the rigors of cutthroat competition in new or turbulent industries. These national regulatory agencies were intended to serve as "managers and coordinators" rather than as policemen, and the business and industrial groups that eventually emerged as bureaucratic clientele organizations were frequently the same groups whose lobbying efforts had helped the create the regulatory agencies in the first place. From their beginnings, therefore, such agencies as the Federal Trade Commission, the Civil Aeronautics

Board, the Atomic Energy Commission, and the Federal Communications Commission had limited and rather clearly defined clienteles, and, says Paul Sabatier, they "were intended—both by their original proponents and their legislative sovereigns—to be 'captured.' "[48] They conformed not to the administrative pattern which has prevailed among municipal bureaucracies but to a clientele-oriented model already well established at other points in the national government.

Where the charter of a regulatory agency did not deliberately make a place for the spokesmen of "special interests," other circumstances might enable the targets of regulation to attain far greater influence in national regulatory agencies than their counterparts did in municipal bureaucracies. In order to understand the difference between urban and national bureaucracies in this respect, one need only consider who was to be regulated in each of the two situations. The objects of federal regulation included bankers, railroads, interstate trucking companies, airlines, and drug manufacturers; in municipal administration they included criminals, drunks, prostitutes, children, and disease carriers. While the regulatory efforts of the national government were generally directed at the wealthy and powerful, those of the municipalities tended to converge on the socially and politically handicapped, who had neither the prestige to command bureaucratic deference nor the influence and organization to make themselves politically useful to administrative agencies. What was characteristic of municipal services, therefore, was not simply the indivisibility of their benefits but the distribution of their costs, which fell heavily on groups that were ill-equipped to shift them elsewhere.

Behind the diffuse public interest that policemen and schoolteachers served, it was possible to discern distinct class interests. A part of the urban bureaucrat's original task—perhaps the most important part— was to protect the persons, property, and moral sensibilities of respectable, usually Protestant, citizens against lower-class tenement dwellers who were coarse, unruly, disease ridden, and frequently foreign. Some optimists even expressed the hope that a strong dose of municipal services might convert tenement dwellers into decent, law-abiding, and serviceable citizens. Not surprisingly, the tenement dwellers often failed to evince much enthusiasm for the products of municipal administration. The benefits of urban services might be indivisible, accessible to the public in general, but considerable segments of the public had no particular interest in them. Municipal services did not arise automatically from the imperatives of urbanization; they had to be imposed. In the creation of public school systems, for example, Michael Katz finds a general pattern of imposition: "In the first place . . . educational reform was imposed by the prominent upon the community. Second, the goals that reform represented the imposition of upper- and middle-class fears and perceptions of social deficiencies. Third, the content of a reformed education represented an imposition of the values of communal leaders on the rest of society."[49]

In national administration, organizations representing "special interests" converted public authority into private property so that they might capture the products of government for their own use while denying access to a larger public. Through municipal bureaucracy, on the other hand, a privileged stratum of the population, with its own vision of the public order of things, converted its private wants into public goods, accessible to everyone regardless of personal preference. The aim was not to seize the fruits of urban bureaucracy for a particular group but to make municipal consumers of the public at large.

Urban Bureaucracy and the Problem of Service Delivery

For consumers of municipal services, the inducements to organize are relatively weak. Benefits accessible to the public-at-large seldom yield powerful incentives to particular members of the public in return for organizational activism. Urban clients who rise up in pressure groups to demand better services will often find that what they win through their organizational efforts may subsequently be enjoyed—without effort—by many of their less energetic neighbors. Because they face such difficulties in capturing the fruits of their own labors, clientele organizations may also face special problems in generating the rewards that are necessary to elicit the exertions of members or supporters. In general, groups that look for organizational resources in the outputs of municipal government are likely to discover that they are mining low-grade ore.

But other arenas in city politics offer far more promising territory for organizational endeavor. While the incentives to organize are usually indivisible, elusive, or diffuse for the consumers of municipal outputs, they can be powerful and distinct for the suppliers of municipal inputs. Those who provide labor, credit, materials, or contractual services to municipal government rarely need worry that their rewards will escape into the hands of the public-at-large. And organizations able to influence the distribution of these highly divisible rewards can therefore offer benefits to their members and supporters which nonmembers and non-supporters do not receive. The result is a superior capacity to attract and retain followers—a more substantial kind of drawing power than municipal consumer groups can derive from dealing in benefits that may be shared by members and nonmembers alike.

This difference in the efficacy of group incentives may help to explain why the organizational center of gravity in city politics has almost always tended to lie on the supply side of municipal government—among the holders of municipal jobs, municipal bonds, and municipal contracts. It was in this setting, rich with patronage, that urban machines once flourished, and when the old machines died away new concentrations of organized power drew nourishment from the same kinds of resources. The political vigor and prominence of today's municipal employee unions, sustained by their control of city jobs, wages, and working conditions, is a recent variation on a well-established urban theme.[50]

Some of the most muscular interest groups in city politics have drawn support from the economy of municipal inputs, and organizations based on the interests of suppliers have become all the more weighty in urban politics precisely because the incentive systems of municipal consumer groups seldom generate enough organizational energy to offset their influence. With the balance of group strength tilted toward the suppliers, municipal governments have developed a decided list in the same direction. In cities, as Norton Long notes, "Legislators and most elected officials show far more interest in contracts, buildings, and jobs, the inputs of the political system, than in the outputs, the delivery of goods and services to the citizen."[51]

In political terms, the most important outputs of municipal government have been its inputs. Like a production line being run in reverse, urban governments often seem to produce public services and facilities primarily for the sake of consuming the raw materials needed to manufacture them. Under some urban regimes of the past—the Tweed Ring, for example—generating business for municipal suppliers has been an unconcealed preoccupation of city government, the chief means for organizing the political support needed to control the electorate and to govern.[52] Recent urban leaders may have been more discreet than Boss Tweed about the compulsion to create public jobs and contracts, but the pressure to satisfy municipal suppliers continues to shape the course of urban government. If today's mayors, for example, have sometimes seemed preoccupied with the construction of convention centers, stadiums, expressways, mass transit systems, and urban redevelopment projects, it is not simply to earn the diffuse thanks of the citizens who will eventually use these facilities but also the more organized and reliable gratitude of the people who finance, design, or build these large-scale projects. On foundations such as these, Robert Moses was able to construct an urban bureaucratic empire.[53]

The imperial possibilities are far more limited for other urban public executives, most of whom find few occasions to build public facilities on

a monumental scale, especially in cities that have stopped growing. If
they are to gain political support outside their own agencies, they must
look primarily to the clients who benefit from their services, not to
suppliers who provide them with raw materials. Since the benefits of
municipal services are usually diffuse and relatively indivisible, however, they are seldom of much use for organizing an agency's clientele
into a stable and cohesive constituency. Unlike many federal administrators, urban executives are frequently unable to cultivate much organized support beyond the precincts of bureaucracy itself, even when
their clients number in the tens of thousands. Although their classic
account of New York City's bureaucracy is highly sensitive to the influence of organized interests in urban administration, Sayre and Kaufman discover few organized bureaucratic constituencies as they call the
roll of the city's line agencies: "The Fire Commissioner has no helpful
constituency to assist him in any aspirations he may have for leadership
and initiative.... The Commissioner of Buildings has few opportunities
to cultivate active or helpful constituencies or to create a favorable
climate of public opinion that would provide him with support or bargaining power." The hospitals commissioner cannot "derive many opportunities for leadership from his relationships to interest groups in the
Department's constituency.... Police Commissioners never quite succeed in identifying the hard core either of their supporting groups or of
the opposition groups with whom they must come to terms. The formations and their attitudes tend to be fluid and unpredictable."[54]

The distinctive attributes of urban bureacracy have distinctive consequences for executive leadership in urban administration. Handicapped in the construction of external constituencies, the leaders of
municipal bureaucracies often turn inward to seek political support
within their own agencies—and succumb, like New York City's police
commissioners, to the necessity of being "the spokesman and the advocate" for their bureaucratic subordinates, rather than "the leader and
the innovator."[55] In the peculiar setting of urban administration, a public agency frequently becomes its own most valuable political constituency. This tendency toward political self-reliance is encouraged not only
by the absence or weakness of alternative constituencies but by the fact
that city bureaucracies themselves usually contain the makings for
powerfully supportive pressure groups. One of the most readily visible
features of urban line agencies is the large number of service-delivery
employees who stand in massed ranks at the base of the administrative
hierarchy. Well-organized and intensely interested in the political and
financial fortunes of their agencies, policemen, sanitation workers,
teachers, welfare caseworkers, or firefighters, together with their
families and friends, can make up a significant fraction of the local

electorate. With the possible exception of the U.S. Postal Service, hardly any national bureaucracy is similarly endowed with such an effective army of rank-and-file lobbyists.

In municipal agencies, these battalions of service-delivery workers also call attention to another distinguishing trait of urban bureaucracies—the prominence of service delivery itself as an administrative activity. In the executive branch of national government, there are many agencies that have surprisingly little to do with the direct delivery of public services to the people who consume them. The U.S. Office of Education, for example, has no pupils. The Law Enforcement Assistance Administration has never made an arrest. And the Department of Transportation collects no fares. While federal agencies frequently finance or advise or regulate local service-delivery organizations, only some of the national bureaucracies actually deliver services themselves, and many of these federal service providers can perform their functions without employing vast armies of street-level operatives to deal directly with individual clients. Since the clients of federal agencies are often arrayed in nonfederal or nongovernmental organizations, national bureaucracies can sometimes delegate the business of service delivery to formal constituency associations. The Department of Agriculture, for example, has relied on commodity associations to regulate the production and marketing activities of farmers, and even the Office of Education depends on its own organized constituency of state and local school officials to administer its federal aid programs.[56]

Some of the functions that street-level bureaucrats perform for municipal governments are fulfilled for national agencies by independently organized constituency groups which lend assistance not only in the work of enforcement and implementation but in other more basic tasks of administration. One fundamental objective of almost any bureaucratic organization is to create a degree of predictability and uniformity in the behavior of its clients, and in these things a national agency with a stable and organized clientele can take much for granted. The very fact that the clients have assembled themselves in organizations presupposes a certain structuring of behavior and a uniformity of purpose or attitude.[57] But urban administrators can seldom rely on such presuppositions. The clientele for a municipal bureaucracy is usually heterogeneous and diffuse and rarely comes packaged in formal associations. Without the mediating services of constituency organizations, a city agency that aims to regularize the conduct of its clients must do the job itself—by sending its own agents into the field to cope with the behavior and attitudes of the clients individually and directly. The prominence of service-delivery workers and their activities in city administration therefore reflects, in part, the same distinctively urban conditions that help to shape the political strategies of top-level municipal executives. While many national bureaucracies can rely on external constituency organizations to bring clients to agencies, most city departments cannot and must depend instead on large forces of street-level employees to carry the agencies to their clients.

Municipal agencies, of course, are also community-based institutions that conduct public business on the same streets where ordinary citizens lead their private lives, and since they stand in such close proximity to the ultimate consumers of public services, perhaps it is only natural that they should be more preoccupied than remote national agencies with the business of service delivery. As self-evident as it may seem to us, however, the idea that municipal government should be chiefly concerned with the direct delivery of public services is a rather recent development in the history of cities, far from the minds of the men who originally designed this country's municipal corporations.[58] The notion that city officials are "closer to the people" than national officials—questionable in itself—does not mean that municipal government necessarily becomes the vehicle for conveying public services to their ultimate consumers. Nor does it explain, by itself, the emphasis on street-level operations in urban agencies or the bottom-heavy character of municipal bureaucracy that results from it.

In these respects, as in many others, it is the special nature of municipal outputs and municipal clienteles that helps to account for the distinctive structure of urban administration—and for a distinctive pattern of bureaucratic behavior. The street-level public servants who figure so prominently in the conduct of municipal business are also notable for the manner in which they conduct it. As described by Michael Lipsky, the street-level pattern of administrative behavior exhibits several conspicuously unbureaucratic tendencies—broad discretion ungoverned by clearly defined administrative directives and exercised in a frequently contentious atmosphere, with much more passion and bias than Max Weber would have been willing to allow. Conflict and ambiguity seem to be present to a far greater extent in the jobs of these urban service-delivery workers than in the activities of bureaucratic foot soldiers elsewhere. Such conditions, as Lipsky suggests, may be found in many administrative settings, but they are relatively salient in the bottom ranks of several urban bureaucracies, and the understanding of them is a fundamental element in any analysis of city administration.[59]

Above all, the working behavior of the city's street-level agents seems to be shaped by the character of the services in which they deal. Most of these front-line administrators, of course, provide services of more than one kind. In fact, the variety of duties performed is one of the things that distinguishes these bureaucrats from production workers in other large organizations, but not all of the functions performed are equally decisive elements in the street-level administrative regime. In his study of the police, for example, James Q. Wilson excludes from consideration the "service" functions of patrolmen—rescuing cats, giving directions to lost travelers, liberating small children from locked bathrooms. Such activities, says Wilson, "are intended to please the client and no one else. There is not reason in principle why these services could not be priced and sold on the open market," and the fact that they are provided by the police is "only a matter of historical accident and community convenience."[60] The "service" functions, in other words, are not essential to the policeman's role, and it follows that what *is* essential—the work of law enforcement and order maintenance—can be distinguished precisely because there *are* reasons why it could not be "priced and sold on the open market." These functions are unmarketable because, like most of the important urban services, their benefits are relatively indivisible and could not be captured by anyone in particular, and it is therefore rather unlikely that anyone in particular would be willing to pay for them through voluntary purchases.

The same kinds of diffuse and indivisible benefits that color the character of municipal administration in general also help to define the work of policemen and other street-level bureaucrats, and they hold at least a clue to the difficulties that may lie in store for some of these service-delivery workers. In the first place, benefits that are diffuse or that can be captured by no one in particular do not promise to gratify anyone in particular; the clientele for these benefits may therefore be elusive or apathetic. In the second place, if marketable services are "intended to please the client," then a characteristic feature of the street-level bureaucrat's unmarketable labors is that they are *not* intended to please the client. Frequently, the particular people who receive these services are *not* intended to please the client. Frequently the particular people who receive these services are not the ones who are supposed to benefit from them. The criminal suspect arrested by a policeman, for example, is obviously not the intended beneficiary of the arrest.

In effect, the policeman has two "clienteles" which may sometimes be quite distinct from one another. There is the clientele with whom he must deal face-to-face (but need not please), and there is the clientele he is supposed to please (but may not be able to identify). In national adminstration, the people who receive public services and the ones who benefit from them are usually the same, but in urban administration the recipients and the beneficiaries are often separate, and each of these clienteles can be associated with a different sort of street-level problem. Since the beneficiaries are a diffuse public-at-large, just who should be

pleased becomes a matter of some uncertainty, and there may be considerable doubt, as a result, about what conduct is appropriate for
service-delivery workers. Since the recipients of services are *not* the
ones to be pleased, conflict and tension are likely to be inherent in
relationships between street-level bureaucrats and the people with
whom they deal.

Such hostilities are routinely encountered in certain types of municipal employment. The jobs of policemen, schoolteachers, and others,
says Michael Lipsky, are all shaped in part by "structural factors that
may contribute to the inherent inability of some bureaucracies to provide objective, nondiscriminatory service, to recognize the existence of
biased behavior, and to respond to pressure from some client groups."
The climate of resentment, insensitivity, and mutual anatagonism has
more than one source in the conditions of street-level work. Some urban
service-delivery employees, for example, routinely operate in the face of
"distinct physical and psychological threats," among citizens who may
acknowledge only bureaucratic power and not bureaucratic authority.
But the citizens, for their part, are frequently nonvoluntary recipients of
the bureaucrat's attentions. They do not come forward like customers in
an open market to purchase services that they have selected from a
range of possibilities designed to please them. Instead, they receive
treatment that they may not have sought, whose benefits are intended
not simply for them but for the public-at-large. And, since urban
service-delivery workers do not tailor public services to fit the wants of
the individual clients with whom they deal, it is evident that these
clients "do not serve as primary bureaucratic reference groups" for
street-level operatives.[61]

Those who provide diffuse or indivisible benefits to the public-at-
large can frequently expect to generate some measure of animosity and
ill-will among the particular members of the public whom they encounter directly, and in cities street-level bureaucrats often confront
this hostility without the reassuring certainty of clearly defined objectives or unambiguous rules that specify how they should proceed. In
part, the uncertainties faced by the street-level bureaucrat reflect the
vagaries of the street itself; a policeman on the beat, for example, is
expected to cope with a variety of unpredictable situations that could
not be anticipated or provided for in any book of formal rules and regulations.[62] But a similar indeterminacy also extends into the more orderly
environment of the classroom or the welfare office. The schoolteacher
must accommodate diverse and usually diffuse expectations about the
functions of educators and education,[63] and, although the rulebook is a
constant companion for welfare administrators, a majority of the caseworkers interviewed in one survey were convinced that circumstances

made it necessary for them to ignore the rules and that their work required the simultaneous pursuit of seemingly inconsistent objectives.[64] Although collecting garbage or fighting fires may give rise to few uncertainties about the business at hand, many street-level bureaucrats must operate in the face of ambiguous, contradictory, or unattainable expectations concerning the nature of their business and its purposes.[65]

Perhaps it is significant that policemen, schoolteachers, and welfare caseworkers—the service-delivery workers whose tasks seem to be most ill-defined—all have something to do with the moral regulation of the city's population, the maintenance of their community's standards for decent, respectable, and orderly conduct. The policeman enforces these standards; the teacher transmits them to succeeding generations; and the welfare worker attempts to "rehabilitate" those city dwellers who have become incapable of living their lives as upstanding and productive citizens. In an urban environment, where diverse sorts of people must live together in close quarters, the preservation of a common code of civility and morality is a most important kind of business. But it is also a nearly impossible business. Urban diversity itself implies moral heterogeneity. In a big city, there is seldom any moral consensus for street-level bureaucrats to uphold, and it is no wonder that the jobs of those charged with the task are shadowed by uncertainty and ambiguity. The task is a doubtful one, not simply because morality is a controversial subject in cities but because the intended beneficiaries of moral regulation are themselves so difficult to identify. On rare and fleeting occasions—as in antipornography campaigns, for example—they may organize themselves into discrete groups with specific interests. But, far more frequently, they remain an anonymous, invisible, and open-ended clientele whose wants are seldom clearly specified. Indivisible benefits designed to suit this diffuse public can easily become indefinable benefits, and the street-level bureaucrats who deal in these goods may therefore be left at sea.

In a national bureaucracy, uncertainty of this sort might be resolved in favor of a more proximate clientele who actually receive public services or administrative treatment—the farmers, broadcast corporations, railroads, or manufacturers directly subject to bureaucratic supervision or regulation. But for urban agencies, organized around functions rather than clienteles, it is much more difficult to engineer such solutions. The proximate clients themselves are likely to comprise a rather disparate groups, and many of them—like welfare recipients or criminal suspects—may lack the political standing to command the attention of administrative officials. Street-level bureaucrats risk the animosity of these service recipients because they presumably take their cues from the interests of a broader public. But this wider group of beneficiaries is an unorganized and largely undefined clientele whose hazy interests provide scarcely any guidance for the functions of service delivery. Among street-level bureaucrats, conflict and ambiguity are two faces of the same dilemma, and much of the behavior of the service-delivery workers may be understood as an attempt to cope with it.

Confronted by a complex, amorphous, and confusing clientele that seldom organizes itself into distinct groups, street-level workers commonly attempt to organize the clientele in their own minds and so make their tasks more manageable. The practitioners of each street-level craft tend to develop their own simplified, informal classification systems so that they can quickly recognize those service recipients who may be troublesome, dangerous, undeserving, or unlikely to respond to treatment.[66] From the perspective of the clients, the categories may seem crude stereotypes that fail to take account of the special circumstances of the individual citizens or their problems. But for the bureaucrats, they are essential labor-saving devices, aids to comprehension that permit them to routinize their work and to reduce the impossible burdens of making their decisions case by case. The need for such informal simplifying devices might be less acute if public agencies in cities could be organized around specific types of clienteles, as they frequently are in national government, and if the clients had categorized themselves by gathering together in various organized interest groups. These organizational arrangements, common in the federal bureaucracy, help to structure the clientele and its demands, and so diminish uncertainties that can tax the decision-making capabilities of administrators. In urban administration, these institutional aids are largely nonexistent, and street-level bureaucrats must invent their own informal shortcuts as substitutes.

Other commonly observed features of street-level administration might conceivably be understood in similar terms. Studies of police behavior in cities, for example, reveal that patrolmen have an especially pronounced concern about their ability to establish personal influence and authority over the people with whom they deal.[67] Some citizens, of course, can be dangerous, and this threat undoubtedly helps to explain the policeman's strong interest in achieving a commanding personal presence. But it may be significant also that policemen, like some other street-level bureaucrats, frequently find it difficult to invoke the formal and impersonal authority of rules and regulations because important parts of their jobs, designed to serve the uncertain interests of largely invisible beneficiaries cannot be specified clearly in formal rules and regulations. Establishing one's personal authority, therefore, becomes more critical to these service-delivery workers than it is for other, more conventional bureaucrats who can routinely resort to the authority of explicit regulations.

So sensitive are street-level bureaucrats where personal authority is concerned that they are apt to react with surprising vehemence when they feel that it has been called into question. Policemen, for example, seem to regard the use of force not simply as a protection against assault but as a defense against disrespect. Patrolmen themselves express the notion clearly: "If a fellow called a policeman a filthy name, a slap in the mouth would be a good thing, especially if it was out in public where calling a policeman a bad name would look bad for the police."[68] What citizens may regard as police brutality, police officers themselves perceive as a necessary means to avoid losing the personal respect of the people with whom they must deal—and with it, the ability to perform many of the tasks to which they have been assigned. Schoolteachers, whose ill-defined functions often leave them similarly detached from the impersonal authority of rules and regulations, are also inclined to take strong measures when their personal authority is threatened by personal insults or obscenities: "I realized that I couldn't leave this boy in the classroom after doing such a thing. I don't know who heard him or how many heard him but I know they just knew that something was wrong, and if they had heard what came out of his mouth they would lose all respect for me. So I had to show them that I would not stand for any nonsense and take him down to the highest authority, the principal."[69]

In the service of the public-at-large, many street-level bureaucrats must execute the uncertain mandates of an indefinite clientele whose preferences are rarely structured through the activities of organized pressure groups. Unable to operate from a sturdy foundation of clear public authority, they have to rely heavily on resources of their own— chiefly, the personal influence and respect that they can command among the clients whom they meet face-to-face. Occasionally, their preoccupation with personal authority may lead to outbursts of personal assertiveness for which these clients can see no explanation, especially since personal severity is often accompanied by official laxity. Policy behavior, for example, sometimes exhibits a curious combination of excessive pugnacity and unauthorized restraint. Patrolmen seem inclined to deal roughly with offenders, but also to underenforce the law,[70] and the concern for personal authority may lie behind both those tendencies. A policeman who deliberately declines to enforce the law not only avoids possible antagonism but also places the offenders in his debt and therefore increases his personal influence with potentially troublesome clients.[71] The dictates of public policy and the diffuse interests of a remote public are likely to carry little weight in the face of a street-level bureaucrat's immediate, perhaps urgent need to maintain personal command of diverse service recipients and to make them and their problems manageable. In effect, these service-delivery workers take their cues not from the clients with whom they deal or from the clients who benefit from their activities but from the special demands of their own jobs, and the result is a distinctive kind of bureaucratic tension.

The chief mission of an urban bureaucracy is service delivery, and its activities are therefore concentrated among municipal clients and consumers. But the political center of gravity for municipal administration usually lies among the suppliers and producers, whose organizational advantages have already been outlined. The result is that the mission of service delivery tends to become the "problem" of service delivery, and a focus of organizational stress. The political constituency and the administrative clientele—usually identical for the domestic agencies of national government—are frequently quite distinct from one another in urban bureaucracy. Signs of this disjunction appear at all levels of the administrative hierarchy, from the political strategies of top-level executives to the coping strategies of street-level bureaucrats. They are manifestations of a general bureaucratic and political pattern that is common in cities, less common in the administrative structures of state governments, and less widespread still in national bureaucratic institutions. But it is also a pattern whose nature and distribution have obviously been modified by recent changes, both urban and national.

Directions of Change

One or two generations ago, students of urban society tackled the city as a whole in an effort to develop a general theory of urbanism. They seem to have approached the enterprise by first asking themselves what it was that distinguished an urban society from a nonurban society. By exploring the contrasts between "ideal-typical polar concepts" of rural and urban, such social scientists as Louis Wirth attempted to identify the distinctive characteristics of city life and then composed a network of hypotheses concerning the relationships among them.[72] The notion of comparing rural and urban societies made especially good sense in a time when one of the most striking urban phenomena was the migration of rural and peasant populations to big cities. Under the circumstances, there must have been something almost tangible about the confrontation between rural and urban "ideal-typical polar concepts." The rural-urban continuum was not just a theoretical abstraction but a path that millions traveled.

Today the continuum carries much less traffic, and, as a device for understanding the significant dimension of social and political change, the framework of rural-urban contrasts no longer seems so helpful. In this country at least, the process of urbanization has all but run its course. Yet even while it was in full swing, social scientists had already begun to shift their attentions to another, increasingly noticeable kind of transformation. A preoccupation with the urbanization of the village gradually gave way to a concern with the nationalization of the city. One by one, functions traditionally reserved for urban communities have been taken up by organizations that do not put down roots in cities, or in any local domain. The growth of an extra-local presence in the local community was a trend already recognized in major community studies of the 1920s and 1930s.[73] To many observers, it seemed that local economies and local cultures were becoming mere tributaries of a national economy and culture.[74]

Urban politics has undergone a similar transformation. As state, national, and metropolitan governments have come to exercise greater authority in local affairs, the prestige and authority of municipal government appear to have faded,[75] and the range of its concerns has steadily diminished. Differences of functional scope between the governments of older cities and those of younger cities testify to the historical progress of a trend toward the contradiction of municipal jurisdictions.[76]

The shifting of municipal functions to state or national institutions may signify not only a narrowing of the urban political arena but also a change in its character. During the 1960s, when the federal government entered an interventionist phase in urban policy, the signs and directions of this change disclosed themselves more clearly than they usually do. What was notable about the federal efforts was the extent to which they sought to transform municipal institutions by mobilizing municipal clienteles. For a time, "citizen participation" became the slogan and the common denominator in a national, multifront war on urban deprivation and deterioration. The Community Action Program, the Model Cities Program, and other urban ventures of the federal government attempted not only to cope with problems of city decay and city poverty but to create organized constituencies to support these efforts. In effect, the policies of the Great Society transplanted a national, clientele-oriented pattern of administration to the nation's municipalities. The programs were intended not for the public at large but for particular segments of the public, and their organizational arrangements created an official role for client groups or their representatives in administrative decision making.

The urban environment, of course, imposed a few changes of its own on the clientele-centered structure of national administration. Where the clientele was an "unmobilized multitude," federal emissaries could expect to find few ready-made, organized interest groups, and the task of manufacturing these administrative adjuncts therefore became a major preoccupation for the national government's urban programs. The results was a shift in the technique of constructing bureaucratic alliances, a movement whose end product, says Eugene Lewis, was the "new co-option": "In the past, administrative organizations became the objects of the 'affections' of organized groups in society that could bring some sort of reward and punishment to their intended. The new co-option involves the identification of a group of people according to some ascribed criteria (such as distance from an arbitrary poverty line), the creation of an agency or agencies to meet the discovered group's needs, and a commitment of some resources to organizing the discovered group into a clientele and constituency."[77]

In the federal government, the process of "discovering" clienteles, made fashionable during the days of urban mobilization, continued long after national attention had moved from cities to other subjects. Federal policy has done much to convert population categories—consumers, the handicapped, women, the elderly—into self-conscious, organized interest groups. And pressure groups themselves seem to have caught the spirit of the new co-option. The recent emergence of public interest lobbies in national government represents an attempt to provide an unorganized multitude with a distinct voice. The lobbies do not arise from previously organized groups in society but seek to create an organized interest where none existed before. To some extent, of course, almost all political lobbies must bring into being the groups that they claim to represent, but public interest organizations constitute an extreme case of the phenomenon, and their distinctiveness in this respect has brought them considerable attention as institutional innovations in American politics.[78] Yet their functions, rhetoric, and organization seem to have been anticipated by the municipal reform and good government organizations of several generations past. Like today's public interest lobbies, the urban good government groups were formed to assert the claim that they spoke for the best interests of a diffuse and unorganized public-at-large—a claim that was symptomatic of the singular character of city politics and administration. Such organizational patterns, once associated with municipal politics, seem to appear with increasing frequency in national government. It is too soon to judge whether and to what extent these echoes of urban politics were set off by the federal government's intimate contacts with municipal institutions during the 1960s, but there are certainly hints that the nationalization of city politics may be accompanied by an "urbanization" of national politics.

On balance, however, it is clearly municipal politics that has been reshaped more completely by the experience of federal-local interaction, and the general effect of the encounter has probably been a further bureaucratization of the urban polity. Although the federal government initiated its urban offensive of the 1960s with a campaign of citizen mobilization, the end products of the effort have not been so populist as its beginnings—or its early critics—sometimes suggested. There is some evidence that federally sponsored community action programs actually did increase the responsiveness of local institutions to the interests of citizens who were poor or who belonged to racial minorities,[79] but "maximum feasible participation" was a notion subject to so many different interpretations that it could easily be adapted to other interests as well.[80]

Especially important was the interest of federal granting agencies in rationalizing their work—an interest that occasionally threatened to collide with the requirements of democratic participation. But since federal policy did not specify clearly just what kind of participation was feasible, and how much was maximum, there was usually sufficient flexibility to define participation so that it could be reconciled with the demands of administrative rationality.[81] In some respects, moreover, citizen participation might actually help to reinforce administrative authority and stability. Bureaucratic decisions, unsanctified by the electoral process, might be endowed with a certain democratic legitimacy if they could be made in consultation with "the community."[82] Perhaps most significant was the fact that federally sponsored community organizations provided not only a forum for the expression of citizen demands but a mechanism for structuring and channeling them. Explicit arrangements for citizen participation could, therefore, afford public agencies some protection against the unpredictability of an unorganized and turbulent urban clientele.

For national agencies administering urban programs, such aids to organizational stability are highly valuable. To achieve an orderly allocation of their time and resources, federal officials need to establish a stable flow of projects requesting funds and a steady stream of reliable information about local events. Yet the managers of national urban programs often encounter disorder and instability among the local clients of federal assistance. An inclusive and undifferentiated constituency, largely untamed by the discipline of organization, does not provide a favorable background for bureaucratic routinization. Federal urban policy has often sought to subdivide this sprawling clientele into more homogeneous groupings whose demands might be more predictable and more manageable, and it has attempted in several other ways to manufacture the conditions for administrative orderliness. Apart from organizing their own local constituencies, federal agencies have sometimes attempted to generate a sustained local demand for their own services. When local institutions are incapable of producing the regular succession of grant proposals on which bureaucratic stability depends, a federal agency can attempt to stimulate this steady flow of projects by sending out "teams that suggest the kind of projects desired and that may even help to draw them up." In other situations, the federal supplier of urban assistance may employ preexisting bureaucratic institutions in a metropolitan area as bulwarks against the uncertainties of an urban environment. Like the donor of foreign aid to a developing country, it "seeks oases of calm and stability in the form of autonomous organizations that do not have to follow civil service regulations and that control their own funds. The donor establishes genial relations with subunits in the recipient nation. They have a supportive relationship: one spends and the other supplies the money."[83]

The common element in these varied national strategies for urban intervention is a consistent tendency toward bureaucratic rationalization and stability—a movement whose crowning achievement to date has probably been the Federal Revenue Sharing Program, which attempts to reduce the diverse and irregular demands of urban constituencies to an arithmetic formula. To guard against the disruptive uncertainties of city politics, national urban policy seems to have operated increasingly from the shelter of "artificially" organized clienteles, the autonomy of established bureaucratic strongholds, or the security of mathematical calculations. One result of these administrative defense measures, according to Jeffrey Pressman, has been to create or reinforce arenas of decision making that are relatively detached from the urban polity as a whole.[84] They are the local outposts of national agencies and national programs, affected as much by the political climate in Washington as by the atmosphere in Cleveland or Indianapolis, and their emergence may formalize the decomposition of urban communities already far gone toward fragmentation. "Enterprises that operate at the national level," observes Herman Turk, "may have little reason to establish many relationships with one another at the local level or with other local organizations."[85] As local manifestations of national institutions, the bureaucratic arenas of urban governance tend to grow into disconnected subgovernments, and the urban public at large is transformed into a patchwork of distinct "publics."

In some respects, the drift toward bureaucratic routinization simply carries forward a political tradition that already has a long history in

American cities. Its earlier expressions include the turn-of-the-century reformers' drive for the "systematization and rationalization" and the struggles of political bosses to create the conditions for stability and predictability in municipal affairs. But these precedents do not anticipate some aspects of bureaucratic politics in today's disjointed urban communities. Bosses and reformers sought to tame an unruly political system; contemporary urban bureaucracies seem more inclined to detach themselves from it.

The unifying ambitions of municipal reformers and the centralizing efforts of municipal bosses appear to have been left behind as city bureaucracies look for sources of support and stability beyond the city limits, in a variety of national institutions and federal agencies, and as they fortify their local strongholds with organized interest groups or special clienteles. Studies of recent revenue-sharing and block-grant programs have already detected some increase of local interest-group activity in connection with the distribution of divisible federal largesse by local authorities.[86] In some cities, publicly financed but privately run community corporations have emerged as important organizational auxiliaries for municipal agencies. And, of course, federal grant programs have done much to convert the cities themselves into pressure groups competing for favored treatment by national authorities. Revenue-sharing, block grants, and earlier federal urban policies have served not only to transfer federal money to municipal treasuries but also to transfuse the cities with a national pattern of bureaucratic, interest-group politics whose outlines and outcomes have been clarified by the work of Grant McConnell.

The emergent political end product of this nationalization process seems to lie beyond the framework that was established by the traditional contention between bosses and reformers. The conflict between the machine and its enemies was a struggle about the control and nature of the public arena in cities. The boss catered to private interests in order to create a unified urban polity. The ideology of the reformer, though tinged by private interests itself, contained an image of a public order. But recent political movements in cities seem to point only to a withering away of the municipality as a public sphere. In an age of bureaucratic privatism, the diffuse urban "public-at-large" appears to become increasingly superfluous, both as an ideological concept and as a basis for the power of unorganized minorities. Urban bureaucracies seem to be developing a closer resemblance to their clientele-oriented counterparts in the federal government. Experience with this administrative regime at the national level gives little reason to hope that it will enhance the democratic responsiveness of government at the local level.

What is likely to be enhanced is the fragmented and bureaucratic character of city politics. What is likely to be lost is the distinctive legacy of "publicness" which had consistently forced its way to the surface of city politics—through the private regardingness of machine bosses and municipal reformers' zeal for government-as-business.

Notes

1. See Robert Lineberry and Ira Sharkansky, *Urban Politics and Public Policy*, 3d ed. (New York: Harper & Row, 1978), p. 268; Carl A. McCandless, *Urban Government and Politics* (New York: McGraw-Hill Book Co., 1970), p. 276.

2. Theodore Lowi, "Machine Politics—Old and New," *New Interest*, no. 9 (Fall 1967), pp. 83–92.

3. Ibid., pp. 87, 83.

4. Grant McConnell, *Private Power and American Democracy* (New York: Alfred A. Knopf, Inc., 1966), p. 161.

5. Lincoln Steffens, *The Shame of the Cities* (New York: Hill & Wang, 1957), pp. 1–17.

6. See, e.g., Edward Banfield and James Q. Wilson, "Public-regardingness as a Value Premise in Voting Behavior," *American Political Science Review* 58 (December 1964): 876–87; Robert L. Lineberry and Edmund P. Fowler, "Reformism and Public Policies in American Cities," *American Political Science Review* 61 (September 1967): 701–16; Edward C. Banfield, *Political Influence* (New York: Free Press, 1961), chap. 8; Raymond Wolfinger, *The Politics of Progress* (Englewood Cliffs, N.J.: Prentice-Hall, Inc., 1974), chap. 4.

7. Martin Shefter, "The Emergence of the Political Machine: An Alternative View," in Willis Hawley and Michael Lipsky (eds.), *Theoretical Perspectives on Urban Politics* (Englewood Cliffs, N.J.: Prentice-Hall, Inc., 1976), p. 14.

8. Edward Banfield and James Q. Wilson, *City Politics* (Cambridge, Mass.: Harvard University Press, 1963), p. 234.

9. Demetrios Caraley, *City Government and Urban Problems* (Englewood Cliffs, N.J.: Prentice-Hall, Inc., 1977), p. 248.

10. Robert L. Lineberry, *Equality and Urban Policy: The Distribution of Municipal Public Services* (Beverly Hills, Calif.: Sage Publications, 1977); Sharon Krefetz, *Welfare Policy Making and City Politics* (New York: Praeger Pubs., 1976); Frank Levy et al., *Urban Outcomes: Schools, Streets, and Libraries* (Berkeley: University of California Press, 1974).

11. Douglas Fox, *The Politics of City and State Bureaucracy* (Pacific Palisades, Calif.: Goodyear Publishing Co., 1974), p. 1; see also Eugene Lewis, *The Urban Political System* (Hinsdale, Ill.: Dryden Press, 1973), p. 151; Herbert Jacob and Michael Lipsky, "Outputs, Structure and Power: An Assessment of Changes in the Study of State and Local Politics," *Journal of Politics* 30 (May 1968): 510–38.

12. David Rogers, *110 Livingston Street: Politics and Bureaucracy in the New York City School System* (New York: Vintage Books, 1969), p. 267; Norman I. Fainstein and Susan Fainstein, *Urban Political Movements* (Englewood Cliffs, N.J.: Prentice-Hall, Inc., 1974), pp. 182–83.

13. Wallace Sayre and Herbert Kaufman, *Governing New York City* (New York: W. W. Norton & Co., 1965), pp. 709–16; Paul E. Peterson, *School Politics Chicago Style* (Chicago: University of Chicago Press, 1976), pp. 123–24.

14. Jerome Skolnick, *Justic without Trial* (New York: John Wiley & Sons, 1967), p. 13.

15. Francis E. Rourke, *Bureaucracy, Politics, and Public Policy*, 2d ed. (Boston: Little, Brown & Co., 1976).

16. J. Leiper Freeman, *The Political Process: Executive Bureau–Legislative Committee Relations* (Garden City, N.Y.: Doubleday, 1955).

17. Matthew Holden, "The Politics of Urbanization," in *People and Politics in Urban Society*, ed. Harlan Hahn (Beverly Hills, Calif.: Sage Publications, 1972), pp. 562–63.

18. Roger Lane, *Policing the City: Boston, 1822–1855* (Cambridge, Mass.: Harvard University Press, 1967), chap. 3; James F. Richardson, *The New York Police: Colonial Times to 1901* (New York: Oxford University Press, 1970), chap. 2; Bayrd Still, *Milwaukee: The History of a City* (Madison: State Historical Society of Wisconsin, 1948), p. 232; Robert M. Fogelson, *The Fragmented Metropolis: Los Angeles, 1850–1930* (Cambridge, Mass.: Harvard University Press, 1967), p. 35. It should be noted that simple differences in the size of the political arena may provide one explanation for the varying role of organized interest groups in city and in national politics. In national government, e.g., the constituency may be sufficiently large and heterogeneous to support a wide variety of vigorous pressure groups. In a city, on the other hand, there may not be enough people sharing the same interest to sustain a permanent lobbying organization. Only at the level of the nation as a whole are there enough musical instrument makers, for instance, to make a permanent organization of instrument producers worthwhile. This straightforward line of explanation undoubtedly helps to explain some portion of the difference between city politics and national politics, but it overlooks the fact that under the regime of clientelism the effective constituencies for many national bureaucracies are much smaller than the nation as a whole. Yet, even within these reduced political arenas, one frequently finds a surprisingly broad array of durable and vigorous clientele groups—industry, trade, commodity, consumer, and labor organizations. The proliferation of organized interest groups within such national bureaucratic constituencies is all the more remarkable since the constituencies themselves are certainly more homogeneous in social and economic terms than the population of any major city. Mere size of constituency does not seem to be sufficient to account for the reported variations in interest group strength, durability, and activity between city and nation.

19. Richard Schott, *The Bureaucratic State: The Evolution and Scope of the American Federal Bureaucracy* (Morristown, N.J.: General Learning Press, 1974), p. 9; see also James Q. Wilson, "The Rise of the Bureaucratic State," *The Public Interest*, no. 41 (Fall 1975), pp. 87–89.

20. Francis E. Rourke, "The Department of Labor and the Trade Unions," *Western Political Quarterly* 7 (December 1954): 658–59; Lloyd M. Short, *The Development of National Administrative Organization in the United States* (Baltimore: Johns Hopkins Press, 1923).

21. Wilson, pp. 89–90; Morton Keller, *Affairs of State: Public Life in Late Nineteenth Century America* (Cambridge: Belknap Press, 1977), pp. 410–12.

22. Luther Gulick, "Notes on the Theory of Organization," in *Papers on the Science of Administration*, ed. Luther Gulick and L. Urwick (New York: Institute of Public Administration, 1937), pp. 25–26.

23. McConnell (n. 4 above), p. 162.

24. Theodore Lowi, "The Public Philosophy: Interest Group Liberalism," *American Political Science Review* 61 (March 1967): 12.

25. Edward C. Banfield and James Q. Wilson, *City Politics* (n.8 above), pp. 104–7; Robert K. Merton, *Social Theory and Social Structure*, rev. ed. (New York: Free Press, 1968), pp. 126–27.

26. Shefter (n. 7 above), p. 27.

27. Frank Kent, *The Great Game of Politics* (Garden City, N.Y.: Doubleday, 1926), p. 92.

28. Douglas Yates, *Neighborhood Democracy* (Lexington, Mass.: Lexington Books, 1973), p. 15.

29. Milton Kotler, *Neighborhood Government: The Local Foundations of Political Life* (Indianapolis: Bobbs-Merrill Co., 1969), p. 14.

30. Moise Ostrogorski, *Democracy and the Organization of Political Parties*, 2 vols. (New York: Macmillan, 1902), 2:161–204.

31. Norton Long, *The Polity* (Chicago: Rand McNally & Co., 1962), p. 53.

32. Ostrogorski, 2:196–97.

33. George Antunes and Kenneth Mladenka, "The Politics of Local Services and Service Distribution," in *The New Urban Politics*, ed. Louis H. Masotti and Robert L. Lineberry (Cambridge, Mass.: Ballinger Publishing Co., 1976), p. 151; see also Robert L. Lineberry and Ira Sharkansky, *Urban Politics and Public Policy*, 2d ed. (New York: Harper & Row, 1974), pp. 80–81, 93; Betty H. Zisk, *Local Interest Politics: A One-Way Street* (Indianapolis: Bobbs-Merrill Co., 1973), pp. 132–44.

34. Samuel P. Hays, "The Politics of Reform in Municipal Government in the Progressive Era," in *Bosses and Reformers: Urban Politics in America, 1880–1920* ed. Blaine A. Brownell and Warren E. Stickle (Boston: Houghton Mifflin Co., 1973), p. 148.

35. Ibid., p. 144.

36. Banfield and Wilson, *City Politics*, p. 139.

37. Robert Agger, Daniel Goldrich, and Bert Swanson, *The Rulers and the Ruled* (New York: John Wiley & Sons, 1964), p. 21.

38. See Raymond Wolfinger and John Osgood Field, "Political Ethos and the Structure of City Government," *American Political Science Review* 60 (June 1966): 306–26.

39. McConnell; Lowi, "The Public Philosophy"; see also Grant McConnell, *The Decline of Agrarian Democracy* (Berkeley: University of California Press, 1953); and Theodore Lowi, *The End of Liberalism* (New York: Free Press, 1969).

40. Holden, pp. 567–68.

41. Lane, pp. 29–35; Richardson, pp. 24–29.

42. Carl Kaestle, *The Evolution of an Urban School System: New York City, 1750–1850* (Cambridge, Mass.: Harvard University Press, 1973), p. 112.

43. Ibid., chap. 4; see also Michael Katz, *The Irony of Early School Reform: Educational Innovation in Mid-Nineteenth Century Massachusetts* (Cambridge, Mass.: Harvard University Press, 1968), pp. 116–24.

44. Mancur Olson, Jr., *The Logic of Collective Action: Public Goods and the Theory of Groups* (Cambridge, Mass.: Harvard University Press, 1965); David J. O'Brien, *Neighborhood Organization and Interest-Group Processes* (Princeton, N.J.: Princeton University Press, 1975).

45. A view of urban services that seems sharply different from this one has been suggested by Douglas Yates, "Service Delivery and the Urban Political Order," in *Improving Urban Management*, ed. Willis Hawley and David Rogers (Beverly Hills, Calif.: Sage Publications, 1976), pp. 147–74. Yates maintains that urban services are distinctive precisely because they are so highly divisible, but the illustrations offered by Yates seem to demonstrate how indivisible the *benefits* of urban services usually are: "A block that is clean enough for a teenager who uses the street as both eating place and playground may not be clean enough for a homeowner or a shopkeeper" (p. 154). Few if any urban services would qualify, by the standards of economists, as pure public goods. Even national security, the archetypal public good, can be provided in differing amounts to different regions or communities. Government services, therefore, are not simply divisible or indivisible. They exhibit varying levels of divisibility, and the outputs of local governments appear to

be relatively indivisible by comparison with those of state or national governments. For
some interesting evidence bearing on this point, see Paul E. Peterson, "The Politics of
Taxation and Expenditure: A Unitary Approach" (paper presented at the annual meeting
of the American Political Sciences Association, New York, September 1978), pp. 15–20, 59.

46. Rourke, *Bureaucracy, Politics and Public Policy*, p. 2.

47. Marver Bernstein, *Regulating Business by Independent Commission* (Princeton,
N.J.: Princeton University Press, 1955).

48. Paul Sabatier, "Social Movements and Regulatory Agencies: Toward a More
Adequate—and Less Pessimistic—Theory of "Clientele Capture,'" *Policy Sciences* 6
(September 1975): 303; see also Louis Jaffe, "The Independent Agency: A New
Scapegoat," *Yale Law Journal*, vol. 65 (June 1956).

49. Katz, p. 131; for a parallel view of welfare services, see Richard Cloward and
Frances Piven, *Regulating the Poor: The Functions of Public Welfare* (New York: Pan-
theon Books, 1971); a similar perspective on police services is presented by Allan Silver,
"The Demand for Order in Civil Society: A Review of Some Themes in the History of
Urban Crime, Police and Riot," in *The Police: Six Sociological Essays*, ed. David J.
Bordua (New York: John Wiley & Sons, 1967), pp. 1–24.

50. On the power resources of municipal employee unions, see Raymond Horton,
Municipal Labor Relations in New York City: Lessons of the Lindsay-Wagner Years (New
York: Praeger Pubs., 1973).

51. Norton Long, *The Unwalled City: Reconstituting the Urban Community* (New
York: Basic Books, 1972), p. 114.

52. Shefter (n. 7 above); Alexander Callow, *The Tweed Ring* (Oxford: Oxford University Press, 1966).

53. Robert Caro, *The Power Broker: Robert Moses and the Fall of New York* (New York:
Vintage Books, 1975), chap. 12.

54. Sayre and Kaufman (n. 13 above), pp. 268, 271–72, 278, 291.

55. Ibid., p. 292.

56. Gary Orfield, *The Reconstruction of Southern Education* (New York: John Wiley &
Sons, 1969), pp. 57–58; see also Philip Foss, *Politics and Grass* (Seattle: University of
Washington Press, 1960).

57. E. Pendleton Herring, *Public Administration and the Public Interest* (New York:
McGraw-Hill Book Co., 1936), pp. 34–35.

58. See John C. Teaford, *The Municipal Revolution in America: Origins of Urban
Government, 1650–1825* (Chicago: University of Chicago Press, 1975); Ernest S. Griffith,
History of American City Government: The Colonial Period (Oxford: Oxford University
Press, 1938).

59. Michael Lipsky, "Toward a Theory of Street-Level Bureaucracy," in *Theoretical
Perspectives on Urban Politics*, ed. Willis Hawley and Michael Lipsky (Englewood Cliffs,
N.J.: Prentice-Hall, Inc., 1976), pp. 197–98.

60. James Q. Wilson, *Varieties of Police Behavior* (Cambridge, Mass.: Harvard University Press, 1968), pp. 4–5.

61. Lipsky, pp. 196–97.

62. Wilson, *Varieties of Police Behavior*, pp. 66–67.

63. James G. Anderson, *Bureaucracy in Education* (Baltimore: Johns Hopkins Press,
1968), p. 128; Wayne C. Gordon, "The Role of the Teacher in the Social Structure of the
High School," *Journal of Educational Sociology* 29 (September 1955): 30–40.

64. Peter Rossi, Richard Berk, and Bettye Eidson, *The Roots of Urban Discontent:
Public Policy, Municipal Institutions, and the Ghetto* (New York: John Wiley & Sons,
1974), pp. 377–79; see also Jerry Jacobs, "Symbolic Bureaucracy: A Case Study of a
Social Welfare Agency," *Social Forces* 47 (June 1969): 413–22.

65. Lipsky, p. 200.

66. Ibid., pp. 201–5; Jerome H. Skolnick, *Justice without Trial: Law Enforcement in a Democratic Society* (New York: John Wiley & Sons, 1966), pp. 45–48.

67. Wilson, *Varieties of Police Behavior*, pp. 32–33; see also Michael Banton, *The Policeman in the Community* (London: Tavistock, 1964).

68. William Westley, *Violence and the Police* (Cambridge, Mass.: M.I.T. Press, 1970), p. 126.

69. Estelle Fuchs, *Teachers Talk: Views from Inside City Schools* (Garden City, N.Y.: Anchor Books, 1969), pp. 47–48.

70. Wilson, *Varieties of Police Behavior*, p. 49.

71. Concerning the relationships between underenforcement and personal influence in a different context, see Alvin W. Gouldner, *Patterns of Industrial Bureaucracy* (New York: Free Press, 1964), pp. 173–74.

72. Albert J. Reiss, Jr., ed., *Louis Wirth: On Cities and Social Life* (Chicago: University of Chicago Press, 1964), pp. 60–83; 222–23; see also Robert Redfield, "The Folk Society," *American Journal of Sociology* 52 (January 1947): 293–308.

73. See Maurice Stein, *The Eclipse of Community: An Interpretation of American Studies* (New York: Harper & Row, 1964).

74. Arthur J. Vidich and Joseph Bensman, *Small Town in Mass Society: Class, Power and Religion in a Rural Community*, rev. ed. (Princeton, N.J.: Princeton University Press, 1968), chap. 4.

75. Peter H. Rossi and Alice S. Rossi, "An Historical Perspective on the Functions of Local Politics," in *Social Change in Urban Politics*, ed. Daniel Gordon (Englewood Cliffs, N.J.: Prentice-Hill, Inc., 1973), pp. 49–60.

76. Roland Liebert, *Disintegration and Political Action: The Changing Functions of City Governments in America* (New York: Academic Press, 1976), chap. 3.

77. Lewis (n. 11 above), p. 170.

78. See Jeffrey M. Berry, *Lobbying for the People: The Political Behavior of Public Interest Groups* (Princeton, N.J.: Princeton University Press, 1977).

79. James J. Vanecko, "Community Mobilization and Institutional Change: The Influence of the Community Action Program in Large Cities," *Social Science Quarterly* 50 (December 1969): 609–30.

80. On the multiple meanings of citizen participation and community action, see Daniel P. Moynihan, *Maximum Feasible Misunderstanding* (New York: Free Press, 1969), pp. 168–69; Sherry R. Arnstein, "A Ladder of Citizen Participation," *Journal of the American Institute of Planners* 35 (July 1969): 216–24.

81. J. David Greenstone and Paul E. Peterson, *Race and Authority in Urban Politics* (New York: Russell Sage Foundation, 1973), pp. 220–22.

82. Elliott A. Krause, "Functions of a Bureaucratic Ideology: 'Citizen Participation,'" *Social Problems* 16 (Fall 1968): 129–43.

83. Jeffrey Pressman and Aaron Wildavsky, *Implementation* (Berkeley: University of California Press, 1973), p. 137.

84. Jeffrey Pressman, *Federal Programs and Urban Politics: The Dynamics of the Aid Process in Oakland* (Berkeley: University of California Press, 1975), chap. 3.

85. Herman Turk, "Interorganizational Networks in Urban Society: Initial Perspectives and Comparative Research," *American Sociological Review* 35 (February 1970): 3.

86. Richard P. Nathan and Charles F. Adams, Jr., *Revenue Sharing: The Second Round* (Washington, D.C.: Brookings Institution, 1977), pp. 118–20, 131; Garth Magnum and David Snedeker, "The Realities of Manpower Planning," *Manpower* 6 (August 1974): 3–7; James W. Singer, "The Private Sector for Hire," *National Journal*, vol. 11 (February 1978).

Eight ★

Federalism,
Economic Development,
and Redistribution

Paul E. Peterson

The problems encountered in the implementation of antipoverty programs in the 1960s—Johnson's Great Society—were rooted in conflicts inherent in the structural arrangements of a federal system of government. These programs, with their emphasis on special assistance to the poor and needy, demonstrated a stronger commitment to redistribution by the central government of the United States than was evident at any other time in its history, save perhaps for the New Deal. However, this egalitarian thrust was implemented through a federal system whose local units did not—indeed, could not—share the federal commitment. Research on poverty has repeatedly revealed the limits on the effectiveness of many programs aimed at reducing poverty in the United States. But in general these studies have not appreciated the structural limitations that the federal system itself placed on Great Society programs. To do so would require the reconstruction of a theory of federalism.

We no longer have a theory of federalism. The word has become at once so encompassing and so vacuous that any multitiered decision-making system can be entitled a federation. Even contractual relationships between central governments and private business firms are now considered to be an element of federalism.[1] Once the concept of federalism is stripped of any distinctive meaning, we lack the basic criteria for the appropriate division of governmental responsibilities among layers of government. Federalism is what federalism does. Even more, we have no orienting concepts that can assist us in explaining the patterns of conflict and cooperation among government levels.

This paper is a revised version of chap. 4 of *City Limits* by Paul E. Peterson (Chicago: University of Chicago Press, 1981).

In this essay, I shall argue that concepts taken from economics provide the opportunity for reviving a structural approach to the study of federalism, thereby providing a more comprehensive explanation for many of the difficulties faced by the antipoverty programs of Johnson's Great Society. Given a federal system of government, central and local governments perform inherently different political functions. The central government is responsible for regularizing relations with foreign countries, for maintaining the nation's prosperity, and for sustaining social welfare and other redistributive services. Local governments concentrate on operating efficiently those services necessary for maintaining a healthy local economy and society. Because of these differing responsibilities, central and local governments often find themselves engaged in value conflicts over matters of domestic policy. Local governments are primarily concerned with the productiveness of their economy, whereas the central government, while concerned about economic development, is also interested in achieving equality.

Decline of Dual Sovereignty Theory

Traditional theories of federalism took as their point of departure the presence of two sovereigns within a single domain. Each sovereign had power over its citizens with respect to the functions for which it was responsible. Neither had power to interfere with the proper role of the other sovereign. A constitution defined the distribution of powers between the dual sovereigns.

Sovereignty was divided between a central state and a local republic in order to avoid both internal and external threats to liberty. Small republics limited the possibility of internal despotism, because citizens knew and understood affairs of state that touched them closely. They could readily be called upon to participate in the defense of their freedoms. The small republic, however, could be easily overcome by external enemies. Only through joining together in a federation with other republics could a common defense be maintained. The permeability of the small republic to external forces justified its relinquishing certain powers to a higher sovereign.[2]

This dual sovereignty theory of federalism linked governmental structure to political processes and policy outcomes. It provided a rationale for the proper division of powers between the central state and the local republics within a federation. It gave federalism a core definition: the presence of a contractual arrangement—a constitution—that divided powers among the sovereigns. Although changing circumstances would require continuous interpretation of that constitution, the theory provided the necessary conceptual apparatus for doing so.

In the United States constitutional interpretations after the Civil War expanded the powers allocated to the central government so that the concept of dual sovereignty, somewhat forced even in 1789, became increasingly difficult to sustain. At the close of the Civil War, the "civil rights" amendment to the Constitution decisively asserted the pre-eminence of the federal prerogative. By 1937 the Supreme Court recognized the interstate effects of almost all commerce, thereby greatly broadening the federal power to regulate business and commercial activities (*NLRB* v. *Jones & Laughlin Corp.*). Also, the Court legitimated almost all forms of federal grants-in-aid to states and localities (*Stewart Machine Co.* v. *Davis*). However valid the dual sovereignty theory remained in principle, it had little applicability to a country that came to believe that its liberties were as safe, if not safer, in the hands of the central government.

The most creative adaptation in federal theory to these constitutional changes was Morton Grodzins's metaphor of the "marble cake."[3] Grodzins showed that virtually all governmental activities are affected by decisions taken at national, state, and local levels. Power was both widely diffused and widely shared. The overall pattern had become marked more by cooperation and mutual assistance than by confrontations between dual sovereigns. Drawing upon the emergent behavioral tradition, Grodzins showed that governmental interrelations were characterized by endless processes of sharing and exchange. The resulting formation had, like a marble cake, no discernible structure at all. The metaphor diffused rapidly in the literature of federalism. It fitted nicely with the contemporary process-oriented focus of the political science discipline as a whole,[4] and it seemed to give point and direction to descriptive studies of intergovernmental relationships. More innovative writers added their own metaphoric variations: picket fence, upside-down cake, harlequin ice cream brick, or what have you.[5]

The Substitution of Metaphor for Theory

But, however apt and appealing the analogy may be, comparing federalism to a structureless piece of pastry is not theory. It suggests flux, change, and complexity when the purpose of theory is to identify simplicity, pattern, and order. The metaphor directs attention toward individuals, groups, and processes, when the essence of federalism is a stable relationship among structures of government. Students of federalism have written persuasive descriptive analyses, but they have (1) failed to give a distinctive meaning to federalism, (2) failed to preserve any distinctions among functions appropriate to each level of gov-

ernment, and (3) failed to identify any pattern to cooperative and conflictual elements in the federal system.

First, and most important, their definitions of federalism are so vague
that it is impossible to distinguish federal arrangements from relationships between central and field offices in a unitary government. Daniel
Elazar's efforts are more careful than most, but even he defines
federalism "as a mode of political organization that unites smaller
polities within an overarching political system by distributing power
among general and constituent governments in a manner designed to
protect the existence and authority of both national and subnational
political systems, enabling all to share in the overall system's
decision-making and executing processes."[6]

By this all-encompassing definition, even the the U.S. Forest Service
is a federal system. Its decision-making processes are divided between
central and field offices, which are united by a handbook of rules and
regulations that protect the existence and authority of each jurisdic-
tional level. From a different perspective, Kaufman has judged the
forest service to be a highly centralized agency of the central government.[7] But certainly the concept of federalism, when applied in this
way, begins to encompass almost all political relationships. Perhaps
that is Elazar's intent, for he goes on to say that federalism "is more
than an arrangement of governmental structures; it is a mode of political
activity that requires certain kinds of cooperative relationships through
the political system it animates."[8] This free-flowing assertion is certainly in keeping with the current emphasis on political process, but it
does little to focus the study of intergovernmental relationships. To be
sure, modern interpreters of American federalism are understandably
concerned not to define federalism in narrow, constitutional terms. To
see the essence of federalism as the division of powers among constituent units as defined by a written constitution places the study of
federalism in a strait jacket at a time when intergovernmental relationships are marked by patterns hardly foreseen by the earliest interpreters of the American Constitution. But modern federal theorists have
not supplied a sufficiently focused substitute for traditional definitions
of federalism in order that a distinctive, middle-range theory of intergovernmental relationships could emerge.

Second, without a definition of federalism, modern writers have been
unable to state the characteristic and appropriate function of each level
of government. In a fascinating commentary, Martin Diamond observed
that Grodzins "was driven by the difficulty of defining localness toward
rejecting any standard for distributing functions between state and national government.[9] He came to argue that 'Local Is as Local Does.'"
The theory degenerates into sheer description. And, once again, it be-

comes impossible to distinguish the federal system from a decentralized administrative structure.

Perhaps it is unkind to suggest that modern theorists are also left without a standpoint from which to study intergovernmental relationships. After all, Grodzins, Elazar, and other of Grodzins's students have commented extensively on the federal "partnership" and have given intelligent accounts of a cooperative sharing of power among governmental levels.[10] But even though their empirical studies are lucid and helpful, general theoretical explanations of the pattern of cooperation and conflict among governmental levels have not emerged. When the concept of the marble cake was first developed, intergovernmental relationships were so poorly understood that sheer descriptive accounts were useful. But the social scientific studies of the "creative federalism" of Johnson's antipoverty programs have hardly improved on early efforts. The results of the Great Society experiment have left many disturbed about the quality of the sharing among federal partners, but few have expressed their uncertainties at a high level of theoretical abstraction.

Toward a New Theory of Federalism

There can be no return to a theory of dual sovereignty; the work of Grodzins has surely laid that moribund notion to rest.[11] But a new theory, like the traditional theory of dual sovereignty, must do three things. First, it must provide a definition that clarifies the way in which a federal system is distinguished from a decentralized administrative structure. Second, it must specify characteristic and appropriate activities of the central and local governments within the federal arrangement. Third, the theory must account for persistent patterns of conflict and cooperation among the various levels of government.

Federalism is a system of government in which powers are divided between higher and lower levels of government in such a way that both levels have a significant amount of separate and autonomous responsibility for the social and economic welfare of those living within their respective jurisdictions. Within the federation, the central government assumes responsibility for relations with foreign countries and determines the exchange relationships among the component units of the federation. The central government may exercise numerous additional powers, but for the system to remain a federation lower levels of government must have at least two crucial powers.

First, lower levels of government must have a significant amount of control over the recruitment of their own political and administrative leadership. If local leaders are selected by officials of the central government, or if recruitment processes are governed by such stringent, centrally determined criteria that the local community has no effective choice, then local government is without power to take responsibility for the well-being of its inhabitants. Second, local government must have the power to tax its citizens in order to provide a range of government services that can enhance the well-being of the community. If local government is totally dependent upon centrally determined grants, it has very limited responsibility for the determination of the well-being of the local community. It will always be dependent on external sources of funds and, consequently, will always feel a need for more such funds. Because such funds do not come directly from the local community's own resources, the monies require strict central government supervision. Once it is no longer dependent on local resources, the local government loses the capacity to act responsibly on its own behalf, and thus becomes simply an agent of the central government.

Federalism is thus to be distinguished from simple decentralization, which can occur without the granting of either recruitment or financial powers to lower decision-making levels. For example, the U.S. Forest Service grants considerable decision-making autonomy to its field offices, though they do not gather their revenues from local sources or act independently in the recruitment of personnel. Were the central administrators of the forest service or any other department or agency to lose these two powers to their district offices, the organization could scarcely be considered a single governmental unit. Indeed, these are precisely the circumstances for which the term "federalism" is appropriately reserved and that at one time might have been characterized as dual sovereignty. Within a federal system, the objectives of central and local governments stand in contrast to one another. In the next sections, we shall describe the way in which structural arrangements have generated distinctive objectives on the part of national and local governments.

Local Government and the Local Economy

When forced to choose between equality and promoting the local economy, local governments in a federal system place greater weight on economic productivity. This choice is not due to a local power elite or to the biases inherent in small constituency politics; instead, it is a function of the external socioeconomic context in which local governments operate. Unlike national governments, local governments have little control over external socioeconomic forces. Just as an individual firm in a competitive economy cannot control its sources of supply or the de-

mand for its products, so local governments cannot control the movement of capital and labor across their boundaries. Local governments
are open systems that can be easily permeated by external forces and
are therefore particularly sensitive to external changes. In responding to
external forces, local governments act to protect an overriding set of
interests. Just as a private firm wishes to maximize its profits, so the
local community seeks to maximize its economic well-being.

Local leaders can be expected to try to safeguard the economic prosperity of the local community for at least three reasons. First, economic
prosperity is necessary for protecting the fiscal base of local government. In the United States, taxes on local sources and charges for local
services remain an important source of local government revenues.
Although transfers of revenue to local units from federal and state governments increased throughout the postwar period, as late as 1974–75
local governments still raised almost 60 percent of their own revenue.[12]
Raising revenue from a community's own economic resources requires
continuing local economic prosperity. Second, good government is good
politics. By pursuing policies that contribute to the economic prosperity
of the local community, the local politician selects policies that redound
to his or her own political advantage. Third and most important, local
officials usually have a sense of community responsibility. They know
that, unless the economic well-being of the community can be maintained, local business will suffer, workers will lose employment opportunities, cultural life will decline, and city land values will fall relative to other areas. To avoid such a dismal future, public officials try to
develop policies that assist the prosperity of their community—or, at the
very least, do not seriously detract from it.

Governments make decisions that maximize this goal within the
numerous environmental constraints with which they must contend. As
policy alternatives are proposed, each is evaluated according to how
well it will help to achieve local economic prosperity. Although information is imperfect and local governments cannot be expected to select the
best alternative on every occasion, policy choices will be constrained to
those few that can plausibly be shown to be conducive to the community's economic prosperity. Internal disputes and disagreements may affect policy on the margins, but the major contours of local revenue
policy will be determined by this larger objective, as shaped by factors
in the community's environment.

In attempting to maximize their economic prosperity, local communities are competing with each other. Each must attract productive
capital and labor to its area, and to achieve that end the conditions for
productive economic activity must be as favorable in one community as
they are in competing communities. Otherwise, there will be a net out-

ward flow of productive resources, leaving a community with a declining economic future. Significantly, local governments can do little directly to control the flow of productive resources; for example, they cannot establish tariff walls or control human migration in the same way that nation-states can. Efficiency is all the more important, therefore, in the design of their policies, so that they protect and enhance the productive capacity of the community.

Central Government and Social Equality

By comparison with local governments, central governments are more concerned about a reasonable balance between developmental and redistributive objectives. This is not to say that central governments are uninterested in the economic capacities of their societies. For one thing, they have assumed the responsibility for managing the domestic economy through manipulation of fiscal and monetary policies. They also promote economic growth through large-scale capital investments in transportation systems, research and development, and, now more than ever, the exploitation of energy and other natural resources. As a result, many federal programs are as concerned with developmental objectives as are programs carried out by states and localities. But these developmental concerns are often coupled with a continuing concern for achieving some degree of equity in social relationships. Tax, welfare, housing, health, and educational policies of the central government are formulated with questions of equality and redistribution often carrying as much weight as questions of economic stability and growth. The commitment to redistributive objectives is due in part to the availability of powers that curb the impact of the external world environment on the nation's economy. The most important of these powers is the capacity to issue passports and visas. Through the exercise of these powers, almost all highly industrialized countries have in recent years carefully restricted immigration. As ethically disturbing as these laws often are, without them many residents of less-advantaged countries would move to the industrialized areas, overwhelming their high-wage economies and swamping their social welfare systems. The case of the Vietnamese "boat people" provides a particularly poignant example of the dilemma faced by liberal-minded citizens in wealthy countries.

If control over human migration is vital, national governments also protect their economies from worldwide forces through a host of controls over the movement of capital, goods, and services. Tariffs, quotas, a national currency, control over exchange rates, and the capacity to fund its own indebtedness are among the powers a national government uses to increase its autonomy from external forces. Not all countries can use these devices with equal effectiveness. The United States is particularly fortunate in that foreign trade amounts to less than 10 percent of its total economic activity. Smaller countries with less self-contained economies have much less scope for autonomous action. But all except the smallest and most dependent—perhaps Hong Kong is the limiting case—have economies less permeable than those for which local governments are responsible.[13]

Where governments have the capacity to redistribute, political forces in relatively open, pluralist polities will generate demands for the same. Competition for popular support will provide political parties with an important incentive to advocate the redistribution of income from smaller numbers of high-income groups to the larger numbers having less income. Although the surge for redistribution may be episodic and in response to external impacts such as the major depression of the 1930s and the mobilization of black discontent in the 1960s, competitive politics in industrial societies periodically brings such redistributive pressures to bear on the policies of central governments.

Once a policy has been promulgated, an agency is founded and administrative staff responsible for implementing the policy develops a loyalty to the substantive mission of the program.[14] As part of the government, the agency has a legitimate claim on a continuing—perhaps slightly increasing—portion of the national budget. To perpetuate its program, the staff solicits the backing of organized elements serviced by its program, who campaign on its behalf in Congress, in other parts of the executive, in the news media, and among the public-at-large.

National policies are thus loaded with a variable mix of developmental and redistributive objectives. Some programs are promulgated at a time when the nation is primarily concerned with economic growth, and such programs are apt to take an almost exclusively developmental turn. Other programs are passed when the political forces favoring redistribution have gained unusual strength. The Elementary and Secondary Education Act of 1965 is, of course, the most dramatic example in education of the federal interest in redistribution. Other governmental policies, formulated under more ambiguous circumstances, may have a more mixed set of orientations. But, on balance the redistributive orientation is greater at the national than at the local level.

Differences in Policies in
Central and Local Governments

Because the interests of local and central governments are different, the pattern of public policies promulgated by the two levels of government is different. Most clearly, central and local governments tend to rely on contrasting principles for raising revenue.[15] The central government depends largely on the ability-to-pay principle and therefore raises most of its revenues through a progressive income tax, taxes on corporate earnings, and excise taxes on luxury commodities. Local governments, on the other hand, rely more on the benefits-received principle, which specifies that individuals should be taxed in accordance with the level of services they receive. As a result, over one-fourth of local revenues are raised through user charges, and the remainder is collected through taxes on property, sales taxes, and nonprogressive income taxes.[16] One need not posit any local power elite to account for this propensity of local governments to favor more regressive taxes. If local communities were to rely on the ability-to-pay principle, there would be a greater disjunction between taxes levied and benefits received, and those paying the most in taxes (who are usually those contributing the most to the local economy) would have strong incentives to migrate elsewhere. Proportional or, preferably, somewhat regressive local taxes come closer to approximating the benefit principle, the principle that is consistent with the economic well-being of the local community.

Second, the expenditures of central and local governments perform different functions. Specifically, the central government assumes the responsibility for financing redistributive policies. As table 1 shows, 47 percent of the domestic budget of the central government was allocated for redistributive purposes even at the beginning of the 1960s. After the declaration of war on poverty, this percentage increased to more than 55 percent. By contrast, the percentage of local revenue used for redistributive policies was only 12.9 percent in 1962. Significantly, even after the emergence of the civil rights movement and its supposed impact on local service delivery systems,[17] this percentage increased over the next decade by less than 1 percent. The role of the states stands midway between that of the central and local governments. States have contributed somewhat less than 35 percent of their budgets to redistributive programs.

The figures in table 2 are even more dramatic. This table shows the percentage of all expenditures devoted to a particular activity contributed by each level of government. As the table shows, not only was the local contribution to redistributive programs scarcely more than 10 percent in 1962, but also the percentage has declined since that time. The fiscal role of the federal government, on the other hand, has become especially significant. And if the political pressures for federalizing welfare policy and health care are any sign, this pattern is likely to continue. As the United States continues to become an increasingly integrated political economy, the redistributive function may well become an almost exclusively federal prerogative.

The distinctively redistributive role of the central government is es-

Table 1
% Distribution among Functions of Direct and Intergovernmental Expenditures by Local, State, and Federal Governments

	Local		
	1962	1967	1973
Redistributive			
Welfare	2.5	2.5	2.0
Hospital and health	6.1	6.7	8.6
Housing	2.4	1.5	0.9
Social insurance	1.9	2.2	2.3
All redistributive	12.9	12.9	13.8
Nonredistributive			
Housekeeping	26.8	26.4	28.5
Utilities	13.2	13.1	11.1
Postal			
Transportation	8.1	6.6	5.7
Natural resources	1.1	1.1	0.7
Interest	4.1	4.4	5.6
Education	33.4	35.2	34.2
Other	0.4	0.3	0.4
Total (%)	100.0	100.0	100.0
Total ($m)	33,591	45,853	77,886

Note: Table adapted from Peterson 1979, table 3. For sources and other notes see citation.

pecially evident in programs supported by federal grants-in-aid. Table 3 shows the distribution by function of intergovernmental revenues from the central and state governments to lower governmental levels. The states allocate most of their intergovernmental moneys for educational purposes, but the primary role of the central government has been to finance the redistributive activities of states and localities. When local governments do provide welfare, hospital, health, and housing services to low-income groups, these services are generally provided through intergovernmental grants from the federal government. Even in 1973, after the establishment of a revenue-sharing program by the Nixon administration, 40 percent of intergovernmental revenues received by states and localities was specifically designated for a redistributive function. The increase in undesignated revenues in that year came largely at the expense of funds for educational and other purposes, not as a substitute for redistributive activities.

The responsibility for financing public policies in the American federal system is not distributed casually among all levels of government. Instead, central and local governments characteristically assume differ-

from their own Fiscal Resources, 1962, 1967, 1973
(% Total Expenditures by Each Level of Government)

State			Federal (Domestic Only)		
1962	1967	1973	1962	1967	1973
6.2	6.4	11.2	12.2	11.9	12.6
7.4	7.2	6.2	3.3	3.7	3.5
0.2	0.2	0.4	1.5	1.9	3.4
14.4	9.4	17.0	29.7	34.0	35.6
28.2	23.2	34.8	46.7	51.5	55.1
12.4	12.9	8.4	4.6	4.5	3.8
			7.0	7.2	5.1
17.8	16.0	11.3	6.2	5.8	4.2
2.9	3.5	2.3	19.3	9.9	7.8
2.2	2.3	2.7	12.3	12.1	9.9
33.6	39.5	38.4	3.2	7.2	8.2
3.0	2.6	2.2	0.8	1.8	5.8
100.1	100.0	100.1	100.1	100.0	99.9
29,356	45,288	89,504	58,960	86,852	186,172

ent functional responsibilities. Local governments allocate services in accord with community needs and, where spillover effects are modest, engage in developmental activities to promote the local economy. In addition to its responsibilities for overall economic growth and for developmental policies that have widespread repercussions, the national government bears the primary responsibilities for redistribution.

Intergovernmental
Cooperation and Conflict

Given the structural differences between federal and local governments, intergovernmental programs that require mutual action will have different experiences, as they are implemented in the federal system, depending on whether they are developmental or redistributive in character. Where the national policy is developmental, local and national goals will overlap and the policy will be executed with a good deal of cooperation and mutual accommodation. But where the central government is

Table 2
% Distribution among Governments of Direct and Intergovern-
mental Expenditures by Local, State, and Federal Governments

		Local		
		1962	1967	1973
Redistributive	Welfare	8.5	7.8	4.3
	Hospital and health	33.2	32.2	35.4
	Housing	46.7	29.3	9.7
	Social insurance	2.9	2.9	2.2
All redistributive		10.8	9.7	7.4
Nonredistributive	Housekeeping	58.7	55.4	60.2
	Postal			
	Utilities	100.0	100.0	100.0
	Transportation	23.3	19.7	20.1
	Natural resources	3.0	4.7	3.3
	Interest	14.9	14.8	17.2
	Education	48.9	40.0	34.9
	Other	8.6	5.4	2.2

Note: Table adapted from Peterson 1979, table 4. For sources and other notes, see citation.

pursuing a more redistributive objective, its goals are likely to conflict with those of local governments. The national interest in equity will conflict with the local interest in efficiently developing its local economy. As a result, the processes of implementing the national program will be considerably more complicated.

These differences between developmental and redistributive programs are exemplified by the objectives and administrative arrangements for the National Defense Education Act (NDEA) Title III and the Elementary and Secondary Education Act (ESEA) Title I. Conceived shortly after Sputnik was launched in 1958, NDEA Title III was a developmental policy that probably had nothing other than positive effects on local economies but at the same time contributed little to educational equity. Federal funds under NDEA Title III were expended for the purpose of enhancing instruction in mathematics, science, and foreign languages, the very programs of greatest interest to the academically oriented, university-bound, middle-class segment of local communities. With higher-quality local school services, the community had additional resources for persuading higher-income families and new industries to move into and remain in the community. Moreover, since states and localities had to match every federal dollar with a state or local dollar, the communities with the greatest fiscal resources were the best placed to take advantage of the program.

from Their Own Fiscal Resources, by Function: 1962, 1967, 1973 (% Expenditures for Each Function By All Governments)

State			Federal			Total		
1962	1967	1973	1962	1967	1973	1962	1967	1973
18.4	20.1	28.7	73.1	72.1	67.2	100.0	100.0	100.2
35.2	34.0	29.6	31.6	33.8	35.0	100.0	100.0	100.0
2.5	3.8	4.5	50.7	66.9	85.8	99.9	100.0	100.0
18.9	12.3	18.2	78.1	84.8	79.6	99.9	100.0	100.0
20.6	17.2	21.5	68.6	73.2	71.1	100.0	100.0	100.1
23.7	26.6	20.4	17.5	17.8	19.4	99.9	99.8	100.0
			100.0	100.0	100.0	100.0	100.0	100.0
45.1	47.3	45.0	31.6	33.0	34.9	100.0	100.0	100.0
6.7	14.9	12.0	90.3	80.4	84.7	100.0	100.0	100.0
6.9	7.6	9.6	78.2	77.6	73.2	100.0	100.0	100.0
43.0	44.4	45.0	8.1	15.6	20.0	100.0	100.0	99.9
60.1	41.1	15.3	31.3	53.5	82.5	100.0	100.0	100.0

Title I of ESEA, passed in 1965 at the height of the civil rights movement, has quite an opposite focus. As enacted by Congress and implemented by the Office of Education, the moneys were to be for learning-deficient children from low-income families. In many ways, the program has greatly increased the possibility of achieving improved equity in education, but its effect on local economies has been far more problematic. Except for any decrease in social unrest in the community, the program provides no particular resources to prosperous middle-class families whose contributions to local commercial activity and to the community tax base are so important. And if in any particular locale the program succeeds in providing quality services to low-income people, it only makes the community more attractive to low-income families elsewhere, who will be tempted to move into the community from other parts of the country. The very achievement of national goals by a local community only increases its economic disabilities.

Just as these two programs differed in their objectives, so they differed in the manner of their implementation. In the case of the developmental policy, NDEA Title III, the federal "partnership" operated as a model of cooperation and mutual reinforcement. Even though the law required that states match each federal dollar with a state dollar for the same program, within one year every state except Arizona had voted to participate in the program.[18] The Office of Education chose to distribute

Table 3
% Intergovernmental Expenditures by State and Federal
Governments, by Function, 1962, 1967, 1973

	State			Federal		
	1962	1967	1973	1962	1967	1973
Redistributive						
Welfare	16.3	15.2	18.4	31.6	28.2	29.0
Hospital and health	1.8	1.6	2.1	2.2	2.7	4.2
Housing	.3	.4	.4	4.1	4.5	5.1
Social insurance				6.0	3.8	1.9
All redistributive	18.4	17.2	20.9	43.9	39.1	40.2
Nonredistributive						
Housekeeping				.9	.9	2.1
Transportation	12.2	9.9	7.4	36.3	27.4	13.2
Natural resources	.2	.2	.2	1.8	1.6	1.6
Education	59.4	62.2	57.1	15.1	26.1	20.8
Other and undesignated	9.7	10.6	14.4	2.0	4.9	22.0
Total	99.9	100.1	100.0	100.0	100.0	100.0
$(m)	10,906	19,056	40,822	7,735	10,027	41,666

Note: Table adapted from Peterson 1979, table 5. See citation for sources and other notes.

the moneys among the forty-nine states with hardly any guidance about the purposes of the act. In drawing up its plan, the state had only "to list its priorities to reimbursing local projects and to describe the kinds of local projects and the standards for equipment it would help pay for."[19] Since national standards and priorities were not clearly defined, the states "in their plans mostly stuck to bland and general descriptions... some said that in effect standards would be as high as the program called for."[20] Indeed, it was left to a private publishing house to produce a catalogue that listed the equipment it felt was sure to qualify for state and federal reimbursement. In short, "federal aid was [not only] unencumbered by federal control, ... it was also innocent of scientific guidance and advice from Washington."[21]

After NDEA Title III expenditures were allocated and programs implemented, the Office of Education did little to monitor the way in which its resources were being utilized. States reported their Title III science activities only in terms of dollars and projects; they were not called upon to demonstrate the ways in which these dollars had improved science education.[22] Evaluation of program impact was virtually nonexistent. Yet these program "inadequacies" had few political repercussions. Popular at both the national and local levels, the program expanded as part of the growing role of the federal government in education.

Implementation of the redistributive program, Title I of ESEA has taken a dramatically different course.[23] Although all states have been eager to participate in the program from the beginning, this might be attributed to the lack of any matching requirement in the legislation. In the first six months of operation, the Office of Education followed its past practice of giving very little guidance about the way in which funds were to be allocated. But before the end of first year, the Office of Education became increasingly concerned about the substantial divergence of state programs from the objectives stated in the Title I legislation. In order to better achieve the redistributive goals of the act, the office began to limit the amount of expenditures on structural renovation, new equipment, and other "hardware"; required that the money be concentrated in schools with large numbers of children from low-income families; and specified that within these schools the moneys be spent on children with learning deficiencies. It also required that local educational authorities establish parent advisory councils that could participate in program development. Above all, it insisted that moneys for educational services be denied to segregated school districts in the rural South.

The success that the Office of Education has had in securing state and local compliance with these and numerous other administrative regulations governing the distribution of Title I funds has been mixed. During the first few years, the Office of Education had a small staff, poor-quality data on the performance of local districts, only limited experience in the supervisory role that Title I seemed to require, and a history of cordial relations with fellow school professionals at state and local levels that it was hesitant to disrupt. It therefore found it difficult to preclude local modification of Title I priorities. In many parts of the country, Title I funds were distributed throughout the system rather than concentrated on schools with high proportions of needy children; elsewhere, they were used to preserve segregated schooling rather than to enhance integrated educational experiences. Moreover, parent advisory councils seldom became effective parts of the Title I policymaking process.

As the Office of Education, and more recently the Department of Education, has become more experienced in administering the program, it has become better able to insure that funds are used in schools attended primarily by low-income children.[24] However, the Office of Education has had continuing difficulties in insuring that Title I funds are supplemental funds rather than substitutes for what otherwise would have been spent by state and local sources. Moreover, school districts seem reluctant to concentrate funds in specific schools, consequently lessening their impact. Most recently, local school administrators have begun to campaign for the replacement of Title I with an unencumbered block-grant funding arrangement.

Federalism and the Great Society

The structural difference between central and local governments also helps account for many of the difficulties encountered in the implementation of other Great Society programs. The zeal for reform was not coupled with an adequate understanding of the American federal system. Instead, it was felt that one could make federalism "creative" by lubricating it with federal dollars; not surprisingly, supporters drew upon the language of the marble cake theorists of American federalism to justify and rationalize the mechanisms for redistribution they adopted. In the words of one:

> Federalism means a relation, co-operative and competitive, between a limited central power and other powers that are essentially independent of it. In the long American dialogue over states' rights, it has been tacitly assumed that the total amount of power was constant and, therefore, any increase in federal power diminished the power of the states and/or "the people." Creative federalism starts from the contrary belief that total power—private and public, individual and organizational—is expanding very rapidly. As the range of conscious choice widens, it is possible to think of vast increases of federal government power that do not encroach upon or diminish any other power. Simultaneously, the power of states and local governments will increase.[25]

Consistent with this view of federalism, Great Society reforms were largely executed through state and local governments. In 1965 Congress enacted twenty-one new health programs, seventeen new educational programs, fifteen new economic development programs, twelve new programs to meet city problems, four new programs for manpower training, and seventeen resource development programs. All were implemented through joint action between the federal and one or more of the lower levels of government.[26] Federal intergovernmental transfers to state and local governments increased from $7.7 billion in 1962 to $41.7 billion in 1973. In 1962 intergovernmental transfers constituted 27 percent of the budget of local government; by 1973 these transfers constituted 37.1 percent.[27] Great Society programs were federal programs, formulated and financed by central departments but administered and executed by state and local governments.[28]

Time has not treated "creative federalism" generously. Many of the Great Society programs proved to be disappointments in practice, and, instead of the cooperative partnership that had been envisaged, conflict, confusion, and simple abandonment of original objectives occured in most of the more visible programs.

By far the least successful of government programs aimed at the poor were those complex programs of service delivery financed centrally but administered locally. The Economic Opportunity Act, the Elementary and Secondary Education Act, manpower development programs, model city programs, the "New Towns" program, urban economic development programs, health maintenance organizations, juvenile deliquency prevention policies, and a host of similar schemes were the liveliest, most imaginative, and most highly touted of the government's efforts at redistributing social and economic opportunities in the United States. But these antipoverty programs seem to have had the smallest long-range impact on low-income groups in the United States. Robert Haveman, former director of the Institute for Research on Poverty at the University of Wisconsin and a cautiously optimistic evaluator of the poverty policies of the federal government, has concluded that, "while poverty was reduced during the decade (after 1965), it is difficult to attribute this result directly to the programs that were an explicit part of the war."[29]

Some have suggested that these so-called antipoverty programs were never intended to reduce poverty in America. They were only symbolic programs designed to pacify an unruly urban population in a time of social unrest. But this view is contradicted by the evident commitment and capacity of American society to reduce overall levels of absolute poverty. To explain adequately the extent to which antipoverty efforts were singularly unhelpful in achieving their objectives, one must look for more specific sources of goal displacement and program frustration. In this regard, it is notable how little research attention has been given to the fact that almost all of the antipoverty programs were centrally financed and locally administered.

Throughout the reassessment of antipoverty efforts, the premises upon which creative federalism rested have seldom been questioned. To explain the limited success of these redistributive programs, three rival hypotheses have been advanced: (1) the power of local ruling elites, (2) the complexity of intergovernmental relationships, and (3) the differential constituencies of central and local governments. Each offers a plausible but, in the end, inadequate explanation for the regularity with which national programs have been frustrated at local levels.

Local Ruling Elites

In both popular and academic literature, the favored explanation for the difficulties faced by Great Society programs is the power of local ruling elites. Local politics, it is said, has been dominated by power structures consisting of bankers and businessmen who, together with a few conservative labor leaders and politicians beholden to them, dictate the major contours of local policy.[30] More sophisticated versions of this explanation do not claim that the ruling elite makes each and every local decision but only that its presence precludes redistributive issues from reaching the agenda of local politics. Its power is used to keep policies that are of interest to low-income groups and racial minorities from ever reaching a threshold of public awareness in the local community.[31]

A study of Baltimore's community action program provided Bachrach and Baratz with an opportunity to apply this perspective directly to the implementation of the most visible of the antipoverty programs.[32] In this study, they contend that the politics of community action in Baltimore was marked by "non-decision-making." They concluded that the efforts by black leaders "to transform the covert grievances of the black population into issues was . . . abortive, in part because they lacked arenas where they could practice the politics of conflict as distinct from the politics of confrontation, and in part because they had no access to key centers of decision-making. In short, the prevailing mobilization of bias blocked black leaders' attempts to arouse their would-be constituents to political action and thereby assured that blacks would remain 'locked-out' of the political system."[33] To support this conclusion, they note that Baltimore lacked an open-occupany ordinance, discriminated against blacks in public and private employment, and funded the antipoverty program only frugally.[34]

About some matters Bachrach and Baratz are certainly correct. If Baltimore resembled other local governments, then the civil rights movement and the war on poverty did not dramatically change the course of local public policy to the extent that low-income minorities received greatly expanded benefits from locally financed redistributive programs. On that score, the evidence to the contrary presented in table 1 seems conclusive. But the mechanisms precluding achievement of this objective do not seem to square with the "non-decision-making" model. Indeed, the empirical materials in the study testify to the earnestness and persistence with which redistributive issues came to the regular attention of Baltimore's leaders. As the authors point out, "By the end of 1967 the CAA (Community Action Agency) with its black director in the forefront, was operating at full tilt and practically in the open to organize the black poor for political action."[35] Unless one is prepared to accept Bachrach and Baratz's penchant for stretching the concept of "non-decision" so that it coincides with its opposite—the mayor's decision to establish a series of biracial task forces, for example, is labeled "an extremely effective non-decision"[36]—one can hardly claim that a ruling elite excluded issues of race and poverty from the agenda of local politics.

Fundamentally, the ruling elite hypothesis is unable to cope with the signal accomplishment of antipoverty programs: their capacity to open up local political systems to previously excluded groups. Although the socioeconomic impact of the programs was limited, they did improve the opportunities for political participation by blacks and other racial minorities. Led by the "maximum feasible participation" focus of the community action program, most of the Great Society service-delivery programs contained features that required the active involvement of representatives of low-income groups and racial minorities in the deliberative process. Although these policies varied by locale and program, the overall impact was greatly to increase both the involvement of minorities as organized supporters of antipoverty programs and their recruitment to positions of administrative responsibility. The war on poverty was most successful in changing the agenda of local politics. Matters of concern to minority groups became regular, if not pervasive issues in city politics. Even more significant, black leaders and groups representing minority interests became permanent elements in the institutionalized bargaining process through which local policy was formulated.[37]

Unfortunately, improved access to local politics did not thereby radically alter the socioeconomic well-being of racial minorities and low-income groups.[38] But to attribute this to the power of a ruling elite once again misguides poverty research. If the issue were simply to place on the agenda of local politics the problems of poor minorities, then the programs of the Great Society would certainly have ended poverty and racism in America. But if there are limits inherent in the functions that local governments can perform, even "maximum feasible" political participation by minorities and the poor does not alter these limits.

Organizational Complexity

Quite another interpretation of the Johnson antipoverty programs derives from an understanding of the variety, the complexity, and the changeability of political and organizational relationships in a pluralist system. From this perspective, intergovernmental relationships do not consist simply of encounters between federal officials and local elites; on the contrary, at all levels of government (federal, regional, state, and local) are numerous public and private agencies, with overlapping jurisdictions and competing clientele, that must be consulted in the course of implementing government policy. Any of these entities can act as a "veto group" to frustrate the execution of policy—or at least to delay its implementation until the original purposes are substantially modified.

As familiar as this pluralist view of American politics has become,[39]

Pressman and Wildavsky's imaginative utilization of these ideas in their analysis of the innovative programs of the Economic Development Administration (EDA) is worthy of special consideration.[40] The study is a detailed analysis of the problems that beset the EDA when it sought to improve minority employment opportunities in Oakland, California, by funding a number of public improvement projects in that city. After beginning with high hopes, large projected budgetary outlays, and the appearance of cooperation on the part of both federal and local officials, EDA was frustrated by numerous delays; almost no detectable progress toward the original objective was made. Although the specific problems encountered are discussed in fascinating detail, Pressman and Wildavsky also reach for a more general explanation for the failure of this and other Great Society programs: "What seemed to be a simple program turned out to be a very complex one, involving numerous participants, a host of differing perspectives, and a long and tortuous path of decision points that had to be cleared. Given these characteristics, the chances of completing the program with the haste its designers had hoped for—and even the chances of completing it at all—were sharply reduced."[41] The problems of the Great Society were thus the problems encountered by any government program in a pluralist political system in which many participants influence policy. Differences must be negotiated, plans must be delayed, and policies must be modified. The solution is either to develop more simple programs, abandon federal efforts to intervene in socioeconomic relationships, or accept that long delays and major revisions are inevitable.

Although the case study is written with incisiveness and energy, in the end the argument cuts too deeply. Inasmuch as it applies to all government programs, it does not provide an adequate explanation for the particular problems encountered by the redistributive programs of the Great Society. In the first place, complexity was not a feature unique to the antipoverty programs of the Johnson administration. Many programs that have become a routinized feature of the federal system—for example, those for highways, rivers and harbors, land reclamation, and airport construction—are equally complex but have nonetheless been incorporated into the ongoing political processes of the federal system. National and local objectives have in these cases been similar enough that, whatever problems they may have encountered in particular cases, few can make claim that the programs have failed. Indeed, local governments avidly compete for resources for these programs. Complexity is not a sufficient explanation for the diffidence with which localities participated in antipoverty programs.

Second, Pressman and Wildavsky's assertion that programs failed because participants had diverse views with respect to complex phenomena is at best a very low-level theoretical statement.[42] In this respect, Pressman and Wildavsky resemble the students of "marble cake" federalism, who find relationships too complicated to identify critical elements patterning the complexity. For example, even though the empirical material in the Oakland study makes it quite clear that the "feds" were concerned primarily with redistribution (e.g., employing minorities) and the "locals" were concerned primarily with obtaining aid for economic development, Pressman and Wildavsky provide no general explanation for this patterning of the differences between the two levels of government.

Differential Constituencies

Constituency theory offers the promise of identifying patterns to conflicts between central and local governments. In its most general formulation, constituency theory argues that political leaders pursue objectives desired by those who select them for office. Regarding the differences between central and local governments, McConnell has argued that the central government, with a larger constituency, can be expected to serve broader and more diffuse interests.[43] In local government, which has a smaller constituency, it is easier for dominant economic interests to control policy to the exclusion of weaker, less well-organized interests. In government with a larger constituency, the mutual checking of powerful interests and the need to build coalitions of diverse interests permit consideration of weaker, broader, more diffuse concerns, perhaps including even those of the poor.

One of the best case studies of the failure of a Great Society program is quite convincingly interpreted within the tradition of constituency analysis. In her study of the "New Towns in Town" program initiated in late 1967, Derthick documents in detail the processes by which a program, originally planned to provide low-income housing through low-cost distribution of surplus federal land, failed to build any new homes for the poor at all.[44] In a thoughtful concluding chapter, Derthick emphasizes the differences in the value commitments of national and local governments and then relates them to their differing constituencies: "In shared programs, both the federal government and local governments have a political function: both play a part in defining the objectives of public action and in responding to differences of value, interest, and opinion. The federal government, being removed from particular and parochial conflicts, is better able to express idealistic and progressive objectives. Local governments, more deeply engaged in these conflicts, are better able to respond to the actual preferences of active political interest."[45]

Although Derthick correctly identifies differing value commitments on the part of national and local institutions, she leaves unstated the exact mechanisms by which local constituencies generate demands that differ from national policies. In Derthick's case study, for example, interest groups and constituency pressure, far from constraining policy choice, were notable for their absence. Although some local officials may have anticipated opposition to a low-income housing program, even that hypothetical opposition does not account for the position of big-city mayors, who could also have anticipated support from sizable low-income and minority constituencies.

Beyond Federalism

If I have identified the limits that economic contexts place on local decision making, my argument still allows room for political action. The structural arrangements that limit the possibility of local redistribution and impede the effectiveness of intergovernmental programs are not an irrevocable concomitant of the national political economy. Once the governmental arrangements which structure our political life are adequately understood, the possibility for effective political reform emerges. Not only are alternative governing structures possible, but they in fact exist in societies not fundamentally dissimilar from our own. The introduction of a number of structural changes would basically alter the peculiarly American set of arrangements which impede the effectiveness of redistributive programs. If these changes would not insure equality, they would at least provide one structural precondition that would make greater equity more possible.

1. *The full faith and credit of the federal government should stand behind all state and local government indebtedness.* This policy innovation would remove the threat of bankruptcy, which is the last and final constraint on local government fiscal policies. Although many factors direct local attention to a city's economic limits, the one constraint which cities simply cannot ignore is their standing in the credit market. As cities see their bond ratings slip first from AA to BBB and then slide to a point where no viable credit options exist at all, a crisis in local politics generally develops. Whatever the city's past political orientation, public attention is now focused on restoring economic order to the city's household. Redistributive programs in such an atmosphere become especially vulnerable to the budgetary ax, because these programs contribute little, if anything, to the economic well-being of the community. Were the issue of a city's credit removed from city politics, the most important constraint on local redistribution would be removed.

Were the federal government to institute this policy, it would, of course, also have to place its own controls on local government debt management. In the United States, capital investments by local government are regulated by the private bond market; if the investment is desired by local officials (and, in some places, by local voters), then credit can be obtained as long as both the purpose of the investment and the stability of the local government meet the standards of the financial community. Under the arrangements suggested here, any such proposal would have to be considered by an agency of the federal government. The agency would have the responsibility of determining whether the proposed policy was technically sound, likely to be of benefit to the community, and consistent with overall national policies. In making its decisions, this agency would wish to consider both the nation's overall strategy for economic growth and questions of balance among different areas of the country. For example, it could provide a coherent framework to address complex issues such as "reindustrialization" and dilemmas inherent in "investment and disinvestment" decisions.

Although many might balk at the creation of such an awesome power in the nation's capital, in Britain "local authorities must obtain the consent of the [appropriate central department] before exercising their borrowing powers."[46] For example, whenever a local educational authority (LEA) in England and Wales wishes to build a new school, it must include the proposed capital investment in its building program, which is submitted annually to the Department of Education and Science. The department exercises control over LEA decisions in three ways: (1) by giving or withholding approval of specific building proposals, (2) by imposing minimum standards of accommodation, and (3) by limiting the costs that can be incurred in the construction of the school. Only after permission has been granted in these areas can the LEA obtain capital financing for its building program. While some may object that such regulations, in application, will inevitably be cumbersome and rigid, Griffith's careful analysis of the way in which the regulations work in practice concludes on the optimistic note that, "as they are operated, the regulations are not unduly restrictive, . . . experimentation is perfectly possible . . . and . . . generally, therefore, the regulations provide a proper and necessary level of performance which it would be undesirable to lower while not, in administrative practice, being so strictly applied as to stifle the development of new ideas."[47]

2. *The federal government should institute a revenue-sharing plan that would attempt to equalize per capita fiscal resources available to each state and local government.* As the economy of a local community declined, its claim on the United States Treasury would increase. As the economy of the community improved, increasing its local fiscal re-

sources, its portion of revenue-sharing resources would decline. Such a policy would greatly reduce the local government's fiscal incentive to promote economic growth through either tax concessions to business firms or cutbacks in services to low-income residents. Improvements in the local economy might still be pursued, but the local government itself would receive fewer fiscal benefits.[48] Every increase in local revenue sources would be offset by a declining portion of federal revenue.

The technical difficulties of this policy innovation are so great that it would probably be impossible to achieve this objective in its entirety. For one thing, the amount given to each lower-tier government would have to take into account the range of functional responsibilities it performed. At present the distribution of functions varies widely from state to state and among areas within states. In some parts of the country the state assumes a large responsibility for financing public services; in other parts of the country over two-thirds of the services are paid for out of local government accounts. In some places, notably New York City, one single government is responsible for the full array of services provided by the local government. In other places, notably Chicago, service delivery is shared among municipal government, county government, a sanitary district, a board of education, a park district, a regional transportation authority, and a host of other specialized districts. A revenue-sharing plan would have to either standardize the structural arrangements through which local governments exercised their responsibilities or find a formula for resource distribution that took into account the great variability presently experienced.

The costs of local government also vary from one part of the country to another. Heating costs are greater in the Northeast; labor costs are greater in central cities than in rural areas; transportation costs are greater in the Mountain states; capital costs, including the purchase of land, are higher in more densely populated areas; and concentrations of poor people in certain areas greatly increase the welfare and social service costs of these communities. A formula that equalized the per capita resources of local governments but did not find some way of accommodating the variable costs faced by local governments would leave their fiscal well-being still dependent upon their local economy.

In addition, it would be difficult to determine an acceptable standard for determining what local resource capacity might be. The amount of revenue that could be raised by a specific property tax rate is one possibility. But localities would then have an incentive to underestimate the value of their property and to remove significant portions of their property from tax rolls (through, say, tax concessions to businesses or institutions which seemed to have an eleemosynary purpose). Also, a community may have economic resources which are not readily apparent in land values but which nonetheless yield considerable income or sales tax revenues. The capacity of resort areas to tax receipts paid largely by tourists is one example.

Difficulties such as these require careful research attention. Yet these technical problems, which probably preclude an ideal solution, should not obscure the fact that at the present time federal policies in the United States do very little to equalize the resources available to local governments. By contrast, many European governments, which have for decades struggled with these technical problems, seem to have worked out programs of intergovernmental assistance which in large measure have freed localities from the economic and fiscal constraints that so dominate local policymaking in the United States. In Britain the primary mechanisms for equalizing local fiscal resources are the general grant and rate deficiency grant. All authorities share in the general grant, which allocates resources among authorities according to population size, population density, number of school-age children, and other indicators of local fiscal needs. The rate deficiency grant compensates those authorities whose local taxes at any given rate raise fewer revenues per capita than can be raised nationally at that rate. Since London and other southern coastal areas enjoy a large share of the nation's resources, four-fifths of the local authorities share in the rate deficiency grant, and for some local governments 40 percent of their revenue comes from this source.[49] When taken together, government grants have such an equalizing effect on local expenditures that the coefficient of variations in expenditures among local authorities is less than 0.1 in England and Wales as compared with 0.32 among the fifty states of the United States.[50] Moreover, variation in British local government expenditures is only weakly and inconsistently explained by variations in the wealth of local communities.[51]

3. *Minimum standards of service provision should replace existing grants-in-aid programs.* Many of the existing federal programs, which generate continuous intergovernmental disputes, endless administrative difficulties, and contradictory principles of resource distribution could be eliminated in favor of a comprehensive revenue-sharing plan. Local governments would then be able to allocate resources among service sectors in a way consistent with local needs and preferences. To guard against the misuse of federal funds, the national government might find it appropriate to set minimum standards of service provision in order for local governments to become eligible for revenue sharing. Also, programs of welfare assistance might be appropriately administered directly by the national government in much the way the Social Security program directly operates. Since only a small percentage of welfare assistance is at present provided locally, national direction in this policy

area could be achieved without much sacrifice in local autonomy. Taken as a whole, the restructuring of federal arrangements would leave local governments with far greater flexibility to experiment widely and to respond differentially to local interests and concerns.

Many will object that these proposals are technically impractical, constitutionally questionable, and politically infeasible. National politics today is concerned primarily with economic development, energy conservation, and government deregulation. Yet, inasmuch as the liberal impulse has not evaporated altogether, it could find renewed substance almost overnight for reasons that cannot now be anticipated. Even in today's conservative atmosphere, we find steady increases in federal responsibilities for health, welfare, and education policy. The first step toward political feasibility is identification of the objectives worth pursuing. Liberal reform is in retreat today, not least because it has lost intellectual vitality and creative ingenuity. Before discarding a proposal for its political unattractiveness, the substantive merits first must be addressed.

But even if fully promulgated, these policy innovations will not introduce an egalitarian utopia, where the needs of low-income groups are carefully met by liberally minded public officials.[52] The choice between productivity and redistribution, or, in an older terminology, the choice between liberty and equality, will continue to require a search for an appropriate balance among competing values where no final resolution is possible. With the amelioration of one problem, new difficulties will emerge, compelling both scholarly and practical attention. The proposed structural changes will nonetheless permit the trade-off between equality and productivity to be debated within a local framework that at least resembles the one that shapes our national debates. Whatever possibilities there are for a more equal distribution of the nation's resources will be explored almost as assiduously at local as at national levels. Once the structural impediments to local redistribution are set aside, a new range of local policies will become possible. Even more, local political life itself may acquire a new meaning.

Notes

1. D. J. Elazar et al., eds., *Cooperation and Conflict: Readings in American Federalism* (Itasca, Ill.: F. E. Peacock Publications, 1969).

2. M. Diamond, "On the Relationship of Federalism and Decentralization." In D. J. Elazar et al., eds. (n. 1 above), pp. 72–80.

3. M. Grodzins, *The American System* (Chicago: Rand McNally & Co., 1966).

4. D. Truman, *The Governmental Process* (New York: Alfred A. Knopf, Inc., 1951); J. D. Greenstone, "Group Theories," in *Handbook of Political Science II*, ed. F.

Greenstein and N. Polsby (Reading, Mass.: Addison-Wesley Publishing Co., 1975), pp. 243–318.

5. U.S. Congress, Senate Committee on Government Operations, Subcommittee on Intergovernmental Relations, "The Federal System as Seen by Federal Aid Officials" in Elazar et al., pp. 331–38; D. S. Wright, "Revenue Sharing and Structural Features of American Federalism," *Annals of the American Academy of Political and Social Science* 419 (1975): 100–119.

6. D. J. Elazar, *Amerian Federalism: A View from the States* (New York: Thomas Y. Crowell Co., 1966).

7. H. Kaufman, *The Forest Ranger* (Baltimore, Md.: Johns Hopkins Press, 1960).

8. Elazar, p. 2.

9. M. Diamond, p. 79.

10. Grodzins; Elazar; Elazar et al.

11. Grodzins.

12. U.S. Department of Commerce, Bureau of the Census, *Local Government Finances in Selected Metropolitan Areas and Large Counties: 1974–75* (Washington, D.C: Government Printing Office, 1976).

13. Greater autonomy allows for greater redistribution from the better off to the less well off. It may be, however, that even in an entirely self-contained economy there remain trade-offs between efficiency and equality. Too high and too progressive a rate of taxation to finance too elaborate a welfare state may weaken incentives for capital formation. Yet, some minimum standard of welfare provision seems necessary to insure a steady, healthy, capable working population. These are highly debatable issues beyond the scope of our analysis. See J. O'Connor, *The Fiscal Crisis of the State* (New York: St. Martin's Press, 1973). But there is one set of constraints on local redistribution that does not restrict decision making at the national level: taxpayers cannot easily flee to other jurisdictions while incoming recipients flood the social delivery system. In this regard, national governments have a much greater capacity to redistribute goods and services than do local governments.

14. J. D. Greenstone and P. E. Peterson, *Race and Authority in Urban Politics*, (Chicago: University of Chicago Press, Phoenix Books, 1976), chap. 7.

15. R. A. Musgrave, *The Theory of Public Finance* (New York: McGraw-Hill Book Co., 1959).

16. P. E. Peterson, "A Unitary Model of Local Taxation and Expenditure Policies in the United States," *British Journal of Political Science* 9 (1979): 281–314.

17. F. F. Piven, "The Urban Crisis: Who Got What, and Why," in *Urban Politics and Public Policy*, 2d ed., ed. S. M. David and P. E. Peterson (New York: Praeger, 1976), pp. 318–38.

18. P. E. Marsh and R. A. Gortner, *Federal Aid to Science Education: Two Programs* (Syracuse, N.Y.: Syracuse University Press, 1963), p. 53.

19. Ibid., p. 40.

20. Ibid., p. 41.

21. Ibid., p. 42.

22. Ibid., p. 87.

23. F. M. Wirt and M. W. Kirst, *The Political Web of American Schools* (Boston: Little, Brown & Co., 1972); J. F. Murphy, "Title I of ESEA: The Politics of Implementing Federal Education Reform," *Harvard Education Review* 41 (1970): 35–63; G. Orfield, *The Reconstruction of Southern Education: The Schools and the 1964 Civil Rights Act* (New York: John Wiley & Sons, Interscience, 1969); J. F. Hughes and A. O. Hughes, *Equal Education: A New National Strategy* (Bloomington, Ind.: Indiana University Press, 1972); R. J. Goetell, "Federal Assistance to National Target Groups: The ESEA Title I Experi-

ence," in *The Federal Interest in Financing Schooling,* ed. M. Timpane (Cambridge, Mass.: Ballinger Publishing Co., 1978), pp. 173–208.

24. U.S. Congress, House, Subcommittee on Elementary, Secondary, and Vocational Education of the Committee on Education and Labor, *Title I Funds Allocation: Hearing on H.R. 15,* 95th Cong., 1st sess., 1977.

25. M. Ways, "Creative Federalism and the Great Society," in Elazar et al., eds. (n. 1 above).

26. A. W. Macmahon, *Administering Federalism in a Democracy* (Oxford: Oxford University Press, 1972), p. 84.

27. Peterson (n. 16 above).

28. "We have not in recent years had much of an extension of domestic programs run directly by the national government, but we have had a great extension of programs operated by states and localities with federal funds and with varying... degrees of federal policy control" (M. D. Reagan, *The New Federalism* [Oxford: Oxford University Press, 1972], p. 12).

29. R. H. Haveman, ed., *A Decade of Federal Antipoverty Programs: Achievements, Failures and Lessons* (New York: Academic Press, 1977), p. 2.

30. F. Hunter, *Community Power Structure* (Chapel Hill: N.C.: University of North Carolina Press, 1953). For a collection of readings from this literature and a general bibliography, see W. D. Hawley and F. M. Wirt, eds., *The Search for Community Power* (Englewood Cliffs, N.J.: Prentice-Hall, Inc., 1968).

31. P. Bachrach and M. S. Baratz, "Two Faces of Power," *American Political Science Review* 56 (1962): 947–52.

32. P. Bachrach and M. S. Baratz, *Theory and Practice* (Oxford: Oxford University Press, 1970).

33. Ibid., pp. 79–80.

34. Ibid., p. 97.

35. Ibid., p. 89.

36. Ibid., p. 71.

37. Greenstone and Peterson (n. 14 above); P. E. Peterson and J. D. Greenstone, "Racial Change and Citizen Participation: The Mobilization of Low-Income Communities through Community Action." In R. Haveman, ed. (n. 29 above).

38. Chicago Urban League, "The Current Economic Status of Chicago's Black Community" (mimeographed).

39. Truman (n. 4 above); D. Riesman, *The Lonely Crowd* (New Haven, Conn.: Yale University Press, 1950); R. Dahl, *Who Governs?* (New Haven, Conn.: Yale University Press, 1961).

40. J. L. Pressman and A. Wildavsky, *Implementation* (Berkeley: University of California Press, 1973).

41. Ibid., p. 94.

42. A. S. McFarland, *Power and Leadership in Pluralist Systems* (Stanford, Calif.: Stanford University Press, 1969).

43. G. McConnell, *Private Power and American Democracy* (New York: Alfred A. Knopf, Inc., 1966).

44. M. Derthick, *New Towns in Town: Why a Federal Program Failed* (Washington, D.C.: Urban Institute, 1972).

45. Ibid., p. 101.

46. J. A. Griffith, *Central Departments and Local Authorities* (Toronto: University of Toronto Press, 1966), p. 76.

47. Ibid., p. 165.

48. As long as localities are allowed to levy differential tax rates, differing economic

bases would still yield certain fiscal dividends. If a community wished to provide services at a higher rate than federal subsidies allowed, it could expand its services above the federal minimum more easily the larger its economic base. In other words, egalitarian objectives would be easily undermined if federal minimums were set very low, and most communities provided services above them. State foundation programs in education have failed to equalize local fiscal resources for this very reason. See J. E. Coons, W. H. Clune, and S. D. Sugarman, *Private Wealth and Public Education* (Cambridge, Mass.: Harvard University Press, 1970).

49. Griffith, p. 74.

50. In Britain, the coefficient of variation for total spending in 1965–66 by county boroughs for welfare, children, health, education, and library service per 10,000 population was .11. See N. Boaden, *Urban Policy-making* (Cambridge, Mass.: Cambridge University Press, 1971), p. 14. The coefficient of variation of expenditure for primary school education per 1,000 population by all local authorities, 1961–63, was .14; for secondary education the coefficient was .11. See B. Davies, *Social Needs and Resources in Local Services* (London: Gresham Press, 1968), pp. 277, 283. Although larger coefficients of variation occur when less expensive public services are examined, there is little variation in expenditures for education, the largest of local authority services, and for overall expenditure totals. In other words, local authorities have a fairly fixed amount of resources available (as compared to states and localities in the United States), but they vary in their allocation of resources among public services. Information on the United States is given in Paul E. Peterson, *City Limits* (Chicago: University of Chicago Press, 1981), chap. 3.

51. Alt found negative associations between wealth and expenditures on education, housing, and fire services; he found positive correlations between wealth and expenditures on police, children's services, libraries, highways, local health facilities, and welfare. Partial coefficients never attained a value larger than .21; in other words, for no public service did the wealth of the community account for more than 4 percent of the variance in expenditures. See J. E. Alt, "Some Social and Political "Correlates of County Borough Expenditures," *British Journal of Political Science* 1 (1971): 49–62. After an extensive review of British literature on determinants of expenditure, Newton concludes that "there is no statistically significant relationship between community wealth, however it is measured, and community spending on performance for a great many services." Although he says that wealthier communities tend to spend "marginally more on planning and parks," they "tend to spend rather less on the aged, mothers and young children, and special education, and to have a lower total per capita expenditure." See K. Newton, "Community Performance in Britain," *Current Sociology* 26 (1976): 49–84.

52. Even if fully implemented my proposals would still leave localities marginally dependent on their own economic base. In addition, the fiscal incentive is only one of several factors that discourage local officials from attending to the needs of low-income minorities. Even in Britain Griffith reports less enthusiasm for redistributive programs on the part of local authorities: "Only in the rarest cases do the Department of Education and Science need to persuade a local education authority to build more schools or the Ministry of Transport to cajole city engineers... to produce bigger and better highway proposals.... In housing the difference is fundamental.... In this area the sense of urgency and the need for a continuing drive for slum clearance have come from the department (Griffith [n. 46 above], pp. 256–57).

Index ★

Agriculture
  Liberalism, money, and the situation of
    organized labor, 185–86
Almond, Gabriel
  Private power and American democ-
    racy, 46
American Association of Railroads
  Taxation policy for highways, 156
American Association of State Highway
  Officials, 147–50
  Maintenance of federal-state relations,
    157–59
  Taxation policy for highways, 156
  Truck weight and size limits, 159–60
American Automobile Association, 147
  Relocation assistance, 164–66
  Taxation policy for highways, 156
  Truck weight and size limits, 159–60
American Construction Council
  Commerce's role in the marketplace,
    121
American Farm Bureau Federation
  Private power and American democ-
    racy, 45
American Federation of Labor
  Liberalism, money, and the situation of
    organized labor, 177–80
American Federation of Labor–Congress of
  Industrial Organizations, 197
American Road Builders Associations, 147
American Trucking Association, 147
  Relocation assistance, 164–66

  Taxation policy for highways, 154–56
  Truck weight and size limits, 159–60
Anderson, Dwight
  Lincoln, Wilson, Nixon, and presiden-
    tial self-sacrifice, 77–79
Antipoverty programs
  Federalism and the Great Society, 262–
    68
Apologetic pluralism
  Conflictual evolution of American politi-
    cal science from . . . to trilateralism
    and Marxism, 34–67
  Elements of . . . , 38–42
  Pluralism and the Third World, 42–43
  Revisionist approach to political parties
    and elections, 49–50
  Trilateralism, 52–55
Arnold, Peri E.
  Ambivalent Leviathan: Herbert Hoover
    and the positive state, 109–36
  Atomic Energy Commission, 224

Bachrach, P.
  Federalism and the Great Society, 264
Bailey, Stephen
  Conflictual evolution of American politi-
    cal science, 34
Baltimore, Maryland
  Federalism and the Great Society, 264
Banfield, Edward
  Conservative reaction to pluralism, 50

Urban bureaucracy in urban politics, 211

Baratz, M.S.
Federalism and the Great Society, 264

Biester, Edward, 101–2

Billboards
Highway beautification, 163–64

"Birth of a Nation"
Lincoln, Wilson, Nixon, and presidential self-sacrifice, 86–87

Boggs, Hale
Taxation policy for highways, 155

Booth, John Wilkes
Assassination of Lincoln, 76

Bowles, Samuel
Trilateralism, 55

Bretton Woods
Liberalism, money, and the situation of organized labor, 182, 188, 189–90

Brownlow, Louis, 128

Bryce, James
Background of pluralism, 37

Brzezinski, Zbigniew
Trilateralism, 52

Bureaucracy
Urban bureaucracy in urban politics, 209–45

Burnham, Walter Dean
Revisionist approach to political parties and elections, 50

Burns, Arthur, 94

Burns, James M.
Commerce's role in the marketplace, 121

Business interests
Problems of corporate power, 48–49

Buzhardt, Fred, 95

Cabinet Committee on Price Stability, 195

Calhoun, John C.
Jacksonian politics: liberal consensus or liberal bipolarity, 20–26

Capitalism
Conflictual evolution of American political science, 34–67
Expansion and crisis of advanced . . . , 59
Marxism, 56
1970s: crisis of world . . . , 51–52
State autonomy, 58–59
Trilateralism, 52–55

Truncated politics in advanced . . . , 56–57

United States exceptionalism, 60–62

Carter, Jimmy
Liberalism, money and the situation of organized labor, 199
Trilateralism, 53

Central government
Differences in policies in central and local governments, 254–57
Intergovernmental cooperation and conflict, 257–61
Toward a new theory of federalism, 253–54

Chapin, Dwight, 102

Chicago, Illinois
Beyond federalism, 270

Chicago Civic Federation, 177

Christian imagery
Lincoln, Wilson, Nixon, and presidential self-sacrifice, 73–74, 77–78

Civil Aeronautics Board, 223–24

Clay, Henry
Jacksonian politics: liberal consensus or liberal bipolarity, 24–25

Commodities
Commerce's role in the marketplace, 115–23

Cox, Archibald, 72

Crenson, Matthew A.
Urban bureaucracy in urban politics, 209–45

Dahl, Robert
Elements of apologetic pluralism, 40, 42
Private power and American democracy, 47

Dahrendorf, Ralf
Private power and American democracy, 46

Daugherty
Commerce's role in the marketplace, 116

Dean, John, 93, 96

Declaration of Independence
Lincoln, Wilson, Nixon, and presidential self-sacrifice, 76

Democracy
Background of pluralism, 36–38
Elements of apologetic pluralism, 38–42
Private power and American democ-

racy, 45
Trilateralism, 52–55
Derthick, M.
   Federalism and the Great Society, 267–
      68
Deutsch, Karl
   Pluralism and the Third World, 42
Diamond, Martin
   Federalism, economic development,
      and redistribution, 249
Dickens, Charles
   Background of pluralism, 37
Drake, J. Walter
   Commerce's role in the marketplace,
      118

Economy
   Federalism, economic development,
      and redistribution, 246–75
   Liberalism, money, and the situation of
      organized labor, 173–206
   Separation of . . . and polity, 56–59
Economy Act of 1932, 126
Education departments
   Urban bureaucracy and the problem of
      service delivery, 231–34
Ehrlichman, John, 95, 97
Eisenhower, Dwight D.
   Allocation formula for highway funds,
      150
   Highway politics since 1956, 161–63
   Liberalism, money, and the situation of
      organized labor, 193
   Taxation policy for highways, 154–57
Eisenstadt, S. N.
   Decay of pluralism abroad, 51
Elazar
   Federalism, economic development,
      and redistribution, 249–50
Elementary and Secondary Education Act
   Intergovernmental cooperation and con-
      flict, 258–61
Ellsberg, Daniel, 72, 91
Emancipation
   Jacksonian politics: liberal consensus or
      liberal bipolarity, 22–26
   Lincoln, Wilson, Nixon, and presiden-
      tial self-sacrifice, 75
Empiricism
   McConnell's empiricist criteria and the
      political sense of "public," 12–15

Employment Act of 1946, 189

Falk, Richard,
   Trilateralism, 54
Fallon, George
   Allocation formula for highway funds,
      150–53
   Highway politics since 1956, 162
   Relocation assistance, 165
   Taxation policy for highways, 155
Fallon Committee
   Taxation policy for highways, 155–57
Farm organization
   Liberalism, money, and the situation of
      organized labor, 185–86
Farmer Union, 185
Farmer's Equity, 185
Federal Communications Commission, 224
Federal Open Market Committee, 191–92,
      195–97
Federal Reserve Board
   Liberalism, money, and the situation
      of organized labor, 175–97
Federal Revenue Sharing Program, 239
Federal Trade Commission, 223–24
Federalism
   Federalism, economic development,
      and redistribution, 246–75
Federalist Papers
   Background of pluralism, 36
Ford, Gerald R.
   Lincoln, Wilson, Nixon, and presiden-
      tial self-sacrifice, 73–74
Foreign policy
   Wilson's . . . , 80–89
   Nixon's . . . , 89–91
Frazer, Douglas, 199
Frost, David
   Interview with Nixon, 73, 96–97

Garson, David
   Conflictual evolution of American politi-
      cal science, 34–67
General Motors
   Settlement with United Auto Workers,
      1948, 190
Gettysburg, Pennsylvania
   Dedication of cemetery, 77
   Wilson's speech at, 1913, 85
Gold standard
   Liberalism, money, and the situation of

organized labor, 175–82
Gore, Albert
    Allocation formula for highway funds,
        150–54
Great Britain
    Beyond federalism, 269–71
    Liberalism, money, and the situation of
        organized labor, 180–81
Great Society
    Federalism, economic development,
        and redistribution, 246–47
    Federalism and the . . . , 262–68
Greenstone, J. David
    Elements of apologetic pluralism, 39
    Public, the private, and American de-
        mocracy, ix–xiv
    Transient and the permanent in Ameri-
        can politics, 3–33
Griffith, D. W., 79
Grodzins, Morton
    Federalism, economic development,
        and redistribution, 248–50
Group theory
    Conflictual evolution of American politi-
        cal science, 34–67
Gulick, Luther, 128

Haig, Alexander, 95
Haldeman, H. R., 93, 95, 97
Hamilton, Charles, 100
Hartz, Louis
    Consensual interpretation of American
        liberalism, 19–22
    Jacksonian politics: liberal consensus or
        liberal bipolarity, 22–26
Hays, Samuel
    Form and function in urban bureaucra-
        cies, 220
Helper, Hinton
    Jacksonian politics: liberal consensus or
        liberal bipolarity, 23
Herring, E. Pendleton
    Conflictual evolution of American politi-
        cal science, 34
Highway beautification, 163–64
Highway politics
    1955–56, 149–60
    Political change in America, 139–72
    Since 1956, 161–68
Highway Users Federation for Safety and
    Mobility, 147

Highways
    Highway politics and reactive policy-
        making, 139–72
    Highway politics in 1955–56, 149–60
    Orfield's interpretation of American pol-
        itics, 145–49
    Political logic of McConnell, 141–44,
        146–49
Hildreth, Richard
    Jacksonian politics: liberal consensus or
        liberal bipolarity, 23, 26
Hiss, Alger, 95–96
Hoepli, M. H., 118
Hofstadter, Richard
    Background of pluralism, 37
Holden, Matthew
    Urban bureaucracy in urban politics,
        213–14
Holmes, John
    Jacksonian politics: liberal consensus or
        liberal bipolarity, 24
Hoover, Herbert
    Ambivalent Leviathan: . . . and the am-
        bivalent state, 109–36
    Commerce's role in the marketplace,
        115–23
    Interest in management of public orga-
        nizations, 123–30
Hoover Commissions
    Administrative order and public power,
        123–30
Hoover Farm Board, 186
House. See U.S. House
Humphrey-Hawkins Full Employment Act,
    197, 199
Hunter, Floyd
    Elements of apologetic pluralism, 38
Huntington, Samuel
    Decay of pluralism abroad, 51

Indochina
    Pluralism and the Third World, 44
Industry
    Commerce's role in the marketplace,
        115–23
Interest groups
    Highway politics and reactive policy-
        making, 139–72
    Liberalism, money, and the situation of
        organized labor, 173–206
    Political logic of McConnell, 143–44

Interstate Highway Program
Founding of . . . , 160–61
Political change in America, 140

Jacksonian politics
Hartz's consensual interpretation of
American liberalism, 19–22
. . . : liberal consensus or liberal bipolarity, 22–26
Jefferson, Thomas
Jacksonian politics: liberal consensus or
liberal bipolarity, 24
Jesus Christ
Lincoln, Wilson, Nixon, and presidential self-sacrifice, 73–74, 87, 99
Johnson, Lyndon B.
Federalism, economic development,
and redistribution, 246–47
Federalism and the Great Society, 262–68
Highway beautification, 163–64
Highways politics since 1956, 161
Liberalism, money, and the situation of
organized labor, 166–68
Mass transit, 166–68
Joint Commission on Reorganization. See
U.S. Joint Commission on Reorganization

Kaestle, Carl
Form and function in urban bureaucracies, 222
Kahn, Ronald C.
Political change in America: highway
politics and reactive policymaking,
139–72
Katz, Michael
Form and function in urban bureaucracies, 224–25
Kaufman, Herbert
Federalism, economic development,
and redistribution, 249
Urban bureaucracy and the problem of
service delivery, 227
Kennedy, John Fitzgerald
Highway politics since 1956, 161
Liberalism, money, and the situation of
organized labor, 193, 195–96
Relocation assistance, 164–65
Kent, Frank
Form and function in urban bureau-

cracy, 217
Kesselman, Mark
Conflictual evolution in American political science, 34–67
Key, V. O.
Revisionist approach to political parties
and elections, 49
Klein, Julius, 117
Kornhauser, William
Elements of apologetic pluralism, 40–41
Kotler, Milton
Form and function in urban bureaucracies, 218
Ku Klux Klan, 76–87

Labor
Liberalism, money, and the situation of
organized labor, 173–206
Lewis, Eugene
Urban bureaucracies and directions of
change, 237
Lewis, John L., 183
Liberalism, American
Liberalism, money, and the situation of
organized labor, 173–206
Standards, interests, and the concept of
"Public," 3–33
Lincoln, Abraham
. . . , Wilson, Nixon, and presidential
self-sacrifice, 71–108
Presidency and assassination, 74–80
Wilson's dedication of memorial, 83
Lindblom, Charles
Conservative reaction to pluralism, 50
Lipset, Seymour M.
Private power and American democracy, 46
Lipsky, Michael
Urban bureaucracy and the problem of
service delivery, 229, 231
Lobbies. See Interest groups
Local government
Beyond Federalism, 268–72
Differences in policies in central and
local governments, 254–57
Federalism, economic development,
and redistribution, 246–75
Federalism and the Great Society, 262–68
Intergovernmental cooperation and conflict, 257–61

Toward a new theory of federalism, 251–53
Locke, John
Hartz's consensual interpretation of American liberalism, 19–22
Jacksonian politics: liberal consensus or liberal bipolarity, 22–26
Long, Norton
Form and function in urban bureaucracies, 219
Urban bureaucracy and the problem of service delivery, 227
Lowi, Theodore
Form and function in urban bureaucracies, 220
Lukas, Anthony, 89
Luther, Martin, 93

McConnell, Grant
Empirical and conceptual elements in analysis of American politics, 8–9
Federalism and the Great Society, 267
Herbert Hoover and the positive state, 109, 112, 117
Highway politics in 1955–56, 149–61
Highway politics since 1956, 161–68
Pluralism and the Third World, 44–45
Political change in America, 139–72
Political logic, 141–44, 146–49
Political sense of "public," 12–15
Private power and American democracy, 45–48
Problem of corporate power, 48–49
Self-development and substantively public regarding social practices, 15–18
Standards and the social sense of "public," 9–12
Transient and the permanent in American politics, 3–33
Urban bureaucracy in urban politics, 210–16
McCormack, John, 155
"Machine" politics
Urban bureaucracy in urban politics, 209–45
Madison, James
Background of pluralism, 36
Elements of apologetic pluralism, 38
Mailer, Norman, 91–93
Marxism, 56

Conflictual evolution of American political science, 34–67
Pluralism to trilateralism and . . . , 52–55
Mass transit, 166–68
Merriam, Charles, 128
Michel
Background of pluralism, 37
Mills, C. Wright
Elements of apologetic pluralism, 38
Private power and American democracy, 47
Mitchell, John, 91
Monarchy
Lincoln, Wilson, Nixon, and presidential self-sacrifice, 71–76
Monetary system (U.S.)
Liberalism, money, and the situation of organized labor, 173–206
Moses, Robert
Relocation assistance, 164–65
Urban bureaucracy and the problem of service delivery, 226
Municipal government
Form and function in urban bureaucracies, 214–25
Urban bureaucracies and problem of service delivery, 225–35
Urban bureaucracy in urban politics, 209–45

Nast, Thomas, 98
National Association of Manufacturers, 187
National Defense Education Act
Intergovernmental cooperation and conflict, 258–61
National Highway Users Conference, 147
National Labor Relations Board
Liberalism, money, and the situation of organized labor, 184–88, 199
National Labor Relations Board v. Jones & Laughlin Corp., 248
National Recovery Act (NRA)
Liberalism, money, and the situation of organized labor, 183–88
Nazism
Elements of apologetic pluralism, 38
New Deal
Hartz's consensual interpretation of American liberalism, 20–21
Liberalism, money, and the situation of organized labor, 182–89

New Haven, Connecticut
Elements of apologetic pluralism, 40
New York City
Beyond federalism, 270
Form and function in urban bureaucra-
cies, 214, 216
Urban bureaucracy and the problem of
service delivery, 226–27
New York Federal Reserve Bank, 181
Nixon, Patricia, 97
Nixon Pay Board, 193
Nixon, Richard Milhous
Highway beautification, 164
Highway politics since 1956, 162
Liberalism, money, and the situation of
organized labor, 193
Lincoln, Wilson, Nixon, and presiden-
tial self-sacrifice, 71–108
Mass transit, 166–68
Presidency, 89–103
Taping system, 94–95

Odegard, Peter
Conflictual evolution of American politi-
cal science, 34
Old Testament imagery
Lincoln, Wilson, Nixon, and presiden-
tial self-sacrifice, 77–78
Orfield, Gary
Highway politics in 1955–56, 149–61
Highway politics since 1956, 161–68
Interpretation of American politics,
145–49
Political change in America, 139–72
Organization of the Executive Branch. See
Hoover Commissions
Organizations
Hoover's interest in management of
public . . . , 123–30
Organized labor. See Labor
Orren, Karen
Liberalism, money, and the situation of
organized labor, 173–206
Ostendorf, Lloyd, 100
Ostrogorski, Igor
Background of pluralism, 37
Ostrogorski, Moise
Form and function in urban bureaucra-
cies, 218–19

Packenham, Robert

Pluralism and the Third World, 43
Paine, Thomas, 72
Palmerston, P. L., 117
Parker, Theodore
Transcendentalist view of human com-
munity, 7–8
Transience and permanence in political
analysis, 3–7
Transient and the permanent in Ameri-
can politics, 3–33
Pentagon Papers
Ellsberg's release of, 91
Permanence
. . . and transience in American politics,
3–33
Petersen, Henry
Interview with Nixon, 98
Peterson, Paul E.
Federalism, economic development,
and redistribution, 246–75
Philippines
American suppression of indepen-
dence, 81
Plowden, Edmund, 71, 94
Pluralism
Background of . . . , 36–38
Conflictual evolution of American politi-
cal science, 34–67
Pluralism. See also Apologetic pluralism
Police departments
Form and function in urban bureaucra-
cies, 214, 221–22
Urban bureaucracy and the problem of
service delivery, 230–34
Policymaking
Political change in America, 139–72
Politics (U.S.)
McConnell's political logic, 141–44
Orfield's interpretation of, 145–49
Political change in America, 139–72
Polity
Separation of economy and . . . , 56–59
Positive state. See State (the)
Presidents, U.S.
Administrative order and public power,
123–30
Foundations of the positive state in
America, 112–13
Lincoln, Wilson, Nixon, and presiden-
tial self-sacrifice, 71–108
Political logic of McConnell, 143–44

Pressman, Jeffrey L.
    Federalism and the Great Society, 266–67
    Urban bureaucracies and directions of change, 239
"Private"
    Concept of . . . in American politics, 6–7
    McConnell's concept of . . . , 8–13
"Public"
    Concept of . . . in American politics, 6–7
    McConnell's concept of, and empiricist criteria, 8–15
    Philosophical sense of . . . , 9–12
    Self-development and substantively public regarding social practices, 15–18
    Standards, interests, and concept of . . . , 3–33
    Substantive standards, inclusiveness and the concept of . . . , 18
Public management
    Hoover's interest in management of public organizations, 123–30
Public Works Committee (House and Senate)
    Highway politics, 147
    Highway politics in 1955–56, 149–60
Pueblo, Colorado
    Wilson's speech at, 1919, 84–86
Pullman Strike, 1894, 176–77
Pumpkin Papers, 95–96

Rayburn, Sam, 155
Rehnquist, William, 91–92
Republican government
    Background of pluralism, 36
Revisionism
    Revisionist approach to political parties and elections, 49–50
Richard II, 99–100
Richard III, 76
Rockefeller, David
    Trilateralism, 52
Rogin, Michael Paul
    Lincoln, Wilson, Nixon, and presidential self-sacrifice, 71–108
Roosevelt, Franklin Delano
    Commerce's role in the marketplace, 121–22
    Elements of apologetic pluralism, 38
Roosevelt, Theodore, 99
Rourke, Francis

Form and function in urban bureaucracies, 223
Sabatier, Paul
    Form and function in urban bureaucracies, 224
St. Clair, James, 95
Sayre, Wallace
    Urban bureaucracy and the problem of service delivery, 227
Schattschneider, E. E.
    Conflictual evolution of American political science, 34
Schott, Richard
    Form and function in urban bureaucracies, 215
Schumpeter, Joseph
    Background of pluralism, 36–38
    Elements of apologetic pluralism, 41
Schwartz, Gary
    Allocation formula for highway funds, 150
Senate. See U.S. Senate
Shakespeare, William, 99–100
Shefter, Martin
    Form and function in urban bureaucracy, 217
Sherman Act
    Commerce's role in the marketplace, 116
Shils, Edward
    Decay of pluralism abroad, 50
Slavery
    Jacksonian politics: liberal consensus or liberal bipolarity, 22–26
    Lincoln, Wilson, Nixon, and presidential self-sacrifice, 75–79
Social practices
    Self-development and substantively public regarding . . . , 15–18
    . . . and philosophical sense of public, 9–12
Social standards
    . . . and philosophical sense of public, 9–12
Socialist policies
    Hartz's consensual interpretation of American liberalism, 19–22
South (U.S.)
    Jacksonian politics: liberal consensus or liberal bipolarity, 22–26
Sovereignty

Decline of dual sovereignty theory, 247–48

Stalinism
Elements of apologetic pluralism, 38

State (the)
Foundations of the positive state, 111–13
Herbert Hoover and the positive state, 109–36

State autonomy
Limits and extent of, 58–59

State government
Federalism, economic development, and redistribution, 246–75

Stephens, Alexander, 79

Stewart Machine Co. v. *Davis*, 248

Sullivan, Eileen
Conflictual evolution of American political science, 34–35

Tammany Hall (New York City)
Form and function in urban bureaucracies, 217, 220
Urban bureaucracy and the problem of service delivery, 226–27

Taylor, Charles
Conflict, change, and political permanence, 28

Taylor, John
Jacksonian politics: liberal consensus or liberal bipolarity, 24–25

Third World
Challenge and response in the 1960s, 43–45
Conflictual evolution of American political science, 34
Decay of pluralism abroad, 50–51
Pluralism and the . . . , 42–43

Tocqueville, Alexis Charles
Hartz's consensual interpretation of American liberalism, 19–20

Trade associations
Commerce's role in the marketplace, 115–23

Transcendentalism
Parker's transcendentalist view of human community, 7–8

Transience
. . . and permanence in American politics, 3–33
. . . in Parker's political analysis, 3

Trilateral Commission

Conflictual evolution of American political science, 35
Trilateralism, 52–55

Trilateralism
Conflictual evolution of American political science, 34–67
Trilateralism, 52–55

Trucks
Truck weight and size limits, 159–60

Truman, David
Conflictual evolution of American political science, 34
Elements of apologetic pluralism, 39–40, 42

Truman, Harry S.
Administrative order and public power, 129

Turk, Herman
Urban bureaucracies and directions of change, 239

Unions
Liberalism, money, and the situation of organized labor, 173–206

United Auto Workers
Settlement with General Motors, 1948, 190

U.S. Bureau of Foreign and Domestic Commerce
Commerce's role in the marketplace, 117–23

U.S. Bureau of Public Roads
Founding of interstate highway program, 160–61
Highway beautification, 163–64
Highway politics, 147

U.S. Bureau of Standards
Commerce's role in the marketplace, 117–23

U.S. Department of Commerce
Commerce's role in the marketplace, 115–23
Hoover and the positive state, 113–14

U.S. Forest Service
Federalism, economic development, and redistribution, 249, 251

U.S. House
Orfield's interpretation of American politics, 145–46
Political logic of McConnell, 143–44

U.S. Joint Commission on Reorganization
Administrative order and public power,

123–30
U.S. Office of Education
  Intergovernmental cooperation and con-
    flict, 258–61
U.S. Office of Environmental and Urban
  Systems
  Highway politics since 1956, 163
U.S. Presidents. *See* Presidents, U.S.
U.S. Senate
  Orfield's interpretation of American pol-
    itics, 145–46
  Political logic of McConnell, 143–44
U.S. Supreme Court
  Commerce's role in the marketplace,
    116
Urban bureaucracy
  Form and function in . . . , 214–25
  . . . and problem of service delivery,
    225–35
  . . . in urban politics, 209–45

Vietnam
  Pluralism and the Third World, 44

Wages
  Liberalism, money, and the situation of
    organized labor, 199
Wagner Act
  Liberalism, money, and the situation of
    organized labor, 183
Watergate
  Lincoln, Wilson, Nixon, and presiden-
    tial self-sacrifice, 72–73, 91–103
Webb, James
  Administrative order and public power,
    129
Webster, Daniel
  Jacksonian politics: liberal consensus or
    liberal bipolarity, 23
Whig Party
  Hartz's consensual interpretation of

American liberalism, 20–21
  Jacksonian politics: liberal consensus or
    liberal bipolarity, 22–26
White House
  Lincoln, Wilson, Nixon, and presiden-
    tial self-sacrifice, 75–76
"Why Are We in Vietnam?" 91–93
Wildavsky, A.
  Federalism and the Great Society, 266–
    67
Wills, Garry, 96
Wilson, Edmund
  Lincoln's speech to the Young Men's
    Christian Lyceum, 75, 92
Wilson, James Q.
  Conservative reaction to pluralism, 50
  Urban bureaucracy and the problem of
    service delivery, 230
  Urban bureaucracy in urban politics,
    211
Wilson, Woodrow
  Lincoln, Wilson, Nixon, and presiden-
    tial self-sacrifice, 71–108
  Presidency and foreign policy, 80–89
Winthrop, John
  Lincoln, Wilson, Nixon, and presiden-
    tial self-sacrifice, 73–74
Wirth, Louis
  Urban bureaucracies and directions of
    change, 235
Wolfe, Alan
  Trilateralism, 55
World War I
  Lincoln, Wilson, Nixon, and presiden-
    tial self-sacrifice, 85–86
Wright, Charles Alan, 97

Young Men's Christian Lyceum
  Lincoln's speech to, 74–79

Zolberg, Aristide
  Decay of pluralism abroad, 51